VISUAL QUICKSTART GUIDE

FLASH 5

for Windows and Macintosh

Katherine Ulrich

 Peachpit Press

Visual QuickStart Guide
Flash 5 for Windows and Macintosh
Katherine Ulrich

Peachpit Press

1249 Eighth Street
Berkeley, CA 94710
(510) 524-2178
(800) 283-9444
(510) 524-2221 (fax)

Find us on the World Wide Web at:
http://www.peachpit.com

Published by Peachpit Press, a division of Addison Wesley Longman,
in association with Macromedia Press.
Copyright © 2001 by Katherine Ulrich

Editor: Clifford Colby
Production coordinators: Lisa Brazieal and Kate Reber
Copyeditor: Kathy Simpson
Compositors: Owen Wolfson and Melanie Haage
Cover design: The Visual Group
Indexer: James Minkin
Tech readers: Erika Burback, Jeremy Clark, Peter Alan Davy, Jonathan Duran, Janice Pearce, and Lisa Young

Trademarks
Macromedia is a registered trademark and Macromedia Flash and Flash are trademarks of Macromedia. Visual QuickStart Guide is a trademark of Peachpit Press, a division of Addison Wesley Longman.

Throughout this book, trademarked names are used. Rather than put a trademark symbol in each occurrence of a trademarked name, we state we are using the names only in an editorial fashion and to the benefit of the trademark owner and with no intention of infringement on the trademark.

Notice of liability
The information in this book is distributed on an "As Is" basis, without warranty. While every precaution has been taken in the preparation of the book, neither the author nor Peachpit Press shall have any liability to any person or entity with respect to any loss or damage caused or alleged to be caused directly or indirectly by the instructions contained in this book or by the computer software and hardware products described in it.

ISBN 0-201-71614-3

9 8 7 6 5 4 3 2

Printed and bound in the United States of America.

Dedication

To Perry Whittle. His continuing support, both moral and technical, makes it possible for phantom mountains to resume their natural proportions as molehills.

Thank you

Special thanks to my calm and careful editor Cliff Colby and Peachpit Executive Editor Marjorie Baer, for their confidence in me and their guidance through the whole process of bringing this book into being; to copyeditor Kathy Simpson, for keeping me on the straight and narrow wordwise and exercising her eagle eyes on my spelling and punctuation; to Lisa Brazieal, for the arduous task of putting it all into readable and visually appealing pages; and to Erika Burback, Jeremy Clark, Peter Alan Davy, Jane DeKoven, Jonathan Duran, Erica Norton, Janice Pearce, and Lisa Young for technical advice and review.

TABLE OF CONTENTS

INTRODUCTION

Back when the Web was emerging from its academic cocoon and spreading its wings into the consciousness of the wide world, the Internet was drab. Any splash of color, any graphic image was a refreshing oasis in a vast desert of text against plain gray backgrounds. As the Web grew and its focus shifted, Web sites became vehicles for personal expression, for instruction, for commerce. Web designers longed to expand the graphic content of their sites. Many designers simply forged ahead, adding bitmaps with abandon. Unfortunately, in the process, these designers abandoned their viewers to endless waiting.

Although the bitmap formats that are standard for Web graphics—JPEG, GIF, and PNG—provide compression to make the images as small and fast to download as possible, download times for sites containing lots of images can slow to an audience-losing crawl. Web designers craved a better, more efficient way to send graphics over the Internet. Macromedia Flash provides that efficiency.

What Makes Flash a Special Web-Design Tool?

Flash satisfies designers' cravings for more graphics and more control over those graphics by providing a way to deliver vector images over the Web. Vector images keep file sizes down, and they are scaleable, which means that you can maintain control of what a Web site looks like when your viewer resizes the browser window, for example, making the whole thing stay in proportion as the window grows or shrinks. In addition, Flash provides streaming capability. Streaming allows some elements to display immediately upon download while more information continues to arrive over the Internet.

Animation in Flash is not limited to cartoon characters like Bugs Bunny and The Simpsons. Flash animations also encompass navigation elements, such as buttons and menus. And Flash doesn't limit you to creating animation only for the Web. You can license Flash Player and distribute Flash movies on CD-ROM. You can create stand-alone projectors and distribute them via e-mail or on disk. You can export Flash to other formats, such as QuickTime or Windows .AVI movies. But Web-site creation and enhancement has become Flash's primary focus.

Although this book can't teach you to create a complete user interface for your Web site, what it will teach you about using Flash to create graphics, animation, and interactivity will go a long way toward helping you develop expressive, creative, exciting Web sites. Whether you need a banner ad that grabs the viewer's attention, a button for moving around within your site or linking to other URLs, or a fun animated cartoon, this book will get you started quickly, helping you use Flash's tools to add activity and interactivity to your Web site.

What Is Streaming?

Most viewers lack the patience to wait for an entire site to download, especially one that has big bitmaps or sounds. Flash streams the content of your Web site over the Internet. Streaming means that once some of the vector art of your site has downloaded, Flash can display it while the rest of your data continues to download. As Flash plays the first frames of your movie, subsequent frames keep coming into your viewer's computer, and Flash feeds them out at the specified frame rate. If you plan your movie right, the frames coming in never catch up to the frames being displayed, and your viewer sees only a continuous flow of images.

Figure i.1 For a computer to draw a bitmapped graphic, it must receive a set of instructions for each dot (each bit of data) that makes up the image. Instructions for a vector graphic describe lines and curves that make up the image mathematically. The bitmapped line (left) appears much rougher than the vector line (right). You can't enlarge the bitmapped line without losing quality. But you can make the vector line as big as you like; it retains its solid appearance.

Vectors Versus Bitmaps

The data that creates vector graphics and the data that creates bitmapped graphics are similar, in that they are both mathematical instructions to the computer about where and how to create images on-screen. Bitmaps, however, are lengthier and result in a less versatile graphic; vector graphics are compact and fully scaleable.

Bitmap instructions break a whole graphic into little dots and must tell the computer about each dot; vector instructions describe the graphic mathematically as a series of lines and arcs (**Figure i.1**). Picture a 1-inch black horizontal line on a field of white. For a bitmap, the instructions would go something like this: Make a white dot, make a white dot, make a black dot, make a black dot, make a black dot, make a black dot, and so on. These instructions would repeat until you'd strung together enough black dots to make a 1-inch line. Then the white-dot instructions would start again and continue until the rest of the screen was filled with white dots. The vector instructions would simply be a mathematical formula for a straight line, plus the coordinates that define the line's position on-screen.

About Flash

Flash began life as Future Splash Animator, a nifty little program for creating and animating vector art. In 1997, Macromedia acquired Future Splash, changed the name to Flash, and promoted the program as a tool for creating graphic content for the World Wide Web. Flash excels as a Web-site-design tool because it brings together in one place all the tools you need: tools for creating graphics; tools for animating those graphics; tools for creating interface elements and interactivity; and tools for creating the HTML necessary to display your graphics, animations, and interface elements as a Web page via a browser.

Standard illustration programs, such as Macromedia FreeHand and Adobe Illustrator, rely on Bézier curves to create vector shapes. Flash offers similar tools but also provides natural drawing tools that let you deal with vectors in a more immediate way, without manipulating curve handles or special points on a line. Flash's natural drawing tools provide a spontaneity that appeals to many artists. Flash's natural drawing tools also appeal to nonartists—those of us who can't draw a straight line to save our lives.

Flash helps beginners create simple animated graphics, but anyone who is familiar with animation can use Flash's tools to create quite complex animations. Flash's scripting language, ActionScript, is easy enough to use that beginners can add simple interactivity controls but powerful enough that serious scripters can create highly sophisticated interactive elements.

With each new generation of Flash, Macromedia has added features and functions that expand the program's capabilities as an animation machine and interactivity creator while preserving the easy-to-use drawing tools and assisted animation and scripting features.

How Flash Animates

Flash uses standard animation techniques to create the illusion of movement. You create a series of still images, each slightly different from the next. By displaying the images rapidly, one after another, you simulate a continuous flow of movement. Flash's animation tools help you create, organize, and synchronize the animation of multiple graphic elements and sounds.

Flash Movie Formats

Flash is both an authoring environment for creating animation and a playback system for making that content viewable on a local computer or in a Web browser. Flash files are often referred to as movies, whether they are in the authoring environment or in final playable form. You create animation and interactivity in Flash-format files. In the Windows world, these files have the extension .fla. To create viewable movies, you convert the authoring files to Flash Player format; these files have the extension .swf. Another name for the playable format is SWF (pronounced *swif*).

How Flash Delivers

Flash includes a publishing feature that creates the necessary HTML code to display your animation in a Web browser. The publishing feature also automates alternative methods of delivering your movie—as animated GIF images, for example, or as a QuickTime movie or RealPlayer file.

Figure i.2 Macromedia Dashboard (available from the Help menu) provides movies that contain new information about Flash, as well as links to online Flash resources.

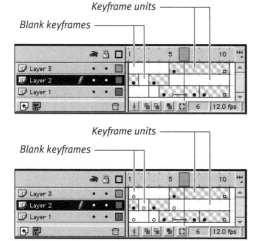

Figure i.3 In Flash 5, the Timeline creates a strong visual link between keyframes and related frames that continue to display the same content (the *keyframe unit*). Solid bullets indicate content in a keyframe; hollow squares indicate the end frame of the unit. When there is no content in a given keyframe unit, nothing appears in the Timeline (top). You can opt to see hollow bullets in blank keyframes (bottom) by setting Flash 4 Frame Drawing as a preference.

Flash 5: What's New?

Flash 5 sports an updated interface that brings Flash closer in look and feel to other Macromedia products. Some of the most exciting additions appear in the interactivity department, with the new ActionScript language. Teaching the full power of ActionScript is beyond the scope of this book. But knowing that it's there may spur you to learn the basics so that you can later soar with the full flexibility of Flash.

The following section lists some new features that beginning and intermediate users of Flash will especially appreciate.

Macromedia Dashboard

Macromedia Dashboard, accessible from Flash's Help menu, brings updated information about Flash directly to your desktop in a Flash movie (**Figure i.2**). Macromedia plans to post new Dashboard content on a regular basis. The Dashboard also provides links to various Web-based resources for Flash developers.

Enhanced Timeline

Flash 5 offers two styles each for viewing and selecting frames in the Timeline. The default frame-drawing and frame-selection styles clarify the relationship between keyframes and in-between frames that extend the keyframe's content (**Figure i.3**). This makes it easy to identify and manipulate blocks of frames containing the same elements.

Panel Interface

In Flash 4, many of the tools for setting the attributes and parameters for graphic elements and animations were hidden in the Toolbar (appearing only when the appropriate tool was selected) or within dialog boxes that required you to navigate a series of menus or commands. Flash 5 makes most of these tools available in *panels*—dockable windows that can stay open on the desktop for quick access during the authoring process (**Figure i.4**).

Movie Explorer

One panel, the Movie Explorer, displays a hierarchical, editable overview of an entire Flash file (**Figure i.5**). You can use it to navigate the Timeline of your movie, search for elements within your movie, and even print a list of movie contents. It also serves as a gateway to editing movie content.

Customizable Keyboard Shortcuts

You can add shortcuts for operations that lack them, change existing shortcuts to ones that works better for you, and save and load different shortcut sets.

Bézier Tools

Flash 5's pen tool allows you to define lines and shapes by placing a series of anchor points to create a path. The subselection tool allows you to manipulate the lines and curves of the path by repositioning anchor points and adjusting their Bézier handles. You can also use the subselection and pen tools to modify shapes created with Flash's natural drawing tools.

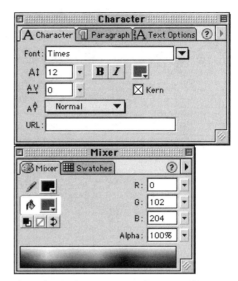

Figure i.4 Flash 5's panels can be grouped in a window (click a tab to bring the panel to the front). You can also dock separate panel windows to minimize the space they take up on your desktop.

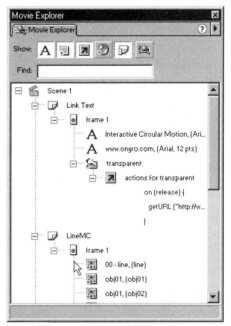

Figure i.5 The Movie Explorer panel is an interactive road map of your movie. Use it to sort and filter content, search for particular kinds of content, and even edit content. You can print the hierarchical list for a hard-copy overview of your movie.

Shared Libraries

In previous versions of Flash, you could create a library of graphic elements, bitmaps, and sounds. That content was available for reuse within a single movie file; reused library elements add little to a published movie's file size. Flash 5 extends that idea, allowing multiple movies to share library elements and adding fonts to the list of sharable items.

MP3 Audio Import

Flash 4 allowed you to compress and export audio in MP3 format. Now Flash 5 also lets you import MP3 files to keep your Flash files small during the development phase.

Enhanced ActionScript

Macromedia has expanded ActionScript, producing a full-fledged scripting language based on JavaScript. Using ActionScript to manipulate variables, expressions, and editable text fields, you can create highly interactive Web sites that can actually communicate with and capture information from your viewers.

Two of the more advanced ActionScript functions (just to tempt you to learn all this book has to offer and then move on) are XML objects and the Debugger. The XML and XMLSocket objects allow you to convert ActionScript to XML and to bring XML data into your Flash movie for manipulation. The Debugger allows you to troubleshoot ActionScripts interactively from inside Flash Player even as it runs in a browser over the Web.

How to Use This Book

Like all Visual QuickStart Guides, this book seeks to take you out of the passive reading mode and help you get started working in the program. The exercises in the book teach you to use Flash's features. The book is suitable for beginners who are just starting to use Flash and for intermediate-level Flash designers. The initial chapters cover the basics of creating graphic elements by using Flash's unique set of drawing tools. Next, you learn how to turn graphic elements into animations. After that, you learn the basics of using ActionScript and sounds to make your movies interactive. Finally, you learn to use Flash's Publish feature to create the HTML that you need to put your Flash movies on the Web.

Cross-Platform Issues

Macromedia designed Flash's authoring environment to have, as much as possible, the same interface on the Macintosh platform that it does on the Windows platform. Still, differences exist where the user interfaces of the two platforms diverge. When these differences are substantial, this book describes the procedures for both platforms. Illustrations of dialog boxes come from both platforms, but generally, there is no special indication as to which platform is shown. If a given feature differs greatly between the two platforms, it is illustrated in both platforms. If a feature is available only on one platform, that is noted in the text.

Keyboard Shortcuts

Most of Flash's menu-based commands have a keyboard equivalent. That equivalent appears in the menu next to the command name. When this book first introduces a command, it also describes the keyboard shortcut. In subsequent mentions of the command, however, the keyboard shortcut usually is omitted. You'll find a complete list of these commands in Appendix A.

Contextual Menus

Both the Macintosh and Windows platforms offer contextual menus. To access one of these contextual menus, Control-click (Mac) or right-click (Windows) an element in the Flash movie. You'll see a menu of commands that are appropriate for working with that element. For the most part, these commands duplicate commands in the main menu; therefore, this book does not generally note them as alternatives for the commands described in the book. The book does point out when using the contextual menu is particularly handy or when a contextual menu contains a command that is unavailable from the main menu bar.

The Artwork

The Flash graphics in this book are simple and easy to draw. In most cases, the examples are based on simple geometric shapes, which means that you can spend your time seeing the Flash features in action instead of re-creating fancy artwork. To make it even easier for you to follow along, Flash files containing the graphic elements that you need for each task are available on the Peachpit Web site *http://www.peachpit.com/vqs/flash/*.

System Requirements

You can create Flash 5 content on the Macintosh and Windows platforms. As a Flash author, you must consider not only the requirements for creating and viewing Flash movies on your own system but also the requirements for viewers of your movie. The following sections list the system requirements for both activities.

To create and edit Flash 5 movies on a Macintosh:

Processor: PowerPC

Operating system: Mac OS 8.5 or later

RAM: 32 MB

Free disk space: 40 MB

Monitor: 256 colors, 800-by-600 resolution

To create and edit Flash 5 movies in Windows:

Processor: 133 MHz Intel Pentium

Operating system: Windows 95, 98, Me, or later; NT 4.0, 2000, or later

RAM: 32 MB

Free disk space: 40 MB

Monitor: 256 colors, 800-by-600 resolution

To play Flash 5 movies via browser on a Macintosh:

Processor: PowerPC recommended

Operating system: Mac OS 8.1 or later

Browser/player: Netscape 3 or later, or Microsoft Internet Explorer 3 or later plus Netscape-compatible plug-in

Other: For movies that rely on Flash Player, Java Edition (a Java-enabled browser)

SYSTEM REQUIREMENTS

To play Flash 5 movies via browser in Windows:

Operating system: Windows 95, 98, Me, or later; NT 4.0, 2000, or later

Browser player: Netscape 3 or later, plus Netscape-compatible plug-in or Internet Explorer 3 or later and ActiveX control

Other: For movies that rely on ActiveX controls, Internet Explorer 3 or later and Windows 95 or later, or NT or later; for movies that rely on Flash Player, Java Edition (a Java-enabled browser)

To play Flash 5 movies via browser under Linux:

Processor: Pentium

Operating system: Redhat 5.1 or 5.2, Slackware 3.5

Browser player: Netscape 3 or later, with standard installation settings

To play Flash 5 movies via browser under Solaris:

Processor: Sparc with 24-bit color

Operating system: Solaris 2.5 or 2.6

Browser player: Netscape 3 or later, with standard installation settings

About Flash Player

Early on, the need for viewers of Flash content to use a player was considered to be a drawback to creating Web content with Flash. Designers feared that users would be reluctant to spend time downloading another helper application for their browsers. But Flash has become the de facto standard for vector art and animation on the Web, and Flash Player for Netscape Navigator and Microsoft Internet Explorer is now widely distributed.

Flash Player is available with the current versions of the two most popular Web browsers (Netscape and Explorer). Flash Player also comes with the latest versions of both the Macintosh and Windows operating systems, and it is built into the applications of America Online and EarthLink. Macromedia estimates that more than 200 million people are equipped to view Web sites created with Flash technology.

The Flash Editor

Before you get started drawing and creating animations in Macromedia Flash, it's helpful to take a look around the editing environment and begin to recognize and manipulate its components. When you open Flash from the File menu or by double-clicking the application icon, you enter the Flash editing environment, and Flash creates a new blank document. Each document consists of three basic items: a Timeline, a record of every frame, layer, and scene that makes up your movie; a Stage, the actual area in which your movie displays; and a work area, a space that extends beyond the Stage on all sides but is outside the visible frame of the final, published movie. In addition, the Flash editor offers various panels, libraries, windows, and tools that help you accomplish your work.

What does the Flash editing environment look like? And how do you access tools and different views? This chapter presents a quick tour of the elements you see when you open a Flash document. Subsequent chapters explain in more detail what is what as you really get into using each element.

Understanding Flash Basics

The way Flash works—in terms of installing the application, creating new documents, closing documents, and saving files—presents nothing unusual to the experienced computer user. The Flash installation software guides you through each step of the installation process, and the procedures for launching the application and creating and saving documents are all standard. Because both the Macintosh and Windows platforms offer users a variety of ways to organize their computers and workflow—such as using shortcuts (Windows), using aliases (Mac), and creating your own hierarchical setup for storing applications and data—it's impossible to cover all the ways you might set up and access files on your computer. But here are the basics of working with Flash.

When you install the program, it's best to copy the installer to your hard drive.

To install Flash:

1. In the Finder (Mac) or on the desktop (Windows), navigate to the installer icon (**Figure 1.1**).

2. Double-click the installer icon.

   The installer window opens to a splash screen for Flash 5 (**Figure 1.2**).

3. Click the Continue button.

   The installation software walks you through all the necessary steps for installing Flash. The installer asks you to read and accept a licensing agreement and to tell it where to place the working software on your system. Don't forget that you need the serial number to install the program. Keep that serial number in a safe place; you will have to reenter it should you ever need to reinstall Flash.

Figure 1.1 The icon of the Flash 5 installer.

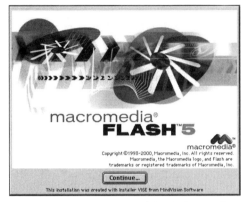

Figure 1.2 The opening screen of the Flash 5 installer software.

✔ Tip (Mac)

- Those of you using the Mac OS should increase Flash's memory allocation. This will reduce the number of memory-related problems you encounter while working on large Flash files.

Figure 1.3 The Flash 5 application icon.

Figure 1.4 To create a new document in Flash, choose File > New.

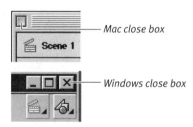

— Mac close box

— Windows close box

Figure 1.5 Clicking the close box closes a Flash document.

To launch Flash:

1. In the Finder (Mac) or from the desktop (Windows), navigate to the Flash icon (**Figure 1.3**).

2. Double-click the Flash icon.

Flash launches and opens a new blank document.

To create a new document:

1. Launch Flash.

2. From the File menu, choose New (**Figure 1.4**).

Flash opens a new blank document.

To close a document:

◆ In the top-left corner of the open document (Mac) or in the top-right corner of the document (Windows), click the close box (**Figure 1.5**).

To save changes to a document:

◆ From the File menu, choose Save.

UNDERSTANDING FLASH BASICS

3

Touring the Flash Editor

A document consists of a Timeline, which holds your movie's frames, layers, and scenes; a Stage, where your movie is displayed; and a work area, which extends beyond the Stage on all sides but remains outside the visible frame of the final movie as it plays (**Figure 1.6**).

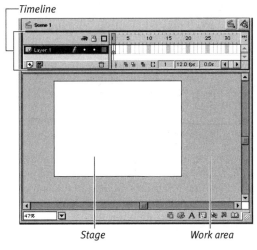

Timeline

Stage *Work area*

Figure 1.6 A new document opened in Flash consists of the timeline, the Stage, and the work area.

About the Timeline

If you think of your Flash movie as a book, the Timeline would be its interactive table of contents: Each scene is like a chapter, each frame is like a page. Imagine that you could point to Chapter 10 in the table of contents, and the book would flip open to the first page of that chapter. In Flash, when you click a frame in the Timeline (or when the playhead enters a frame), that frame appears in your document window.

A Flash movie is much more complex than a book, of course. Each movie "page" may actually be several transparent sheets stacked one on top of the other. Flash keeps track of these "sheets" in what it calls *layers*. And the whole "book" appears to be in motion as you move through the table of contents, with some unseen hand flipping the pages.

The Timeline is a vital and complex organizational and navigational tool. You will use it extensively when you actually create animations. Then you'll need to go more deeply into its components. For now, you only need to understand the Timeline generally; you'll learn more about it in Chapter 8.

Figure 1.7 identifies the major Timeline elements. You can dock the Timeline to any side of a Flash window or float it on top as a separate window.

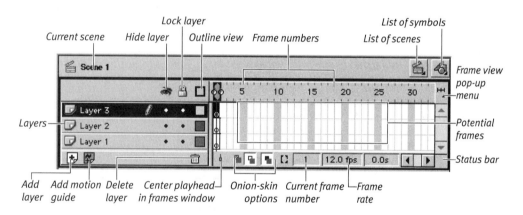

Figure 1.7 The timeline is the complete record of your movie. It represents each scene, frame, and layer that makes up the movie. Frames appear in chronological order. Clicking any frame in the Timeline takes you directly to that frame and displays its contents on the Stage.

To create a separate Timeline window:

1. Click inside the gray bar at the top of the Timeline, and drag away from the document window (**Figure 1.8**).

   A dotted line represents the Timeline palette's position.

2. Release the mouse button where you want the Timeline to be.

To dock the Timeline:

1. Click the gray bar at the top of the Timeline, or click any of the draggable window edges (Mac), and drag the Timeline to the edge of the document window.

2. Release the mouse button when the pointer is at the edge of the window.

   The Timeline resizes to the appropriate vertical or horizontal dimensions to fit the window (**Figure 1.9**).

✔ Tip

- Docking the Timeline vertically gives you easy access to several layers at a time. Docking the Timeline horizontally increases the number of easily accessible frames.

  Although the Timeline appears in any new document you create, you can hide the Timeline to give more room to your Stage.

To hide the Timeline:

- From the View menu, choose Timeline; or press ⌘-Option-T (Mac) or Ctrl-Alt-T (Windows) to toggle between hiding and showing the Timeline.

✔ Tip

- To hide a floating Timeline quickly, simply click the close box of the floating Timeline window.

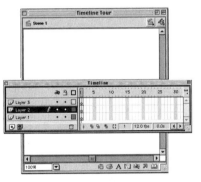

Figure 1.8 Drag the Timeline by its top gray bar (top) and then release the mouse button. The Timeline floats in its own window (bottom).

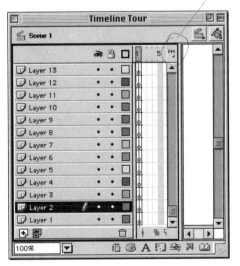

Figure 1.9 Vertical docking gives you access to many layers in the timeline but greatly reduces the number of frames accessible without scrolling.

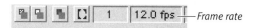

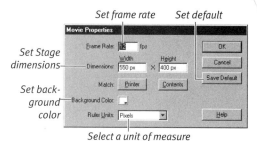

Figure 1.10 Double-clicking the frame-rate box in the status bar is a quick way to access the Movie Properties dialog box.

Set frame rate   Set default

Set Stage
dimensions

Set back-
ground
color

Select a unit of measure

Figure 1.11 The Movie Properties dialog box is where you set all the parameters for viewing the Stage. Selecting a unit of measure for the rulers resets the unit measurement for all the Stage's parameters. Clicking the color box pops up the current set of colors from which you can choose. Clicking Save Default sets the parameters for all new documents you create.

Figure 1.12 Choose a unit measurement from the Ruler Units pop-up menu.

✔ Tip

■ If you want a banner that's 1 inch tall and 5 inches wide but don't know what that size is in pixels (the standard units of measure used for working on the Web), Movie Properties can figure it out for you. First, set Ruler Units to inches. Enter 1 in the Width field and 5 in the Height field. Then return to Ruler Units and choose pixels. Flash does the math for you and sets the Stage dimensions. (Note that Flash uses screen pixels in its calculations, which means that an inch in your movie may differ from an inch in the real world, depending on the resolution of the monitor on which you view the Flash movie.)

About the Stage

The Stage is the area containing all the graphic elements that make up a Flash movie. Think of it as the screen on which you will project your movie. At your local movie house, the screen is whatever size the management could afford to buy for the available space. In Flash, you control how big the screen is, and what color it is, through the Movie Properties dialog box.

To access the Movie Properties dialog box:

Do one of the following:

◆ From the Modify menu, choose Movie; or press ⌘-M (Mac) or Ctrl-M (Windows).

◆ In the Timeline's status bar, double-click the frame-rate box (**Figure 1.10**).

The Movie Properties dialog box appears (**Figure 1.11**).

To set the units of measure:

1. In the Movie Properties dialog box, click the Ruler Units pop-up menu.

A list of units appears (**Figure 1.12**).

2. Select the units you prefer to work in.

Flash uses these units to calculate all measured items on the Stage: rulers, grid spacing, and dimensions.

3. Click OK.

ABOUT THE STAGE

You have three options for setting the size of your Stage.

To set the size of your Stage:

1. To create a movie with specific dimensions, open the Movie Properties dialog box and enter values for Width and Height in the appropriate fields of the Dimensions section (**Figure 1.13**).

2. Click OK.

   Flash automatically assigns the units of measure currently selected in Ruler Units (see "To set the units of measure" earlier in this chapter).

   or

1. To create a Stage just big enough to cover all the elements in your movie, in the Match section of the Movie Properties dialog box, click the Contents button (**Figure 1.14**).

2. Click OK.

   Flash calculates the minimum Stage size required to cover all the elements in the movie and enters those measurements in the Width and Height fields of the Dimensions section.

   or

1. To set the Stage size to match the maximum print area currently available to you, in the Match section of the Movie Properties dialog box, click the Printer button.

2. Click OK.

   Flash gets the paper size from the Page Setup dialog box, subtracts the current margins, and puts the resulting measurements in the Width and Height fields of the Dimensions section.

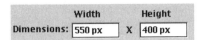

Figure 1.13 To assign new proportions to your Stage, enter a width and height in the Dimensions section of the Movie Properties dialog box.

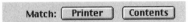

Figure 1.14 To make your Stage just big enough to enclose the objects in your movie, click the Contents button in the Match section of the Movie Properties dialog box.

✔ Tip

■ When you click the Stage, it becomes the active area. When you click the Timeline, it becomes active. Flash outlines the active area with a dark line.

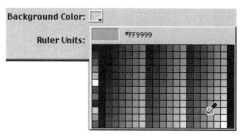

Figure 1.15 To assign your Stage a new color, choose one from the Background Color pop-up menu in the Movie Properties dialog box.

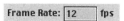

Figure 1.16 Enter a frame rate for your movie in the Frame Rate section of the Movie Properties dialog box.

Figure 1.17 To save the settings you've chosen as Flash's default, click the Save Default button in the Movie Properties dialog box.

To set the background color:

1. In the Background Color section of the Movie Properties dialog box, click the color box to pop up your choices (**Figure 1.15**).

2. Select a color.

   The color you selected appears in the color box.

3. Click OK.

   The Stage now appears in this color in your current document.

Frames are the lifeblood of your animation, and the *frame rate* is the heart that keeps that blood flowing at a certain speed. Flash's default setting is 12 frames per second—a good setting for work viewed over the Web. (By comparison, the standard frame rate for film movies is double that.) You'll learn more about frame rates in Chapter 8.

To set the frame rate:

1. In the Frame Rate section of the Movie Properties dialog box, type a value in the entry field (**Figure 1.16**).

2. Click OK.

To save your settings as the default:

◆ In the Movie Properties dialog box, click the Save Default button (**Figure 1.17**).

   The current settings for the parameters in the Movie Properties dialog box become the default for any new documents.

ABOUT THE STAGE

Using Grids

A *grid* is a set of crisscrossing vertical and horizontal lines that acts as a guide for drawing and positioning elements, the way that graph paper functions in the nondigital world. Flash also uses the grid to align objects when you activate the Snap to Grid feature. The grid does not appear in your final movie.

To make grids visible:

Do one of the following:

◆ From the View menu, choose Grid > Show Grid.

◆ Press ⌘-apostrophe (') (Mac) or Ctrl-apostrophe (') (Windows) .

  A checkmark indicates that this feature is on. Flash displays a set of crisscrossing lines as part of the Stage (**Figure 1.18**).

To set grid color:

1. From the View menu, choose Grid > Edit Grid, or press ⌘-Option-G (Mac) or Ctrl-Alt-G (Windows).

  The Grid dialog box appears (**Figure 1.19**).

2. Click the Color box.

  The pointer changes to an eyedropper tool, and a pop-up box of swatches appears (**Figure 1.20**).

3. Position the eyedropper tool over a color swatch or over an item on the Stage.

  (For more information on selecting colors, see Chapter 3.)

4. Click the swatch or item on the Stage.

  The selected color appears in the Color box. Flash uses the selected color to create the grid lines on the Stage.

5. Click OK.

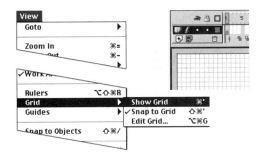

Figure 1.18 Choosing View > Grid > Show Grid (left) makes the grid lines visible on the Stage (right).

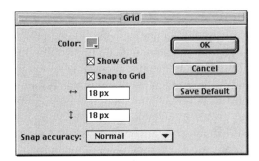

Figure 1.19 Choose View > Grid > Edit Grid to open the Grid dialog box and change grid parameters.

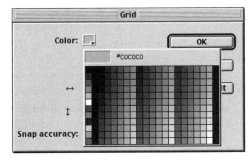

Figure 1.20 To select a new grid color, with the eyedropper pointer, click anywhere in the pop-up set of swatches or on the Stage. The pop-up color-swatch menu displays the currently selected color set.

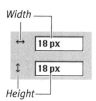

Width

18 px

18 px

Height

Figure 1.21 Enter values in the Width and Height fields to set grid spacing.

To set grid spacing:

1. Follow Step 1 in the preceding exercise to open the Grid dialog box.

2. Enter a value in the Width field.

3. Enter a value in the Height field (**Figure 1.21**).

   The width and height values define the spacing of the grid. Note that the grid need not consist of perfect squares.

4. Click OK.

Using Rulers and Guides

Rulers and guides aid you in drawing objects with precise sizes, shapes, and positions on the Stage.

To display rulers:

◆ From the View menu, choose Rulers, or press ⌘-Option-Shift-R (Mac) or Ctrl-Alt-Shift-R (Windows).

Ruler bars appear on the left side and top of the Stage (**Figure 1.22**). To change ruler units, see "About with the Stage" earlier in this chapter.

To hide rulers:

◆ With rulers visible on the Stage, choose View > Rulers, or press ⌘-Option-Shift-R (Mac) or Ctrl-Alt-Shift-R (Windows).

To place a guide:

1. With rulers visible, position the pointer over the vertical or horizontal ruler.

   If you are using a tool other than the arrow tool, the pointer changes to the arrow.

2. Click and drag the pointer onto the Stage.

   As you click, a small directional arrow appears next to the pointer, indicating which direction to drag (**Figure 1.23**).

3. Release the mouse button.

   Flash places a vertical or horizontal line on the Stage (**Figure 1.24**).

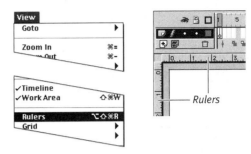

Rulers

Figure 1.22 Choosing View > Rulers (left) makes rulers visible on the Stage (right).

Figure 1.23 As you drag a guide line from the ruler bar, a direction indicator appears next to the arrow tool.

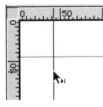

Figure 1.24 You can position individual vertical and horizontal guides anywhere you want on the Stage.

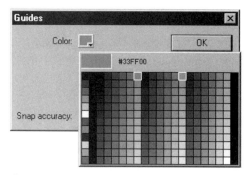

Figure 1.25 With the eyedropper tool, click one of the swatches in the pop-up menu to select a color from the currently loaded color set. You can also click elements on the Stage to sample their colors.

To reposition a guide:

1. From the Toolbox, select the arrow tool.

2. On the Stage, position the arrow tool over the guide you want to reposition.

   The direction arrow appears next to the arrow pointer, indicating that the guide can be dragged.

3. Click and drag the guide to a new location.

4. Release the mouse button.

✔ Tips

■ To remove a guide, drag it completely off the Stage.

■ To avoid accidentally repositioning guides, choose View > Guides > Lock Guides or press ⌘-Option-; (Mac) or Ctrl-Alt-; (Windows). The directional arrow no longer appears next to the arrow tool when you place it over a guide line, and the guides cannot be moved. To unlock the guides, choose View > Guides > Lock Guides or press the keyboard shortcut again.

To set guide color:

1. From the View menu, choose Guides > Edit Guides, or press ⌘-Option-Shift-G (Mac) or Ctrl-Alt-Shift-G (Windows).

   The Guide dialog box appears.

2. Click the Color box.

   The pointer changes to an eyedropper tool, and a pop-up box of swatches appears (**Figure 1.25**).

3. Using the eyedropper tool, click a color swatch or an item on the Stage to select a new guide color.

4. Click OK.

   Flash applies that color to any existing guides and uses it for creating new guides.

Working with Snapping

Flash's Snap feature helps you align objects as you position them on the Stage. With Snap turned on, Flash forces the edge or center of an object to sit directly on top of a grid or guide line as soon as you position the object within a user-specified distance from that line. Flash can also snap objects to other objects.

To snap objects to grids:

◆ From the View menu, choose Grid > Snap to Grid, or press ⌘-Shift-' (Mac) or Alt-Shift-' (Windows).

or

1. Choose View > Grid > Edit Grid.

2. In the Grid dialog box, check the Snap to Grid checkbox (**Figure 1.26**).

3. Click OK.

   A checkmark appears next to the Snap to Grid command in the menu. As you drag an object near a grid line, Flash highlights potential snap points with a circle.

To set parameters for snapping to grid:

1. Choose View > Grid > Edit Grid.

2. In the Grid dialog box, choose a parameter from the Snap Accuracy pop-up menu (**Figure 1.27**).

3. Click OK.

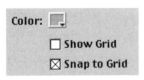

Figure 1.26 Check the Snap to Grid check box to turn on snapping.

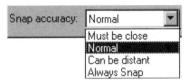

Figure 1.27 Choose a Snap Accuracy setting to determine how close an object must be to the grid before Flash snaps the object to the grid line. Choosing Always Snap forces the edge or center of an object to lie directly on a grid line.

To snap objects to guides:

◆ From the View menu, choose Guides > Snap to Guides, or press ⌘-Shift-; (Mac) or Ctrl-Shift-; (Windows).

or

1. Choose View > Guide > Edit Guides.

2. Check the Snap to Guides checkbox.

3. Click OK.

To set parameters for snapping to guides:

1. Choose View > Guides > Edit Guides.

2. In the Guides dialog box, choose a parameter from the Snap Accuracy pop-up menu.

3. Click OK.

To turn off snapping to grids:

1. Choose View > Grid > Edit Grid.
The Grid dialog box appears.

2. In the Grid dialog box, uncheck the Snap to Grid check box.

To turn off snapping to guides:

1. Choose View > Guides > Edit Guides.
The Guide dialog box appears.

2. In the Guides dialog box, uncheck the Snap to Guides check box.

3. Click OK.

WORKING WITH SNAPPING

About the Toolbox

The Toolbox contains Flash's drawing tools and other tools you'll need to create and manipulate graphics for animation. The Mac and Windows operating systems handle the Toolbox slightly differently. ~~In Windows, you can dock the Toolbox on either side of the application window.~~ In Mac OS, the Toolbox always floats as a separate window.

To view the Toolbox:

◆ From the Window menu, choose Tools.

A checkmark indicates that the Toolbox window is open. The Toolbox window appears on the desktop (**Figure 1.28**).

To relocate the Toolbox:

1. Click the gray (Mac) ~~or blue (Windows)~~ bar at the top of the Toolbox window, and hold down the mouse button.

2. Drag the Toolbox to the desired location.

To turn on Tooltips:

1. From the Edit menu, choose Preferences.

2. In the Preferences dialog box, select the General tab.

3. Check the Show Tooltips checkbox (**Figure 1.29**).

    When the Tooltips feature is on (as it is by default), Flash pops up an identifying label whenever you position the pointer over a tool icon and don't click it (**Figure 1.30**).

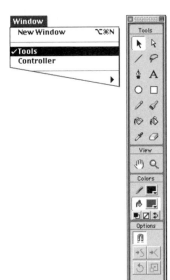

Figure 1.28 To access Flash's drawing tools, choose Window > Tools (left). The Toolbox window appears on your desktop (right).

Figure 1.29 Turn on Tooltips by checking Show Tooltips in the General tab of the Preferences dialog box.

Figure 1.30 When the Tooltips feature is on, an icon label appears whenever the pointer rests over an icon for a few seconds.

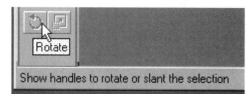

Show handles to rotate or slant the selection

Figure 1.31 In Windows, additional Tooltip information appears at the bottom of the application window when you activate the Status bar (choose Window > Toolbars > Status).

Figure 1.32 In Windows, you can drag the Toolbox to either side of the application window to dock it.

✔ Tip

- In Windows, you can display additional Tooltip information at the bottom of the application window by displaying the Status toolbar. Choose Window > Toolbars > Status (**Figure 1.31**).

To create a floating Toolbox (Windows):

1. Click anywhere in the docked Toolbox that's not actually a tool button, and hold down the mouse button.

2. Drag the Toolbox away from the edge of the window.

   An outline version of the floating Toolbox appears.

To dock the Toolbox (Windows):

- ◆ When the Toolbox is floating, drag it to the right or left edge of the application window. Flash snaps the Toolbox to the edge of the application window (**Figure 1.32**).

✔ Tip

- Double-clicking the title bar of a floating Toolbox automatically docks it to whichever side of the window it was last docked.

Viewing Graphics at Various Magnifications

Flash offers several ways to adjust the magnification of elements on the Stage.

To view objects at actual size:

◆ From the View menu, choose Magnification > 100% (**Figure 1.33**), or press ⌘-1 (Mac) or Ctrl-1 (Windows).

or

1. In the Stage's Zoom Control field, enter 100%.

   At 100%, Flash displays objects as close as possible to the size they will be in the final movie. (Some monitors and video cards may display slightly different sizes.)

2. Press Return (Mac) or Enter (Windows).

To zoom in or out on the Stage:

1. In the Zoom Control field (at the bottom-left corner of the Stage), enter the desired percentage of magnification.

   To zoom in, enter a percentage larger than 100. To zoom out, enter a percentage smaller than 100 (**Figure 1.34**).

2. Press Return (Mac) or Enter (Windows).

✔ Tip

■ Click the triangle icon next to the Zoom Control to open a menu that duplicates the View > Magnification submenu. Choose a percentage from this menu to change magnification immediately. This menu also lets you choose Show Frame and Show All modes. Choose Show Frame to display the full Stage area in the current window; choose Show All to display just the elements on the Stage.

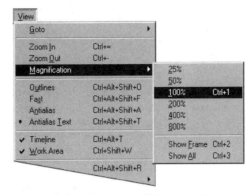

Figure 1.33 Choose 100% magnification to display graphics at the size they will be in the final movie.

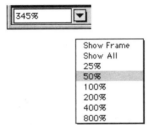

Figure 1.34 Enter a percentage greater than 100 in the Zoom Control field to magnify objects on the Stage. The pop-up menu to the right of the entry field offers several common magnification levels.

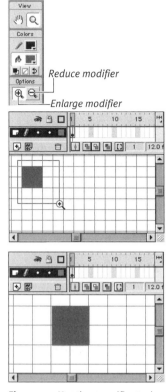

Reduce modifier

Enlarge modifier

Figure 1.35 Use the magnifier tool (top) to draw a selection rectangle around an element (middle). Flash places the element at the center of the enlarged view (bottom).

To zoom in on specific areas of the Stage:

1. In the Toolbox, select the magnifier tool (or press M or Z on the keyboard).

   The pointer changes to a magnifying glass.

2. Choose the Enlarge modifier.

3. Move the pointer over the Stage, and select the area to magnify in one of two ways:

   ◆ Click the area or element you want to enlarge. Flash doubles the percentage of magnification in the Zoom Control field and places the spot you clicked at the center of the viewing window.

   ◆ Click and drag to create a selection rectangle that encloses the element you want to view. Flash fills the window with your selected area (**Figure 1.35**).

To zoom out:

◆ In the Toolbox's Zoom Control field, enter a percentage less than 100.

   or

1. In the Toolbox, select the magnifier tool.

2. Choose the Reduce modifier.

3. Move the pointer over the Stage, and click the element or the area you want to see more of (or view at a smaller size). Flash halves the percentage of magnification specified in the Zoom Control field.

✔ Tips

■ To switch the magnifier tool temporarily from Enlarge to Reduce, and vice versa, hold down the Option (Mac) or Alt (Windows) key.

■ Oddly enough, even in Reduce mode, you can drag a selection rectangle to create a magnified view.

■ To access the magnifier tool in Enlarge mode temporarily, press ⌘-spacebar (Mac) or Ctrl-spacebar (Windows). To access the tool in Reduce mode, press ⌘-Shift-spacebar (Mac) or Ctrl-Shift-spacebar (Windows).

VIEWING GRAPHICS AT VARIOUS MAGNIFICATIONS

About Panels

In earlier versions of Flash, you set the properties and attributes of elements (such as fill color, line style, and font) by using tools and modifiers in the Toolbar or various dialog boxes. Flash 5 puts many of these settings in *panels*—windows that can stay open on the desktop for quick access as you work. You use panels to set the attributes to be used by tools in creating new elements. You can also use panels to modify the attributes of selected elements. You'll learn to use individual panels in later chapters of this book. For now, you will learn general features of panels and how to manage the panel environment.

To open a panel window:

1. From the Window menu, choose Panels.

    A submenu of panel choices appears. (**Figure 1.36**).

2. From the Panels submenu, choose the desired panel—for example, Mixer.

    or

◆ In the Launcher bar in the bottom-right corner of the Stage, click the desired panel button (**Figure 1.37**).

    Flash opens a window containing that panel and any other grouped panels (**Figure 1.38**).

✔ Tip

■ The preceding techniques work to open a panel that is not currently open or to bring a panel to the front if you've grouped several panels in one window. If a panel is already open, and foremost in its window, using these techniques closes the panel.

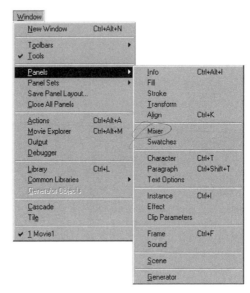

Figure 1.36 Choose Window > Panels to open a list of panel choices.

Figure 1.37 The Launcher bar allows you to open commonly used panels and windows with a single click.

Figure 1.38 In the default panel layout, clicking Mixer in the Launcher bar opens the Color Mixer and the Swatches panels in a single window.

To close a panel window:

◆ Click the panel window's close box.

✔ Tips

■ To close all the currently open panel windows, choose Window > Close All Panels or Alt-click (Windows) any panel window's close box.

■ To hide all the currently open windows (including the Toolbar and any open Library windows), press the Tab key. Press Tab again to show the windows.

To reposition a panel window:

◆ Click the window's title bar, and drag the window to a new location.

✔ Tip

■ When you position one panel window so that one of its edges lies right next to the edge of another panel window, Flash docks the two windows. It's not a permanent connection, but it ensures that the two take up as little space together as possible.

To resize a panel window:

◆ Click and drag the bottom-right corner of the window (Windows) or the resize handle (Mac).

ABOUT PANELS

Working with Grouped Panels

You can group several panels in one or more windows to save space on your desktop. By default, Flash automatically groups certain panels to make similar types of attributes available simultaneously. The panels that control text attributes (Character, Paragraph, and Text Options), for example, open together in the default panel set layout.

To open the default panel set:

◆ From the Window menu, choose Panel Sets > Default Layout.

Flash opens four windows containing groups of panels (**Figure 1.39**). Each window bears the name of the panel tab that is foremost in the window.

To separate panels:

1. Follow the preceding steps to open the default panel set.

2. In one of the panel windows, click a panel tab and drag it away from its window.

Flash displays an outline of the window and tab as you drag.

3. Release the mouse button.

The panel appears in its own window (**Figure 1.40**).

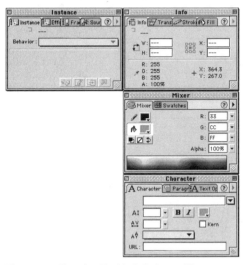

Figure 1.39 Choosing Flash's default panel layout opens four frequently used panel groups along the right side of the desktop.

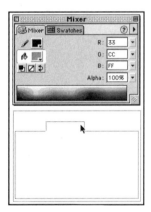

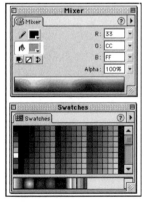

Figure 1.40 To separate a panel from a group, drag one panel tab away from the window until you see the outline of the window with a tab (top); then release the mouse button to create a separate panel window (bottom).

WORKING WITH GROUPED PANELS

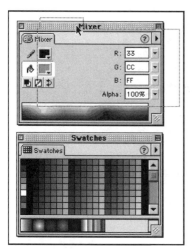

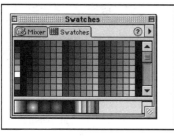

Figure 1.41 To group panels, drag one panel tab over another. When the outline shows just a tab shape (top), release the mouse button. The new tab appears at the front of the target window (bottom).

Panels vs. Windows

The distinction between panels and windows in Flash seems to be somewhat arbitrary. The important thing to remember in managing your screen real estate is that any item that has a tab can be combined in a window with other tabbed items or can be separated into its own window. Actions, for example, appears directly within the Window menu. But choosing Window > Actions opens a window containing an Action tab, and you can drag that tab to combine it with any open panels.

To combine panels in one window:

1. With two or more panel windows open on the desktop, click a panel tab and drag it away from its window.

    Flash displays an outline of the window and tab as you drag.

2. Drag the tab on top of another open panel window.

    The outline changes to show just the tab; the rectangle disappears.

3. Release the mouse button.

    The tab you dragged now appears as the front item in the second window (**Figure 1.41**). The attributes of the front panel appear in the window.

4. Click the tab of any panel to bring its attributes to the front of the window.

✔ Tips

- Flash adds new panel tabs to the right of any tabs already in a panel window. To change the tab order, drag the panel whose tab you want to be at the far left to a separate window and then drag the remaining panels into that window in the order in which you want the tabs to appear from left to right.

- If you are short on screen real estate, try creating a set of pseudo-drop-down panels. Combine all the panels in one wide window and place it at the top of your desktop. Double-click the window's title bar to collapse the window to just the title bar and panel tabs. Double-click again to expand the window.

- You can close grouped panels from the Window menu, but the behavior is a bit tricky. To close the entire group, from the Window > Panels menu, choose the panel that is foremost in the window of grouped panels that you want to close.

Using Custom Panel Sets

Flash lets you save and restore any number of customized panel configurations. A custom panel layout stores information about which panels are open, which are grouped, how large each panel or group window should be, and where to place those windows on the desktop.

To create a custom panel layout:

1. Open the panels you want to work with.

2. Group, resize, and reposition the panels as you desire.

3. From the Window menu, choose Save Panel Layout (**Figure 1.42**).

   The Save Panel Layout dialog box appears.

4. Enter a name for your layout (**Figure 1.43**).

5. Click OK.

   Flash saves the current panel configuration and makes it available in the Panel Sets submenu. Whenever you launch Flash, it opens the panel set that was active during your previous work session.

Figure 1.42 Choose Window > Save Panel Layout to create a custom panel set.

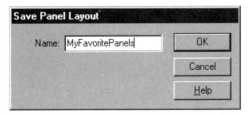

Figure 1.43 Enter a name for your custom layout in the Save Panel Layout dialog box.

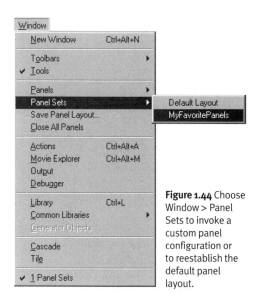

Figure 1.44 Choose Window > Panel Sets to invoke a custom panel configuration or to reestablish the default panel layout.

The Mystery of Default Panel Groups

When you use the default panel layout, Flash automatically groups some panels and windows. Choosing Window > Panels > Mixer, for example, opens the Mixer and the Swatches panel tabs in one window. Choosing Window > Actions opens a window containing both the Actions tab and the Movie Explorer tab. The logic by which Flash groups panels in the default layout is not always apparent from the Window menu. The groupings are basically, but not entirely, indicated by the lines that separate the menu items. Here's a rundown of the windows and panels that Flash groups by default:

◆ Info, Transform, Stroke, Fill

◆ Instance, Effect, Frame, Sound

◆ Mixer, Swatches

◆ Character, Paragraph, Text Options

◆ Actions, Movie Explorer

✔ Tips

■ Create different panel layouts for different tasks. You can create a set that lines up panels along the bottom of your desktop for tasks that require you to access the Timeline at the top of the Stage. You can create another set that lines the panels along the top of the desktop, covering the Timeline, when you need more room to create objects on the Stage.

■ Assign a custom keyboard shortcut to the panel layouts you use most frequently (see "Customizing Keyboard Shortcuts," below).

■ If you discover a useful panel layout, you can share it with your friends and coworkers. They just need to put the file in the Flash 5 application folder in the folder called Panel Sets.

■ Take care in naming panel sets. If you create a new panel layout with the same name as an existing set, Flash overwrites the existing panel set file.

To invoke a custom panel set:

1. From the Window menu, choose Panel Sets.

   A submenu appears, listing Default Layout and any custom panel layouts you have saved (**Figure 1.44**).

2. From the submenu, choose the desired custom set.

   Flash closes whatever panels you have open and configures your desktop with the custom setup.

To remove a custom panel set:

1. In the Finder (Mac) or on the desktop (Windows), navigate to the Panel Sets folder within the Flash 5 application folder.

2. Delete the file that bears the name of the panel set you want to remove.

Customizing Keyboard Shortcuts

The Flash 5 shortcut set lets you quickly access the drawing tools and most menu commands from the keyboard. But what if your favorite operation lacks a shortcut or uses key combinations that you find awkward? You can create your own set of combinations, add shortcuts to items that lack them, and change the assigned key command.

Flash comes with four additional shortcut sets that let you implement the same keyboard shortcuts as Macromedia's Fireworks or FreeHand 9 or Adobe's Illustrator or Photoshop.

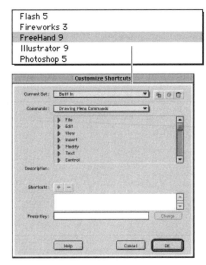

Figure 1.45 Use the Current Set menu in the Customize Shortcuts dialog box to switch to a different set of shortcuts.

Entering Values in Panel Fields

Many panels require you to enter a value in a field. You can always type a new value using the keyboard. When you are modifying selected items on the Stage, you must press Enter after typing to apply the new value to selected items.

Sliders for entering values quickly and interactively accompany many fields. A small black triangle to the right of a panel's entry field hides a pop-up slider for that field. Often, dragging a slider allows you to interactively preview new values for items selected on the Stage. The following methods of operation work for most sliders.

◆ **Click and Drag** Click and hold the small triangle; you can start dragging the slider's lever right away. Release the mouse button. Flash enters the current slider value in the field and—in most cases—applies that value to selected objects automatically.

◆ **Click and Click** Click the small triangle once; the slider pops up and stays open. You can drag the slider's lever or click various locations on the slider, to choose a new value. Flash enters the value in the field. To apply the value to selected items, you must click somewhere off the slider. Click another entry field, click elsewhere on the panel, or click the Stage.

Figure 1.46 When creating custom shortcuts you must work on a copy of one of the sets that comes with Flash. Click the Duplicate Set button to copy the set displayed in Current Sets.

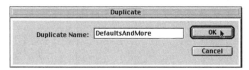

Figure 1.47 Enter a name for the set in the Duplicate dialog box.

Figure 1.48 The Commands menu offers three categories of items to which you can assign keyboard shortcuts.

To switch among shortcut sets:

1. From the Edit menu, choose Keyboard Shortcuts.

   The Customize Shortcuts dialog box appears.

2. From the Current Set menu, choose one of the listed shortcut sets (**Figure 1.45**).

3. Click OK.

   Flash loads the new shortcuts. The new key combinations appear in menus and Tooltips.

To create a custom shortcut set:

1. Follow the steps in the preceding exercise to select a set of keyboard shortcuts.

   The selected set forms the basis of your new set.

2. Click the Duplicate Set button (**Figure 1.46**).

   The Duplicate dialog box appears.

3. Enter a name for your custom shortcut set (**Figure 1.47**).

4. Click OK.

   Flash makes the new set available in the scrolling Commands window. You can now add more shortcuts and delete existing ones.

To assign a new shortcut:

1. From the Edit menu, choose Keyboard Shortcuts.

   The Customize Shortcuts dialog box appears.

2. From the Current Sets menu, choose the set you want to modify.

3. From the Commands menu, choose one of the following options (**Figure 1.48**):

continues on next page

CUSTOMIZING KEYBOARD SHORTCUTS

- To modify a command used in Flash's editing environment, choose Drawing Menu Commands.

- To modify a command used in Flash's movie-testing environment, choose Test Movie Menu Commands.

- To modify a command that accesses a drawing tool, choose Drawing Tools.

A scrolling list of the selected commands and their current assigned keyboard shortcuts appears in the Commands window.

4. In the Commands window, select the name of the command or tool you want to modify.

An overview of the item appears in the Description area of the dialog box (**Figure 1.49**). Any existing shortcuts for that item appear in the scrolling Shortcuts list and in the Press Key field.

5. Click the Add button.

Flash creates an <empty> entry in the Shortcuts list and enters <empty> in the Press Key field (**Figure 1.50**).

6. On the keyboard, press the keys you want to use as a shortcut to access the item.

Flash enters the shortcut in the Press Key field.

7. Click the Change button to update the shortcut set.

Flash replaces <empty> with the key combination in the scrolling commands list (**Figure 1.51**).

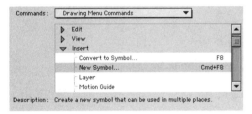

Figure 1.49 Menu-related commands appear in a hierarchical list. To expand or collapse entries in the list, click the triangle to the left of each menu name.

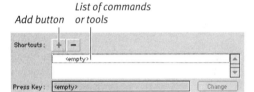

Figure 1.50 Select a command or tool in the Commands window to see its description. Click the Add button to define a new shortcut.

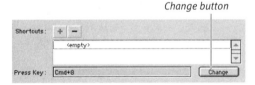

Figure 1.51 Click the Change button to confirm any additions.

Remove button

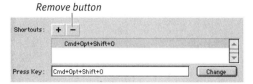

Figure 1.52 Clicking the Remove button deletes a selected shortcut.

✔ Tips

■ Shortcut keys for menu commands must be function keys or include the ⌘ character (Mac) or the Ctrl character (Windows).

■ You can assign multiple shortcuts to a single command or tool.

■ You cannot alter Flash's default shortcuts set directly. To customize Flash's standard set of keyboard commands, first duplicate the set named Flash 5 and then add and remove shortcuts in the duplicate set.

To remove a shortcut:

1. Follow steps 1 through 4 in the preceding exercise.

2. Click the Remove button (**Figure 1.52**). Flash removes the shortcut from the scrolling commands list.

✔ Tip

■ To change an existing shortcut for a selected command or tool, double-click the shortcut name in the scrolling Shortcuts list. Flash highlights the shortcut in the Press Key field. Enter your new key combination, and click the Change button.

CUSTOMIZING KEYBOARD SHORTCUTS

CREATING SIMPLE GRAPHICS

This chapter teaches you to use Macromedia Flash's drawing tools to create basic shapes from lines and solid colors or, in Flash terminology, *strokes* and *fills*.

Flash also lets you import graphics from other programs. If you create graphics in a program such as Macromedia FreeHand or Adobe Illustrator, you can import them into Flash for animation (see Chapter 7).

For the first time, in version 5, Flash offers the option of drawing with Bézier curves, using the new pen tool. The pen works similarly to the Bézier tool in other graphics programs. For those who are unfamiliar with Bézier tools or who want to sketch freely, Flash continues to offer its natural drawing tools, with various levels of assistance. Flash's assistance can change a basically straight line that bobbles a bit to one that's perfectly straight. Flash also can smooth curves so that they flow beautifully instead of in jaggy fits and starts.

You can edit all shapes, even those drawn with the natural drawing tools, with the Bézier subselection tool. You also can correct a shape by tugging on its outline. (To learn about editing shapes, see Chapter 3.)

Touring the Toolbox

In Flash 5, the Toolbox looks a bit different than it did in Flash 4 (**Figure 2.1**). The biggest changes are the addition of the pen and subselection tools and the removal of many tool modifiers and options. The modifiers for setting most tool attributes now live in panels. You can open the precise panels you need for the work you are doing at any instant; and the panels can remain visible and ready to access no matter what tool you have selected in the Toolbox.

The Toolbox still contains modifiers for Stroke and Fill color, and three new buttons let you quickly set the default stroke (black) and fill (white), choose no color for stroke or fill, and swap the current stroke and fill colors.

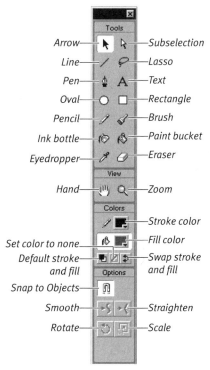

Figure 2.1 The Toolbox contains tools for drawing, editing, and manipulating graphic elements in Flash. The options section displays modifiers appropriate to the currently selected tool.

What Are Strokes and Fills?

Stroke and *fill* are two terms you will encounter often in graphics programs, and Flash is no exception. What do these terms mean? Basically, a stroke is an outline, and a fill is a solid shape. Picture a coloring book in pristine condition, with simple black lines creating the pictures: Those lines are strokes. When you fill in the areas outlined by strokes —say, with crayon—that colorful area is the fill. In a coloring book, you always start with an outline and create the fill inside it. In Flash, you can work the other way around—start with a solid shape and then create the outline around it as a separate object.

Flash's oval and rectangle tools allow you to create an elements that's just a stroke or just a fill or to create the stroke and fill elements simultaneously. The line tool, as you might guess, creates only strokes. The pen tool can create both strokes and fills.

The concept of fills and strokes is a bit trickier to grasp in relation to the brush tool. This tool creates fills. Though these fills may look like lines or brush strokes, they are really shapes you can outline with a stroke. Flash provides special tools for adding, editing, and removing strokes and fills: the ink bottle, the paint bucket, and the faucet eraser. Chapter 3 discusses these tools in greater detail.

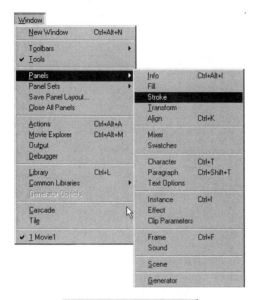

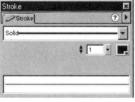

Figure 2.2 Choose Window > Panels > Stroke (top) to display the Stroke panel (bottom).

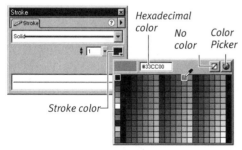

Hexadecimal color

No color

Color Picker

Stroke color

Figure 2.3 Clicking the stroke-color box opens a set of color swatches and provides the eyedropper tool for selecting a new color.

Setting Stroke Attributes

A line has three attributes: color, thickness (or *weight*), and style. The Stroke panel lets you set all three. Any tools that create strokes use the settings that currently appear in the Stroke panel. In addition to setting stroke color in the panel, you can set stroke color from the Toolbox.

To access the Stroke panel:

◆ If the Stroke panel is not currently open, from the Window menu, choose Panels > Stroke.

The Stoke panel appears on the desktop (**Figure 2.2**).

To set stroke color:

1. Access the Stroke panel.

2. Click the stroke-color box.

The pointer changes to an eyedropper tool, and a set of swatches appears (**Figure 2.3**).

3. To select a color, *do one of the following:*

◆ To select the color directly below the tip of the eyedropper, with the eyedropper tool, click a swatch or an item on the Stage.

◆ In the hexadecimal-color field, enter a value.

◆ To define a new color, click the Color Picker button. (For more information on defining colors, see Chapter 3.)

The selected color appears in the stroke-color box. Flash uses that color to create lines when you use the line tool or any other tool that creates strokes.

✔ Tips

■ You can set stroke color without opening the Stroke panel. In the Toolbox, with any tool selected, click the stroke-color box. The eyedropper tool and a set of swatches appear (**Figure 2.4**). Select a color, and Flash updates the stroke-color box in both the Toolbox and the Stroke panel.

■ To set the stroke color to black quickly, click the Default stroke-color button in the Toolbox.

To set a line weight in the Stroke panel:

1. Access the > Stroke panel.

2. In the panel line-weight field, enter a number between 0.25 and 10 (**Figure 2.5**).

✔ Tips

■ For easy entry of line weights, click the triangle to the right of the line-weight field. (A slider pops open.) Drag the slider's lever to choose a value between 0.25 and 10 points. (Flash previews the changes in the preview window as you drag the slider lever.) Click elsewhere in the panel window or on the Stage to close the slider and apply the new line weight.

■ For even quicker changes, just click and drag the slider triangle. When you release the slider's lever, Flash applies the new weight immediately.

■ In Flash, the hairline setting is considered to be a line style, not a line weight. In symbols, hairlines do not change thickness when you resize the symbol. Other lines in symbols grow thicker or thinner as you scale them up or down. (To learn about symbols, see Chapter 6.)

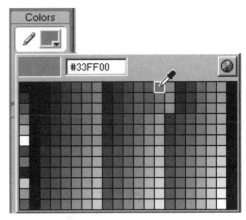

Figure 2.4 Click the stroke-color box in the Toolbox to open a set of color swatches similar to those available in the Stroke panel.

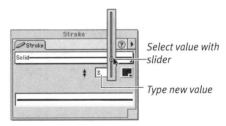

Figure 2.5 Entering a new value in the line-weight field sets the thickness for strokes created by tools that create strokes.

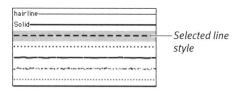

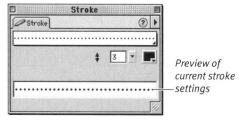

Selected line style

Preview of current stroke settings

Figure 2.6 Choose a line style from the pop-up menu in the Stroke panel.

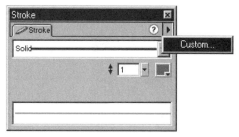

Figure 2.7 Choose Custom from the Stroke panel's Options menu to access the Line Style dialog box.

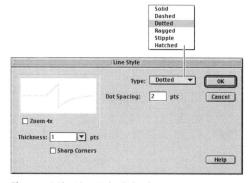

Figure 2.8 The Line Style dialog box contains a pop-up menu for selecting the type of line you want to customize. The dialog box shown here is for Dotted lines.

To select a line style:

1. In the Stroke panel, click the Style menu (**Figure 2.6**).

   A list of seven styles (hairline, solid, dashed, dotted, ragged, stippled, and hatched) appears.

2. Select a style.

   A graphic representation of that style appears in the line-style field.

You can modify these styles—creating, for example, a custom dotted-line style with lots of space between dots or a stippled line with a highly random pattern.

To customize a line style:

1. In the Stroke panel, click the triangle in the top-right corner of the window.

   The Options menu appears.

2. Choose Custom (**Figure 2.7**).

   The Line Style dialog box appears.

3. From the Type menu in the Line Style dialog box, choose a style—for example, Dotted.

   The parameters appropriate to the currently selected line style appear in the dialog box (**Figure 2.8**).

4. In the Dot Spacing field, enter a number between 1 and 20 points.

   This value specifies the amount of space that appears between the dots in the dotted line.

5. To select a thickness value, *do one of the following:*

   ◆ Enter a value from 1 to 10 in the line-thickness field.

   ◆ Choose a value from the pop-up menu.

continues on next page

SETTING STROKE ATTRIBUTES

6. If you want Flash to place a dot at the tip of each corner when you draw a line, choose Sharp Corners.

7. Click OK.

Your custom dotted-line style appears in the preview window of the Stroke panel.

✔ Tips

■ Line-style custom settings remain in effect until you customize that style again or quit Flash. Define a custom dashed line that has really long dashes, and you'll get the same long dashes the next time you choose the dashed line from the Style menu in the Stroke panel.

■ Changing the line weight doesn't affect any other custom settings you've applied. If you want to use your customized long dashes with a thinner line, just enter a new line-weight value directly in the Stroke panel; you don't need to choose Custom and go back to the Line Style dialog box.

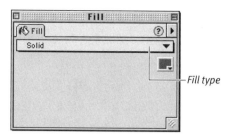

Figure 2.9 Choose Window > Panels > Fill to open the Fill panel.

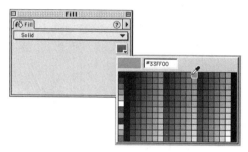

Figure 2.10 Click the fill-color box to access the eyedropper tool and swatches for selecting a new fill color.

Setting Fill Attributes

There are five fills: none, solid, linear gradient, radial gradient, and bitmap. You set the fill type and any related attributes in the Fill panel. For a solid fill, for example, you can set the color. Any tools that create fills use the Fill panel's current settings. You can also choose some fills from the Toolbox. The following exercises deal with solid fills; you'll learn about gradients and bitmaps in Chapter 3.

To access the Fill Panel:

◆ If the Fill panel is not open, from the Window menu, choose Panels > Fill.

The Fill panel appears (**Figure 2.9**).

To select a fill type:

◆ From the Fill panel's Fill menu, choose a fill type—Solid, for example.

The attributes for that fill appear in the panel below the menu.

To select a solid fill color from the Fill panel:

1. In the Fill panel, with Solid selected as the fill type, click the fill-color box.

The pointer changes to an eyedropper tool, and a set of swatches appears (**Figure 2.10**).

2. To select a color, *do one of the following:*

◆ To select the color directly below the tip of the eyedropper, click a swatch or an item on the Stage.

◆ Enter a value in the hexadecimal-color field.

◆ To define a new color, click the Color Picker button. (For more information on defining colors, see Chapter 3.)

The new color appears in the fill-color box.

✔ Tip

■ You can set fill color without opening the Fill panel. In the Toolbox, with any tool selected, click the fill-color box. The eyedropper tool and a set of swatches appear. Select a color, and Flash updates the fill-color box in both the Toolbox and the Stroke panel.

Using the Line Tool

Flash offers a tool that does nothing but draw perfectly straight line segments. By putting together several line segments, you can create a shape made of several straight sides, such as a pentagon or star.

To draw line segments:

1. In the Toolbox, select the line tool by clicking the line icon, or press N (**Figure 2.11**).

2. Move the pointer to the spot on the Stage where you want your line to begin.

    The pointer changes to a crosshair as it moves over the Stage area.

3. Click and drag to pull a line segment out from your starting point (**Figure 2.12**).

    Flash displays an outline preview of the line, a simple form that doesn't show the line's color, style, and weight settings.

4. Release the mouse button when the line is the right length and in the right position.

    Flash draws a line segment on the Stage, using the current stroke-color, line-style, and line-weight settings (see "Setting Stroke Attributes" earlier in this chapter).

✔ Tips

- The line is not set until you release the mouse button. You can shorten, lengthen, and reorient the line's direction or angle by dragging until you release the mouse button.

- Holding down the Shift key as you draw a line constrains it to the vertical, horizontal, or 45-degree angle position.

- If you're using a narrow line thickness, you may need to zoom in to see it accurately on screen. Thin lines may look identical on screen unless you zoom in; they will print accurately, though.

Figure 2.11 Click the line icon in the Toolbox to select the line tool.

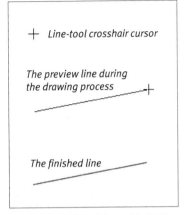

Line-tool crosshair cursor

The preview line during the drawing process

The finished line

Figure 2.12 Click and drag with the line tool's crosshair cursor. Flash previews the line as you draw. Release the mouse button, and the line takes on the attributes you assigned to the strokes in the Stroke panel.

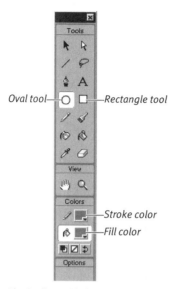

Figure 2.13 The Toolbox with the oval tool selected.

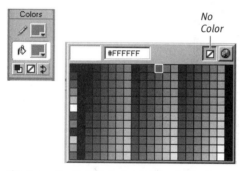

Figure 2.14 The No Color button appears in the pop-up set of fill swatches. Choosing No Color as the fill color with the oval tool allows you to create oval outlines.

Figure 2.15 When the fill-color box is selected in the Colors section of the Toolbox, clicking the No Color button allows whatever tool you select to create a shape with no fill.

Using the Oval and Rectangle Tools

Flash provides separate tools for drawing ovals and rectangles. The tools work quite similarly; both can draw a shape as an outline (just a stroke) or as a solid object (a fill). You can also create a filled object with an outline stroke simultaneously.

To draw an oval outline:

1. In the Toolbox, select the oval tool, or press O (**Figure 2.13**).

2. To activate the fill-color box, in the Colors section of the Toolbox, select the paint-bucket icon.

3. To set fill color to None, *do one of the following:*
   - Click the fill-color box, and in the set of swatches that appears, click the No Color button (**Figure 2.14**).
   - In the Colors section of the Toolbox, click the No Color button (**Figure 2.15**).

4. Use the current stroke color and line weight or select new ones (see "Setting Stroke Attributes" earlier in this chapter).

5. Move the pointer over the Stage.
   It turns into a crosshair.

continues on next page

6. Click and drag to create an oval with the size and proportions you want (**Figure 2.16**).

Flash displays an outline preview of the oval as you drag.

7. Release the mouse button.

Flash draws an outline oval.

✔ Tip

■ To draw a perfect circle, hold down the Shift key while you drag the crosshair cursor. Flash makes the oval grow with the proportions of a perfect circle.

To draw a rectangular fill:

1. In the Toolbox, select the rectangle tool, or press R (**Figure 2.17**).

2. To select the stroke-color box, in the Colors section of the Toolbox, click the pencil icon.

3. To set stroke color to None, *do one of the following:*
  ◆ Click the stroke-color box, and in the swatch window, click the No Color button.
  ◆ In the Colors section of the Toolbox, click the No Color button.

4. Use the current fill color, or select a new one (see "Setting Fill Attributes" earlier in this chapter).

5. To open the Rectangle Settings dialog box, *do one of the following:*
  ◆ In the Options section of the Toolbox, click the Round Rectangle Radius button.
  ◆ Double-click the rectangle tool.
  The Rectangle Settings dialog box appears (**Figure 2.18**).

6. Enter a value of 0 points.

This setting creates a rectangle with sharp 90-degree angles at the corners.

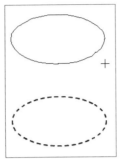

Figure 2.16 Click the Stage, and drag to create an oval. You see a preview outline of your shape (top). Release the mouse button, and Flash creates an oval outline using the current color, thickness, and style settings (bottom).

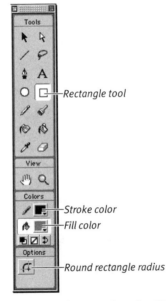

Rectangle tool

Stroke color

Fill color

Round rectangle radius

Figure 2.17 The rectangle tool and its modifier. The Round Rectangle Radius modifier lets you specify how blunt the rectangle's corners are.

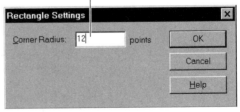

Corner radius value

Figure 2.18 Enter a value of 0 in the Rectangle Settings dialog box to create a rectangle with sharp corners. Enter a larger value to round the corners of your rectangle.

Figure 2.19 As you drag the rectangle tool, Flash creates an outline preview of a rectangle (top). To complete the fill shape, release the mouse button (bottom).

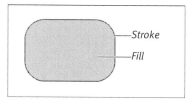

Stroke

Fill

Figure 2.20 A rounded rectangle with stroke and fill.

7. Click OK to close the dialog box.

8. Move the pointer over the Stage.
   It changes to a crosshair.

9. Click and drag to create a rectangle with the size and proportions you want.
   Flash displays an outline preview of the rectangle as you drag.

10. Release the mouse button.
    Flash draws a rectangular fill, using the color currently set in the Fill panel (**Figure 2.19**).

✔ **Tip**

■ To create a perfect square, hold down the Shift key as you draw your rectangle. Flash constrains the rectangle to the proportions of a perfect square.

To draw a rounded rectangle with fill and stroke:

1. In the Toolbox, select the rectangle tool.

2. Make sure that you have selected a fill and stroke color other than No Color (see Setting Stroke Attributes" and "Setting Fill Attributes" earlier in this chapter).

4. Click the Round Rectangle Radius button.

5. In the Rectangle Settings dialog box, enter the desired corner-radius setting, and click OK.

6. Click and drag on the Stage with the crosshair cursor to create a rectangle.

7. Release the mouse button.
   Flash creates a filled rectangle in the color currently set in the Fill panel and gives it a stroke the color, thickness, and style currently set in the Stroke panel (**Figure 2.20**).

✔ Tips

- Flash accepts corner-point settings ranging from 0 to 999 points. This value equals the radius of the imaginary circle that creates the rounded corner. A larger value creates a more-rounded corner.

- To reset the rectangle tool's corner radius to 0 quickly, Shift-double-click the rectangle tool or Shift-click the Round Rectangle Radius button.

- You can change a rectangle's corner radius as you draw. Drag on the Stage with the rectangle tool to create your shape. Before releasing the mouse button, press the up-arrow key to reduce the corner radius value; press the down-arrow key to increase it. Now release the mouse button to complete your shape.

- The Round Rectangle mode of the rectangle tool makes it easy to draw capsule shapes in Flash. Use a large corner-radius setting—say, 300 points. This high setting ensures that a smooth arc connects the two shorter sides of the rectangle and the longer sides remain flat. Note that if you draw four sides of equal length using this high corner-radius setting, you'll wind up with something more like a circle than a square.

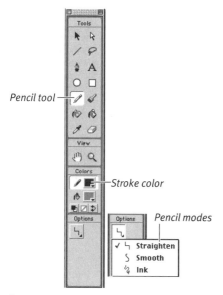

Figure 2.21 With the pencil tool selected, the Toolbox displays a pop-up menu of pencil modes.

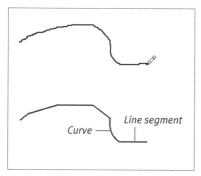

Figure 2.22 With the pencil in Straighten mode, when you draw a squiggle, Flash previews it for you. When you release the mouse button, Flash applies straightening, turning your rough squiggle (top) into a set of straight line segments and smooth curves (bottom).

Using the Pencil Tool with Assistance

Flash's pencil tool offers two freeform line-drawing modes—Straighten and Smooth—that help you draw smooth, neat shapes.

Straighten mode eliminates the small blips and tremors that can mar quick hand sketches. Straighten refines your line into straight line segments and regular arcs. This mode also carries out what Flash calls *shape recognition*. In Straighten mode, Flash evaluates each rough shape you draw, and if the shape comes close enough to Flash's definition of an oval or rectangle, Flash turns your rough approximation into a version of the shape neat enough to please your high-school geometry teacher.

Smooth mode helps you by transforming your rough drawing into one composed of smooth, curved line segments.

To use Straighten mode for freeform drawing:

1. In the Toolbox, select the pencil tool.
   The pencil tool modifiers appear at the bottom of the Toolbox (**Figure 2.21**).

2. From the Pencil Mode pop-up menu, choose Straighten.

3. Move the pointer over the Stage, and it turns into the pencil icon.

4. Click and draw a squiggle (**Figure 2.22**). Flash previews your rough line.

5. Release the mouse button.
   Flash recasts the line you've drawn with fewer vectors. Notice that it turns your line into a set of straight line segments and regular curves.

To use Straighten mode for drawing rectangles and ovals:

1. With the pencil tool in Straighten mode, click and quickly draw a rectangle or circle (**Figure 2.23**).

You don't need to close the shape completely; leave a slight gap between the first and last points of your line.

2. Release the mouse button.

Flash recognizes the shape and creates a perfect rectangle or oval, connecting the ends of your line and completing the shape for you.

✔ Tip

■ Tolerance settings are all-important here. You can set Flash to change almost anything ovoid into a circle and anything slightly more oblong into a rectangle. Take a little time to play around with the settings in the Editing tab of the Preferences dialog box (see "Controlling the Amount of Assistance You Get" later in this chapter) to find the degree of accuracy that's right for you.

Smooth mode does not recognize shapes or connect line segments; it simply smoothes out the curves you draw.

To draw smooth curves:

1. With the pencil tool selected, choose Smooth from the Pencil Mode pop-up menu.

2. Move the pointer over the Stage; then click and draw a wavy line.

3. Release the mouse button.

Flash eliminates any vectors that aren't needed to define the basic shape (**Figure 2.24**).

Notice that Flash turns your line into a set of smooth curved segments instead of straight line segments.

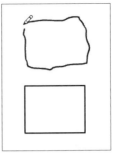

Figure 2.23 In the pencil tool's Straighten mode, when you draw a rough rectangle (top) and release the mouse button, Flash turns your shape into a rectangle with straight sides and sharp corners. You can also rough out oval shapes and have Flash fix them the same way.

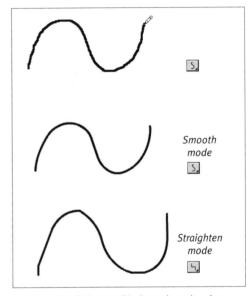

Smooth mode

Straighten mode

Figure 2.24 With the pencil in Smooth mode, when you draw a wavy line (top), Flash turns it into a series of smooth curves (middle). Compare a similar shape drawn with the pencil set to Straighten mode (bottom).

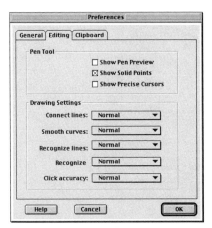

Figure 2.25 Choose Edit > Preferences, and select the Editing tab to set the amount of assistance Flash gives you in smoothing and recognizing shapes.

Must be close
Normal
Can be distant

Figure 2.26 Connect Lines controls how close the beginning and ending points of an oval or rectangle must be before Flash closes them for you.

Off
Rough
Normal
Smooth

Figure 2.27 Smooth Curves determines how much Flash alters the curve you've drawn to make it smoother.

Off
Strict
Normal
Tolerant

Figure 2.28 Recognize Lines determines how close to straight a line must be before Flash removes all curves and changes it to a straight line segment.

Off
Strict
Normal
Tolerant

Figure 2.29 Recognize Shapes determines how nearly ovoid or rectangular a shape must be for Flash to transform it to a perfect oval or rectangle.

Strict
Normal
Tolerant

Figure 2.30 Click Accuracy determines how close you must get to a line segment with the arrow pointer to select that segment.

Controlling the Amount of Assistance You Get

Flash helps you by straightening line segments, recognizing shapes, and smoothing curves as you draw them with the various pencil-tool modifiers discussed in the preceding sections. The degree of assistance depends on the settings you pick in the Editing tab of the Preferences dialog box. The settings are relative to the resolution of your monitor and the amount of magnification you're using to view the Stage. At 100 percent magnification with the setting Can Be Distant, for example, Flash recognizes and closes an oval that has a gap of 8 to 10 pixels between its beginning and ending points. But bump up the magnification to 400 percent, and Flash refuses to close a gap of 8 to 10 pixels. You must get the shape's end points within around 2 pixels of each other before Flash will recognize the gap and close the shape for you.

To set the degree of assistance:

1. From the Edit menu, choose Preferences. The Preferences dialog box appears.

2. Choose the Editing tab of the Preferences dialog box (**Figure 2.25**).

3. In the Drawing Settings section of the dialog box, choose one of the options from the pop-up menu (**Figure 2.26** through **Figure 2.30**).

    Your choices range from turning the feature off to having Flash give you the highest degree of assistance.

Using the Pencil Tool Without Assistance

The pencil tool's Ink mode allows you to bypass the assistance features and draw without correction or shape recognition. Ink mode leaves all the little bumps, twists, and turns of your rough sketch intact.

To use Ink mode to draw irregular, unsmoothed lines:

1. With the pencil tool selected, from the Pencil Mode pop-up menu, choose Ink.

2. Move the pointer over the Stage; then click and draw a squiggle (**Figure 2.31**).

3. Release the mouse button.

   Flash recasts the line you've drawn so that it looks less jaggy, but Flash does not straighten lines or smooth curves.

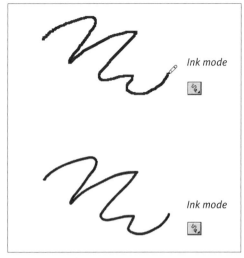

Figure 2.31 Flash turns a squiggle drawn in the pencil's Ink mode (top) into a vector graphic (bottom), with minimal smoothing and straightening of its curves and line segments.

Figure 2.32 Select the pen tool to create paths.

Figure 2.33 The x next to the pen icon indicates that you are about to start a new path. Click to place the first anchor point.

Using the Pen Tool: Straight Line Segments

With most Flash tools, the math goes on behind the scenes. You draw a line or a shape, and Flash takes care of placing points that define the line segments and curves that make up that shape. The pen tool brings the process to center stage. The pen tool lets you place defining points (called *anchor points*) and adjust the curvature of the lines connecting them (using controllers called *Bézier handles*). You learn more about curves and handles in the following section of this chapter and in Chapter 3.

The *path*—the whole series of points and connecting lines created by the pen tool— is the skeleton of your object. When you've completed a path, Flash fleshes it out by applying a stroke to it.

For the following exercises set the pen tool to show previews as you create your path. Choose Edit > Preferences, select the Editing tab, and check the Show Pen Preview checkbox.

To draw straight line segments with the pen tool:

1. In the Toolbox, select the pen tool, or press P (**Figure 2.32**).

2. Set stroke attributes for your path.

3. Move the pointer over the Stage.

   The pen icon appears with a small x next to it (**Figure 2.33**). The x indicates that you are ready to place the first point of a path.

4. Click where you want your line segment to begin.

   The pointer changes to a hollow arrowhead; a small circle indicates the location of the anchor point on the Stage.

5. Reposition the pen tool where you want your line segment to end.

Flash extends a preview of the line segment from the first point to the tip of the pen as you move around the Stage.

6. Click.

Flash completes the line segment, using the selected stroke attributes. The anchor points appear as solid squares (**Figure 2.34**).

7. Repeat steps 5 and 6 to draw a series of connected line segments.

To end an open path:

To end a line segment or series of segments, *do one of the following*:

◆ Double-click the last point in your path.

In the Toolbox, click the pen tool (or any other tool).

◆ From the Edit menu, choose Deselect All, or press ⌘-Shift-A (Mac) or Ctrl-Shift-A (Windows).

◆ On the Stage, ⌘-click (Mac) or Ctrl-click (Windows) away from your path.

To create a closed path:

1. With the pen tool selected, click three areas on the Stage to place three anchor points in a triangular layout.

Flash completes two legs of your triangle with strokes.

2. Position the pointer over your first anchor point.

Flash previews a line segment for the third side of the triangle. A small hollow circle appears next to the pen icon (**Figure 2.35**).

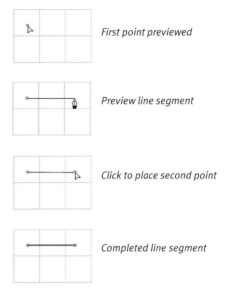

First point previewed

Preview line segment

Click to place second point

Completed line segment

Figure 2.34 Flash previews points as you place them (top) and adds a stroke to the path as soon as you complete a segment (bottom).

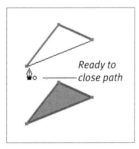

Ready to close path

Figure 2.35 To close a path, position the pen tool over an existing anchor point (top). The circle next to the pen icon indicates that you are directly on top of the path. Click to complete the path (bottom).

3. Click.

Flash closes the shape, adding a stroke to the triangle's third side and filling the triangle with the currently selected fill color.

4. Move the pointer away from your anchor points.

A small x appears next to the pen icon, indicating that you are free to place the first anchor point of a new path.

✔ Tip

■ You can close a path anywhere along a line (or curve) segment. Position the pen over a the path between anchor points. A small circle appears next to the pen icon. Click to close the path. Double-click to close the path *and* fill the resulting shape.

USING THE PEN TOOL: STRAIGHT LINE SEGMENTS

Using the Pen Tool: Curved Line Segments

In the preceding exercise, you simply clicked to lay down anchor points, and Flash created straight line segments connecting those points. To create curved segments, you must activate the points' Bézier handles. You do this by clicking and dragging when you place a point. As you drag, the handles extend out from the anchor point.

As you learn to create curves with the pen tool, it helps to have a grid visible on the Stage. To display the grid, choose View > Show Grid.

To draw an upward curve with the pen tool:

1. With the pen tool selected, move the pointer over the Stage.

   The pen icon appears with a small x next to it. The x indicates that you are ready to place the first point of a path.

2. Click a grid intersection where you want your curve segment to begin, and hold down the mouse button.

   Flash places a preview point on the Stage; the pointer changes to a hollow arrowhead.

3. Drag the pointer in the direction in which you want your curve to bulge.

   Two handles extend from the anchor point, growing in opposite directions as you drag.

4. Release the mouse button, and reposition the pointer to the right of your original point.

   The pen icon returns, and Flash previews the curve you are drawing.

5. Click and drag in the opposite direction from the curve's bulge.

   As you drag, the preview of the curve changes.

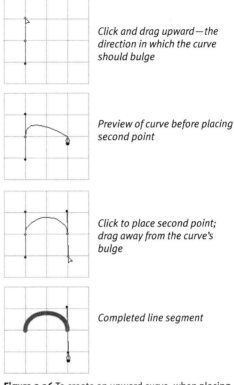

Click and drag upward—the direction in which the curve should bulge

Preview of curve before placing second point

Click to place second point; drag away from the curve's bulge

Completed line segment

Figure 2.36 To create an upward curve, when placing the first anchor point, click and drag toward the top of the Stage. Before you click and drag your second point, the preview looks lopsided. You adjust the curvature as you drag the Bézier handle. Drag toward the bottom of the Stage.

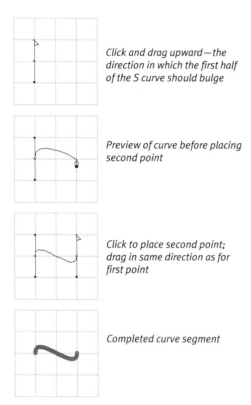

Click and drag upward—the direction in which the first half of the S curve should bulge

Preview of curve before placing second point

Click to place second point; drag in same direction as for first point

Completed curve segment

Figure 2.37 Click and drag your first point upward to start an S curve. Click and drag your second point in the same direction. Release the mouse button to finish the curve.

6. When the curve preview looks the way you want, release the mouse button.

Flash completes your curve segment with a stroke (**Figure 2.36**).

You can end the path here (as described in the preceding section) or repeat steps 2 through 6 to add more curves to your path.

To draw an S curve with the pen tool:

1. Follow steps 1 and 2 in the preceding exercise.

2. Drag the pointer in the direction in which you want the left side of the curve to bulge.

3. Release the mouse button, and reposition the pointer to the right of your original point.

4. Click and drag in the same direction you went in step 2.

Flash creates a horizontal S shape centered between the anchor points you placed (**Figure 2.37**).

✔ Tips

■ When you create symmetrical curves, use grid lines to help position anchor points and Bézier handles.

■ Don't worry about fine-tuning each curve as you draw; just get down the basic outlines. It's often easier to adjust points and curves when you have a rough version of the object to work on. You learn to modify paths in Chapter 3.

■ One of the tricks of drawing with the pen tool is visualizing the way a shape's curves and lines must look before you place points and adjust handles. To get the hang of it, try creating paths that trace existing objects. Lock the layer that contains your template shapes. Add a new layer, and practice re-creating the shapes, using the locked layer as a guide. (You learn about using layers in Chapter 5.)

USING THE PEN TOOL: CURVED LINE SEGMENTS

Using the Paint Bucket

The paint bucket lets you fill the inside of a closed shape with a solid color. You can also use the paint bucket to change the color of an existing fill. The oval and rectangle tools automatically create closed shapes that are easy to fill. If you draw a shape yourself, it may have some small gaps. You can have Flash ignore these gaps and fill the basic shape anyway.

In addition to solid colors, the paint bucket tool can fill shapes with gradients or bitmapped patterns (see Chapter 3).

To fill an outline shape with a solid color:

1. In the Toolbox, select the paint bucket tool by clicking the paint bucket icon, or press K.

   The paint bucket icon appears high-lighted on the Toolbox, and tool modi-fiers for fills appear in the Options section of the Toolbox (**Figure 2.38**).

2. From the Toolbox's fill-color box or the Fill panel, select a color.

3. Click the paint bucket's hot spot (the tip of the drip of paint) somewhere inside an outline shape (**Figure 2.39**).

   The shape fills with the currently selected fill color (**Figure 2.40**).

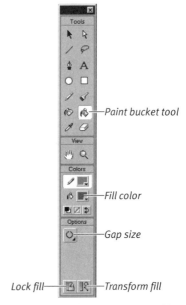

Figure 2.38 The paint bucket tool and its modifiers.

Figure 2.39 The hot spot on the paint bucket tool is the little drip at the end of the spilling paint. It changes to white when you move the paint bucket over a darker color.

Figure 2.40 Clicking inside an outline shape with the paint bucket (left) fills the shape with the currently selected color (right).

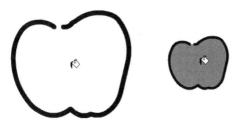

Figure 2.41 The Gap Size pop-up menu controls Flash's capability to fill shapes that aren't fully closed.

Figure 2.42 The paint bucket cannot fill this apple shape with the setting of Close Large Gaps and a magnification of 100 percent (left). But in a 50 percent view, the paint bucket with the same large-gap closure setting recognizes this shape as complete and fills it.

To set gap closure:

1. With the paint bucket selected, from the Toolbox's Gap Size menu, choose a setting (**Figure 2.41**).

   Flash presents four options for filling gaps.

2. Choose the amount of assistance you want.

   If you draw your shapes precisely, Medium or Small Gap closure serves you best; you don't want Flash to accidentally fill areas that are not meant to be shapes. If your drawings are rougher, choose Close Large Gaps. This setting enables Flash to recognize less-complete shapes.

✔ Tips

- You may be unaware that your shape has any gaps. If nothing happens when you click inside a shape with the paint bucket, try changing the Gap Size setting.

- Gap-closure settings are relative to the amount of magnification you're using to view the Stage. If the paint bucket's largest gap-closure setting fails at your current magnification, try again after reducing magnification (**Figure 2.42**).

USING THE PAINT BUCKET

Using the Brush Tool in Normal Mode

Flash's brush tool offers a way to create free-flowing swashes of color. These shapes are actually freeform fills drawn without a stroke. The brush tool enables you to simulate the type of artwork you'd create in the real world with a paintbrush or marking pen. A variety of brush sizes and tip shapes helps you create a painterly look in your drawings.

If you have a pressure-sensitive drawing tablet, the brush can interact with it to create lines of varying thickness as you vary the pressure in your drawing stroke, simulating real-world brush work.

To create freeform fill shapes:

1. In the Toolbox, select the brush tool, or press B (**Figure 2.43**).

   The various brush modifiers appear at the bottom of the Toolbox.

2. From the Toolbox's fill-color box or the Fill panel, select a fill color.

   Use the default settings for the Brush Size and Brush Shape for now. You'll learn how to change them in the next task.

3. From the Brush Mode pop-up menu, choose Paint Normal (**Figure 2.44**).

   The other paint modes allow your paint strokes to interact in various ways with other lines and shapes on the Stage. You learn more about using these modes in Chapter 4.

4. Move the pointer over the Stage.

   The icon changes to reflect the current brush size and shape.

5. Click and draw on the Stage.

   Flash previews your brushwork in the currently selected fill color (**Figure 2.45**).

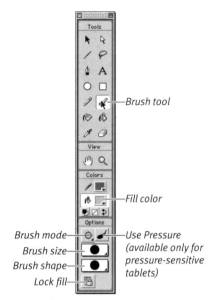

Figure 2.43 The brush tool and its modifiers.

Brush tool

Fill color

Brush mode — Use Pressure (available only for pressure-sensitive tablets)

Brush size

Brush shape

Lock fill

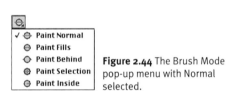

Figure 2.44 The Brush Mode pop-up menu with Normal selected.

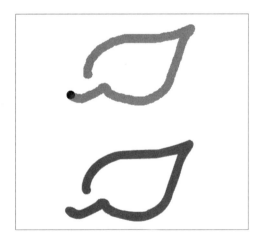

Figure 2.45 Drawing with the brush creates a preview of your shape (top); Flash recasts the shape as a vector graphic with the currently selected fill color.

Figure 2.46 The Brush Size pop-up menu.

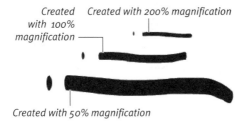

Created with 100% magnification *Created with 200% magnification*

Created with 50% magnification

Figure 2.47 Flash created these three brushstrokes with exactly the same brush size — only the magnification level of the Stage changed for each stroke.

Figure 2.48 The Brush Shape pop-up menu.

6. When you complete your shape, release the mouse button.

Flash creates the final shape.

To change the brush size:

1. With the brush tool selected in the Toolbox, click the Brush Size pop-up menu.

A list of eight circles representing brush sizes appears (**Figure 2.46**).

2. Select the size you want.

3. Release the mouse button.

A circle the size you selected appears in the Brush Size box in the Toolbox. This circle is the size Flash will use as you work with the brush tool.

✔ Tip

■ You can change the size of your brush stroke by changing the magnification at which you view the Stage. To create a fat stroke without changing your brush-tip settings, set the Stage view to a small percentage. To switch to a thin stroke, zoom out to a higher percentage (**Figure 2.47**). Be sure to check your work in 100 percent view.

To change the brush shape:

1. With the brush tool selected in the Toolbox, click the Brush Shape pop-up menu.

A list of nine tip shapes appears (**Figure 2.48**).

2. Select the shape you want.

The shape you picked appears in the Brush Shape box in the Toolbox. This shape is the tip Flash will use as you work with the brush tool.

If you have a pressure-sensitive drawing tablet attached to your computer, the Toolbox displays an additional brush modifier that lets you take advantage of your tablet.

To use a pressure-sensitive tablet:

◆ With the brush tool selected in the Toolbox, click the Use Pressure modifier. The modifier is highlighted.

You have activated the pressure-sensitive capabilities of your pen, and you can draw lines that vary in thickness according to the amount of pressure you use (**Figure 2.49**). Applying more pressure makes your brush stroke fatter. Applying less pressure keeps the brush stroke thin. Note that Flash will not create a brush stroke fatter than the currently selected brush size.

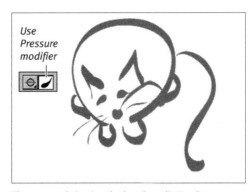

Figure 2.49 Selecting the brush tool's Use Pressure modifier activates the pressure-sensitive capabilities of a connected pressure-sensitive pen and graphics tablet. You can then produce lively lines of varying thickness simply by applying more or less pressure as you draw. Flash created all the lines in this cat with a single brush size and shape.

Text tool

Figure 2.50 Select the text tool in the Toolbox to start creating text fields on the Stage.

Mac   Windows

Figure 2.51 The text tool pointer.

Resize handle for text box without word wrap

Text box

Figure 2.52 The round resize handle indicates that the text box does not have word wrap turned on.

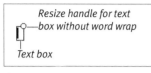

Figure 2.53 As you continue to enter text, the text box grows horizontally to accommodate it. The text will not wrap.

Using the Text Tool

The text tool lets you control all sorts of text attributes, including text and paragraph styles.

To create a single line of text for use as a graphic element:

1. In the Toolbox, select the text tool, or press T (**Figure 2.50**).

   For this task, use the current settings for type and paragraph styles. You learn to change these settings in upcoming tasks.

2. Move the pointer over the Stage.

   The pointer turns into a crosshair with a letter A in the bottom-right corner (**Figure 2.51**).

3. Click the Stage in the spot where you want your text to start.

   Flash creates a text box containing a blinking insertion point, ready for you to enter text (**Figure 2.52**).

4. Start typing to enter your text.

   The text box grows to accommodate whatever you type (**Figure 2.53**).

5. When you finish typing, click elsewhere on the Stage (if you want to create another piece of text) or change tools.

   Flash hides the text box, leaving just the text visible. When you select another tool, Flash selects the text box automatically so that you can reposition it or change its attributes directly.

To create a text box with set width and word wrap:

1. With the text tool selected in the Toolbox, click the Stage in the spot where you want your text to start.

   Flash creates a text box with a round resize handle.

2. Move your pointer over the resize handle.

   The pointer changes to a double-headed arrow.

3. Click and drag the handle until your text box is as wide as you want it (**Figure 2.54**).

   The resize handle changes to a square.

4. Release the mouse button.

   The blinking insertion point appears in the text box.

5. Enter your text.

   Flash wraps the text to fit inside the column that the text box defines. The box automatically grows taller (not wider) to accommodate your text.

✔ Tips

- To reposition a text box with the text tool active, position the pointer along the edge of the text box. The pointer changes to the selection arrow. You can now click and drag the text box to a new location.

- If you enter so much text on one line that the end of the text box starts to disappear off the Stage, you can fix the problem.

   You can either drag the text box to the left using the selection arrow or choose View > Work Area (Shift-⌘-W [Mac], Ctrl-Shift-W [Windows]) and reduce magnification until you can see the resizing handle. You can then force the text to wrap by resizing the text box.

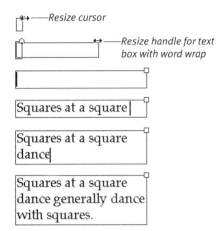

Figure 2.54 Click and drag the resize handle to create a text box with a specific width. The handle changes to a square, indicating that the text you enter will wrap to fit the column width of the text box. The text box continues to grow in length—but not width—as you enter more text.

What Is Editable Text?

The term *editable text* has two meanings in Flash. First, you can modify text within the Flash authoring environment. As you create text elements for your movie, you can go back and change your typeface, pick a new text color, select another font size, fix typos—you name it (Flash calls this type of text *static text*). Second, text can be modified in a movie playing in the Flash Player. Through the use of actions and variables, your movie can retrieve user input and put it to work in various ways (Flash calls such text *input text*). Or you, the creator, can use editable text fields to update and provide new information in a movie (Flash calls such text *dynamic text*).

In this chapter, you learn about using static text, which is strictly a graphic element in the final movie. To find out more about input text and dynamic text, check out Chapter 15.

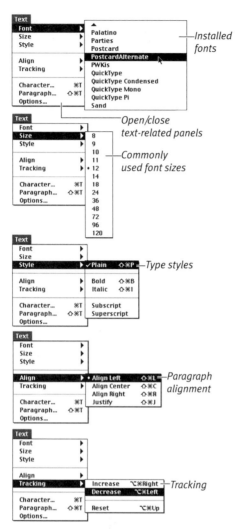

Figure 2.55 The Text menu presents several options for applying type attributes to selected text.

Setting Text Attributes

Flash offers two ways to set text attributes: the Text menu and the text-related panels. From the Text menu, you can set the font, size, style, paragraph alignment, and tracking of selected text. The Text menu also lists commands for opening the three text-related panels: Character, Paragraph, and Text Options. These panels allow you not only to modify selected text, but also to set the attributes to be used by the text tool the next time you create a text box. You learn to use the panels in subsequent exercises.

To set attributes via the Text menu:

1. Following the steps in the preceding exercises, create a text block on the Stage.

2. With the text tool selected, highlight some or all of your text to select it.

3. From the Text menu, choose the attribute you want to modify (**Figure 2.55**).
   Flash applies the new setting to your type.

✔ Tip

■ Whenever you select text, Flash puts all the attributes of that text into the text-related panels—for example, the Character panel. In other words, selecting text loads the text tool with that text's attributes. Keep blocks of text with formatting you use often in the work area and just click to re-create their settings for the text tool.

Setting Character Attributes

The Character panel allows you to set the attributes of your text that deal specifically with type: the typeface, font size, spacing between letters, color, and style. You can define text as a superscript or subscript. You can also create live links between text and URLs in this panel.

You can set character attributes in advance so that as you type, the text tool applies them automatically, or you can apply character attributes to existing text. The text tool always uses whatever settings currently appear in the Character panel.

To access the Character panel:

If the Character panel is not currently open, *do one of the following:*

◆ From the Window menu, choose Panels > Character.

◆ In the Launcher bar at the bottom of the Stage, click the Show Character button.

The Character panel appears (**Figure 2.56**).

To select text to apply character attributes:

Do one of the following:

◆ With the text tool selected, click and drag over existing text to highlight just a portion of text.

◆ With the arrow tool selected, click a text box to select all the text within it.

✔ Tip

■ You can select multiple text boxes with the arrow tool and modify them all at the same time. (You learn more about selections in Chapter 3.)

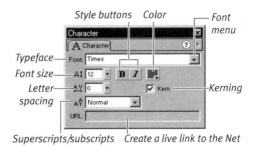

Figure 2.56 Choosing Window > Panels > Character is one way to open the Character panel, where you set the type attributes to be created by the text tool.

Preview window   *Font menu*

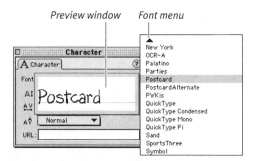

Figure 2.57 The font list in the Character panel lets you see a preview of each typeface as you move the pointer through the list.

The following exercises assume that you have selected text to modify.

In the Character panel choose a typeface in one of two ways.

To choose a typeface:

1. Click the triangle to the right of the Font field.

A scrolling list of your installed fonts appears, together with a font-preview window (**Figure 2.57**).

2. Move the pointer over a font name.

The preview window displays the name in the selected font.

3. Click to select the currently highlighted font.

The selected font name now appears in the Font field.

or

1. Click and drag in the Font field to highlight the current font name.

2. Enter the name of the font you want to use.

✔ Tips

■ Although the Toolbox's Font field is not case-sensitive, you do need to type accurately. If Flash can't find the name you type, it doesn't warn you. The name you typed remains intact, but the system substitutes another font.

■ You can set text attributes in text-related panels at any time; the text tool doesn't have to be selected. When you next select the text tool, it uses the current panel settings.

To set font size:

1. In the Character panel's Font Size field, enter the desired point size.

2. Press Enter.

✔ Tips

■ For easy entry of new font sizes, click the triangle to the right of the Font Size field. (A slider pops open.) Drag the slider's lever to choose a value between 8 and 96 points. (Flash previews the changes on the Stage as you drag the slider lever.) Press Enter.

■ To enter font sizes of 97, 98, or 99 points, you must type the value in the Font Size field.

■ For even quicker changes, just click and drag the slider triangle. When you release the slider's lever, Flash confirms the new font size, you don't need to press Enter.

To choose a text color:

1. In the Character panel, click the fill-color box (note that text in Flash is a fill).

   The pointer changes to an eyedropper, and a set of swatches appears (**Figure 2.58**).

2. To select a color, *do one of the following:*

   ◆ To select the color directly below the tip of the eyedropper, with the eyedropper tool, click a swatch or an item on the Stage.

   ◆ Enter a value in the hexadecimal-color field.

   ◆ To define a new color, click the Color Picker button. (For more information on defining colors, see Chapter 3.)

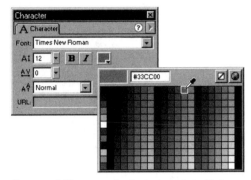

Figure 2.58 Choose a color for text created with the text tool from the Character panel's stroke-color box.

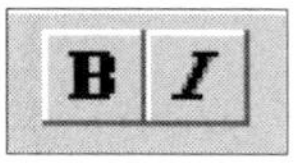

Figure 2.59 Access bold and italic styles by clicking the Bold and Italic buttons in the Character panel.

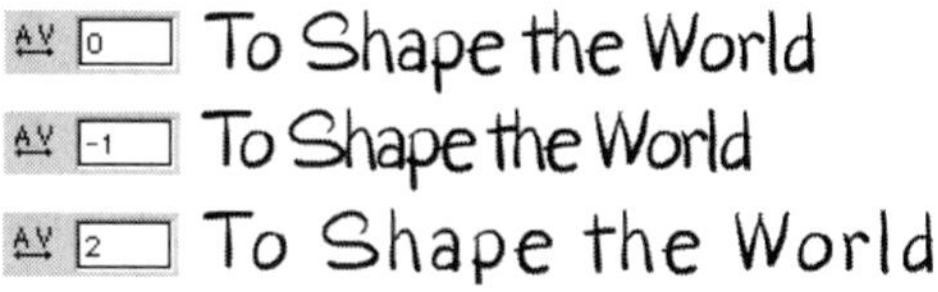

$\underline{A}\underline{V}$ ⃞0⃞ To Shape the World

$\underline{A}\underline{V}$ ⃞-1⃞ To Shape the World

$\underline{A}\underline{V}$ ⃞2⃞ To Shape the World

Figure 2.60 Enter a negative tracking value to bring characters closer together. Enter a positive value to space characters out. Enter 0 for no tracking.

To choose a type style:

In the Character panel, *do one of the following:*

◆ To create boldface type, click the Bold button (**Figure 2.59**).

◆ To create italic type, click the Italic button.

   To create type that is both boldface and italic, click the Bold and Italic buttons.

   When creating bold and italic styles, Flash simply modifies the current typeface; Flash doesn't select a bold or italic typeface in the family of fonts you've chosen.

Flash's Tracking feature allows you to control tracking, the amount of space between letters in a chunk of selected text.

To apply tracking:

1. Within a text box in a Flash document, select the text to track.

2. In the Character panel's Tracking field, enter the desired point size.

   A negative value reduces the space between the letters; a positive value increases it (**Figure 2.60**).

3. Press Enter.

SETTING CHARACTER ATTRIBUTES

✔ Tips

- For easy entry of new values, in the Character panel's Tracking field, click the triangle to the right of the field. (A slider pops open.) Drag the slider's lever to a value between –59 and 59. (Flash previews the changes on the Stage as you drag the slider lever.) Press Enter.

- For even quicker changes, just click and drag the slider triangle. When you release the slider's lever, Flash confirms the new tracking value; you don't need to press Enter.

- You can increase tracking of selected text in 0.5-point increments by choosing Text > Tracking > Increase or by pressing ⌘-Option-left arrow (Mac) or Alt-Ctrl-right arrow (Windows).

- To decrease tracking in 0.5-point increments, press ⌘-Option-left arrow (Mac) or Alt-Ctrl-right arrow (Windows).

- Add the Shift key to the keyboard shortcuts for narrower and wider tracking; this method increases or decreases space in 2-pixel increments.

- You can also track interactively by using the keyboard shortcuts. The space between letters continues to expand or contract as long as you hold down the key combination.

What Is Kerning?

Kerning is the spacing between a pair of letters. Because of the way fonts are constructed, with each letter a separate element, some pairs of letters look oddly spaced when you type them. The space between a capital *T* and a lowercase *o*, for example, may seem too large because of the white space below the T's crossbar. To make the characters look better, you can reduce the space between them, or *kern in* the pair. Some letters may seem to be too close together —say, a *t* and an *i*. You can *kern out* the pair so that it looks better.

Font designers often build into their fonts special information about how to space troublesome pairs of letters. Flash takes advantage of that embedded kerning information when you check the Kerning checkbox in the Font dialog box. It's a good idea to turn kerning on to make your type look its best.

You can simulate kerning manually in Flash, instead of using the embedded kerning or in addition to it. Select the character pair that you want to kern; then use Flash's Tracking feature to bring the letters closer together or move them farther apart.

SETTING CHARACTER ATTRIBUTES

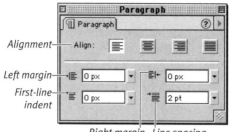

Figure 2.61 The Paragraph panel allows you to set attributes such as alignment, indents, margins, and space between lines of text.

Figure 2.62 The Alignment buttons allow you to format the text of a paragraph in four ways. A graphic representation of the selected paragraph alignment style appears on each button in the Paragraph panel.

Setting Paragraph Attributes

Flash allows you to work with paragraph formatting much as you would in a word processor. The Paragraph panel allows you to set right and left margins, a first-line indent, line spacing, and alignment (flush left, flush right, centered, or justified) (**Figure 2.61**). You can set paragraph attributes in advance so that as you type, the text tool applies them automatically. And you can apply paragraph attributes to existing text. The text tool uses whatever settings currently appear in the Paragraph panel. The following exercises describe how to modify existing text.

To set paragraph alignment:

1. To make your selection, *do one of the following:*
- ◆ With the text tool selected, click within the paragraph you want to modify.
- ◆ With the arrow tool selected, click a text box to select all the paragraphs within it.

2. In the Paragraph panel, *do one of the following* (**Figure 2.62**):
- ◆ To align text left, click the first alignment button.
- ◆ To center text, click the second alignment button.
- ◆ To align text right, click the third alignment button.
- ◆ To justify text (force all lines except the last line of a paragraph to fill the full column width), click the fourth alignment button.

To select text to modify margins, indentation, and line spacing:

Do one of the following:

◆ With the text tool selected, click anywhere within the paragraph you want to modify.

◆ With the text tool selected, click and drag to select multiple paragraphs within one text box.

◆ With the arrow tool click the text box to select all the paragraphs within the box.

✔ Tip

■ To select all the paragraphs within a text block, click with the text tool anywhere inside the text block. Choose Edit > Select All. Flash highlights the entire text block.

To set margins:

1. In the Character panel, in the Left Margin or Right Margin field, enter the desired margin size.

   The units of measure used for the margin are the ones set in the Movie Properties dialog box (see Chapter 1).

2. Press Enter, or click the Stage (**Figure 2.63**).

   Flash uses the values that you enter to create margins from the left and right sides of the text box. Your audience will not see the margins unless you are creating text they can edit, in which case you can make the border of the text box visible.

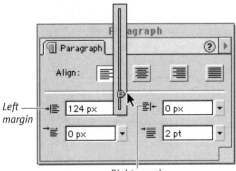

Figure 2.63 You can enter a value for right and left margins directly in the appropriate field or use the slider to select a value.

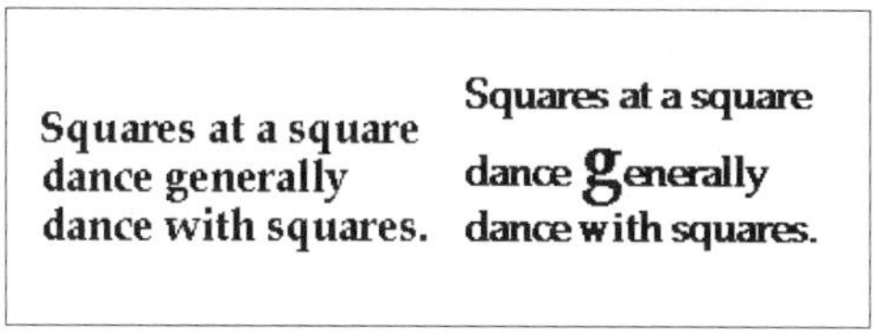

Squares at a square
dance generally
dance with squares.

Squares at a square
dance **g**enerally
dance with squares.

Figure 2.64 The line spacing for the text block on the left is set to 0 points. The space you see between lines is the space included as part of the font. Because the text is all one size, the spacing above and below the middle line of text is the same. In the text block on the right—with the same 0-point line spacing—one letter is a larger point size. Flash increases the space between lines to make room for the larger text.

✔ Tip

- For easy entry of new values when you have the text tool selected, click the triangle to the right of the Margin field. (A slider pops open.) Drag the slider's lever to choose a value between 0 and 720 pixels. Click the Stage to confirm the new margin value. With this slider, you cannot press Enter to confirm the value.

To set a first-line indent:

◆ In the Indentation field, use the value-entry techniques described in the preceding exercise to enter a value for indenting the first line of text in the paragraph.

Flash calculates the indent from the left edge of the text box.

To set line spacing:

◆ In the Line Space field, use the value-entry techniques described earlier in this chapter to enter a value for the amount of space you want between lines of text.

If your text contains various point sizes, Flash bases the spacing between two lines on the larger font (**Figure 2.64**).

✔ Tip

- Points are the most common unit of measure for working with type, and regardless of what units you've set in the Movie Properties dialog box, Flash always enters the line-spacing value with the abbreviation pt (for points).

SETTING PARAGRAPH ATTRIBUTES

MODIFYING SIMPLE GRAPHICS

3

One method of modifying Macromedia Flash graphics is to select one or more shapes and edit them by changing their attributes (such as color, size, and location) in the appropriate panels.

You can also modify the shape of an element. Some operations—such as straightening lines, adjusting Bézier curves, and assigning new attributes via panels—require that the element be selected. Other operations, such as reshaping a line segment or curve with the arrow tool, require the element to be deselected. A few operations allow you to edit the element whether it is selected or not—using the paint bucket tool to change a fill color, for example.

This chapter covers using the arrow, lasso, and subselection tools to select and modify the elements you learned to make Chapter 2. You also learn about using panels to modify elements' attributes.

Setting Selection Preferences

Flash allows you to select elements in several ways. You can click an element with the arrow tool or draw a selection outline.

When you use the arrow tool, it can take you several selection actions to select an entire line, because each segment and curve of a line is a separate element that you must select. Adding to a selection is a common operation, and Flash gives you two ways to do it: shift selection and additive selection.

The shift-selection method is common to many software programs. In Shift Select mode, you use the Shift key as a modifier while selecting an item to add it to any selection that is already active on the Stage. When you turn off Shift Select mode, selections become *additive*, which means that any new selections get added to current selections.

You always remove individual items from a selection by Shift-clicking.

Flash's default setting is Shift Select. You set the selection method in the General tab of the Preferences dialog box.

To set a selection method for the arrow tool:

1. From the Edit menu, choose Preferences. The Preferences dialog box appears.

2. Choose the General tab (**Figure 3.1**).

3. In the Selection Options section, check or uncheck the Shift Select checkbox.

4. Click OK.

    In Shift Select mode (Flash's default setting), you must Shift-click to add items to the current selection. With Shift Select turned off, each new item you click with the arrow tool gets added to the current selection.

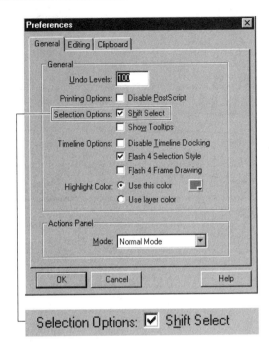

Figure 3.1 Select the General tab in the Preferences dialog box to choose a selection method.

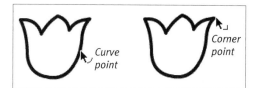

Figure 3.2 As you prepare to select a line, Flash indicates what kind of point the pointer is located over

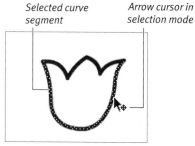

Figure 3.3 When you click the line to select it, Flash highlights that line segment.

Selecting Lines with the Arrow Tool

Using the arrow tool to select lines and outline shapes may be a bit confusing at first. What you think of as being a single element—say, a swooping squiggly line or a square—may actually be several connected segments. Flash divides lines that you draw with the pencil tool into curves and segments that it defines as vectors. This means you may need to make multiple selections to select a single item with the arrow tool.

Flash covers selections with a pattern of tiny dots. Make sure that all the parts of the line or outline you intend to select display this highlighting.

To select a single line segment:

1. In the Toolbox, select the arrow tool (or press V on the keyboard).

2. Move the pointer over a portion of the line (**Figure 3.2**).

   Flash appends a little arc or a little right-angle icon to the arrow. These icons indicate that the arrow is over a point in a line segment and show what type of point it is: a curve or a corner point. (For more information about points, see "Reshaping Lines" later in this chapter).

3. Select the line.

   Flash highlights the selected segment (**Figure 3.3**).

To select multiple line segments:

1. In the Toolbox, select the arrow tool.

2. To select the segments you want to include, *do one of the following:*

- ◆ If you are using Flash's default selection style (Shift Select), Shift-click each segment you want to select. Flash adds each new segment to the highlighted selection (**Figure 3.4**).

- ◆ If you turned off the Shift Select option in Preferences, click each segment you want to include. Flash adds each new segment to the highlighted selection.

To select multiple connected line segments as a unit:

1. In the Toolbox, select the arrow tool.

2. Double-click any segment in the series of connected line segments.

Flash highlights all the segments (**Figure 3.5**).

✔ Tip

- ■ To switch to the arrow tool temporarily while using another tool, press ⌘ (Mac) or Ctrl (Windows). The arrow tool remains in effect as long as you hold down the modifier key.

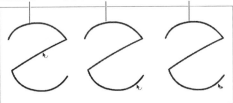

First segment selected   Second segment added to selection   Third segment added to selection

Figure 3.4 This graphic element consists of three segments. To select the entire element, you can click (or Shift-click, depending on your Preferences setting) each segment. Note that the line segments need not be connected, as they are in this example; they can be anywhere on the Stage.

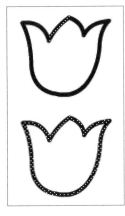

Figure 3.5 After single-clicking (top), you select one segment of this outline. After double-clicking (bottom), you select the entire shape.

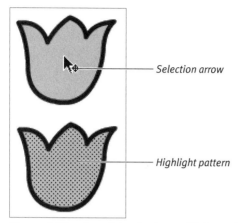

Selection arrow

Highlight pattern

Figure 3.6 When the pointer sits above a filled area, it changes into the selection arrow. Click the fill to select it. A dot pattern in a contrasting color highlights the selected fill.

Edit	
Undo	⌘Z
Redo	⌘Y
Cut	⌘X
Copy	⌘C
Paste	⌘V
Paste in Place	⇧⌘V
Clear	Delete
Duplicate	⌘D
Select All	**⌘A**
Deselect All	⇧⌘A
Cut Frames	⌥⌘X
Copy Frames	⌥⌘C
Paste Frames	⌥⌘V
Edit Symbols	⌘E
Edit Selected	
Edit All	
Preferences...	
Keyboard Shortcuts...	

Figure 3.7 Choose Edit > Select All, or press ⌘-A (Mac) or Ctrl-A (Windows), to select everything on the Stage.

Selecting Fills with the Arrow Tool

You can select filled areas the same way you select lines.

To select multiple filled areas:

1. In the Toolbox, select the arrow tool.

2. Position the pointer over the fill you want to select.

   The selection icon appears next to the arrow pointer.

3. Click the fill.

   Flash highlights the selected fill with a dot pattern (**Figure 3.6**).

4. To select additional fills, do one of the following:

   ◆ If you are using Flash's default selection style (Shift Select), Shift-click each additional fill you want to select.

   ◆ If you turned off the Shift Select option in Preferences, click each fill you want to include.

   Flash adds each newly selected fill to the highlighted selection.

✔ Tip

■ To select everything currently on the Stage, from the Edit menu, choose Select All, or press ⌘-A (Mac) or Ctrl-A (Windows) (**Figure 3.7**).

Using a Selection Rectangle

Flash allows you to select several elements (or parts of elements) in a single operation by drawing a special rectangle around them. The rectangle is not a graphic element; it just defines the boundaries of your selection.

To create a selection rectangle:

1. In the Toolbox, select the arrow tool.

2. Click and drag to pull out a selection rectangle (**Figure 3.8**).

3. Continue dragging until the rectangle encloses all the elements you want to select.

   Be sure to start dragging at a point that allows you to enclose the elements you want within a rectangle drawn from that point.

4. Release the mouse button.

   Flash highlights whatever falls inside the selection rectangle.

✔ Tip

■ If as you drag out your selection rectangle, you realize that it won't include all the elements you want to select and you don't want to add to the selection, drag back toward your starting point and release the mouse button when the rectangle encloses nothing. You can then start over at a new point.

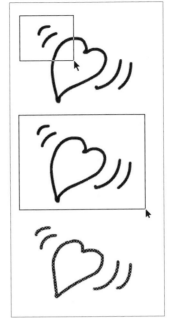

Figure 3.8 Clicking and dragging with the arrow tool creates a selection rectangle (top). Be sure to start from a point that allows you to enclose all the elements you want to select within the rectangle (middle). Release the mouse button, and you've selected those elements (bottom).

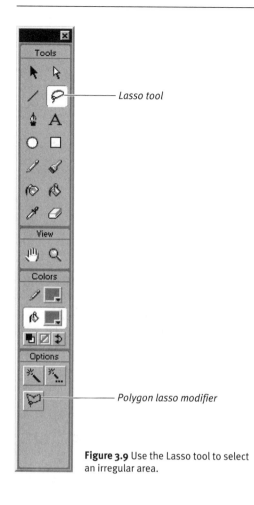

Figure 3.9 Use the Lasso tool to select an irregular area.

Using the Lasso Tool

If the lines or shapes you want to select are located close to other lines, you may have difficulty selecting just the items you want with a rectangle. The lasso tool lets you create an irregularly shaped selection outline.

To select elements with the lasso tool:

1. In the Toolbox, select the lasso tool (or press L on the keyboard) (**Figure 3.9**).

2. Click and draw a freeform line around the elements you want to select (**Figure 3.10**).

3. Close the selection outline by bringing the lasso pointer back over the point where you began the selection line.

4. Release the mouse button.
   Flash highlights whatever falls inside the shape you drew with the lasso.

✔ Tip

■ Flash draws a straight line between the starting point of your lasso line and the point at which you release the mouse button. You can skip the step of closing the shape if you're sure that Flash's closing will include the elements you want.

Figure 3.10
The lasso tool lets you select elements that are oddly shaped or too near other elements to allow use of the selection rectangle (top). Whatever falls within the area you outline with the lasso becomes highlighted and selected when you release the mouse button.

USING THE LASSO TOOL

For complex shapes, you may find it difficult to hold down the mouse button and draw the correct shape with the lasso. For these cases, Flash provides Polygon Lasso mode. The polygon lasso allows you to define the selection area with a series of connected straight-line segments.

To select elements with the lasso tool in polygon mode:

1. With the lasso tool selected, in the Toolbox, select Polygon Lasso mode.

2. Click your way around the shape or elements you want to select.

   Each time you click, the lasso finishes one line segment and adds a new point from which to start another connected line segment (**Figure 3.11**).

3. Close the shape by double-clicking.

   Flash draws a straight line from wherever you double-click to the point where you started creating the selection outline. To be sure you get all the elements you want, double-click directly over your beginning point.

✔ Tips

■ You can combine the regular lasso tool with the polygon lasso in creating a single selection outline. To access Polygon Lasso mode temporarily, hold down Option (Mac) or Alt (Windows) as you click.

■ Warning: Before you complete a selection with the polygon lasso, the lasso sticks to your pointer like gum; it'll even follow you right off the Stage and into the Toolbox. That means you can't change your mind in midselection and choose a new tool. If you get stuck with the polygon lasso tool, just double-click the Stage anywhere to complete the selection.

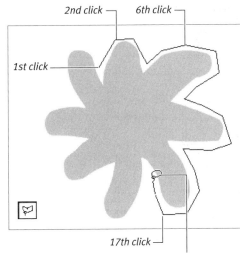

2nd click — *6th click* —

1st click —

17th click —

Positioning polygon lasso for 18th click

Figure 3.11 The polygon lasso tool creates a series of connected line segments to outline whatever element you want to select. Double-clicking finishes the shape by drawing a line from the point where you double-click to the starting point.

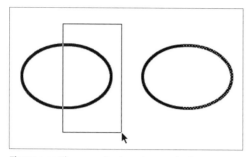

Figure 3.12 The arrow tool creates a selection rectangle that selects a portion of this oval.

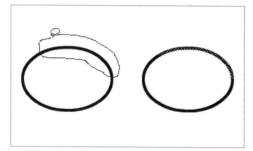

Figure 3.13 The lasso tool (or polygon lasso) gives you greater freedom to select a particular arc of the oval.

Selecting Partial Elements

Sometimes, you want to select just a portion of a line segment, curve, or shape. You can use the arrow tool to draw a rectangle that selects just a slice of an element. The lasso tool and polygon lasso tool are particularly good for this task, because they can select various-shaped portions.

To select part of a line or outline:

1. Select the arrow, lasso, or polygon lasso tool.

2. To make a selection, *do one of the following*:

   ◆ With the arrow tool, click and drag out a rectangle that encloses just a piece of the line or outline, and release the mouse button (**Figure 3.12**).

   ◆ With the lasso, draw a shape that encloses just a piece of the line or outline (**Figure 3.13**).

   ◆ With the polygon lasso, create a series of line segments that enclose just a piece of the line or outline, and double-click to close the shape.

   Flash highlights only what was inside the rectangle or the shape drawn with the lasso.

To select part of a fill:

1. Select the arrow, lasso, or polygon lasso tool.

2. To make a selection, *do one of the following:*

   ◆ With the arrow tool, click and drag out a rectangle that encloses a slice of the element, and release the mouse button (**Figure 3.14**).

   ◆ With the lasso, draw a shape that encloses part of the line or outline (**Figure 3.15**).

   ◆ With the polygon lasso, create a series of line segments that enclose part of the line or outline, and double-click to close the shape (**Figure 3.16**).

   Flash highlights only what was inside the rectangle or the shape drawn with the lasso.

✔ Tip

■ You can use a single selection area to select multiple elements or parts of multiple elements. The lasso and polygon lasso tools offer the most flexibility for grabbing different elements.

Figure 3.14 The arrow tool cuts a swath through this ribbon-shaped fill, selecting just part of each zigzag.

Figure 3.15 The lasso tool selects just a portion of the ribbon shape.

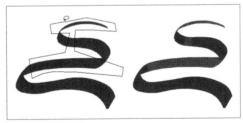

Figure 3.16 The polygon lasso makes it easy to select disparate areas of the ribbon.

Figure 3.17 With the arrow tool selected, position the pointer over the element you want to remove from the selection (left). Shift-click the item to deselect it (middle). Repeat the process to deselect another item (right).

Figure 3.18 Choose Edit > Deselect All to remove selection highlighting from all the graphic elements on the stage.

Deselecting Elements

No matter what method you use to select items, there is just one way to deselect individual elements when you have several selected. You must Shift-click with the arrow tool to remove items from a selection.

To deselect individual items:

1. In the Toolbox, select the arrow tool.

2. Hold down the Shift key.

3. Click any highlighted lines or fills you want to remove from the current selection.

Flash removes the highlighting from the item you just clicked (**Figure 3.17**).

To deselect everything:

◆ From the Edit menu, choose Deselect All, or press Shift-⌘-A (Mac) or Shift-Ctrl-A (Windows) (**Figure 3.18**).

✔ Tip

■ To deselect all elements quickly, click the arrow tool in an empty area of the Stage or work area.

Repositioning Elements Manually

If you aren't happy with the position of an element, you can always move it.

To reposition an element with the arrow tool:

1. Position the arrow tool over the element you want to move.

   The element doesn't need to be selected, although it can be. The arrow tool displays the selection icon as it hovers over the element.

2. Click the element, and drag it to the desired location (**Figure 3.19**).

   An outline preview appears to help you position the element as you drag it.

3. Release the mouse button.

   The element is now selected and in its new location.

✔ Tip

- Turn on rulers (View > Rulers) to help you position your element. As you drag the element around the Stage, guidelines indicating the height and width of the element's bounding box (see the sidebar "How Flash Tracks Elements") appear in the ruler area (**Figure 3.20**).

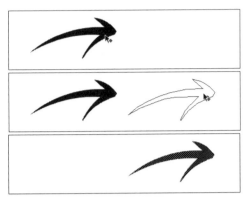

Figure 3.19 Use the arrow tool to select and drag an element to a new location.

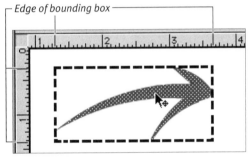

Figure 3.20 The longer lines in the ruler area indicate the edges of the element you are dragging.

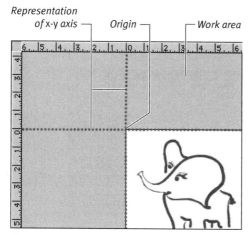

Representation of x-y axis — *Origin* — *Work area*

Figure 3.21 The dotted line here represents the *x-y* axis of the Stage. The origin, the zero point both horizontally and vertically, is the top-left corner of the Stage.

To reposition an element with the arrow keys:

1. In the Toolbox, select the arrow tool.

2. Select the element you want to move.

3. Use one of the four arrow keys on the keyboard to move the element in 1-pixel increments.

   The Up arrow moves the element toward the top of the Stage. The Down arrow moves the element toward the bottom of the Stage. The Right arrow moves the element toward the right side of the Stage. The Left arrow moves the element toward the left side of the Stage.

✔ Tip

■ To beef up the arrow keys' capability to move an element, hold down the Shift key. Each press of the Shift-arrow moves a selected element 8 pixels.

How Flash Tracks Elements

To keep track of an element's size and position on the Stage, Flash encloses each element in a *bounding box*, an invisible rectangle just big enough to enclose the element. Flash then treats the Stage as a giant graph, with the top-left corner of the Stage as the center of the *x* and *y* axis (see **Figure 3.21**). Flash locates elements by means of *x* and *y* coordinates on that graph. The units of measure for the graph are the ones currently selected in the Movie Properties dialog box (to learn more about movie properties, see Chapter 1). The Info panel shows you the *x* and *y* coordinates for an element's current position and also displays the height and width of the element's bounding box. Flash calculates an element's position on the Stage either from the top-left corner of the element's bounding box or from the element's center point (the point at the exact center of the bounding box).

By entering new *x* and *y* coordinates for Height and Width in the Info panel, you can change an element's position and size. (For more information on resizing elements, see "Changing the Size of Elements" later in this chapter).

Repositioning Elements with the Info Panel

Flash's Info panel allows you to reposition a selection by specifying a precise Stage location in *x* and *y* coordinates.

To access the Info panel:

If the Info panel is not currently open, *do one of the following*:

◆ From the Window menu, choose Panels > Info (**Figure 3.22**).

◆ In the Launcher bar at the bottom of the Stage, click the Show Info button.

The Info panel appears.

To reposition an element via the Info panel:

1. With the Info panel open, on the Stage, select the element you want to reposition.

   The coordinates for the element's current position appear in the *x* and *y* fields of the Info panel (**Figure 3.23**).

2. To position the element, *do one of the following*:

   ◆ To position your element by its center point, select the center square in the Info panel's element model.

   ◆ To position your element by its top-left corner, select the top-left square in the Info panel's element model.

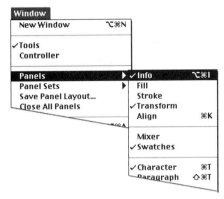

Figure 3.22 Choose Window > Panels > Info to access the Info panel.

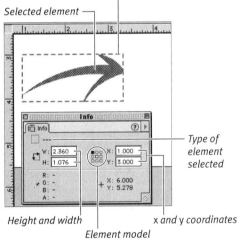

Selected element of bounding box (not really visible in Flash)

Selected element

Type of element selected

Height and width

Element model

x and *y* coordinates

Figure 3.23 Selecting an element puts that element's information in the Info panel (bottom). This element is located 1 inch to the right along the horizontal axis and 3 inches down the vertical axis.

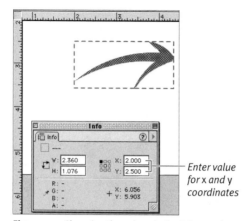

Enter value for x and y coordinates

Figure 3.24 Changing the values in the Info panel changes the location of the selected element. This arrow is now located 2 inches to the right along the horizontal axis and 2.5 inches down the vertical axis (left).

3. Enter a new *x* coordinate for the element's position along the horizontal axis.

4. Enter a new *y* coordinate for the element's position along the vertical axis.

Flash changes the element's horizontal position as soon as you click the *y* field.

5. Press Enter on the keyboard to confirm the new *x* coordinate value.

The element moves to its new position (**Figure 3.24**).

✔ Tip

■ If you change multiple values in the Info panel (as in the preceding task), Flash confirms each change when you click the next entry field. To confirm the last new value quickly, click any other field in the panel or click the Stage.

Performing Basic Editing Tasks: Cut, Copy, Paste

Flash supports the standard cut, copy, and paste operations and also provides some special operations tailored for working with animated graphics.

To delete a selection:

1. Select the elements you want to remove.

2. From the Edit menu, choose Clear (**Figure 3.25**), or press the Delete key.

    Flash removes the selected items.

To cut a selection:

1. Select the elements you want to cut.

2. From the Edit menu, choose Cut (**Figure 3.25**), or press ⌘-X (Mac) or Ctrl-X (Windows).

    Flash copies the selected items to the Clipboard and removes them from the Stage.

To copy a selection:

1. Select the elements you want to copy.

2. From the Edit menu, choose Copy (**Figure 3.25**), or press ⌘-C (Mac) or Ctrl-C (Windows).

    Flash copies the selected items to the Clipboard.

    After you cut or copy an item, it resides in the Clipboard until your next cut or copy operation. You can retrieve the Clipboard's contents with the Paste command.

Edit	
Undo	Ctrl+Z
Redo	Ctrl+Y
Cut	Ctrl+X
Copy	Ctrl+C
Paste	Ctrl+V
Paste in Place	Ctrl+Shift+V
Paste Special...	
Clear	Backspace
Duplicate	Ctrl+D
Select All	Ctrl+A
Deselect All	Ctrl+Shift+A
Cut Frames	Ctrl+Alt+X
Copy Frames	Ctrl+Alt+C
Paste Frames	Ctrl+Alt+V
Edit Symbols	Ctrl+E
Edit Selected	
Edit All	
Preferences...	
Keyboard Shortcuts...	

Figure 3.25 The Edit menu offers all the basic cut, copy, and paste commands as well as some special ones for working with graphics and animations.

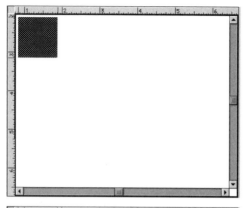

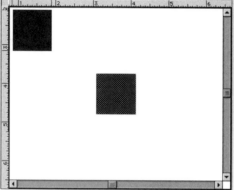

Figure 3.26 Copy a selected graphic element (top) and then choose the Paste command. Flash pastes a copy of the element from the Clipboard to the center of the Stage (bottom).

Figure 3.27 The Duplicate command offsets a copy of the element from the original. The duplicate is the selected element.

To paste the Clipboard's contents in the center of the window:

◆ From the Edit menu, choose Paste, or press ⌘-V (Mac) or Ctrl-V (Windows).

Flash pastes the Clipboard's contents in the center of the current view (**Figure 3.26**).

To paste Clipboard contents in their original location:

◆ From the Edit menu, choose Paste in Place, or press Shift-⌘-V (Mac) or Shift-Ctrl-V (Windows).

Flash pastes the Clipboard contents back into their original location on the Stage. The value of this command will become more apparent when you get into working with layers and animation, when it can be crucial to have elements appear in precisely the same spot but on a different layer or frame.

To duplicate a selection:

1. Select the elements you want to copy.

2. From the Edit menu, choose Duplicate, or press ⌘-D (Mac) or Ctrl-D (Windows).

Flash creates a copy of the selected items. The duplicate appears on the Stage, offset from the original item (**Figure 3.27**). The duplicate is selected so that it doesn't interact with the original. (For more information on interaction between elements, see Chapter 4.) The Duplicate command doesn't change the contents of the Clipboard.

✔ Tip

■ With the arrow or lasso tool active, you can Option-click (Mac) or Ctrl-click (Windows) and drag any selected elements to create a copy.

The Mystery of Paste Special (Windows)

Previous versions of Flash were able to take advantage of the Paste Special command—a feature of the Windows OS that uses embedded OLE objects to create links between a pasted item and its creator program. Flash 5 no longer supports this linking feature, but the Paste Special command still exists under the Edit menu (**Figure 3.28**). The main purpose of the Paste Special has been removed, but it does work slightly differently than the regular paste command. And those differences may be just what you need on occasion (**Figure 3.29**).

A
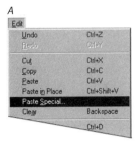

B
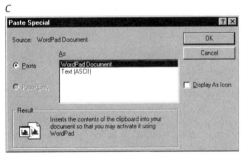

C
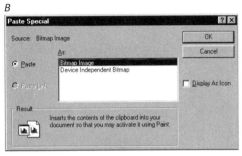

D

Figure 3.28 The Paste Special command is still available from the Edit menu in Flash 5 for Windows (A). The Paste Special dialog box seems to offer you the chance to create linked bitmaps (B) or text (C), but when you actually try to complete the operation by clicking OK, a dialog box appears telling you that Flash 5 no longer supports embedded OLE objects (D).

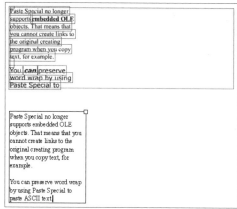

Figure 3.29 When you have copied a block of text to the Clipboard, Flash's Edit >Paste command preserves the word wrap and formatting of copied text by creating lots of separate text boxes (top). The Edit > Paste Special command places the copied text in a single text box that preserves the copied text's word wrap, but you lose the text's formatting (bottom).

Paste Special for Bitmaps

When you copy bitmapped graphics from outside Flash and paste them into a Flash document via the Edit > Paste command, Flash automatically groups the bitmap before placing it on the Stage. It's easy enough to ungroup the bitmap or break it apart, but you can use Paste Special to paste an ungrouped bitmap.

Select all or part of a bitmapped graphic in a non-Flash graphics program. In Flash, from the Edit menu, choose Paste Special: The Paste Special dialog box appears. From the scrolling list of formats, choose Device Independent Bitmap, and then click OK. Flash pastes the ungrouped bitmap on the Stage.

Paste Special for Text

When you copy a block of text from outside Flash and paste it into a Flash document, Flash creates several separate text boxes to preserve the formatting and line breaks of the original text. By using Paste Special you can keep the text as a single block (although you lose any formatting).

Select all or part of a text block in a word-processing program. In Flash, from the Edit menu, choose Paste Special; the Paste Special dialog box appears. From the scrolling list of formats choose Text (ASCII), and then click OK. Flash pastes the text in a single text box the same width as the original.

Editing Existing Elements with Assistance

Rather than have Flash assist you with everything you draw, you may prefer the flexibility of simply sketching with the pencil tool's freeform Ink mode. Flash can always recognize shapes and apply smoothing and straightening after you draw them.

To smooth an existing line:

1. Select the line with curves you want to smooth.

2. To smooth the curves, *do one of the following:*
   - With the Arrow tool selected, in the Toolbox, click the Smooth button (**Figure 3.30**).
   - From the Modify menu, choose Smooth (**Figure 3.31**).

Flash smoothes the curves in the selected line according to the tolerances currently set in the Assistant. By repeated clicking, you can smooth the curves further and ultimately reduce the number of curve segments in the line.

To straighten an existing line:

1. Select the line you want to straighten.

2. To straighten the lines, *do one of the following:*
   - With the Arrow tool selected, in the Toolbox, click the Straighten button (**Figure 3.32**).
   - From the Modify menu, choose Straighten.

Flash straightens the selected line according to the tolerances currently set in General Preferences (see Chapter 2).

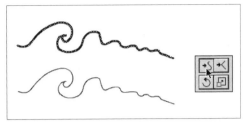

Figure 3.30 With your line selected on the Stage (top) and the arrow tool selected in the Toolbox, click the Smooth button. Flash smooths the line (bottom).

Figure 3.31 Choose Modify > Smooth to smooth curves selected on the Stage.

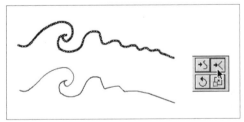

Figure 3.32 With your line selected on the Stage (top) and the arrow tool selected, in the Toolbox, click the Straighten button. Flash straightens the line (bottom).

Number of smoothing commands applied *Number of straightening commands applied*

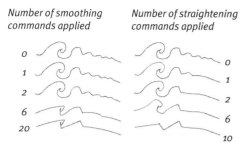

Figure 3.33 Invoking the Smooth and Straighten commands several times can dramatically change the appearance of a line.

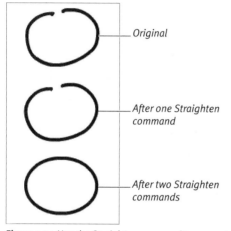

Original

After one Straighten command

After two Straighten commands

Figure 3.34 Use the Straighten command to recognize a shape.

✔ Tip

■ If the line still looks too rough after your first attempt, apply the Smooth or Straighten command again. Repeated smoothing eventually flattens your curves; repeated straightening eventually turns curve segments into straight-line segments (**Figure 3.33**).

To recognize existing shapes:

1. Select your rough version of an oval or rectangle.

2. To make flash recognize your shape, *do one of the following:*

   ◆ With the Arrow tool selected, in the Toolbox, click the Straighten button.

   ◆ From the Modify menu, choose Straighten.

   If the shape is recognizable under the tolerances currently set in General Preferences (see Chapter 2), Flash recasts the shape as a perfect oval or rectangle.

✔ Tip

■ If at first Flash fails to recognize your rough shape, try again. Often, the newly straightened shape falls within the parameters Flash needs to recognize it (**Figure 3.34**).

Moving End Points with the Arrow Tool

You can use the arrow tool to change the length of straight-line and curve segments. You simply grab and reposition the segment's end points.

When you use the arrow tool, the segment you want to modify must not be selected. If it is selected, the arrow tool simply moves the segment as a unit. Always note what kind of icon the arrow pointer is displaying as it hovers over the line you want to modify (**Figure 3.35**).

For the following exercises, make sure the item you want to modify is deselected.

To reposition the end of a line segment with the arrow tool:

1. Position the pointer over the end point of the line.

    The corner-point modifier appears.

2. Reposition the end point.

    The arrow tool now operates like the straight-line tool (the line segment changes to preview mode). Dragging away from the existing line lengthen it; dragging toward the existing line shortens it (**Figure 3.36**).

3. Release the mouse button.

    Flash redraws the line segment.

To reposition the end point of a curve with the arrow tool:

1. Position the pointer over the end point of a curve.

    The corner-point modifier appears.

2. Click and drag the end point to the desired location.

3. Release the mouse button.

    Flash redraws the end of the curve (**Figure 3.37**).

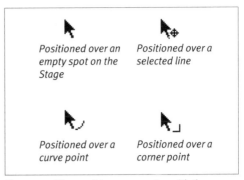

Figure 3.35 The small icons appearing with the arrow pointer indicate what type of graphic element lies beneath the pointer.

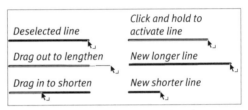

Figure 3.36 You can use the arrow tool to change a line segment's length.

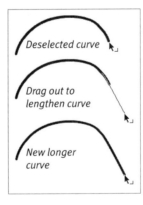

Figure 3.37 You can use the arrow tool to change a curve's length.

Figure 3.38 Use the subselection tool to modify the path of a line segment.

Figure 3.39 When a solid square appears next to the subselection tool, it's ready to select the entire path (left). When a hollow square appears (right), the tool is ready to select and manipulate a single anchor point.

Moving Points with the Subselection Tool

The subselection tool allows you to reveal and manipulate the anchor points that define a line segment or curve. You can then grab and reposition these points to modify lines and curves.

To view a path and anchor points:

1. In the Toolbox, choose the subselection tool (**Figure 3.38**).

   The pointer changes to a hollow arrow.

2. On the Stage, click the line or curve you want to modify.

   Flash selects and highlights the entire path. In Flash's default editing mode, anchor points appear as solid squares in a contrasting highlight color.

To manipulate a particular point, you must select it directly.

To select an anchor point:

1. With the subselection tool selected, position the pointer over the point you want to move.

   The anchor-point modifier (a small hollow square) appears next to the hollow-arrow icon (**Figure 3.39**).

2. Click the anchor point.

   Flash highlights the selected point. At Flash's default setting, selected corner points appear as hollow squares; selected curve points appear as hollow circles with Bézier handles.

   continues on next page

MOVING POINTS WITH THE SUBSELECTION TOOL

✔ Tips

- If you know where a point is in your element, you can skip the step of clicking the path to highlight all the anchor points. To select the point directly, double-click it.

- You can select multiple points on a path directly with the subselection tool. Draw a selection rectangle that includes the points you want to select. Flash highlights the entire path and selects any points that fall within the rectangle.

- To view anchor points as hollow squares and selected points as solid, you need to change Flash's editing preferences. From the Edit menu, choose Preferences. Click the Editing tab in the Preferences dialog box, and uncheck the Show Solid Points checkbox.

To reposition anchor points with the subselection tool:

- With the subselection tool active, click and drag the desired anchor point to a new location.

  Flash redraws the path (**Figure 3.40**).

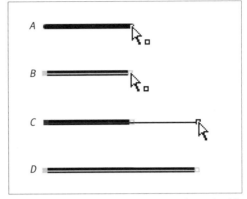

Figure 3.40 When you've selected an anchor point (A), Flash highlights the entire path (B). You can drag the anchor point to lengthen or shorten the path (C). The path and anchor points remain highlighted when you're done (D).

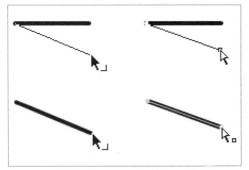

Figure 3.41 Using the arrow tool (left) or subselection tool (right), click the line's end point and drag it to a new position. You can pivot the line and change its angle as you would when creating a line with the straight-line tool. Flash redraws the line. With the subselection tool, when you release the mouse button, the path is selected and its anchor points are highlighted.

Reshaping Lines

Flash makes drawing easy by allowing you to reshape every line or element you create. The arrow tool lets you simply grab a point and give it a tug. The subselection tool gives you precise control of reshaping by allowing you to manipulate anchor points and Bézier control handles directly.

To change the direction of a line segment (arrow or subselection tool):

1. Using the arrow or subselection tool, position the pointer over the line segment's end point.

   The corner-point modifier appears with the arrow tool.

   The anchor-point modifier appears with the subselection tool.

2. Click and drag the end point to a new location that changes the line's direction (**Figure 3.41**).

3. Release the mouse button.

   Flash redraws the line.

About Curve and Corner Points

Flash's arrow and pen/subselection tools let you modify an element's curves and lines. The subselection tool lets you do so by moving the curve and corner points that define the elements and by rearranging the curves' Bézier handles. When you highlight a path with the subselection tool, Flash reveals any curve points' Bézier handles. (Corner points have no handles.)

When you use the arrow tool, Flash hides all the technical stuff. You simply pull on a line to reshape it. Still, the arrow tool does have its own hidden version of curve and corner points, which are evident only in the changing icons that accompany the tool as it interacts with a line or curve.

For the arrow tool, corner points appear at the end of a segment or at the point where two segments join to form a sharp angle. All those other in-between points—even if they fall in the middle of a line segment that happens to be completely flat—are curve points. When you tug on a curve point with the arrow tool, you pull out a range of points in a tiny arc. When you tug on a corner point with the arrow tool, you pull out a single point.

Reshaping Curves with the Arrow Tool

You can reshape a curve, or change a straight-line segment into a curve, by using the arrow tool to push and pull on the curve. You can also reshape curves by using the pen and subselection tools in combination (see "Reshaping Curves with the Subselection Tool" later in this chapter).

In the following exercises for the arrow tool, make sure that the line or curve you want to reshape is deselected when you start each exercise.

To reposition the end of a curve with the arrow tool:

1. Position the arrow tool's pointer over the end point of the curve.

The corner-point modifier appears.

2. Click and drag the end point to a new location.

The last segment of the curve changes direction depending on where you locate the end point. Flash previews the new curve segment as you drag (**Figure 3.42**).

To reshape a curve with the arrow tool:

1. Position the arrow tool's pointer over the middle of a curve segment.

The curve-point modifier appears.

2. Click and drag the curve to reshape it (**Figure 3.43**).

Flash previews the curve you're drawing.

3. Release the mouse button.

Flash redraws the curve.

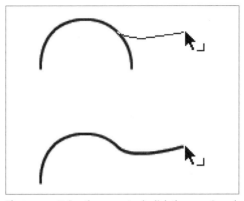

Figure 3.42 Using the arrow tool, click the curve's end point and drag it to a new position. Flash reshapes the end of the curve.

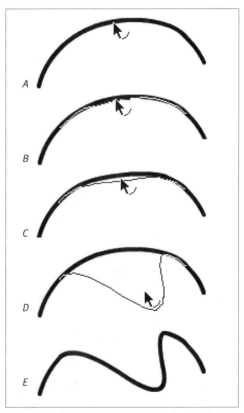

Figure 3.43 Click the middle of a curve (A). Flash activates the curve segment (B). Drag the curve to a new position (C, D). When you release the mouse button, Flash redraws the curve (E).

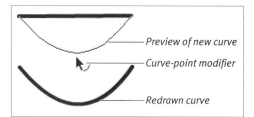

Figure 3.44 Although this line doesn't look curved (top), Flash considers all its middle points to be curve points. Drag one of those points to create a line that *looks* like a curve (bottom).

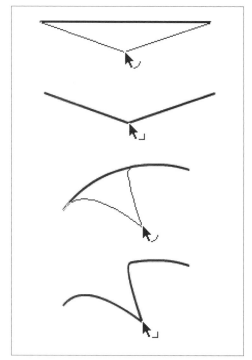

Figure 3.45 Option-click (Mac) or Ctrl-click (Windows) to create a new corner point for editing your line. Dragging a corner point from a straight-line segment creates a sharp V shape (top). Dragging a corner point from a curve creates a V with curving sides that comes to a sharp point (bottom).

To turn a straight-line segment into a curve segment with the arrow tool:

1. Position the arrow tool's pointer over the middle of a line segment.

The curve-point modifier appears.

2. Click and drag the line to reshape it (**Figure 3.44**).

Flash previews the curve that you're drawing.

3. Release the mouse button.

Flash redraws the line, giving it the curve you define.

To create new corner points with the arrow tool:

1. Position the arrow tool's pointer over the middle of a line or curve segment.

The curve-point modifier appears.

2. Option-click (Mac) or Ctrl-click (Windows).

After a brief pause, the arrow tool's modifier changes from the curve-point arc to the corner-point angle.

3. Drag to modify the line or curve segment and add a new corner point (**Figure 3.45**).

RESHAPING CURVES WITH THE ARROW TOOL

Reshaping Curves with the Subselection Tool

The subselection tool lets you manipulate a point's Bézier handles to modify the slope and depth of the curve. You can add and delete points and convert existing curve points to corner points, or vice versa, with the pen tool (see "Converting, Removing, and Adding Points," later in this chapter).

One way to reshape a curve is to change the location of the anchor points that define the curve.

To move a curve point:

1. In the Toolbox, choose the subselection tool.

2. Click a path to select it.

   Flash highlights the entire path of the selected element.

3. Position the pointer over a curve point. The anchor-point modifier appears.

4. Click and drag the point to a new location.

   Flash previews the new curve as you drag (**Figure 3.46**).

After you move a curve point, the path remains selected and Bézier control handles of the point you moved become active so that you can further manipulate the curve.

To reshape a curve with the Bézier handles:

1. With the subselection tool, click the curve you want to modify.

2. Click one of the two anchor points that define the curve you want to modify. Bézier handles appear.

3. Click and drag one of the Bézier handles. The pointer changes to an arrowhead.

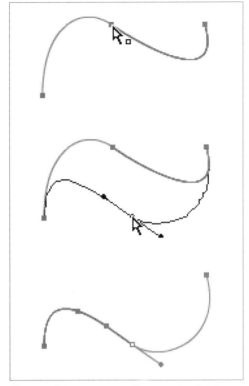

Figure 3.46 One way to modify a curved path is to reposition anchor points with the subselection tool.

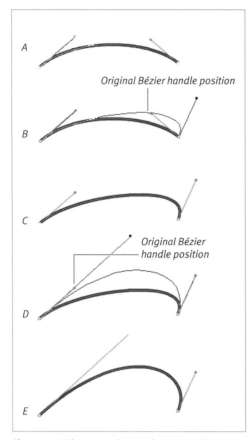

Figure 3.47 When you select anchor points, their Bézier handles appear (A). Leaning a Bézier handle away from a curve (B) makes that curve segment more pronounced (C). Leaning the handle toward the curve flattens that part of the curve. Dragging the Bézier handle away from its anchor point (D) makes the curve deeper (E); dragging the handle toward the anchor point makes the curve shallower.

4. To modify the curve, *do one or more of the following:*

- ◆ To make the curve more pronounced, position the Bézier handle farther from the curve in the direction in which the curve currently bulges.

- ◆ To make the curve flatter, position the Bézier handle closer to the curve.

- ◆ To make the curve bulge in the opposite direction, move the Bézier handle past the existing curve, in the opposite direction from the current bulge.

- ◆ To make the curve deeper, position the Bézier handle farther from the anchor point.

- ◆ To make the curve shallower, position the Bézier handle closer to the anchor point.

Flash previews the new curve as you manipulate the Bézier handle (**Figure 3.47**).

✔ Tips

- ■ To select an anchor point and activate its Bézier handles quickly, use the subselection tool to draw a selection rectangle around the curve you want to modify. Even if the path was not highlighted previously, Flash selects any anchor points that fall within the section and activates their handles.

- ■ You can move selected anchor points with the arrow keys. To move in larger increments, press Shift-arrow key.

- ■ When you have multiple anchor points selected, using the arrow keys moves the selected points as a unit. Dragging one of those points with the subselection tool repositions just that point.

Converting, Removing, and Adding Points

In some graphics programs, you select pen modifiers to convert, remove, and add points. In Flash, the pen tool automatically turns into a modifier as it hovers over a path or an anchor point. The subselection tool can change corner points to curve points. The pen tool can add new points between existing curve points, can "reduce" a curve point to a corner point, and can reduce a corner point to no point at all.

To convert corner points to curve points:

1. Using the subselection tool, click the path you want to modify.

   Flash highlights the path and its anchor points.

2. Position the hollow-arrow pointer over a corner point.

   The anchor-point modifier appears.

3. Click the anchor point to select it.

4. To pull Bézier handles out of the point, Option-drag (Mac) or Alt-drag (Windows) away from the selected corner point.

   Flash converts the corner point to a curve point (**Figure 3.48**).

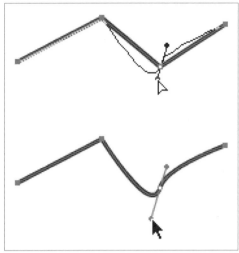

Figure 3.48 To change a corner point into a curve point (one with Bézier handles), use the subselection tool to Option-drag (Mac) or Alt-drag (Windows) a selected corner point (top). You actually pull a Bézier handle out of the point instead of relocating the point. When you release the mouse button, Flash redraws the curve (bottom).

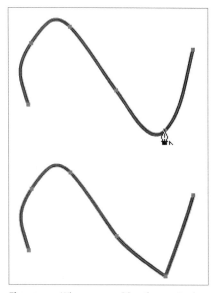

Figure 3.49 When you position the pen tool over a curve point, a small caret appears next to the pointer (top). With the caret modifier active, click the curve point to "reduce" it to a corner point (bottom). Flash redraws the path accordingly.

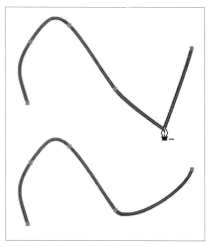

Figure 3.50 When you position the pen tool over a corner point, a small minus sign appears next to the pointer (top). With the minus-sign modifier active, click the corner point to "reduce" it to no point at all (bottom). Flash redraws the path accordingly.

To convert curve points to corner points:

1. With the path you want to modify selected, in the Toolbox, choose the pen tool.

2. Position the pen pointer over a curve point.

   The convert-to-corner-point modifier (a small caret) appears next to the pen icon.

3. Click the curve point.

   Flash converts the curve point to a corner point and flattens the curved path (**Figure 3.49**).

To delete anchor points:

1. With the path you want to modify selected, in the Toolbox, choose the pen tool.

2. Position the pen pointer over a corner point.

   The remove-point modifier (a minus sign) appears next to the pen icon.

   (Note that if the point you want to delete is currently a curve point, you must follow the steps in the preceding exercise to convert it to a corner point.)

3. Click the corner point.

   Flash removes the anchor point and reshapes the path to connect the remaining points (**Figure 3.50**).

✔ Tip

■ You can also delete one or more anchor points by selecting them with the subselection tool and pressing Delete.

To add new anchor points to a curve segment:

1. With the path you want to modify selected, in the Toolbox, choose the pen tool.

   Position the pen pointer over the path between two curve points.

2. The add-point modifier (a plus sign) appears next to the pen icon.

3. Click the path.

   Flash adds a new curve point (**Figure 3.51**).

✔ Tips

- If you need to add points to a straight-line segment, first convert the corner points that define the segment to curve points. Then you'll be able to add another curve point between them.

- To add points to the end of an open path, position the pen pointer over the end of the path. When the x to the right of the pen pointer disappears, click the last anchor point and then continue clicking to add more points.

- You can select an open path with the pen tool by clicking the end anchor point at either end of the path. Flash won't convert or delete the end anchor point; it just highlights the path the same way the subselection tool would.

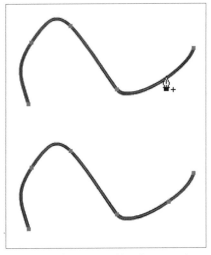

Figure 3.51 When you position the pen tool between existing curve points, a small plus sign appears next to the pointer (top). With the plus-sign modifier active, click the curve to add a new curve point (bottom). (Note that the pen tool cannot add points between corner points.)

Figure 3.52 When you position the pointer over the edge of a fill shape, the arrow tool displays either the curve-point or corner-point modifier. If you then click the edge of the fill, Flash activates part of the outline for reshaping.

Before   *After*

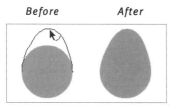

Pull out a curve point

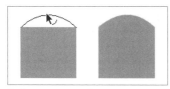

Pull out a curve point

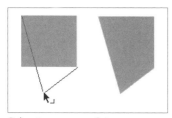

Relocate a corner point

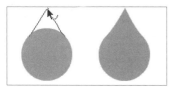

Create a new corner point

Figure 3.53 Take some time to play around with reshaping fills. You can pull points out to create protrusions. You can move points in to create indentations. You can pretty much reshape the fill any way you want.

Reshaping Fills

Although you can't see the outlines of filled shapes unless you give them a stroke, fills do have outlines that act just like any other line. This means you can use the arrow, pen, and subselection tools to reshape fills the same way you reshaped lines and paths in the previous tasks.

To reshape a fill with the arrow tool:

1. With nothing selected, position the arrow tool's pointer over the edge of your filled shape.

   The curve point or corner-point modifier appears (**Figure 3.52**).

2. Click and drag the curve point or corner point to reshape the fill (**Figure 3.53**).

   Flash previews the new outline.

3. Release the mouse button.

   Flash creates the new fill shape.

To reshape a fill with the subselection and pen tools:

1. In the Toolbox, choose the subselection tool.

2. Position the hollow-arrow pointer over the edge of your filled shape.

3. Click.

   Flash highlights the path and anchor points that define the fill shape (**Figure 3.54**).

4. Add, remove, and reposition anchor points and Bézier handles with the pen and subselection tools, as described earlier in this section.

✔ Tip

- To select an entire fill path quickly, use the subselection tool to drag a selection rectangle over any portion of the fill. Unlike the arrow tool, the subselection tool selects the whole shape even if you include just a small portion of it within the selection rectangle. Any curve points that fall within the rectangle display their Bézier handles.

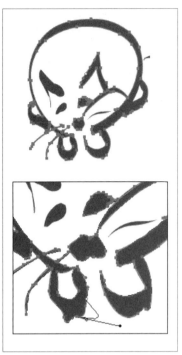

Figure 3.54 Select a fill shape with the subselection tool, and Flash highlights the path (and anchor points) that outline the shape (top). Reposition anchor points and Bézier handles to modify the fill shapes (bottom).

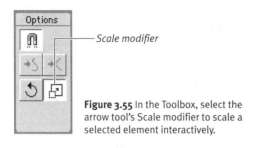

Scale modifier

Figure 3.55 In the Toolbox, select the arrow tool's Scale modifier to scale a selected element interactively.

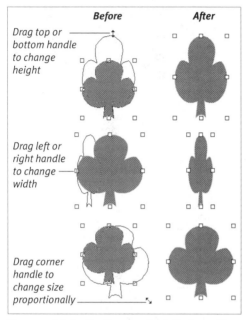

Before   *After*

Drag top or bottom handle to change height

Drag left or right handle to change width

Drag corner handle to change size proportionally

Figure 3.56 Activating the arrow tool's Scale modifier places a set of handles around a selected element. Click and drag the handles to change the size of the element.

Changing the Size of Graphic Elements

Flash gives you several ways to resize, or scale, graphic elements. You can scale selected elements interactively on the Stage, or you can set specific scale percentages or dimensions for your element via menu commands or panels.

To resize a graphic element interactively:

1. With the arrow tool selected in the Toolbox, click the element you want to resize.

Flash selects and highlights the element.

2. In the Toolbar, click the Scale modifier (**Figure 3.55**).

Square handles appear on all four sides and at the four corners of the element's bounding box.

3. Move the pointer over a handle.

The pointer changes to a double-headed arrow indicating the direction in which the element will grow or shrink as you pull or push on the handles.

4. To change the graphic element's width, click and drag one of the side handles.

Dragging toward the center of the element narrows it; dragging away widens it (**Figure 3.56**).

5. To change the element's height, click and drag the top or bottom handle.

Dragging toward the center of the element shortens it; dragging away makes it taller.

6. To change the size of the element proportionately, click and drag one of the corner handles.

Dragging toward the center of the element reduces it; dragging away enlarges it.

continues on next page

✔ Tips

■ You can also activate the scale handles for a selected element by choosing Modify > Transform > Scale.

■ With one exception, you can select a whole graphic element, part of an element, or multiple elements to scale with any of the selection methods discussed at the beginning of this chapter. You cannot use the subselection tool to select an element by its path because when you activate the arrow tool, Flash automatically deselects the selected path.

To resize a graphic element with the Scale and Rotate command:

1. Select the element you want to resize.

2. From the Modify menu, choose Transform > Scale and Rotate.

   The Scale and Rotate dialog box appears (**Figure 3.57**).

3. To resize the element, *do one of the following:*

   ◆ To make the element smaller, in the Scale % field, enter a value less than 100.

   ◆ To make the element larger, in the Scale % field, enter a value greater than 100.

4. Click OK.

You can also resize elements by using the Transform panel.

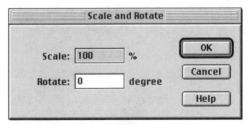

Figure 3.57 You can enter a specific percentage of enlargement or reduction in the Scale and Rotate dialog box.

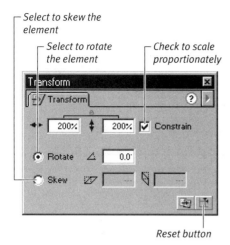

Select to skew the element

Select to rotate the element

Check to scale proportionately

Reset button

Figure 3.58 The Transform panel lets you enter values for scaling, rotating, and skewing selected elements.

To access the Transform panel:

If the Transform panel is not currently open, *do one of the following:*

◆ From the Window menu, choose Panels > Transform.

◆ In the Launcher bar at the bottom of the Stage, click the Show Info button.

The Transform panel appears (**Figure 3.58**).

To resize an element proportionately by using the Transform panel:

1. With the Transform panel open, on the Stage, select the element you want to resize.

   A value of 100% appears in the Scale Width and Scale Height fields of the Transform panel.

2. Check the Constrain checkbox next to the Scale Width and Scale Height fields.

3. Enter a new value in either scale field.

   A value less than 100% shrinks the element; a value greater than 100% enlarges the element. As you enter the value in one field, Flash automatically updates the other field.

4. Press Enter.

   Flash resizes the element.

✔ Tip

■ You can undo your transformation quickly by clicking the Reset button in the bottom-right corner of the Transform panel.

CHANGING THE SIZE OF GRAPHIC ELEMENTS

To resize the width and height of an element separately:

1. With the Transform panel open, on the Stage, select the element you want to resize.

2. In the Transform panel, uncheck the Constrain checkbox.

3. Enter a new percentage in the Scale Width field.

4. Enter a new percentage in the Scale Height field.

5. Press Enter.

   Flash resizes the element.

✔ Tips

- You can scale several elements at the same time. Select all the elements and then use any of the scaling methods described earlier in this section. The elements scale together as a group.

- You can transform a copy of the element by clicking the Copy and Apply Transform Button in the Transform panel.

- You can also resize a selected element by entering specific width and height values in the Info panel (**Figure 3.59**).

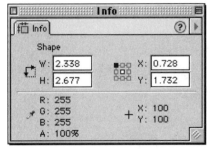

Figure 3.59 You can enter precise dimensions for an element's width and height in the Info panel. This panel doesn't require you to click a button to apply changes; simply click the Stage to apply the values you entered in the panel to the selected graphic element.

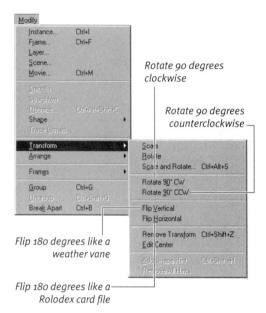

Rotate 90 degrees clockwise

Rotate 90 degrees counterclockwise

Flip 180 degrees like a weather vane

Flip 180 degrees like a Rolodex card file

Figure 3.60 The Modify > Transform menu offers commands for flipping graphic elements vertically and horizontally. It also offers commands for rotating an element in 90-degree increments both clockwise and counterclockwise.

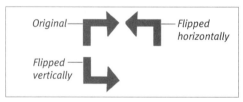

Original

Flipped horizontally

Flipped vertically

Figure 3.61 The result of flipping an element using the Flip commands in the Modify > Transform menu.

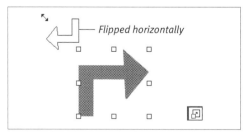

Flipped horizontally

Figure 3.62 The arrow tool's Scale modifier can flip and scale an element simultaneously. Here, Scale is flipping the element both vertically and horizontally.

Reorienting Graphic Elements

Flash lets you rotate, flip, and skew selected elements. You can either manipulate elements freely with the arrow tool's rotate modifier or use a variety of commands to do the job with more precision.

To flip a graphic element:

1. Select the element you want to flip.

2. To reorient the element so that it spins 180 degrees around its vertical central axis like a weather vane, from the Modify menu, choose Transform > Flip Horizontal (**Figure 3.60**).

3. To reorient the element so that it spins 180 degrees around its horizontal central axis like a Rolodex file, from the Modify menu, choose Transform > Flip Vertical.

Figure 3.61 shows the results of the two types of flipping.

✔ Tip

■ You can simultaneously flip and scale elements by using the scale tool. With the selected element in scale mode, drag one handle all the way across the bounding box and past the handle on the other side. To flip a selected element vertically and horizontally, for example, drag the handle in the bottom-right corner diagonally upward, past the handle in the top-left corner (**Figure 3.62**). The flipped element starts out small and grows as you continue to drag away from the element's top-left corner. Flash previews the flipped element; release the mouse button when it's the size you want.

To rotate an element in 90-degree increments:

1. Select the element you want to rotate.

2. To rotate the element, *do one of the following:*

   - To rotate the element counterclockwise 90 degrees, from the Modify menu, choose Transform > Rotate 90° CCW.

   - To rotate the element clockwise 90 degrees, from the Modify menu, choose Transform > Rotate 90° CW.

   Flash rotates the element 90 degrees. You can repeat the command to rotate the element 180 and 270 degrees or back to its starting point.

To rotate an element by a user-specified amount:

1. From the Modify menu, choose Transform > Scale and Rotate, or press ⌘-Option-S (Mac) or Ctrl-Alt-S (Windows).

   The Scale and Rotate dialog box appears (**Figure 3.63**).

2. To enter a value in the degree field, *do one of the following:*

   - To rotate the element counterclockwise, enter a negative value (-1 to -360) in the degree field.

   - To rotate the element clockwise, enter a positive value (1 to 360).

3. Click OK.

   Flash rotates the selected element by the amount you specified.

✔ Tip

- You can also rotate a selected element by specifying the degree of rotation in the Transform panel.

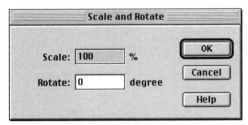

Figure 3.63 The Scale and Rotate dialog box lets you rotate graphic elements in precise increments. Positive values rotate the element clockwise; negative values rotate it counterclockwise.

Vertical skew — *Copy and Apply Transform*

Horizontal skew —

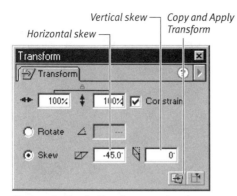

Figure 3.64 Use the Transform panel to skew selected elements. You can set separate values for horizontal and vertical skewing.

To skew an element by using the Transform panel:

1. With the Transform panel open, select the element you want to skew.

2. In the Transform panel, choose Skew.

3. Enter the desired skew values in the horizontal and vertical fields (**Figure 3.64**).

4. To complete the transformation, press Enter.

✔ Tip

■ To skew a copy of the selected element, in the Transform panel, click the Copy and Apply Transform button.

To rotate and skew an element interactively:

1. Select the element you want to resize, using any of the methods described at the beginning of this chapter.

2. Select the arrow tool in the Toolbox; then click the Rotate button (**Figure 3.65**). Round handles appear on all four sides and at the corners of the element's bounding box.

3. To rotate the element, click and drag one of the corner handles.

   The pointer changes to a circular arrow, indicating that the element will rotate as you drag that handle. Drag clockwise to rotate the element clockwise; drag counterclockwise to rotate the element counterclockwise. Flash previews the skewed element as you drag (**Figure 3.66**).

4. To skew the element, click and drag one of the handles on the side, bottom, or top.

   The pointer changes to a double-headed arrow, indicating the direction in which the element will skew as you drag that handle. Flash previews the skewed element as you drag.

5. Release the mouse button.

   Flash redraws the skewed element.

Figure 3.65 Click the arrow tool's rotate modifier to rotate a selected element interactively.

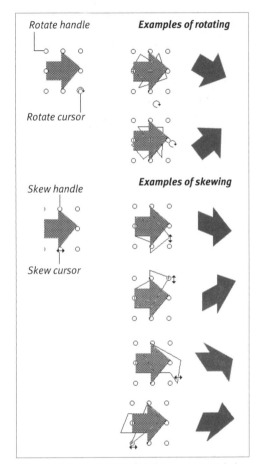

Figure 3.66 A selected graphic element surrounded by round handles is ready to rotate or skew. To rotate the element, drag one of the corner handles (top examples); to skew the element, drag one of the side handles (bottom examples).

Ink bottle

Figure 3.67 The ink-bottle tool applies all the stroke attributes currently set in the Stroke panel.

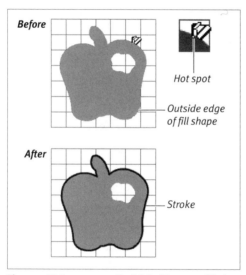

Before

Hot spot

Outside edge of fill shape

After

Stroke

Figure 3.68 As you move the ink bottle over a filled shape, the hot spot appears as a white dot at the end of the ink drip that's spilling out of the bottle. To add a stroke around the outside edge of your fill shape, position the hot spot along that edge (top) and click. Flash adds a stroke with the current attributes set in the Stroke panel (bottom).

Modifying Strokes

Flash provides two methods for modifying the stroke of an existing element. You can select the element and change its attributes in the Stroke panel, or you can use the ink-bottle tool to apply the current Stroke panel settings to unselected elements. Certain modifications, however, you can make only with the ink bottle.

To add a stroke to an element that currently lacks one, you must use the ink bottle.

To add a stroke to the outside of a shape:

1. In the Toolbox, select the ink bottle, or press S on the keyboard (**Figure 3.67**).

2. In the Stroke panel, *set any of the following attributes:*

- ◆ From the Line Style pop-up menu, choose a new style.

- ◆ In the line-weight field, enter a value for the thickness of the stroke.

- ◆ Click the stroke-color box, and choose a new color from the swatch set.

  The stroke-color box in the Toolbox displays the selected color, and the ink bottle is ready to apply the other stroke attributes you set in the Stroke panel. (For more details about setting attributes in the Stroke panel, see Chapter 2.)

3. Move the pointer over the Stage.

The pointer appears as a little ink bottle spilling ink.

4. With the ink bottle's hot spot, click the outside edge of the shape (**Figure 3.68**).

Flash adds a stroke around your shape, using the color, thickness, and style settings from the Stroke panel. Note that you must click near the outside edge to add the stroke to the shape's outside.

When a shape has a hole in it, you can outline the shape of the hole.

MODIFYING STROKES

To add a stroke to the inside of a shape:

1. Follow steps 1 through 3 in the preceding exercise.

2. With the ink bottle's hot spot, click near the inside edge of the shape.

   Flash outlines the hole—the inside edge of the shape—using the current Stroke panel settings. Be sure to click inside the shape but near the hole to outline the inside edge. (**Figure 3.69**).

✔ Tip

- Sometimes, you want to outline both the outside of a shape and the hole inside the shape. The ink bottle does both simultaneously when you click the ink bottle's hot spot in the middle of the shape (**Figure 3.70**).

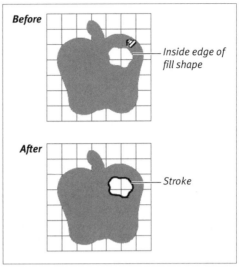

Figure 3.69 Position the ink bottle's hot spot along the inside edge of your fill shape (top) and click. Flash uses the current line attributes set in the Toolbox to outline the hole in your shape (bottom).

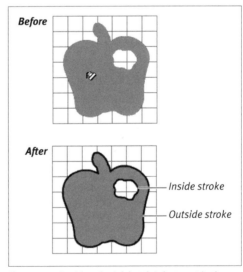

Figure 3.70 Position the ink bottle's hot spot in the middle of your fill shape (top) and click. Flash uses the current stroke attributes to add a stroke around the outside and inside of your shape (bottom).

With nothing selected, click stroke or fill

With fill and stroke selected, click stroke or fill

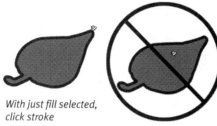

With just fill selected, click stroke

Warning: Clicking a selected fill with unselected stroke does nothing

With part of stroke selected, click selection

Figure 3.71 You don't have to select a stroke to change its attributes—just click the stroke or the unselected fill with the ink bottle. Warning: If you have the fill selected, you must click the stroke itself; you can't click the selected fill to change an unselected stroke.

To modify existing strokes with the ink bottle:

1. In the Stroke panel, set the attributes for color, line weight, and line style.

2. In the Toolbox, select the ink-bottle tool.

3. Click the ink bottle's hot spot on the stroke you want to modify.

When you click the hot spot directly on a stroke to modify it, the stroke can be selected or deselected.

✔ Tips

■ If you leave an element fully deselected, or if you select the whole element (both fill and stroke), you won't need to position the ink bottle's hot spot so carefully. Clicking anywhere in the graphic element modifies its stroke. **Figure 3.71** shows the way the ink bottle interacts with selections.

■ To apply new attributes to the inside and outside strokes of a graphic element, click the middle of the shape with the ink bottle's hot spot.

■ Remember that lines you've created with the straight-line tool and the pencil are also strokes. To change the attributes of an existing line, set the stroke attributes as described earlier in this section and then use the ink bottle tool to click the line you want to modify. The line can be selected or deselected.

■ You don't have to modify an entire stroke. You can select just a piece of a stroke and use the ink bottle to apply changes to just that piece.

■ You can modify multiple strokes at the same time. Select all the strokes you want to change; then click any selected stroke with the ink bottle to modify them all in one fell swoop.

MODIFYING STROKES

To modify selected strokes by using the Stroke panel:

1. Using the arrow tool, select one or more strokes on the Stage.

2. Set the attributes for color, line weight, and line style in the Stroke panel.

   Flash changes all selected strokes as you enter each new attribute in the Stroke panel (**Figure 3.72**).

✔ Tips

- You cannot modify the stroke attributes of a selected path (one selected with the subselection tool). You can, however, modify the stroke attributes of selections created with any other selection methods.

- You can modify the color of a selected stroke without using the ink bottle or without even opening a panel. Click the stroke-color box in the Toolbox, and choose a new color. Any selected strokes update to the new color.

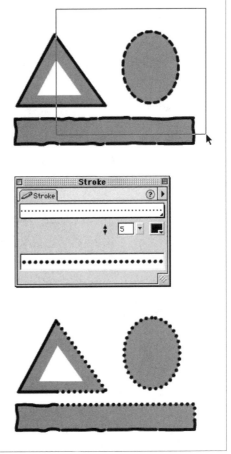

Figure 3.72 Select one or more strokes for modification (top). Set new attributes in the Stroke panel (middle). Flash applies the attributes to all the strokes in your selection (bottom).

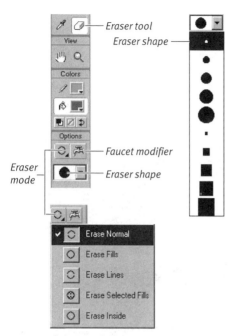

Figure 3.73 The eraser tool and its modifiers.

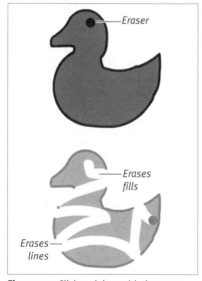

Figure 3.74 Click and drag with the eraser tool in Erase Normal mode to erase all lines and fills.

Using the Eraser Tool in Normal Mode

The eraser tool has five modes that interact with fills and strokes in a variety of ways. This chapter describes using the eraser in Normal mode; the other modes will become more important when you handle complex graphics with multiple elements (see Chapter 4).

In Normal mode, the eraser acts pretty much as you'd expect. When you click and drag it over the Stage, the tool removes any line or fill in its path.

To erase all strokes and fills (Erase Normal):

1. In the Toolbox, select the eraser, or press E on the keyboard (**Figure 3.73**).

   Flash displays the eraser modifiers.

2. From the Eraser Mode pop-up menu, choose Erase Normal.

   A check appears by that mode in the menu, and the Erase Normal icon appears in the Toolbox.

3. From the Eraser Shape pop-up menu, choose a size and shape for the eraser.

   The icon for the selected eraser shape appears in the Toolbox.

4. Move the pointer over the Stage.

   The pointer has the size and shape you selected.

5. Click and drag, or scrub back and forth as you would with an ordinary eraser (**Figure 3.74**).

   Flash removes all the lines you erase.

Using the Faucet Modifier

To speed the erasing of lines and fills, Flash provides the faucet modifier for the eraser tool. The faucet erases an entire fill shape or an entire line with a single click.

To erase a line:

1. In the Toolbox, with the eraser tool selected, click the faucet button (**Figure 3.75**).

   The pointer changes to a dripping-faucet icon.

2. Place the faucet's hot spot (the drop of water) over the line you want to remove (**Figure 3.76**).

3. Click.

   Flash deletes the entire line, even if it's made up of several line segments.

To erase a fill:

1. Select the eraser tool's faucet modifier.

2. Place the faucet's hot spot over the fill you want to remove.

3. Click.

   Flash deletes the fill.

✔ Tip

■ In the Toolbox, double-click the eraser tool to delete the entire contents of the Stage.

—*Faucet mode*

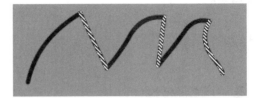

Figure 3.75 The eraser tool's faucet modifier lets you erase entire lines or fills with a single click.

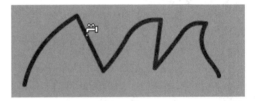

Figure 3.76 This squiggly line contains multiple curve segments, as the selections indicate (top). You can delete the whole line by using the eraser tool's faucet modifier. Click the hot spot of the water drip anywhere on the deselected line (middle); Flash deletes the entire line (bottom).

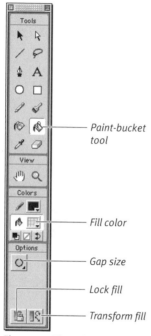

Paint-bucket tool

Fill color

Gap size

Lock fill

Transform fill

Figure 3.77 The paint-bucket tool lets you modify fills without first selecting them.

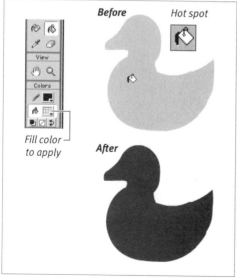

Before Hot spot

Fill color to apply

After

Figure 3.78 Clicking a fill with the paint bucket applies whatever color is selected in the fill-color box. Use this technique to change existing unselected fills.

Modifying Fill Colors

Flash provides two methods for modifying the color of an existing fill. You can select the fill and change its attributes in the Fill panel, or you can use the paint-bucket tool to apply the current Fill panel settings to an existing fill.

To change fill color with the paint bucket:

1. In the Toolbox, select the paint-bucket tool, or press K on the keyboard.

   Modifiers for fills appear in the Options section of the Toolbox (**Figure 3.77**).

2. In the Fill panel, *set the following attributes:*

   ◆ From the fill-type menu, choose Solid.

   ◆ Click the fill-color box, and choose a new color from the swatch set.

   The fill-color box in the Toolbox displays the selected color, and the paint bucket is ready to apply the new fill color.

3. Click the paint bucket's hot spot (the tip of the drip of paint) somewhere inside the fill you want to change.

   The shape fills with the new color (**Figure 3.78**).

To modify selected fills with the Fill panel:

1. Using the arrow tool, select one or more fills on the Stage.

2. In the Fill panel, click the fill-color box, and choose a new color from the swatch set. Flash changes all selected fills to whatever color you selected in the Fill panel (Figure 3.79).

✔ Tips

- Note that changes made with the paint bucket or the Fill panel have no effect on selected strokes. You can safely include strokes in your selection.

- If the selection highlighting makes it too hard to see your color changes, you can hide the highlight temporarily. Choose View > Hide Edges. Just don't forget to turn the feature off later; otherwise, you won't be able to see any selections.

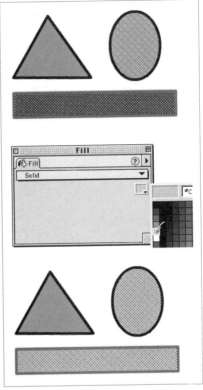

Figure 3.79 Select one or more fills for modification (top). Choose a new color from the Fill panel's fill-color box (middle). Flash changes the color of all the fills in your selection (bottom).

Figure 3.80 To access the Mixer panel, choose Window > Panels > Mixer.

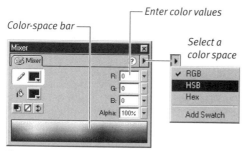

Figure 3.81 The Mixer panel lets you choose a color from the color-space bar or enter values directly to define a color in the RGB, HSB, or Hex color space.

Creating Solid Colors: Mixer Panel

You can define new solid colors for fills and strokes in the Mixer panel. You can do so visually, by clicking a representation of a color space, or numerically, by entering specific values for color components. Always choose the type of color—fill or stroke—before you start defining. Flash updates all the related color boxes with the new color. If you define a new fill color, for example, that color becomes the setting for all the tools that use fills. You can also set a color's transparency in the Mixer panel.

To access the Mixer panel:

If the Mixer panel is not currently open, *do one of the following:*

◆ From the Window menu, choose Panels > Mixer (**Figure 3.80**).

◆ In the Launcher bar at the bottom of the Stage, click the Show Mixer button.

The Mixer panel appears.

To access solid color attributes in the Mixer panel:

1. From the Mixer panel's Options menu, choose a color space (**Figure 3.81**).

    The Mixer panel allows you to define colors values in three color spaces: RGB (red, green, blue), HSB (hue, saturation, brightness), and Hex (hexadecimal).

2. To determine where Flash applies the new color, *do one of the following:*

    ◆ To set a new stroke color, click the pencil icon.

    ◆ To set a new fill color, click the paint-bucket icon.

To define a new color visually in the Mixer panel:

1. With the Mixer panel open, choose a color space.

2. Position the pointer over the desired hue in the color-space bar.

3. Click.

   The crosshair cursor appears, and Flash selects the color within the crosshairs (**Figure 3.82**).

✔ Tip

■ Even if you have set your monitor resolution to 640 by 480, that color-space bar is awfully tiny. You can access a full-size color picker from any color-box (see "Creating Solid Colors: Color Picker" later in this chapter).

To define a new color numerically in the Mixer panel:

1. With the Mixer panel open, choose a color space.

2. To define a new color, *do one of the following:*

   ◆ For RGB and Hex colors, enter values for red, green, and blue in the R, G, and B fields (**Figure 3.83**).

   ◆ For HSB, enter values for hue, saturation, and brightness in the H, S, and B fields.

To define a color's transparency:

1. With the Mixer panel open, define a color.

2. Enter a value in the Alpha field (**Figure 3.84**).

   A percentage of 100 results in a completely solid color; a percentage of 0 results in a completely transparent color.

Sometimes, you might want to match the color of an item you've already created in Flash, for example.

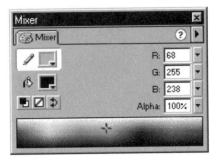

Figure 3.82 Click the color-space bar to choose a new color visually.

Figure 3.83 Enter RGB values to specify RGB or Hex colors; enter HSB values to specify hue, saturation, and brightness. The new color appears in the selected color box.

Figure 3.84 Enter an Alpha value of less than 100 percent to define a transparent color.

To sample and select a color from the Stage:

1. With the Mixer panel open, click the stroke- or fill-color box.

The pointer changes to an eyedropper tool, and a set of swatches appears.

2. Click on any element in a Flash document to select the color directly below the tip of the eyedropper.

After you define a new color, you may want to add it to the Swatches panel so you can use it again. (For more information about the Swatches panel, see "Creating Color Sets" later in this chapter.)

To add a color to the Swatches panel:

1. Use any of the techniques described earlier in this section to define a new color in the Mixer panel.

2. From the Mixer panel's Options menu, choose Add Swatch.

Flash appends the new color to the solid-colors section of the Swatches panel.

✔ Tip

■ You can add new colors to the Swatches panel even if it is closed. But if you want to get the feedback when you add a swatch, open the Swatches panel in its own window. Resize the panel so there's a bit of gray space below the existing swatches. You'll see the new swatch come in.

What Are Hex Colors?

The term *hex color* is short for *hexadecimal color*, which is a fancy way of saying a color defined by a number written in base 16. Hexadecimal coding is the language of bits and bytes that computers speak; it's also the coding you use to specify color in HTML.

If you remember studying bases in high-school math, you'll recall that the decimal system is base 10, represented by the numbers 0 through 9. In hex color, to get the extra six digits, you continue coding with letters A through F.

CREATING SOLID COLORS: MIXER PANEL

Creating Solid Colors: Color Picker

In addition to creating colors in the Mixer panel, you can create colors in the Color Picker window. This window offers a variety of color pickers. HSV (hue, saturation, and value) and HLS (hue, lightness, and saturation) present the available color space in a large circle that's easier to see than the small color-space bar in the Mixer panel. The CMYK Picker, RGB Picker, and HTML Picker work via color sliders. All the pickers display large swatches for comparing the current color with the new color you are defining.

With one exception, you can access the Color Picker from any fill-color or stroke-color box that pops up the current set of color swatches. (The Fill panel's fill-color box doesn't provide access to the Color Picker.) The following exercise shows one way to reach the Color Picker window and work with one of the color spaces.

To access the Color Picker:

1. In the Toolbox or Mixer panel, click the fill-color or stroke-color box.

   A set of color swatches pops up.

2. Click the Color Picker button (**Figure 3.85**).

   The Color Picker (Mac) or Color (Windows) window appears (**Figure 3.86**).

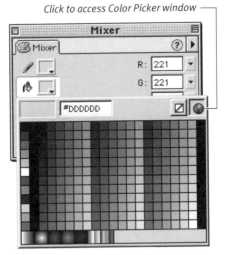

Click to access Color Picker window

Figure 3.85 The Color Picker button appears on most of the swatch sets that you access via the fill- or stroke-color box.

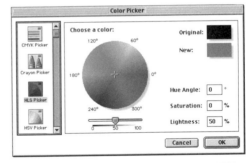

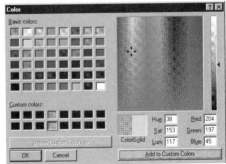

Figure 3.86 The Mac's Color Picker window (top) offers six color pickers. Each picker has a set of sliders and value fields or visual representations of the color space. In Windows, you define a color by entering HLS and RGB values or selecting colors from the color-space window in the Color window (bottom).

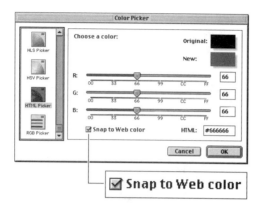

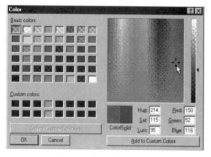

Figure 3.87 On the Mac, define a new Web-safe color using the HTML Picker in the Color Picker window (top). With Snap to Web color checked, Flash restricts the sliders to creating Web-safe combinations. In Windows, define Web-safe colors in the Color window (bottom). Double-clicking the Solid area of the current-color swatch forces the cross-hair to the nearest color that can be represented without dithering.

✔ Tips

■ You can ensure that your new color is safe for Web use. On the Mac, define the color by using the HTML Picker in the Color Picker window. Check Snap to Web color. Flash finds the nearest match for your color from the 216 Web-safe colors (**Figure 3.87**). In Windows, the Color window displays the current color in a split window; half of the window shows a dithered swatch, half shows a solid swatch. Double-click the solid swatch to force Flash to make the color solid, in other words, Web safe.

To define a new fill color with the HLS Picker (Mac):

1. Access the Color Picker from a fill-color box.

2. From the scrolling list on the left side of the window, choose HLS Picker.

   The main portion of the window displays a circular representation of the HLS color space plus the appropriate sliders and entry fields.

3. To define the new color, *do one of the following:*

   ◆ Click and drag the crosshair cursor in the color space.

   ◆ Enter new values in the Hue Angle, Saturation, and Lightness fields.

4. Click OK.

   Flash updates the fill-color box in the Toolbox and relevant panels.

To define a new fill color in the Color window (Windows):

1. Access the Color window from a fill-color box.

2. *Do one of the following:*

   ◆ To define a new color numerically, in the Hue, Saturation, and Luminosity (or Red, Green, and Blue) fields, enter the values for your new color.

   ◆ To define a new color visually, click in the color-space window. The crosshair cursor moves to the spot you clicked and Flash updates the color values in the HLS and RGB fields.

3. Click OK.

   Flash updates the fill-color box in the Toolbox and relevant panels.

Creating New Gradients

In addition to solid colors, Flash works with *gradients*—bands of color that blend into each other. Gradients can be linear (parallel bars of color) or radial (concentric rings of color). Gradients can create interesting visual effects and are useful for adding shading—to make a circle look like a sphere, for example.

Flash defines each gradient with a set of pointers that indicate what color goes where in the lineup of color bands. You define the color for each pointer. By positioning the markers on the gradient definition bar, you control how wide each band of color is. Each gradient can contain as many as eight colors.

You define new gradients in the Fill panel.

To create a three-color linear gradient:

1. Open the Fill panel and the Mixer panel. For this exercise, place the panels in separate windows so you can see what's happening at each step.

2. From the Fill panel's Fill menu, choose Linear Gradient.
   The tools for defining gradients appear (**Figure 3.88**).

3. In the Fill panel, click the fill-color box.

4. From the set of swatches that pops up, select an existing gradient as a starting point.
   The selected gradient appears in the Fill panel with two to eight pointers. (Because a gradient must have at least two colors, the bar always contains at least two pointers.)

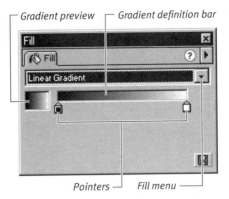

Gradient preview   *Gradient definition bar*

Pointers — *Fill menu* —

Figure 3.88 Select Linear Gradient from the Fill menu to access the tools for defining gradients.

No pointer selected

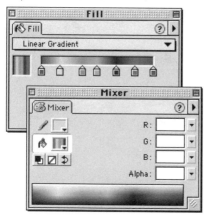

Pointer selected — *Pointer color*

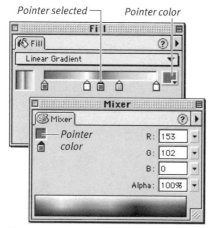

Figure 3.89 When you select one of the gradient's pointers, a pointer-color box appears in the Fill panel, and the Mixer panel displays the current pointer color.

5. To set up the gradient bar for three colors, in the Fill panel, *do one of the following:*

- ◆ If your starting gradient has more than three pointers, click and drag the extra pointers away from the gradient-definition bar to remove them.

- ◆ If your starting gradient has only two pointers, click below the gradient-definition bar to add a new pointer.

6. Click the leftmost pointer for your first color.

When you select a pointer, a pointer-color box appears in the Fill panel, and the Mixer panel replaces its stroke- and fill-color boxes with a color swatch and a gradient-pointer icon. These visual cues indicate that you are currently setting a pointer color (**Figure 3.89**).

7. To define the pointer's color, *do one of the following:*

- ◆ Click the pointer-color box in the Fill panel, and choose a color from the set of swatches that appears.

- ◆ In the Mixer panel, define a new color.

8. Repeat steps 6 and 7 for the middle and rightmost pointers.

continues on next page

9. Drag the pointers to position them on the gradient-definition bar (**Figure 3.90**).

Place pointers closer together to make the transition between colors more abrupt; place them farther apart to spread the transition out over more space.

While you modify the gradient, your changes appear in all fill-color boxes. Check out the one in the Toolbox. Any tool that creates a fill—say, the oval tool—will use your modified gradient.

✔ Tips

■ To choose a gradient for modification, select the existing gradient in the Swatches panel. Flash switches the Fill panel to gradient mode and displays the selected gradient.

■ To increase the size of the gradient-definition bar (so it's easier to add and fine-tune points), resize the Fill panel. As the Fill panel grows, so does the bar.

■ To reverse the direction of a gradient's color transition, drag one pointer over another. In a white-to-black gradient (a white pointer on the left and a black pointer on the right), drag the white pointer to the right past the black one. Your gradient now goes from black to white.

To create a new radial gradient:

1. Open the Fill and Mixer panels.

2. From the Fill panel's Fill menu, choose Radial Gradient.

The tools for defining circular gradients appear. The gradient-definition bar looks the same as it does for linear gradients, but the preview shows your gradient as a set of concentric circles (**Figure 3.91**). The leftmost pointer defines the inner ring; the rightmost pointer defines the outer ring.

Gradient starts with white and blends first to gray and then to black; black fills out the gradient

Move pointers in to increase width of outside bands

Click to add pointers

Figure 3.90 Choose a color for each pointer. The colors and positions of the pointers on the bar define a gradient's color transitions.

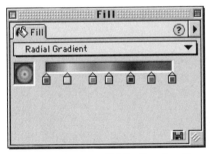

Figure 3.91 Choose Radial Gradient from the Fill menu to create a circular gradient. The preview window translates the horizontal gradient-definition bar into the appropriate circular color transitions.

Figure 3.92 When transparent colors make up part of a gradient, grid lines appear in the pointer, the pointer-color box, and the gradient preview window.

3. Follow steps 3 through 9 in the linear-gradient exercise to define the color transitions in the radial gradient.

✔ Tips

- Gradients can have transparency. You simply use a transparent color in one or more gradient pointers (see "To define a color's transparency" earlier in this chapter). If a gradient has transparency, a grid shows up in the pointer, in the pointer-color box, and in the transparent part of the gradient in the preview window (**Figure 3.92**).

- Each pointer in a gradient can have a different alpha setting. To create fade effects, try creating a gradient that blends from a fully opaque color to a transparent one.

You can save a new gradient by adding it to the Swatches panel.

To add a gradient to the Swatches panel:

1. Create a new gradient using any of the techniques outlined in the preceding section.

2. In the Fill panel, *do one of the following:*
   ◆ From the Options menu, choose Add Gradient.
   ◆ Click the Save button (in the bottom-right corner of the panel).

Flash adds the new gradient to the gradients section of the Swatches panel.

Creating Color Sets

Flash stores a default set of colors and gradients in the system color file, but it stores the colors and gradients used in each document with that document. (In Flash 3 and earlier versions, all colors resided in a system color file.)

Flash lets you define what colors and gradients make up the default set. In addition, you can create and save other color sets and load them into the Swatches panel. This makes it easy to maintain a consistent color palette when you are creating several documents for use in a single movie or on a single Web site.

To access the Swatches panel:

◆ If the Swatches panel is not currently open, from the Window menu, choose Panels > Swatches.

The Swatches panel appears.

To define a new set of colors:

1. Define all the colors and gradients you want in your special color set (see "Creating Solid Colors" and "Creating New Gradients" earlier in this chapter).

   You don't need to define all your colors in a single session, but after you have a set you want to save, move on to step 2.

2. From the Swatches panel's Option menu, choose Save Colors (**Figure 3.93**).

   An export dialog box appears (**Figure 3.94**).

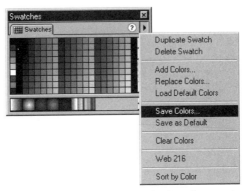

Figure 3.93 The Options menu in the Swatches panel offers commands for working with color sets.

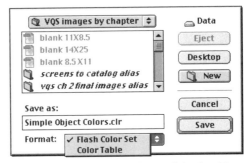

Figure 3.94 Use the Export Color Set dialog box (Mac version shown) to save a set of colors for reuse.

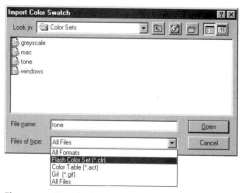

Figure 3.95 Use the Import Color Swatch dialog box (Windows version shown) to reload a saved set of colors.

3. Navigate to the folder where you want to store your color set.

4. Enter a name for your color set file in the Save as field (Mac) or File name field (Windows).

5. From the Format (Mac) or Save As Type (Windows) pop-up menu, *choose one of two formats:*

   ◆ To save colors and gradients in Flash's proprietary Flash Color Set (CLR) format, choose Flash Color Set.

   ◆ To save the colors in Color Table (ACT) format, choose Color Table.

   The ACT format saves only colors (not gradients) but allows you to use those colors in other programs, such as Adobe Photoshop and Macromedia Fireworks.

6. Click Save.

To load a set of colors:

1. From the Options menu in the Swatches panel, *choose one of the following:*

   ◆ To add to the color set currently displayed in the Swatches panel, choose Add Colors.

   ◆ To replace the entire set currently displayed in the Color window, choose Replace Colors.

   The Import Color Swatch dialog box appears (**Figure 3.95**).

   continues on next page

2. To determine what types of files to display, from the List Files of Type pop-up menu (Mac) or Files of Type (Windows) pop-up menu, choose one of the following:

◆ All Formats, which displays CLR, ACT, and GIF files.

◆ Flash Color Set, which displays only CLR files.

◆ Color Table, which displays only ACT files.

◆ GIF, which displays only GIF files.

◆ All Files, which displays files of any format.

Note that the Color Table and GIF formats are for color import only; these formats do not handle gradients. Flash Color Set handles both colors and gradients.

3. Navigate to the file you want.

4. Click Open.

To define the default set of colors:

1. From the Options menu in the Swatches panel, choose Save As Default.

A warning dialog box appears, giving you the chance to cancel the operation at this point (**Figure 3.96**).

2. *Do one of the following:*

◆ To cancel the operation, click No.

◆ To go ahead and create the new default color set, click Yes.

Figure 3.96 This warning dialog box gives you a chance to change your mind after you've chosen Save As Default from the Options menu in the Swatches panel. You can't undo this operation.

Fill control
Stroke control

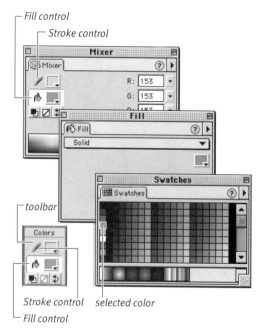

toolbar

Stroke control   selected color
Fill control

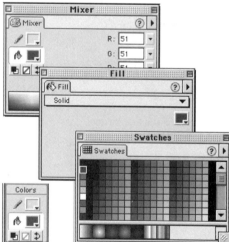

Figure 3.97 Click the stroke or fill button in either the Toolbox or the Mixer panel to tell Flash what type of color you are assigning. You can then select a color in the Swatches panel (top). Flash updates the appropriate color boxes throughout the program (bottom).

✔ Tips

■ The Options menu in the Swatches panel also offers some handy shortcuts for dealing with color sets. To reload the default color set, choose Load Default Colors. To remove all color swatches from the current panel window, choose Clear Colors. To load the standard Web-safe colors, choose Web 216. To arrange colors in order of their luminosity values, choose Sort by Color.

■ To delete a swatch from the current set, in the Swatches panel, select the swatch; then, from the panel's Options menu, choose Delete Swatch.

■ To copy a swatch to modify it—to create a transparent version of the color, for example—in the Swatches panel, select the swatch. Then, from the panel's Options menu, choose Duplicate Swatch.

■ You can also use the Swatches panel to select colors for fills and strokes. The key is first to tell Flash where to apply the new color. You do that by clicking the stroke or fill button in the Colors section of the Toolbox or in the Mixer panel (**Figure 3.97**). Then select a color in the Swatches panel. Flash puts that color into every fill-color or stroke-color box. In the Colors section of the Toolbox, for example, click the paint-bucket icon and then select blue in the Swatches panel. Blue now appears in the fill-color box in the Toolbox, in the Fill panel, in the Character panel, and in the Mixer panel.

■ If the swatches in the Swatches panel are too small for you, resize the panel window. The swatches grow or shrink as you resize the window.

Putting Gradients to Work

In the "Creating New Gradients" section earlier in this chapter, you learned how to create color blends. Flash treats gradients just like any other fill. You use the paint-bucket tool to fill outline shapes with a gradient and the brush tool to create freeform swashes of gradient color.

To fill a shape (or replace a solid fill) with a linear gradient:

1. In the Toolbox, select the paint-bucket tool.

2. From a fill-color box (in the Toolbox, Fill panel, or Mixer panel), choose a linear gradient.

3. Click the paint bucket's hot spot (the tip of the drip of paint) somewhere inside the outline shape or within the existing fill (**Figure 3.98**).

   The shape fills with the linear gradient currently displayed in the fill-color boxes.

To fill a shape (or replace a solid fill) with a radial gradient:

1. In the Toolbox, select the paint-bucket tool.

2. From a fill-color box (in the Toolbox, Fill panel, or Mixer panel), choose a radial gradient.

3. Click the paint bucket's hot spot (the tip of the drip of paint) somewhere inside the outline shape or within the existing fill (**Figure 3.99**).

   The shape fills with the radial gradient currently displayed in the fill-color boxes.

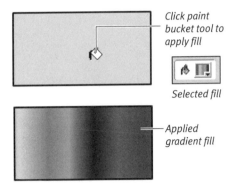

Click paint bucket tool to apply fill

Selected fill

Applied gradient fill

Figure 3.98 You can use the paint-bucket tool to apply a linear-gradient fill.

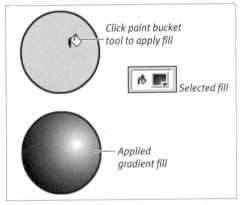

Click paint bucket tool to apply fill

Selected fill

Applied gradient fill

Figure 3.99 The paint-bucket tool can also apply a radial-gradient fill.

Gradients Add Overhead

Gradients are lovely, but they do increase file sizes and thereby slow the loading of published movies. Each area of gradient fill requires an extra 50 bytes of data that a solid fill doesn't need.

Figure 3.100 Deselect Lock Fill modifier to paint with an unlocked gradient.

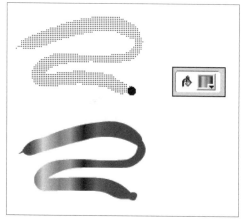

Figure 3.101 A painted shape with a linear-gradient fill.

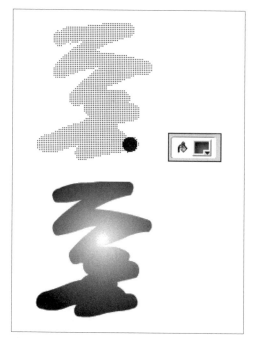

Figure 3.102 A painted shape with a radial-gradient fill.

To paint with an unlocked gradient:

1. In the Toolbox, select the brush tool.

2. Make sure that the Lock Fill modifier is deselected (**Figure 3.100**).

3. From a fill-color box (in the Toolbox, Fill panel, or Mixer panel), choose a gradient.

4. Paint with the brush as described in Chapter 2.

   Flash cannot preview the shape you paint with the gradient you chose, as it can do with solid-color fills. The preview shape has a black-and-white pattern.

5. When you finish your brushstroke, release the mouse button.

   Flash redraws the painted shape, using the gradient currently selected in the fill color box. Flash fills the shape's bounding box (an invisible rectangle that's just the right size to enclose the shape) with the gradient. The painted shape reveals portions of that gradient pattern (**Figures 3.101** and **3.102**).

✔ Tip

- You can also create a single underlying gradient for several shapes on the Stage by using the Lock Fill modifier. With the paint bucket selected, choose a gradient fill. Click the Lock Fill button. Flash creates an underlying hidden rectangle—the same size as the Stage—filled with the locked gradient. Wherever you paint with the locked gradient using the brush tool (or apply the locked fill to a shape using the paint-bucket tool), Flash reveals that hidden gradient.

PUTTING GRADIENTS TO WORK

Modifying Applied Gradients

You can also use Flash's tools to modify a gradient fill.

To move a gradient fill's center point:

1. In the Toolbox, select the paint-bucket tool.

2. Choose the Transform Fill modifier (**Figure 3.103**).

   The pointer changes to the Transform Fill arrow.

3. Position the pointer over the graphic element whose gradient you want to modify.

4. Click.

   Handles for manipulating the element appear (**Figure 3.104**).

5. Drag the center-point handle to reposition the center point of the gradient (**Figure 3.105**).

Figure 3.103 The Transform Fill modifier (left) and the pointer with which you manipulate gradients (right).

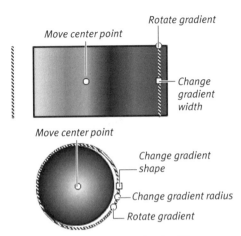

Figure 3.104 Handles for transforming fills appear when you click the fill with the transform-fill arrow.

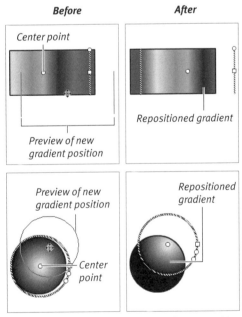

Figure 3.105 Drag the center-point handle to reposition the center of the gradient within your shape.

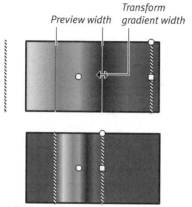

Preview width *Transform gradient width*

Color bands on outer edges of blend get wider

Figure 3.106 With a linear gradient, drag the square handle inward to create a narrower space for a gradient.

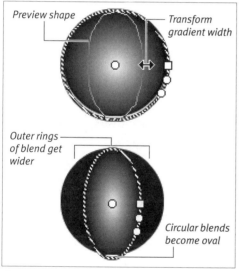

Preview shape *Transform gradient width*

Outer rings of blend get wider

Circular blends become oval

Figure 3.107 With a radial gradient, drag the square handle inward to create a narrower oval for a gradient.

To resize a gradient fill:

1. With the paint bucket in Transform Fill mode, click the graphic element that contains the gradient you want to modify.

2. To change the width of a linear gradient, drag the square handle (**Figure 3.106**).

   The pointer changes to a double-headed arrow. Dragging toward the center of your shape squeezes the blend into a narrower space; dragging away from the center of your shape spreads the blend over a wider space.

3. To change the shape of a radial gradient, drag the square handle (**Figure 3.107**).

   The pointer changes to a double-headed arrow. Dragging toward the center of your shape creates a narrower oval space for the blend; dragging away from the center of your shape creates a wider oval space.

continues on next page

MODIFYING APPLIED GRADIENTS

4. To change the radius of a radial gradient, drag the circular handle next to the square handle (**Figure 3.108**).

The pointer changes to a double-headed arrow within a circle. Dragging toward the center of your shape squeezes the blend into a smaller circular space; dragging away from the center of your shape spreads the blend over a larger circular space.

To rotate a gradient fill:

1. With the paint bucket in Transform Fill mode, click the graphic element with the gradient you want to modify.

2. To rotate the gradient, *do one of the following:*

- ◆ To rotate a linear gradient, drag the round handle (**Figure 3.109**).

- ◆ To rotate a radial gradient, drag the round handle farthest from the square handle.

The pointer changes to a circular arrow. You can rotate the gradient clockwise or counterclockwise.

✔ Tips

- ■ You can click and drag with the paint-bucket tool to rotate the gradient as you apply it. To constrain the gradient angle to vertical, horizontal, or 45-degree angles, hold down the Shift key as you drag.

- ■ When you rotate a gradient interactively with the paint bucket, the modified angle remains part of the selected fill even though the color-fill box continues to display the gradient in its vertical position. You can now switch to the brush tool, for example, and paint with the rotated gradient. To remove the angle modification, use the paint bucket to modify the gradient again or choose another fill.

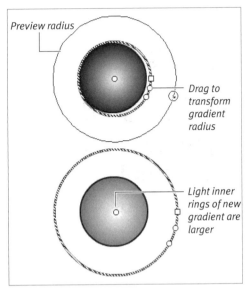

Figure 3.108 With a radial gradient, drag the first round handle outward to create a larger radius.

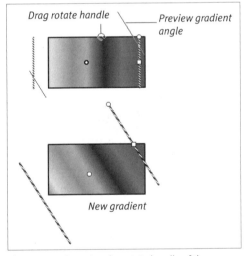

Figure 3.109 Dragging the rotate handle of the gradient spins the gradient around its center point.

Dropper tool pointer   ┌*Dropper tool selected*

*Dropper switches to
paint bucket*

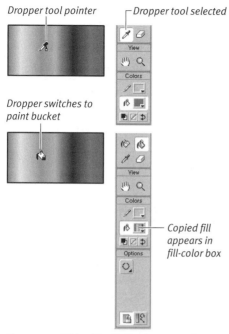

*Copied fill
appears in
fill-color box*

Figure 3.110 Click a fill with the dropper tool to copy that fill to another graphic element.

Applying Attributes of One Graphic Element to Another

To save time, you can copy the fill and stroke attributes of one element and apply them to another element.

To copy fills between graphic elements:

1. In the Toolbox, select the dropper tool, or press I on the keyboard.

2. Move the pointer over the Stage.

The pointer changes to an eyedropper.

3. Position the eyedropper over the fill you want to copy (either a solid color or gradient).

4. Click the fill (**Figure 3.110**).

Flash switches to the paint-bucket tool automatically. The color or gradient you picked up appears in the fill-color box in the Toolbox, Fill panel, and Mixer panel. (Clicking the dropper tool on a fill activates the paint bucket's locked gradient mode.)

5. You can now use the paint bucket to apply the copied fill to a different graphic element (see "Modifying Fill Colors" earlier in this chapter).

APPLYING ATTRIBUTES OF GRAPHICS

To copy stroke attributes:

1. In the Toolbox, select the dropper tool.

2. Position the eyedropper pointer over a line or outline (stroke) whose attributes you want to copy.

3. Click the line (**Figure 3.111**).

Flash switches to the ink-bottle tool. The color, weight, and style attributes of the line you clicked appear in the Stroke panel.

You can use the ink-bottle pointer to apply the copied attributes to a different line (see "Modifying Strokes" earlier in this chapter).

✔ Tips

■ To pick up the color of a stroke or fill and use it for both strokes and fills, Shift-click with the dropper. Flash sets the fill- and stroke-color boxes in the Toolbox and in the various panels to the selected color.

■ Any time you select a stroke or fill with the arrow tool, you actually pick up those attributes and enter them in the relevant panels. If you frequently use certain stroke and fill combinations, keep graphic elements with those settings sitting to one side on the Stage. When you're ready to set those parameters, select the graphic element and start drawing on the Stage or use the ink-bottle or paint-bucket tool to apply the parameters to existing graphic elements.

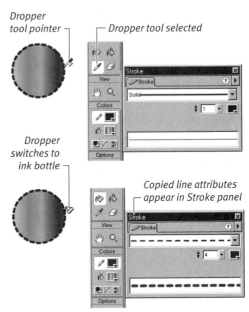

Dropper tool pointer —

— *Dropper tool selected*

Dropper switches to ink bottle —

Copied line attributes appear in Stroke panel

Figure 3.111 Clicking a line with the dropper tool copies the stroke attributes to the Stroke panel. Use the ink bottle tool to apply them to another line.

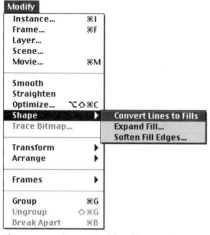

Figure 3.112 Choose Modify > Shape > Convert Lines to Fills to transform strokes into fills.

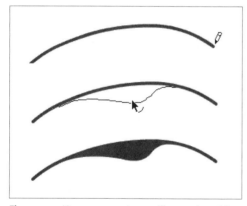

Figure 3.113 You can convert an outline, such as this line drawn with the pencil tool (top), to a fill. It then has its own editable outlines (middle and bottom).

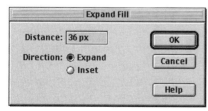

Figure 3.114 The Expand Fill dialog box presents options for resizing a selected fill.

Converting Lines to Fills

Flash lets you convert lines and outlines (strokes) to fills, which you can then edit or fill with gradients. You can expand or contract a shape by a user-specified amount. And you can create soft-edged graphic elements. These conversions increase the number of curves that Flash creates and therefore may increase file size.

To convert a line to a fill:

1. In the Toolbox, select the pencil tool.

2. Draw a simple line on the Stage.

3. Change to the arrow tool, and click the line to select it.

4. From the Modify menu, choose Shape > Convert Lines to Fills (**Figure 3.112**).

   Flash converts the line to a fill shape that looks exactly like the line. You can now edit the shape of the "line's" outline (or apply a gradient) as though you were working with a fill created with the brush tool (**Figure 3.113**).

To expand a fill:

1. In the Toolbox, select the oval tool with no stroke.

2. On the Stage, draw an oval shape.

3. Change to the arrow tool, and click the shape to select it.

4. From the Modify menu, choose Shape > Expand Fill.

   The Expand Fill dialog box appears (**Figure 3.114**).

5. Enter a value in the Distance field.

6. Choose a Direction option.

   Expand makes the shape larger. Inset makes the shape smaller.

continues on next page

7. Click OK.

Flash blows the fill shape up like a balloon (or shrinks it) (**Figure 3.115**).

To soften the edges of a fill:

1. In the Toolbox, select the oval tool with no stroke.

2. On the Stage, draw an oval shape.

3. Change to the arrow tool, and click the shape to select it.

4. From the Modify menu, choose Shape > Soften Edges.

The Soften Edges dialog box appears (**Figure 3.116**).

5. Enter values for Distance and Number of Steps.

6. Choose a Direction option.

Expand makes the shape larger; Inset makes the shape smaller.

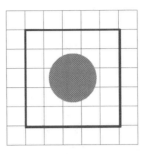

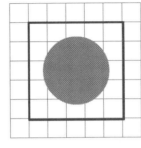

Figure 3.115 Using the Expand Fill command on the selected fill (top) causes its outlines to expand. The grid here is set to 36 pixels.

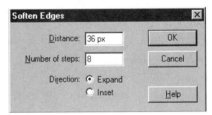

Figure 3.116 The Soften Edges dialog box.

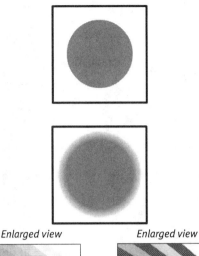

Enlarged view   *Enlarged view*

Figure 3.117 The Soften Edges command creates a purposeful banding effect to give fill shapes a soft edge. The selected circle (top) gets a soft edge in eight steps (middle). Enlarged views show the banding more clearly (bottom left); you can select individual steps of the softened edge (bottom right).

7. Click OK.

Flash divides the expansion or inset value by the number of steps and creates a series of concentric shapes that outline your original shape. The new shapes get progressively lighter in color as they approach the outer edge of the softened shape (**Figure 3.117**).

✔ Tips

- The Expand Fill and Soften Edges commands work best on plain fill shapes (fills without strokes). Small shapes and shapes with convoluted outlines take a longer time to convert, and the results may not be what you expect.

- When you use the Modify > Shape > commands on fills that also have strokes around them, the stroke doesn't expand or shrink to match the expansion or inset. Depending on how far you expand the fill, it will eat into—or totally cover—the stroke.

- If you use one of the Modify > Shape commands to inset the fill of a stroked graphic, you wind up with a blank ring inside the stroke. This could be handy should you ever need to create a secondary outline for a shape, but it's usually not the effect you're looking for.

CONVERTING LINES TO FILLS

COMPLEX GRAPHICS ON A SINGLE LAYER

4

In Chapters 2 and 3, you learned to make simple individual shapes from lines (strokes) and fills by using Macromedia Flash's drawing tools. You learned to make a single oval and a lone rectangle, for example. In your movies, you'll want to use many shapes together, and you'll need to combine strokes and fills in complex ways. You might combine several ovals and rectangles to create a robot character, for example. To work effectively with complex graphics, you need to understand how Flash shapes interact when they are on the same layer or on different layers. In this chapter, you learn how to work with multiple shapes on one layer. To learn more about the concept of layers, see Chapter 5.

Two of Flash's drawing tools—the brush tool and the eraser—offer special modes for use with multiple fills and strokes on a single layer. In this chapter, unless you are specifically requested to do otherwise, leave both tools at their default settings of Paint Normal (for the brush tool) and Erase Normal (for the eraser).

When Lines Intersect Lines

If you draw several lines on the same layer, they interact. Draw a new line across an existing one, and the new line cuts—or, in Flash terminology, *segments*—the old. Segmentation happens whether the lines are the same color or different colors, but it's easiest to see with contrasting colors.

To see how one line segments another:

1. In the Stroke panel, *do the following:*
   - Set the line style to Solid.
   - Set the line weight to 4 points.
   - Set the color to red.

2. In the Toolbox, choose the pencil tool.

3. On the Stage, draw a line.

4. Click the stroke-color box (in the Toolbox or in the Stroke panel), and from the pop-up swatch set, choose a new color.

5. On the Stage, draw a second line; make it intersect your first line at least once.

   Flash segments the line. To see the segments, select various parts of the line with the arrow tool (**Figure 4.1**).

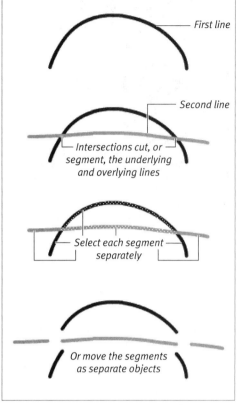

Figure 4.1 When you draw one line across another, every intersection creates a separate segment.

How Do Flash's Editable Objects Interact?

You can think of each frame in a Flash movie as being a stack of transparent acetate sheets. In Flash terms, each "sheet" is a layer. Objects on different layers have a depth relationship: Objects on higher layers block your view of those on lower layers, just as a drawing on the top sheet of acetate would obscure drawings on lower sheets.

Imagine that you have two layers in your movie. If you draw a little yellow square on the bottom layer and then switch to the top layer and draw a big red square directly over the yellow one, the little square remains intact. You simply can't see it while the big red square on the top layer is in the way.

On a single layer, however, objects actually interact with one another, almost as though you were painting with wet finger paint. When fills of different colors interact, the newer fill replaces the older one. Take the preceding example: First draw a little yellow square, and then switch colors and draw a big red square right on top of the little one in the same layer. The little square disappears for good. The red fill replaces the yellow wherever it overlaps the latter.

If the new fill only intersects the old, it still replaces the part where the two overlap. Imagine, for example, using the brush tool to paint the first stroke of the letter X. Now pick up a different color to paint the second stroke of the X. Where the second brush stroke overlaps the first, it eats up that first fill color. You wind up with separate segments of the first stroke on either side of the second stroke where the two intersect.

When fills are the same color, the newer fill simply adds to the shape. If you lay down two brushstrokes in the same color, the second slightly overlapping the first, the edges of the two brushstrokes run together, and you wind up with one wide shape. If you paint both halves of the letter X with the same color, you wind up with a single X-shape object.

When Lines and Fills Interact

Even the invisible outlines that describe painted brushstroke fills can cut other lines. This means that when you draw lines over fills, you can wind up with lots of little segments.

To see how a fill segments a line:

1. In the Stroke panel, *do the following:*

   ◆ Set the line style to Solid.

   ◆ Set the line weight to 4 points.

   ◆ Set the color to red.

2. In the Toolbox, choose the pencil tool.

3. On the Stage, draw a line.

4. Return to the Toolbox, and choose the brush tool.

5. Click the fill-color box (in the Toolbox or in the Fill panel), and from the pop-up swatch set, choose blue.

6. On the Stage, paint a brushstroke that intersects your line twice.

   The brush stroke remains one solid object, but the line turns into three separate segments (**Figure 4.2**).

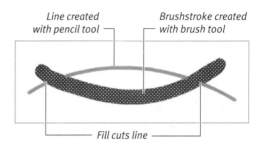

Figure 4.2 When a fill overlays a line, the fill segments the line. As the selection highlighting shows, the fill remains one solid object.

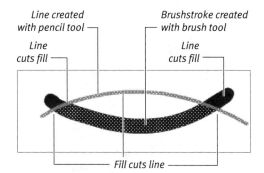

Line created with pencil tool

Brushstroke created with brush tool

Line cuts fill

Line cuts fill

Fill cuts line

Figure 4.3 When a line overlays a fill, the line cuts the fill and the fill's invisible outline cuts the line.

To see how a line segments a fill:

1. In the Toolbox, choose the brush tool.

2. Click the fill-color box (in the Toolbox or the Stroke panel), and from the pop-up swatch set, choose red.

3. On the Stage, paint a brushstroke.

4. Return to the Toolbox, and choose the pencil tool.

5. In the Stroke panel, *do the following:*

   ◆ Set the stroke color to blue.

   ◆ Set the line thickness to 4 points.

   ◆ From the Line Style pop-up menu, choose Solid.

6. On the Stage, draw a line that intersects your brushstroke twice.

   The line cuts the brushstroke into three segments; the invisible outline of the brushstroke cuts the line into five separate segments (**Figure 4.3**).

WHEN LINES AND FILLS INTERACT

When Shapes Interact

The interaction of one fill with another can have one of two results; the outcome depends on what color the two fills are. Fills of the same color simply run together and create a new shape. If the fills are different colors, the one you draw second replaces the first in any areas where the two overlap. You can use these interactions to create complex shapes from several simpler ones.

To add to a fill shape:

1. In the Toolbox, select the brush tool.

2. Click the fill-color box (in the Toolbox or in the Fill panel), and from the pop-up swatch set, choose a color.

3. On the Stage, paint one brushstroke.

4. Using the same color, paint a separate brushstroke that intersects the first one.

   Flash adds the second brushstroke to the first, creating a single new fill shape (**Figure 4.4**).

To subtract one fill from another:

1. In the Toolbox, choose the oval tool.

2. In the Colors section of the Toolbox, click the pencil icon.

   This selects the Stroke control and lets you apply any color selections to strokes.

3. Click the No Color button.

   Flash sets the stroke to none. The oval tool now draws a fill without an outline stroke.

4. Click the fill-color box (in the Toolbox or in the Fill panel), and choose red from the pop-up swatch set.

5. On the Stage, draw a fairly large oval.

6. Back in the Toolbox or the Fill panel, choose a different fill color for the oval tool.

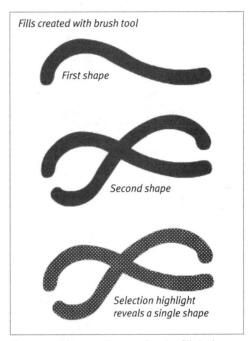

Fills created with brush tool

First shape

Second shape

Selection highlight reveals a single shape

Figure 4.4 When you draw overlapping fills in the same color, Flash puts the two shapes together to create a single shape. (Compare this figure with the overlapping lines in **Figure 4.1**, which cut one another.)

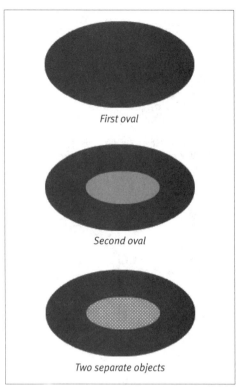

First oval

Second oval

Two separate objects

Figure 4.5 When one fill overlaps another of a different color, the fills don't meld but remain separate. The second oval here replaces the first where they overlap.

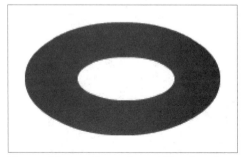

Figure 4.6 Because the smaller oval fill replaces the part of the big oval it covers, deleting the smaller oval leaves a hole in the big one.

7. On the Stage, draw a smaller oval in the middle of your first oval to create concentric ovals.

8. Switch to the arrow tool, and select the smaller oval.

   As the highlighting indicates, fills of different colors are separate objects (**Figure 4.5**).

9. To delete your selection, press Backspace (Mac) or Delete (Windows).

   Removing the smaller oval leaves a hole in the bigger oval, because the fill that overlaps the first fill replaces it (**Figure 4.6**).

✔ Tips

■ Interactions between lines and fills take place not only when you draw a shape but also when you place a copy of a shape or move a shape. Be careful when placing live shapes and lines on a single layer. You can inadvertently add to or delete part of an underlying shape.

■ If you accidentally change an object by drawing on top of it with another color, you can restore the original and keep the new object, too. Select your top shape and press F8 to turn the shape into a symbol. (For more information on creating symbols, see Chapter 6.) Now press ⌘-Z (Mac) or Ctrl-Z (Windows) three times: once to undo the Convert to Symbol command, a second time to undo the selection, and a third time to remove the top shape and restore the bottom shape. Though you undid the conversion of the shape to a symbol, the symbol still lives in the Library. To break apart the symbol, drag an instance of the symbol onto the Stage and press ⌘-Option-B (Mac) or Ctrl-Alt-B (Windows).

WHEN SHAPES INTERACT

Understanding Grouping

Flash does give you ways to force its paint to "dry." When you turn objects into groups (or symbols), they are no longer immediately editable and they stop interacting with other objects. (You can still edit the contents of groups and symbols, but you must invoke special editing modes to modify them.) If you put several groups (or symbols) on the same layer, they merely stack up, one on top of another. (To learn more about symbols, see Chapter 6.)

To create a group:

1. Select one or more objects on the Stage, using any of the methods discussed in Chapter 3 (**Figure 4.7**).

2. From the Modify menu, choose Group, or press ⌘-G (Mac) or Ctrl-G (Windows) (**Figure 4.8**).

   Flash groups the items, placing them within a bounding box (**Figure 4.9**). The visible bounding box lets you know that the group is selected. When the group is not selected, the bounding box is hidden.

To return objects to ungrouped status:

1. Select the group that you want to return to ungrouped status.

2. From the Modify menu, choose Ungroup, or press ⌘-Shift-G (Mac) or Ctrl-Shift-G (Windows).

   Flash removes the bounding box and selects all the items.

✔ Tip

■ If you prefer using a two-key shortcut rather than a three-key shortcut, the command for breaking apart symbols also works to ungroup groups. That command is ⌘-B (Mac) or Ctrl-B (Windows).

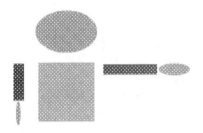

Figure 4.7 The first step in grouping is selecting the objects you want to use in the group.

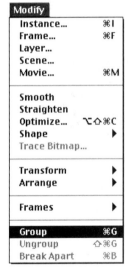

Figure 4.8 Choose Modify > Group to unite several selected objects as a group.

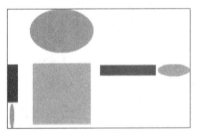

Figure 4.9 When you select the group, a highlighted bounding box appears, surrounding the grouped objects.

Figure 4.10 The oval before grouping.

Working with Grouped Elements

Grouping is useful for keeping elements together as you work with them and other elements on the Stage. Groups make it easy to reposition a set of shapes whose relationships must stay the same. You may also want to group individual shapes to prevent them from interacting with other elements on the same layer. Suppose that you are drawing shapes that make up a face, with eyes, nose, and mouth. You may want to move the facial features around to get just the right look, and you don't want to leave holes in your basic face oval each time. Grouping each element lets you avoid that. Flash makes it easy to edit lines and fills—you simply grab and drag them with the arrow tool—but that means it's also easy to reshape an object accidentally when you meant to move it. Grouping prevents you from editing objects inadvertently.

To prevent interaction between objects on the same layer:

1. In the Toolbox, choose the oval tool.

2. In the Colors section of the Toolbox, click the pencil icon

   This selects the Stroke control and lets you apply any color selections to strokes.

3. Click the No Color button.

   The oval tool now draws a fill without an outline stroke.

4. Click the fill-color box (in the Toolbox or in the Fill or Mixer panel), and from the pop-up swatch set, choose red.

5. On the Stage, draw a fairly large oval (**Figure 4.10**).

6. In the Toolbox, switch to the arrow tool, and select the oval you just drew.

continues on next page

7. To make the oval a grouped element, from the Modify menu, choose Group (**Figure 4.11**).

8. Back in the Toolbox, choose the oval tool and a different fill color.

9. On the Stage, draw a smaller oval in the middle of your first oval (**Figure 4.12**).

When you finish drawing the new oval, it immediately disappears behind the grouped oval (**Figure 4.13**). That's because grouped objects always stack on top of ungrouped objects (see the sidebar "Understanding the Stacking Order of Grouped Objects").

10. Switch to the arrow tool, and reposition the large oval so that you can see the small one (**Figure 4.14**).

11. Deselect the large oval, and select the small oval (**Figure 4.15**).

12. To make the small oval a grouped element, from the Modify menu, choose Group (**Figure 4.16**).

Flash puts the small oval in a bounding box and brings it to the top of the stack. Flash always places the most recently created group on the top of the stack. You can now reposition the two ovals however you like, and they will not interact.

Figure 4.11 The oval after grouping.

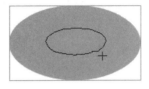

Figure 4.12 Draw a second oval on top of the grouped oval.

Figure 4.13 The ungrouped oval stacks beneath the grouped oval.

Figure 4.14 Drag the grouped oval to make the ungrouped oval visible.

Figure 4.15 Select the small oval.

Figure 4.16 Once grouped, the small oval—the most recently created group—pops to the top of the stack.

Figure 4.17 You can group several shapes that you want to manipulate as a group but keep in the same relationship to one another. The eyes and eyebrows in this face are a single group.

Figure 4.18 It's easy to reposition (top) or resize (bottom) the eyes and eyebrows to create new facial expressions when you've made a group out of them.

To keep multiple items together:

1. Using the drawing tools of your choice, create eight to ten separate shapes in different locations on the Stage.

2. Select three or four elements that you'd like to keep together (**Figure 4.17**).

3. From the Modify menu, choose Group.

4. In the Toolbox, select the arrow tool, and practice moving and modifying the grouped shapes.

   Every action you take now affects the entire group (**Figure 4.18**). If you click one of the grouped shapes, you select them all. If you drag one, you drag the whole group. If you duplicate or resize one, you duplicate or resize the entire group.

✔ Tips

■ You can group grouped objects. If you want to position several items on top of one another, group them as individuals first. Position them as you like. Then group all the items to preserve their relationship.

■ You can lock groups so that you don't accidentally move or modify them. Select the group that you want to lock. From the Modify menu, choose Arrange > Lock. You can no longer select the item. To make it available again, from the Modify menu, choose Modify > Arrange > Unlock All. You cannot unlock locked items selectively.

Controlling the Stacking Order

You can change the stacking order of groups via the Modify > Arrange menu. Notice that the stacking order doesn't require that you actually stack objects on top of one another. If you have two groups on opposite sides of the Stage, their stacking order is not visible, but as soon as you drag the objects so that one overlaps the other, the order becomes apparent.

Each grouped object sits on its own sublayer. You can move objects up or down the stacking order one level at a time, or you can bring an object forward or send it backward through the stack of sublayers. The sublayer containing the live, editable objects is always at the bottom; groups and symbols stack on top of ungrouped elements.

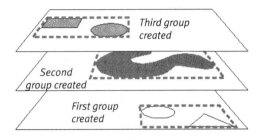

Figure 4.19 This schematic shows Flash's default stacking order for grouped items. The most recently created group is on top. Editable shapes are always on the bottom.

Understanding the Stacking Order of Grouped Shapes

Editable shapes on a single layer always stay on the same layer, cutting one another whenever they inhabit the same space on the Stage. Grouped items (and symbols), however, stack on top of one another. By default, Flash stacks each group that you create on top of the preceding one; the last group created winds up on top of all the others (**Figure 4.19**).

A higher-level group obscures any groups that lie directly beneath it.

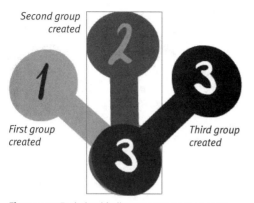

Second group created

First group created

Third group created

Figure 4.20 Each dumbbell represents a separate group.

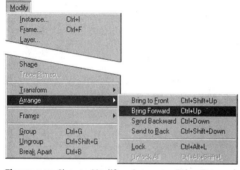

Figure 4.21 Choose Modify > Arrange > Bring Forward to move a selected group up one level in the stacking order.

Figure 4.22 The selected group moves forward in the stacking order one sublayer.

To bring an element forward in the stacking order:

1. On the Stage, select a grouped object (**Figure 4.20**).

2. From the Modify menu, choose Arrange > Bring Forward, or press ⌘-up arrow (Mac) or Ctrl–up arrow (Windows) (**Figure 4.21**).

   Flash brings the selected item up one sublayer in the stacking order (**Figure 4.22**).

CONTROLLING THE STACKING ORDER

To bring an element to the front of the stack:

1. On the Stage, select a grouped object (**Figure 4.23**).

2. From the Modify menu, choose Arrange > Bring to Front, or press ⌘-Shift-up arrow (Mac) or Ctrl–Shift-up arrow (Windows) (**Figure 4.24**).

   Flash brings the selected object to the top of the heap (**Figure 4.25**).

To send an element to a lower level of the stack:

1. On the Stage, select a grouped object.

2. From the Modify menu, choose Arrange > Send Backward, or press ⌘-down arrow (Mac) or Ctrl–down arrow (Windows).

   Flash sends the selected item down one sublayer in the stacking order.

To send an element to the bottom of the stack:

1. On the Stage, select a grouped object.

2. From the Modify menu, choose Arrange > Send to Back, or press Option-Shift-down arrow (Mac) or Ctrl-Shift-down arrow (Windows).

   Flash sends the selected item to the bottom of the heap.

Figure 4.23 Select an item that you want to bring to the very top of the stacking order.

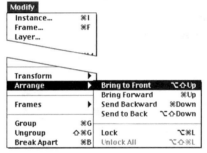

Figure 4.24 Choose Modify > Arrange > Bring to Front.

Figure 4.25 The selected item comes to the front of the stack, regardless of how many groups (or sublayers) lie on top of the selected group.

Movie-editing mode

Click current scene name to
return to movie-editing mode

Group-editing mode

Grayed shapes do
not belong to group
that's being edited

Double-click away from
the group to return to
movie-editing mode

Selected
group being
edited

Figure 4.26 These eyes and eyebrows are a selected group that's being edited. The other objects on the Stage are grayed out to indicate that you can't edit them.

Editing Groups

Although you transform a group as a whole (scale, rotate, and skew it), you can't directly edit the individual shapes within the group, the way that you can an ungrouped shape. To edit the shapes within a group, you must use the Edit Selected command.

To edit the contents of a group:

1. In the Toolbox, select the arrow tool.

2. On the Stage, select the group you want to edit.

3. From the Edit menu, choose Edit Selected. Flash enters group-editing mode (**Figure 4.26**). The word *group* appears in the top-left corner of the document window to indicate that you are no longer in regular movie-editing mode. The bounding box for the selected group disappears, and Flash dims all the items on the Stage that are not part of the selected group. These dimmed items are not editable; they merely provide context for editing the selected group.

To return to movie-editing mode:

Do one of the following:

◆ Double-click the Stage or the work area away from the shapes in the group you're editing.

◆ Click the current scene name in the top-left corner of the document window.

✔ Tips

■ With the arrow tool selected, you can enter group-editing mode quickly by double-clicking a grouped item on the Stage.

■ If in addition to returning to movie-editing mode, you want to work on a different scene, you can simply choose it from the pop-up list of scenes in the top-right corner of the document window. Flash takes you to the new scene in movie-editing mode. (To learn more about scenes, see Chapter 11.)

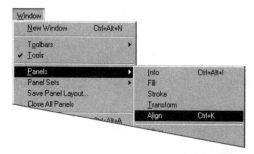

Original object placement   *Align top edges*

Distribute horizontally by right edges   *Align right edges*

Figure 4.27 Flash's Align panel can line up selected objects in various ways. Here are a few alignment choices used on the same set of objects.

Figure 4.28 Choose Window > Panels > Align to open the Align panel.

Aligning Elements

As you get into the process of animation, you'll discover how important alignment can be. Flash's grids, its guides, and its Snap feature (see Chapter 1) help you align objects on the Stage manually. Flash also offers automatic alignment through the Align panel. You can line up selected objects by their top, bottom, left, or right edges or by their centers (**Figure 4.27**). You can align the objects to each other or align them to the Stage—for example, placing the top edge of all selected objects at the top edge of the Stage. Flash can also resize one object to match the dimensions of another—making them the same width, for example.

To access alignment options:

◆ From the Window menu, choose Panels > Align, or press ⌘-K (Mac) or Ctrl-K (Windows) (**Figure 4.28**).

The Align panel appears (**Figure 4.29**). You can apply any of the alignment options to selected objects on the Stage.

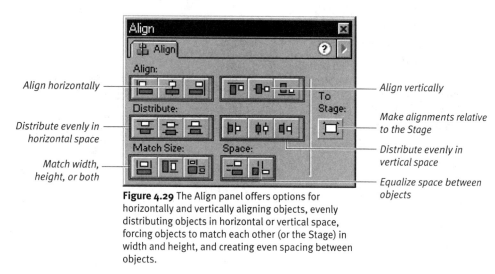

Align horizontally

Distribute evenly in horizontal space

Match width, height, or both

Align vertically

Make alignments relative to the Stage

Distribute evenly in vertical space

Equalize space between objects

Figure 4.29 The Align panel offers options for horizontally and vertically aligning objects, evenly distributing objects in horizontal or vertical space, forcing objects to match each other (or the Stage) in width and height, and creating even spacing between objects.

To align items horizontally:

1. On the Stage, select the items that you want to align.

2. In the Align section of the Align panel (**Figure 4.30**), *choose one of the following options:*
   - ◆ Align left edges
   - ◆ Align centers
   - ◆ Align right edges

   Flash rearranges the selected objects.

To align items vertically:

1. On the Stage, select the items that you want to align.

2. In the Align section of the Align panel (**Figure 4.31**), *choose one of the following options:*
   - ◆ Align top edges
   - ◆ Align centers
   - ◆ Align bottom edges

   Flash rearranges the selected objects.

To match dimensions of items:

1. On the Stage, select the items that you want to change.

2. In the Match Size section of the Align panel (**Figure 4.32**), *do one of the following:*
   - ◆ To expand all items to be the same width as the widest item, choose Match Width.
   - ◆ To expand all items to be the same height as the tallest item, choose Match Height.
   - ◆ To perform both of the preceding actions, choose Match Width and Height.

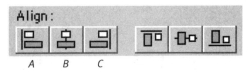

Figure 4.30 You can align objects horizontally by their left edges (A), centers (B), or right edges (C).

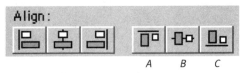

Figure 4.31 You can align objects vertically by their top edges (A), centers (B), or bottom edges (C).

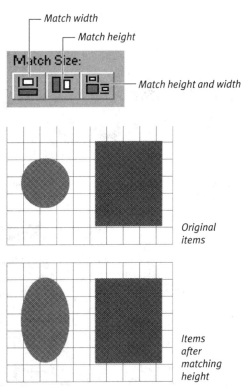

Original items

Items after matching height

Figure 4.32 Choosing the vertical option in the Match Size section of the align dialog box makes two items the same height. Flash matches the shorter one to the taller one.

Shapes with Match Size set to vertical and To Stage selected

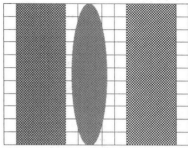

Figure 4.33 Choosing To Stage in the Align panel makes all your alignment choices relative to the edges of the Stage.

To make alignment relative to the Stage:

◆ In the Align panel, choose To Stage (**Figure 4.33**).

Flash makes your alignment choices in the Vertical, Horizontal, and Match Size sections relative to the edges of the Stage. Align to Bottom, for example, puts all the bottom edges of the selected elements at the bottom of the Stage. Matching height makes selected elements as tall as the Stage.

✔ Tips

■ In addition to aligning items horizontally and vertically, you can create equal horizontal or vertical space between three or more items. The buttons in the Distribute section of the Align panel let you equalize the horizontal space between selected elements' left edges, centers, or right edges or equalize the vertical space between selected items' top edges, centers, or bottom edges.

■ Use the Align panel's Space options to create equal horizontal or vertical space between items' inside edges.

■ You can make a series of alignment adjustments to the same set of elements— for example, aligning all selected items by their left edges and then equalizing the vertical space between them. You can even use the alignment options to pull all selected items into one corner of the Stage.

Using the Complex Paint Modes with the Brush

In Chapter 3, you learned about using the brush in Normal mode, in which every stroke with the brush lays down a new fill. As you saw earlier in this chapter, when brush strokes overlap, they interact. Flash offers four special brush modes that restrict the way the new brushstrokes interact with existing editable lines (strokes) and fills. These special modes make it much easier to work with complex graphics made of multiple fills and lines. You can set the brush to paint over lines without affecting them (the fill winds up behind the lines instead of covering them up), to paint only in blank areas of the Stage (existing lines and fills repel the paint), to paint only within a selection (if the brush slips outside the selection, nothing happens), or to paint only within the area where you started your brushstroke (all other areas repel the paint).

To leave lines intact when painting:

1. Create several shapes on the Stage. Use both lines and fills and a variety of colors.

2. In the Toolbox, select the brush tool.

3. Click the fill-color box (in the Toolbox or in the Fill panel); from the pop-up swatch set, choose a color you haven't used in creating the fills and lines on the Stage.

   Testing the brush modes in a new color makes it easy to see what's happening.

4. From the Brush Mode menu, choose Paint Fills (**Figure 4.34**).

5. Start painting; paint over blank areas of the Stage as well as over the items you created.

   When you release the mouse button, Flash creates the new fill without affecting any lines you may have overlapped. These temporarily obscured lines reappear (**Figure 4.35**).

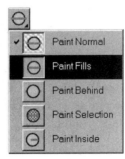

Figure 4.34
The Brush Mode menu lets you choose the way new brushstrokes interact with existing fills and strokes.

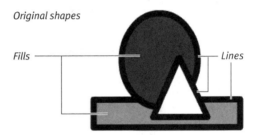

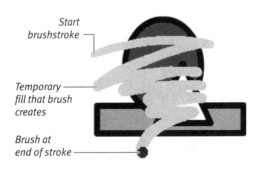

Figure 4.35 When you paint with the brush tool set to Paint Fills, Flash lets you paint over lines without affecting them. Lines pop to the front of the image when you release the mouse button.

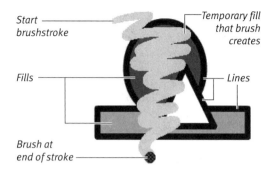

Start brushstroke

Temporary fill that brush creates

Fills

Lines

Brush at end of stroke

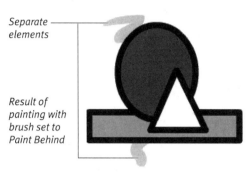

Separate elements

Result of painting with brush set to Paint Behind

Figure 4.36 When you paint with the brush set to Paint Behind, Flash lets you paint over lines and fills without affecting them. Existing lines and fills pop to the front of the image when you release the mouse button.

To leave existing lines and fills intact when painting:

1. With a variety of lines and fills already on the Stage, select the brush tool in the Toolbox.

2. From the Brush Mode menu, choose Paint Behind.

3. Start painting; paint over blank areas of the Stage as well as over the elements you created.

   When you release the mouse button, Flash creates the fill only in blank areas of the Stage (**Figure 4.36**).

✔ Tip

■ The term *Paint Behind* is a bit misleading. You do not actually create fills that lie behind other fills. Rather, Flash allows existing lines and fills to repel, or cut away, any overlapping portions of the new fill you're creating. When you release the mouse button after painting a new fill, that fill appears to sink down behind the other fills on the Stage. When you use this mode, be sure to remember that any existing lines and fills will segment the new fill you create.

How Can You Tell What You're Painting?

Flash cannot accurately preview the fills you create in complex paint modes the way it can in the normal mode. In complex modes, as you hold down the mouse button and paint in one continuous brushstroke, Flash displays your new fill in a temporary form. This temporary fill lies on top of every object it overlaps on the Stage and obscures any fills and lines that lie beneath it. When you release the mouse button, Flash calculates and redraws the new fill according to the paint mode you've selected in the Toolbox.

To restrict paint to selected fills:

1. With a variety of lines and fills already on the Stage, select one or more of the fills but leave some fills unselected.

2. In the Toolbox, select the brush.

3. From the Brush Mode menu, choose Paint Selection.

4. Start painting; paint over blank areas of the Stage as well as over the elements you've created.

   When you release the mouse button, Flash creates the fill only in areas of the Stage you had highlighted as a selection. Your new brushstroke has no effect on selected lines or on lines and fills that lie outside the selection (**Figure 4.37**).

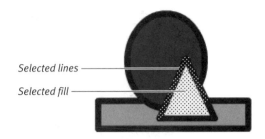

Selected lines ———

Selected fill ———

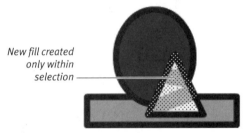

Start
brushstroke ———

Temporary
fill that brush ———
creates

Brush at end
of stroke ———

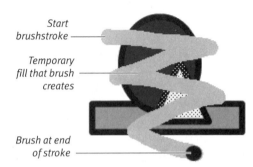

New fill created
only within
selection ———

Figure 4.37 When you paint with the brush set to Paint Selection, Flash ignores any brushstrokes you make outside the selection. In this mode, you cannot affect lines, and any unselected fills you accidentally paint over reappear when you release the mouse button.

To restrict paint to one area:

1. With a variety of lines and fills already on the Stage, in the Toolbox, select the brush tool.

2. From the Brush Mode menu, choose Paint Inside.

3. Start painting from within one shape, extending your brushstrokes to paint outside the shape where you began.

   When you release the mouse button, Flash creates the fill only inside the shape where you first clicked with the brush to begin painting (**Figure 4.38**).

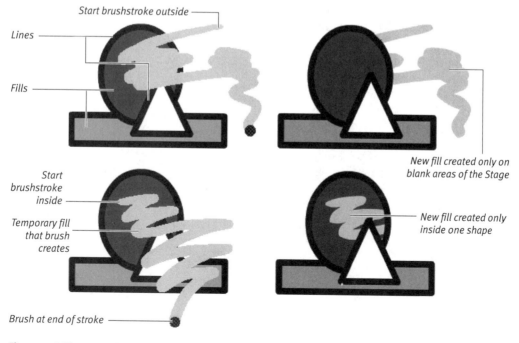

Start brushstroke outside

Lines

Fills

New fill created only on blank areas of the Stage

Start brushstroke inside

Temporary fill that brush creates

New fill created only inside one shape

Brush at end of stroke

Figure 4.38 When you paint with the brush set to Paint Inside, Flash confines the creation of new brushstrokes to the area where you started painting. Painting over lines has no effect, and if your brush slips outside the area in which you started, Flash simply ignores it.

Applying Gradients to Multipart Shapes

As the characters and elements in your animations get more complex, you may wind up creating graphics made up of numerous parts. When applying gradients to multipart graphics, you have the choice of filling each part with its own separate gradient (as you learned to do in Chapter 3) or selecting several parts and applying one gradient to all of them.

To apply one gradient separately to multiple fills:

1. On the Stage, create a graphic made of several fills.

2. Select the fills to which you want to apply the same gradient.

3. Click the fill-color box (in the Toolbox or in the Mixer panel), and from the pop-up swatch set, choose the gradient you want to apply.

   Flash applies the fill to each selected shape separately (**Figure 4.39**). The full range of the gradient appears within each shape.

✔ Tip

■ You can also use the paint bucket to apply separate gradients. Make sure the Lock Fill Modifier is deselected, choose the gradient you want, and then click the shapes to which you want to apply the gradient fills.

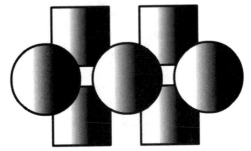

Figure 4.39 With several shapes selected, when you choose a gradient from a fill-color box in a panel, Flash applies the gradient to each shape separately. The full range of the gradient fits within each shape.

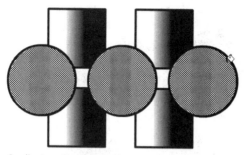

Gradient applied to selection

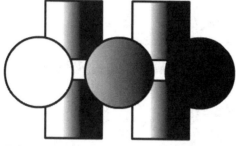

Each shape reveals part of the gradient

Bounding box, not actually visible ⌐

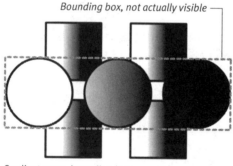

Gradient spans bounding box

Figure 4.40 When you use the paint bucket tool to apply a gradient to multiple selected shapes, none of the selected objects contains the entire color range of the gradient. Each object opens a window onto part of the gradient within a behind-the-scenes bounding box that contains a single gradient.

To spread one gradient across multiple fills:

1. On the Stage, create an object made of several fills.

2. On the Stage, select the fills to which you want to apply the gradient.

3. In the Toolbox, select the paint bucket.

4. Deselect the Lock Fill modifier.

5. Click the fill-color box (in the Toolbox or in the Mixer panel), and from the pop-up swatch set, choose the gradient you want to apply.

   Flash applies the gradient to each shape separately.

6. On the Stage, click any of the selected fills.

   Flash spreads a single gradient across all the selected fills (**Figure 4.40**).

✔ Tip

- You can also spread a single gradient across unselected fills using the paint bucket tool. In the Toolbox, select the paint bucket's Lock Fill Modifier. Click each unselected fill on the Stage. It's as if Flash spreads the gradient across the entire frame (Stage and work area). Each shape you click reveals the portion of the gradient that corresponds to that location in the frame.

APPLYING GRADIENTS TO MULTIPART SHAPES

Using the Eraser Tool with Multiple Shapes

Just as the brush has complex modes for interacting with live fills and lines, the eraser tool offers complex interaction modes. (For a review of the eraser's normal mode, see Chapter 3.)

Flash's eraser has four modes that let you select what to erase; in each mode, the eraser interacts differently with lines and fills. In Erase Fills mode, the tool ignores any lines you drag over. In Erase Lines mode, the reverse occurs: The tool ignores fills and removes only lines. Erase Selected Fills mode ignores lines but also ignores any areas of fill you haven't selected. Erase Inside restricts you to erasing within a single fill: the one where you started erasing.

To erase only fills, leaving lines intact:

1. Create several shapes on the Stage, using both lines and fills and a variety of colors.

2. In the Toolbox, select the eraser.

3. From the Eraser Mode menu, choose Erase Fills (**Figure 4.41**).

4. From the Eraser Shape menu, choose a shape for your eraser.

5. To erase, click and drag over the objects on the Stage.

   When you release the mouse button, Flash removes only the erased fills. Any lines that you erased over reappear (**Figure 4.42**).

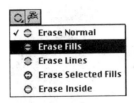

Figure 4.41
The Eraser Mode menu.

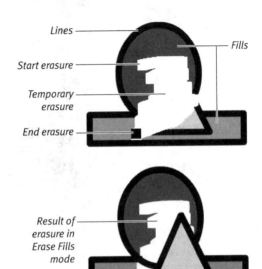

Figure 4.42 When you erase in Erase Fills mode, Flash lets you run the eraser over lines without affecting them. The "erased" lines reappear when you release the mouse button.

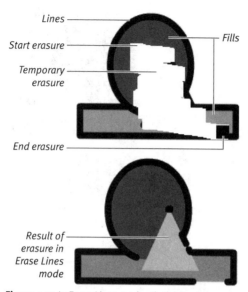

Lines

Start erasure

Temporary erasure

Fills

End erasure

Result of erasure in Erase Lines mode

Figure 4.43 In Erase Lines mode, Flash lets you run the eraser over fills without changing them. The "erased" fills reappear when you release the mouse button.

To erase only lines:

1. Create several shapes on the Stage, using both lines and fills and a variety of colors.

2. In the Toolbox, select the eraser.

3. From the Eraser Mode menu, choose Erase Lines.

4. Click and drag over the objects on the Stage to erase.

   The preview erasure obliterates everything you dragged the eraser over. When you release the mouse button, Flash removes only the erased lines. Any fills you erased over pop back up (**Figure 4.43**).

To erase selected fills:

1. With a variety of lines and fills already on the Stage, select one or more fills, making sure to leave some fills unselected.

2. In the Toolbox, select the eraser.

3. From the Eraser Mode menu, choose Erase Selected Fills.

4. Start erasing; erase over both selected areas and areas you didn't select.

   Flash removes fills only from areas you highlighted as a selection. The eraser has no effect on selected lines or on lines and fills that lie outside the selection (**Figure 4.44**).

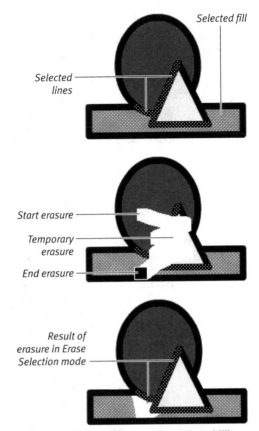

Figure 4.44 When you erase in Erase Selected Fills mode, Flash lets you restrict your erasure to fills in selected areas. Any "erased" lines, as well as any "erased" lines and fills that are not part of the selection, reappear when you release the mouse button.

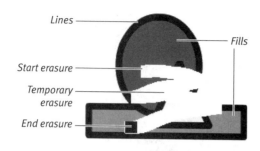

Lines

Fills

Start erasure

Temporary erasure

End erasure

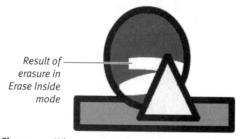

Result of erasure in Erase Inside mode

Figure 4.45 When you erase in Erase Inside mode, Flash lets you restrict your erasure to the fill in which you start erasing. Any other "erased" fills reappear when you release the mouse button.

To restrict erasures to one area:

1. With a variety of lines and fills already on the Stage, select the eraser tool in the Toolbox.

2. From the Eraser Mode menu, choose Erase Inside.

3. Start erasing within one shape, extending your erasure outside the shape where you began.

   Flash erases only inside the shape where you first clicked with the tool to begin erasing (**Figure 4.45**).

How Can You Tell What You're Erasing?

Flash cannot accurately preview erasures in complex erase modes the way it can in Normal mode. In complex modes, as you hold down the mouse button and erase in one continuous stroke, Flash temporarily obliterates everything you dragged the eraser over. When you release the mouse button, Flash redraws the erasure according to the Erase mode you have selected in the Toolbox.

GRAPHICS ON MULTIPLE LAYERS

Macromedia Flash uses two types of spatial organization: (1) the position of elements within the rectangle that is the Stage and (2) the way elements stack up back to front. You create an illusion of three-dimensional depth by overlapping objects. As you learned in Chapter 4, you can create this overlapping effect on one layer by stacking groups and symbols. The more elements your movie contains, however, the more difficult it becomes to manipulate and keep track of the stacking order of items on a single layer. Layers help you bring that task under control.

You could think of a Flash animation as a stack of film: a sheaf of long, clear acetate strips divided into frames. Each filmstrip is analogous to a Flash layer. Shapes painted on the top strip of film obscure shapes on lower strips; where the top strip of film is blank elements from lower strips show through.

When you place items on separate layers, you can easily control and rearrange the way the items stack up. If you have several elements—say, a square, circle, rectangle, and star—each on its own layer, you can play around with which shapes appear to be closer to the viewer by changing the layer order. Placing items on different layers prevents the items from interacting, so you don't need to worry about grouping the items or having one shape inadvertently overwrite another.

Touring the Timeline's Layer Features

Flash graphically represents each layer as one horizontal section of the Timeline and provides several controls for viewing and manipulating these graphic representations. Flash layers offer several features that make it easier to work with graphics on layers, such as viewing the items on layers as outlines and assigning different colors to those outlines so you can easily see which items are on which layers. You can lock layers so you don't accidentally edit their contents, and you can hide layers to make it easier to work with individual graphics in a welter of other graphics. You can create special guide layers for help in positioning elements, masks for selectively hiding and revealing layers, and guides for animating motion along a path. (You learn more about motion paths in Chapter 9.)

Figure 5.1 offers a road map to the salient layer features in the Timeline.

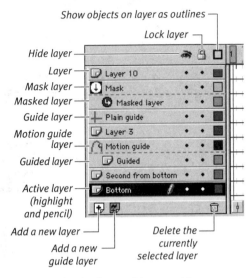

Figure 5.1 The Timeline provides a graphic representation of all the layers in a Flash movie. You can do much of the work of creating and manipulating layers by clicking buttons on the Timeline.

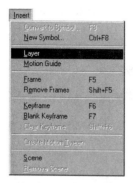

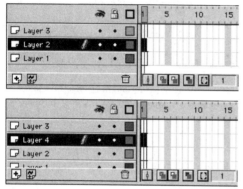

Figure 5.2
Choose Insert > Layer to add a new layer to the Timeline.

Figure 5.3 Select the layer that you want to wind up below the new layer (top); Flash inserts a new layer directly above the selected layer and gives the new layer a default name (bottom).

Figure 5.4 Click the Trash button to delete a selected layer.

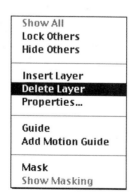

Figure 5.5
The contextual menu for layers gives you easy access to layer commands, including some that you can otherwise access only via buttons—for example, Delete Layer.

Creating and Deleting Layers

You can add new layers as you need them while creating the ingredients of a particular scene in your movie.

To add a new layer:

1. In the Timeline, select a layer.

   Flash always adds the new layer directly above the selected layer, so be sure to choose the layer that you want to lie directly below the new layer. If you want to add a layer below the current bottom layer, create it first and then click and drag it to reposition it at the bottom of the stack.

2. *Do one of the following:*

   ◆ From the Insert menu, choose Layer. (**Figure 5.2**).

   ◆ In the Timeline, click the Add Layer button.

   Flash adds a new layer and gives it a default name—for example, Layer 4 (**Figure 5.3**). Flash bases the number in the default name on the number of layers already created in the movie, not on the number of layers that currently exist.

To delete a layer:

1. In the Timeline, select the layer you want to delete.

2. Click the Trash button (**Figure 5.4**).

   Flash removes that layer (and all its frames) from the Timeline.

✔ Tip

■ The contextual menu for layers offers some choices that otherwise are available only via buttons on the Timeline—for example, the Delete Layer command (**Figure 5.5**). To access this menu, Control-click a layer on the Mac or right-click it in Windows.

To delete multiple layers:

1. In the Timeline, select the first layer you want to remove.

2. ⌘-click (Mac) or Ctrl-click (Windows) every layer you want to remove.

   This method of selection allows you to choose layers that are not right on top of each other (**Figure 5.6**).

3. Click the Trash button.

   Flash removes the selected layers (and their frames) from the Timeline.

✔ Tips

■ Shift-click to select a whole range of layers. Click to select the lowest layer you want to delete. Shift-click the highest layer you want to delete. Flash selects it and all the layers in between.

■ You can drag selected layers to the Trash button to delete them instead of selecting and clicking the Trash button in two steps.

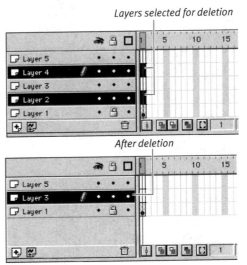

Figure 5.6 To delete noncontiguous layers, ⌘-click (Mac) or Ctrl-click (Windows) the layers you want to add to your selection; then click the Trash button.

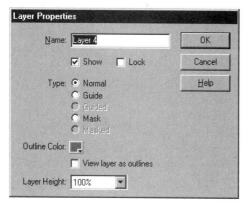

Figure 5.7 You can define a layer's type in the Layer Properties dialog box.

Figure 5.8 You can rename a layer by typing the new name in the Name field of the Layer Properties dialog box.

Controlling Layers via the Dialog Box

Layer properties are the parameters that define the look and function of a layer. You can name layers. You can hide or show layers, lock them to prevent any editing of their contents, and view them in outline form. Flash generally gives you two ways to control each property: set properties in the Layer Properties dialog box or set them via button controls located on the Timeline. Selecting a property in the dialog box doesn't offer any more permanence than setting it on the Timeline, however. Two functions available in the Layer Properties dialog box that lack button equivalents are creating plain guide layers and changing the height of the layer in Timeline view.

To work with the Layer Properties dialog box:

1. From the Modify menu, choose Layer.

   The Layer Properties dialog box appears (**Figure 5.7**).

2. Name the layer or set other layer properties or both as described in the following sections.

3. Click OK.

   Flash applies all the selected settings to the current layer.

To name a layer:

◆ In the Layer Properties dialog box's Name field, type a new name for the layer.

   When you call up the dialog box, the Name field is selected; just start typing (**Figure 5.8**).

   Although Flash numbers layers, renaming them is a good idea. A movie may have dozens of layers, and you'll never remember that Layer 12 contains your company's name and Layer 4 contains its logo.

✔ Tip

■ To access the Layer Properties dialog box quickly, double-click a layer icon in the Timeline.

To set a layer's visibility:

◆ In the Layer Properties dialog box, check the Show checkbox.

When the checkbox is checked, the contents of the layer are visible on the Stage. When the checkbox is empty, the contents of the layer are hidden.

To prevent changes in a layer:

◆ In the Layer Properties dialog box, check the Lock checkbox.

When the checkbox is checked, the layer is locked. Although you can see the objects in that layer, you can't select or edit them. When the checkbox is empty, the contents of the layer are available for editing.

To define the layer type:

◆ In the Layer Properties dialog box, select the radio button corresponding to the layer type you want to use.

Flash divides layers into five types: normal guide, guided, mask, and masked. The default layer type is normal; all the items in a normal layer appear in your final movie.

Flash creates two types of guide layers: guides and motion guides. Lines or shapes on plain guide layers serve as reference points for placing and aligning objects on the Stage. Motion guides allow you to create a path for an animated object to follow (see Chapter 9). You must link the layer containing that animated object—called a *guided layer*—to the motion guide layer. Items on guide layers do not appear in the final movie.

A mask layer hides and reveals portions of linked layers that lie directly below the mask layer. Flash calls such linked layers *masked layers*.

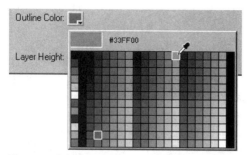

Figure 5.9 Select the color for displaying the outlines of a layer's objects from the pop-up menu in the Layer Properties dialog box.

Layer Height pop-up menu

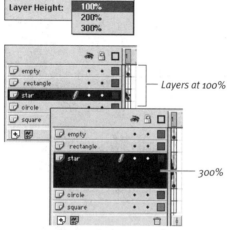

Figure 5.10 Choose a larger percentage from the Layer Height pop-up menu in the Layer Properties dialog box to increase the height of a selected layer.

To view the contents of a layer as outlines:

1. In the Layer Properties dialog box, click the View Layer As Outlines checkbox.

When the checkbox is checked, Flash displays the contents of the layer as outlines. Using different colors for outlines on different layers makes it easier to edit graphics when you have many layers. Flash assigns different default colors for each layer, but you can choose your own.

2. From the Outline Color pop-up menu, choose a color for the outlines on the active layer (**Figure 5.9**).

Flash changes the color swatch to your selected color.

3. Click OK.

Flash displays the graphics on this layer as outlines, using the color you selected.

To change the layer's height in the Timeline:

◆ In the Layer Properties dialog box, choose a percentage from the Layer Height pop-up menu.

Flash offers two enlarged layer views (**Figure 5.10**). The larger layers in the Timeline are especially useful for working with sounds. The waveform of each sound appears in the layer preview in the Timeline, and some sounds are difficult to see at the 100% setting.

✔ Tip

■ You can change the size of the graphic representation of all the layers in the Timeline by choosing a size from the Frame View pop-up menu, located in the top-right corner of the Timeline. The Preview and Preview in Context options display thumbnails of the contents of each frame in the layers.

Controlling Layers via the Timeline

The Timeline represents each layer as a horizontal field containing the layer name and three buttons for controlling the way the layer's contents look on the Stage. You can hide a layer (making all the elements on that layer temporarily invisible), lock a layer (making the contents visible but uneditable), and view the items on the layer as outlines. These controls are helpful when you are editing numerous items on several layers.

To rename a layer:

1. In the Timeline, double-click the layer name.

   Flash activates the text-entry field for the layer name.

2. Type a new name.

3. Press Enter, or click anywhere outside the name field.

To hide a layer:

◆ In the Timeline on the layer that you want to hide, click the bullet in the column below the eye icon (**Figure 5.11**).

   Flash replaces the bullet with a red X, indicating that the layer is hidden. The contents of the layer no longer appear on the Stage. Making a layer invisible does not affect the final movie. When you publish a movie (see Chapter 16), Flash includes all the contents of hidden layers.

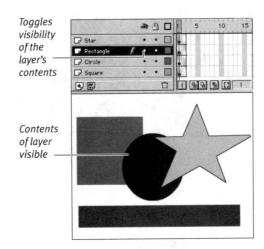

Toggles visibility of the layer's contents

Contents of layer visible

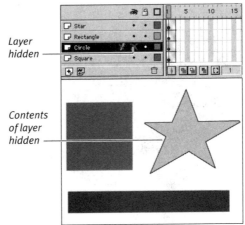

Layer hidden

Contents of layer hidden

Figure 5.11 The column below the eye icon controls the visibility of layers. Each of the original four elements (top) is on a separate layer. Hiding the circle layer makes the circle disappear from the Stage (bottom).

—Locked layer

Figure 5.12 The padlock icon indicates that a layer is locked. The contents of a locked layer appear on the Stage, but you can't edit them.

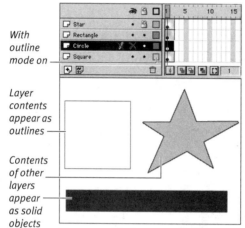

With outline mode on

Layer contents appear as outlines —

Contents of other layers appear as solid objects

Figure 5.13 A hollow square in the outline-mode column indicates that objects on that layer appear as outlines.

To show a hidden layer:

◆ In the Timeline on the layer that you want to show, click the red X in the column below the eye icon.

Flash replaces the X with a bullet and displays the contents of the layer.

To lock a layer:

◆ In the Timeline on the layer that you want to lock, click the bullet in the column below the padlock icon (**Figure 5.12**).

Flash replaces the bullet with a padlock icon. The contents of the layer appear on the Stage, but you can't edit them. Locking a layer does not affect the final movie.

To unlock a layer:

◆ In the Timeline on the layer that you want to unlock, click the padlock icon.

Flash replaces the padlock with a bullet and makes the contents of the layer editable.

To view the contents of a layer as outlines:

◆ In the Timeline on the layer that you want to view as outlines, click the solid square in the column below the square icon (**Figure 5.13**).

Flash replaces the solid square with a hollow square, indicating that the layer is in outline mode. The contents of the layer appear on the Stage as outlines in the color that the square indicates. Placing a layer in outline mode does not affect the final movie.

CONTROLLING LAYERS VIA THE TIMELINE

To view the contents of a layer as solid objects:

◆ In the Timeline on the layer that you want to view as outlines, click the hollow square.

Flash replaces the hollow square with a solid square, indicating that the layer is no longer in outline mode. The contents of the layer appear on the Stage as solid objects.

Working with Layer-View Columns

Flash provides several shortcuts for working with the three layer-view columns in the Timeline. The following tips describe hiding and showing layers; the controls in the Timeline for locking, unlocking, and viewing outlines work the same way.

◆ To hide several layers quickly, click the bullet in the column below the eye icon and drag through all the layers you want to hide. As the pointer passes over each bullet, Flash changes it to a red X.

◆ To show numerous layers quickly, click a red X in the eye column and drag through all the layers you want to show.

◆ To hide all the layers but one, Option-click (Mac) or Alt-click (Windows) the bullet in the eye column of the layer you want to see. Flash puts an X in all the other layers.

◆ To hide all the layers, ⌘-click (Mac) or Ctrl-click (Windows) the eye column of any layer, or click the eye icon in the column header. Flash puts an X in all the layers. To show all the layers, simply ⌘-click or Ctrl-click an X or click the eye icon again.

Active layer ⎯

Use arrow tool to modify shape on inactive layer

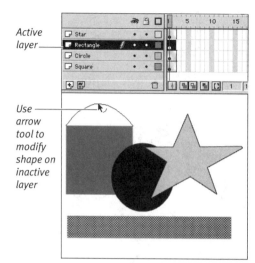

No change to active layer ⎯

Flash redraws shape ⎯

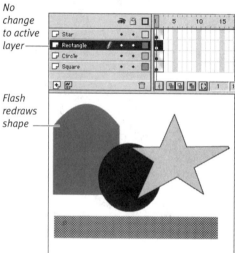

Figure 5.14 Selecting the rectangle makes the rectangle layer the active layer. You can still edit objects on inactive layers by reshaping their outlines with the arrow tool.

Working with Graphics on Different Layers

Unless you lock shapes, or lock or hide layers, the graphics on all layers are available for editing.

To edit shape outlines on inactive layers:

1. Create a document that has four layers.

2. Place a different shape on each layer.

   For this example, place a square on Layer 1, a circle on Layer 2, a rectangle on Layer 3, and a star on Layer 4.

3. In the Toolbox, select the arrow tool.

4. On the Stage, click the rectangle.

   Flash selects the rectangle and makes its layer active.

5. Click a blank area of the Stage.

   Flash deselects the rectangle but keeps its layer active.

6. On the Stage, position the pointer over the outline of the square.

   The curve or corner-point icon appears.

7. Drag the square's outline to reshape it.

8. Release the mouse button.

   Flash redraws the shape (**Figure 5.14**). Rectangle is still the active layer. Flash switches active layers only if you select a shape.

For the next exercise, continue using the document that you created for the preceding task; make sure that the current layer is still the rectangle layer.

To edit fills across layers:

1. In the Toolbox, select the paint bucket tool.

2. Click the fill-color box (in the Toolbox, Mixer panel, or Fill panel), and choose a color you haven't used for any of the shapes on the Stage.

3. Position the paint bucket over the star shape, and click.

   Flash fills the star with the new color (**Figure 5.15**), but the rectangle layer remains the active layer.

✔ Tip

■ To be safe, get into the habit of putting each graphic you create in a separate layer. That way, if you need to tweak the stacking order, you can. Having more layers doesn't increase the file size of your final movie significantly.

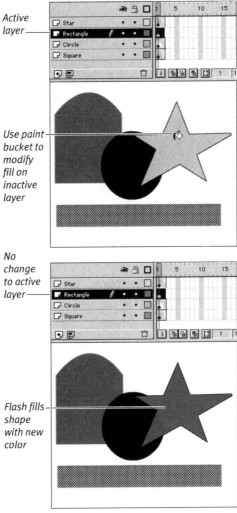

Active layer

Use paint bucket to modify fill on inactive layer

No change to active layer

Flash fills shape with new color

Figure 5.15 Use the paint bucket to change a fill color on an inactive layer.

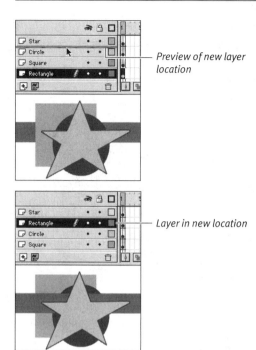

Preview of new layer location

Layer in new location

Figure 5.16 To reorder layers, drag them in the Timeline.

Controlling the Stacking Order of Layers

As you add more layers to your document, you may need to rearrange them so that the objects that should appear in the foreground actually cover objects that appear in the background.

Layers make it easy to change the stacking order of numerous elements at the same time. You can, for example, bring all the elements on one layer to the top of the stack simply by dragging that layer to the top of the list in the Timeline. Doing so brings those elements to the front of the Stage (overlapping any items on other layers) in every frame of the movie.

To reorder layers:

1. In the Timeline, position the mouse pointer over the layer you want to move.

2. Click and drag the layer.

   Flash previews the layer's new location with a thick gray line.

3. Position the preview line in the layer order you want to use (**Figure 5.16**).

4. Release the mouse button.

   Flash moves the layer to the new location and selects it.

Where Do Pasted Objects Go?

A Flash document can have only one layer active at a time. Any new shapes you create wind up on the currently selected or active layer. The same is true of placing copies of shapes or instances of symbols; if you copy and paste an element, Flash pastes the copy on the active layer. When you drag a symbol instance from the Library window, it winds up on the active layer.

Working with Guide Layers

Flash offers two types of guide layers: guides and motion guides. Plain old guides can contain any kind of content: lines, shapes, or symbols. The contents of a regular guide layer merely serve as a point of reference to help you position items on the Stage. Flash doesn't include such guide layers in the final exported movie.

Motion guides, however, do make up part of the final movie. Motion guide layers contain a single line that directs the movement of an animated object along a path. (To learn more about animating with motion guides, see Chapter 9.) Another distinction to remember is that Flash creates motion guides by adding a new layer directly to the Timeline. To create plain guides, you redefine an existing layer as a guide layer.

To create a plain guide layer:

1. *Do one of the following:*

   ◆ To create a new layer, in the Timeline, click the Add Layer button. Flash selects the new layer.

   ◆ Select a layer that already exists.

2. From the Modify menu, choose Layer to display the Layer Properties dialog box.

3. In the Type section, click Guide (**Figure 5.17**).

   You also can rename the layer to identify it as a guide, if you want.

4. Click OK.

   Flash turns the selected layer into a guide layer and places a little crossed-guidelines icon before the layer name (**Figure 5.18**).

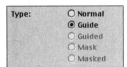

Figure 5.17 Select Guide as the layer type in the Layer Properties dialog box to change a normal layer to a guide layer.

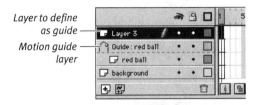

Layer to define as guide

Motion guide layer

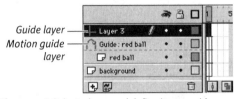

Guide layer

Motion guide layer

Figure 5.18 Select a layer and define it as a guide layer. In the Timeline, Flash identifies the guide layer with a crossed-guideline icon; compare that with the icon for the motion guide layer.

WORKING WITH GUIDE LAYERS

5. From the View menu, choose Guides > Snap to Guides.

Flash forces items that you draw or drag to snap to the lines or shapes on guide layers.

✔ Tips

■ You can create a guide layer quickly by Control-clicking (Mac) or right-clicking (Windows) the layer you want to define as a guide. Choose Guide from the pop-up contextual menu that appears.

■ While dragging an item on the Stage, press G on the keyboard to turn on the Snap feature temporarily. With Snap on, Flash helps you align items on other layers to the lines on the guide layer.

■ When you've placed guide elements where you need them for a certain scene, lock the guide layer so you don't accidentally move the guides as you draw on other layers.

Working with Mask Layers

Mask layers are special layers that allow you to hide and show elements on underlying layers.

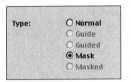

Figure 5.19 Select Mask as the layer type in the Layer Properties dialog box to define a layer as a mask.

To create a mask layer:

1. *Do one of the following:*
   - ◆ To create a new layer, in the Timeline, click the Add Layer button. Flash selects the new layer.
   - ◆ Select a layer that already exists.

   In general, you should create (or select) a layer directly above the layer containing content you want to mask, although you can always create the mask separately and link the masked layers to it later.

2. From the Modify menu, choose Layer to display the Layer Properties dialog box.

3. In the Type section, click Mask (**Figure 5.19**).

   You can also rename the layer to identify it as a mask, if you want.

4. Click OK.

   Flash turns the selected layer into a mask layer and places a little down-arrow icon before the layer name, indicating that the layer will affect linked layers below it (**Figure 5.20**).

Figure 5.20 The mask-layer icon.

To link layers to the mask:

1. In the Timeline, create or select a layer that contains content you want to mask.

2. From the Modify menu, choose Layer to display the Layer Properties dialog box.

3. In the Type section, click Masked.

   You can also rename the layer to identify it as a masked layer, if you want.

Figure 5.21 The masked-layer icon.

4. Click OK.

Flash links the selected layer to the mask layer directly above it and places a little bent-arrow icon before the name (**Figure 5.21**). Flash indents the icon and layer name to indicate that the mask above this layer controls it.

5. Repeat steps 1 through 4, above, to create more linked layers.

One mask can affect many linked layers.

✔ Tip

■ To create new linked layers, in the Timeline, select the layer directly beneath the mask; then follow the steps for creating a new layer. To link existing layers to a mask layer quickly, simply drag them in the Timeline so that they sit directly below the mask itself or one of its linked layers.

The Mystery of Masks

A mask layer is like a window envelope (the ones you get your bills in). There may be whole sheaves of papers covered with numbers inside that envelope, but the outside presents a blank white front with just a little window that lets you see the portion of the bill showing your name and address. The mask layer is the window envelope, and the linked, or masked, layers are the papers inside.

In Flash, you create the window in the envelope by drawing and painting on a mask layer. (As you'll learn in Chapter 11, you can animate that window to create special effects.) Any filled shape on the mask layer becomes a window in the final movie. That window reveals whatever lies on the linked (or masked) layers inside the envelope. Within that envelope, you can have several layers that act just like any other Flash layers.

Here's where it gets a bit tricky. Any areas of the envelope (the mask layer) that you leave blank hide the corresponding areas of all the layers inside the envelope (the masked layers). But the same blank areas of the envelope allow all unlinked layers outside and below the envelope to show through.

To create the mask:

1. Create one or more layers containing graphic elements you want to reveal only through a mask.

2. Create a mask layer above your masked-content layers, and make sure that it's selected, visible, and unlocked.

   The layer should be highlighted in the Timeline, and the eye and padlock columns should contain bullets (not X or padlock icons).

3. Use the paintbrush, oval, or rectangle tool to create one or more fill shapes (**Figure 5.22**).

   Flash uses only fills to create the mask and ignores any lines on the mask layer. The mask may consist of several shapes on the mask layer, but they must all be on the same sublayer. (For more information on how sublayers within a layer work, see Chapter 4.)

   You can use several editable shapes, or you can create one group or symbol that contains all the shapes. If you combine editable shapes and a group or symbol, Flash uses just the editable shapes to create the mask. If you have two or more groups or symbols, Flash uses just the bottom-most group or symbol. (For more details on stacking order for groups and symbols, see Chapter 4.)

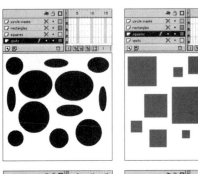

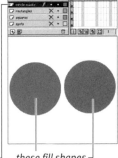

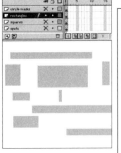

When you define this ——— ...these fill shapes ⌐
layer as a mask...   become the mask

Figure 5.22 The content for the layers that the mask will reveal is just like any other content. You create the mask itself from filled shapes. All the mask elements must be on the same sublevel of the layer. In other words, you must either use only editable shapes or combine all your shapes into a single group or symbol.

✔ Tips

■ To convert a particular layer into a mask and link the layer below it in one step, use the contextual layer menu. Control-click (Mac) or right-click (Windows) the layer you want to be the mask. From the pop-up contextual menu, choose Mask. Flash automatically defines the layer as a mask, links the layer below the selected layer to the mask, and locks both layers so that masking is in effect.

■ No matter what kind of fill (gradient, transparent, opaque) you use to draw your mask, Flash creates a completely open window out of it. It's easier to position a mask made from a transparent fill than one made from a solid. With a transparent mask, you can see the content below to position the mask precisely.

Figure 5.23 The Show Masking command in the contextual menu for layers locks all layers linked to the selected mask.

Masking not on

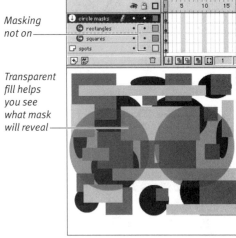

Transparent fill helps you see what mask will reveal

Locking turns masking on

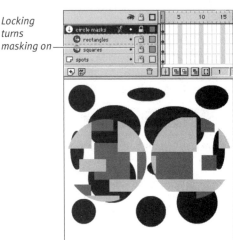

Figure 5.24 After defining the mask and masked layers, you must lock them to see the mask in effect in movie-editing mode.

To see the mask's effect:

◆ Lock the mask layer and all linked layers.

   or

1. Ctrl-click (Mac) or right-click (Windows) a mask (or masked) layer.

2. From the contextual menu, choose Show Masking (**Figure 5.23**).

   Flash automatically locks the mask layer and all the layers linked to it.

   In movie-editing mode, you must lock the mask layer and any masked layers beneath it to see the mask effect (**Figure 5.24**). You can see the effect without locking the layers in one of Flash's test modes (see Chapter 8).

To edit a mask:

1. In the Timeline, select the mask layer.

2. Make sure that the layer is visible and unlocked.

3. Use any of the techniques you learned in preceding chapters to create and edit fills.

✔ Tips

■ If you want to break the connection between a mask and its linked layers, you can simply redefine the layer type for the masked layer in the Layer Properties dialog box.

■ If you delete a mask layer, Flash redefines all the layers linked to it as normal layers.

WORKING WITH MASK LAYERS

Cutting and Pasting Between Layers

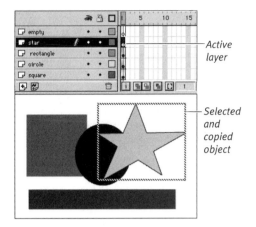

Flash allows you to create and place graphics only on the active layer of a movie. But you can copy, cut, or delete elements from any visible, unlocked layer. You can select items on several layers, cut them, and then paste them all into a single layer. Or you can cut items individually from one layer and redistribute them to separate layers. (The redistribution process is, obviously, more time-consuming, because you have to keep selecting new layers as you place the elements.)

Active layer

Selected and copied object

Flash offers two pasting modes: Paste and Paste in Place. Paste puts elements in the center of the Flash window. Paste in Place puts an element at the same *x* and *y* coordinates it had when you cut or copied it. Paste in Place is useful for preserving the precise relationship of all elements in a scene as you move items from one layer to another.

To use the Paste command across layers:

1. Create a document that contains several layers, leaving one layer empty.

2. Place at least one element on each of the other layers.

   Make a document with five layers, for example. Put a rectangle on one layer, a square on another, a circle on a third, a star on a fourth, and leave the fifth layer empty. To make the items easier to work with, group each one.

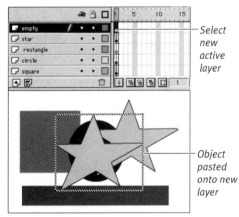

Select new active layer

Object pasted onto new layer

Figure 5.25 Copying a shape from one layer to another involves selecting the shape (top), copying it, selecting the target layer, and then pasting the copy there. The Paste command (middle) positions the pasted shape in the center of the window (bottom).

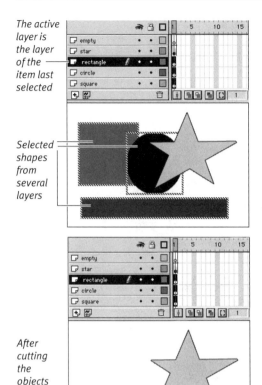

The active layer is the layer of the item last selected

Selected shapes from several layers

After cutting the objects

Figure 5.26 The first step in consolidating items from several different layers on a single new layer involves selecting all the items and cutting them. Later, you'll paste them into the new active layer.

3. Name each layer according to its contents.

   Adding the names Star, Circle, Rectangle, and so on makes it easier to remember which layer contains which items. It also makes it easier for you to see what's going on as you practice moving items across layers in this exercise.

4. On the Stage, select the star.

   Notice that Flash highlights the star's layer in the Timeline.

5. From the Edit menu, choose Copy.

6. In the Timeline, select the empty layer.

7. From the Edit menu, choose Paste.

   Flash pastes the copy of the star in the empty layer, in the middle of the window (**Figure 5.25**). You can now move the star to a new position, if you want.

To use the Paste in Place command across layers:

1. Using the same document as in the preceding exercise, select the rectangle.

2. Using the techniques that you learned in Chapter 3, add the square and the circle to your selection.

3. From the Edit menu, choose Cut.

   Flash removes the three selected shapes (**Figure 5.26**).

4. In the Timeline, select the empty layer.

continues on next page

CUTTING AND PASTING BETWEEN LAYERS

5. From the Edit menu, choose Paste in Place (**Figure 5.27**).

Flash pastes all three shapes back into their original locations on the Stage but on a different layer (**Figure 5.28**). Try hiding the empty layer temporarily; you should no longer see those three objects.

✔ Tips

■ You've already learned that selecting an object on the Stage causes Flash to select that object's layer in the Timeline. As you move objects between layers, it helps to know that selections work the other way around, too. When you select a layer in the Timeline, Flash selects all that layer's objects that are currently on the Stage.

Figure 5.27 Choose Edit > Paste in Place to paste items back into their original positions, but on a new layer.

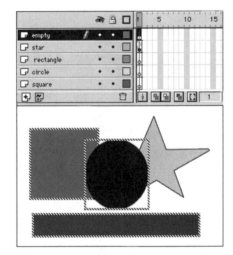

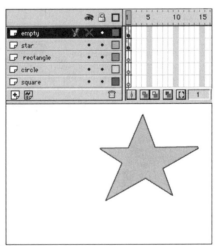

Figure 5.28 The Paste in Place command positions the pasted items in the new layer. Each shape occupies the same coordinates it had on its former layer, but now the shapes are all together in the new layer. Hide the new layer to make sure that you did move the elements from their old layers.

SAVING AND REUSING GRAPHIC ELEMENTS

In the previous chapters, you learned to create and edit static graphics. Your ultimate goal will be to use those graphics in animated movies. And for that, you're likely to want to use items over again. You may want an element to appear several times in one movie, or you may want to use the same element in several movies. Macromedia Flash provides a container for storing graphics that makes it easy to do both. This container is called a *library*.

Every Flash document has its own library, where you can store the elements that go into a movie: text, sounds, animations, rollover buttons, bitmapped graphics, and vector graphics.

Flash 5 offers a new way to share assets (including fonts) among movies: shared libraries. Shared libraries help reduce the amount of material that must be downloaded to a user's system before he or she can view your Flash movies.

In this chapter you learn to work with Libraries and to create symbols that are static graphics. In later chapters you learn about creating animated symbols and buttons (see Chapters 11 and 13), working with bitmapped graphics (see Chapter 7), and adding sounds (see Chapter 14). You also learn about shared libraries and font symbols.

Library Terminology

The general term for an item stored in a Flash library is an *asset*. More specifically, graphics created with Flash's drawing tools and stored in a library are called *symbols*, fonts stored in a library are called *font symbols*, and sounds and bitmaps (which are always stored in a library) are just called *sounds* and *bitmaps*. Flash refers to each copy of a library asset that you actually use in a movie as an *instance* of that asset.

Understanding the Library Window

The Library window offers several ways to view a library's contents and allows you to organize hierarchically the symbols, sounds, fonts, and bitmaps in folders. The Library window provides information about when an item was last modified, what type of item it is, and how many times the movie uses it. The Library window also contains shortcut buttons and menus for working with symbols. Flash has shortcuts for creating new folders, for renaming elements, and for quickly deleting items. Flash remembers whether you had the Library window open during your last work session with a file. If so, it opens the Library window for you next time you open that file.

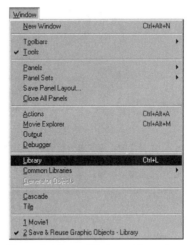

Figure 6.1 Choose Window > Library to open the library of the current Flash document.

To open the library of the current movie:

◆ From the Window menu choose Library, or press ⌘-L (Mac) or Ctrl-L (Windows) (**Figure 6.1**).

The Library window appears on the desktop (**Figure 6.2**).

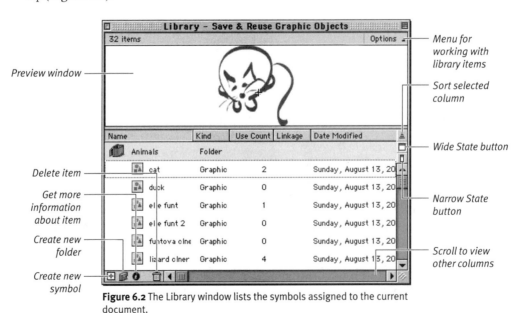

Figure 6.2 The Library window lists the symbols assigned to the current document.

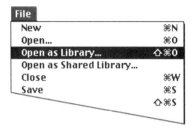

Figure 6.3 The File menu contains the command for opening the library of another file.

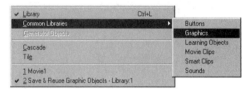

Figure 6.4 The Common Libraries menu gives you quick access to the libraries of Flash documents, located inside the Libraries folder within the Flash application folder.

What Are Common Libraries?

Flash makes a set of libraries available from the menu bar—a sort of library of libraries. Flash 5 ships with six libraries, but you can add your own to the list. The Common libraries menu makes it easy for you to access libraries of symbols, sounds, and bitmaps. The libraries in the Common Libraries menu are simply Flash files that live in the Libraries folder inside the Macromedia Flash folder. Any files you add to the Libraries folder appear in the Common Libraries menu (**Figure 6.4**). Choosing an item from the Common Libraries menu opens only the library, not the file itself.

To open the library of another movie:

1. From the File menu choose Open as Library, or press Shift-⌘-O (Mac) or Shift-Ctrl-O (Windows) (**Figure 6.3**).

2. In the dialog box that appears, choose the name of the file whose library you want to open.

   The Library window appears on the desktop. You can add, delete, or modify elements only in the current movie; when you open another file as a library, you cannot modify the contents of that library. Flash grays out the background, shortcut icons, and most of the Options menu choices in the Library window of a file that's not open.

✔ Tips

■ The variety of menus from which you can open a library of some sort can be daunting at first. Here's the short rundown. To open a library window for the current movie, use Window > Library; to open the library of another file, use File > Open as Library; to open a shared library, use File > Open as Shared library; to open a library from your library of libraries, use the Window > Common libraries menu.

■ One handy way to keep all the symbols, sounds, and bitmaps you're using on a project accessible from the menu bar is to create a special My Project file. As you create symbols or import sounds and bitmaps, add a copy of each item to My Project. Put the file in the Library folder.

■ On the Mac you can put an alias of the file in the Library folder. When you choose the My Project alias from the Window > Common Libraries menu, Flash opens the Library containing all your project's items.

Understanding Library Window Views

You can resize the Library window just as you would any other window, or you can quickly toggle between a wide window and a narrow one. In its wide state, the Library window displays as many as five columns of information about each element (its name, what kind of object it is, how many times it appears in the movie, whether it's exported or imported as a shared asset, and the last modification date). In the narrow view, you generally see the first column of information.

To view the wide Library window:

◆ In the open Library window, click the Wide State button (**Figure 6.5**).

Flash widens the window to accommodate all columns.

To view the narrow Library window:

◆ In the open Library window, click the Narrow State button.

Flash narrows the window to accommodate just the first column.

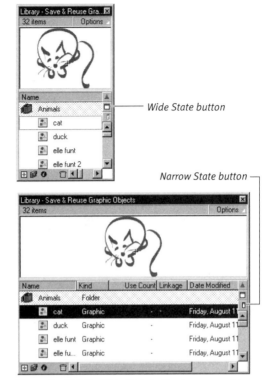

Wide State button

Narrow State button

Figure 6.5 Click the Wide State button to open a wide view of the Library window. Click the Narrow State button to open a narrow view.

Preview new column edge

Drag to resize

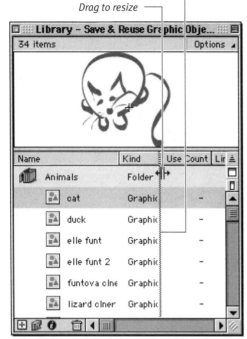

Figure 6.6 Drag the divider between column headers to resize a column.

To resize columns in the Library window:

1. In the open Library window, position the pointer over one of the column-head dividers.

   The pointer changes to a double-arrow divider-moving icon.

2. Click and drag the divider to resize the column (**Figure 6.6**).

✔ Tips

- You can't change the order of the columns in the Library window, but you can hide any middle column you don't need to see. Try hiding the Kind column to save space (the icon preceding each item indicates what type of asset it is). Drag the divider on the right side of the Kind header until it's on top of the left divider.

- By default, the Use Count column doesn't automatically update. To change that, from the Options menu in the Library window, choose Keep Use Counts Updated. (This setting can slow Flash.) To update use counts periodically, from the Options menu, choose Update Use Counts Now as needed.

ABOUT LIBRARY WINDOW VIEWS

Understanding Library Hierarchy

Flash lets you store library elements hierarchically within folders. This makes it easy to organize the elements of movies that contain numerous reused elements. To further aid you in organizing the Library, Flash allows you to sort Library items by column.

To create a library folder:

1. Open the Library window.

2. To select a location, *do one of the following:*
   - To add a root-level folder, select an item at the root level.
   - To add a subfolder, select an item within the folder where you want to add the new subfolder.

3. To create the new folder, *do one of the following:*
   - At the bottom of the window, click the New Folder button (**Figure 6.7**).
   - From the pop-up Options menu in the top-right corner of the window, choose New Folder (**Figure 6.8**).

   Flash creates a new folder, selects it, and activates the text entry field.

4. Type a name for your folder.

5. Press Enter.

Select root-level item to add root-level folder

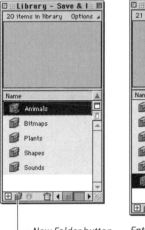

New Folder button   Enter folder name

Select item within a folder to add subfolder

Figure 6.7 To create new folders and subfolders, click the New Folder button.

Figure 6.8 From the Options menu in the Library window choose New Folder.

UNDERSTANDING LIBRARY HIERARCHY

Delete button ⌐

Figure 6.9 Click the Delete button to delete a selected library item.

Figure 6.10 Deleting items in the Library is not undoable. Flash gives you a chance to change your mind with this warning dialog box.

Figure 6.11 Open folders in the Library window to display their contents.

To delete a library folder:

1. Select the folder you want to remove.

2. To delete the folder, *do one of the following:*
   - At the bottom of the window, click the Delete button (the trash-can icon) (**Figure 6.9**).
   - From the pop-up Options menu in the top-right corner of the window, choose Delete.

   Flash displays a dialog box warning that you can't undo the delete operation (**Figure 6.10**).

3. To complete the deletion, *do one of the following:*
   - To stop the operation, click Cancel.
   - To continue, click Delete.

   Deleting permanently removes the folder and its contents from the library. Note that removing items from the library also means removing them from the Stage where you've used them in the movie.

✔ Tip

■ Always carefully check the usage numbers before you delete library items. You don't want to accidentally delete a symbol that you're currently using in a movie, which is especially easy to do if you've nested symbols within symbols. Some earlier versions of Flash would warn you when you tried to delete an item that was in use in a movie. All you get now is the warning that you can't undo deletions from a library.

To open one library folder:

1. In the Library window, select a closed folder.

2. To open the folder, *do one of the following:*
   - Double-click the folder icon.
   - From the Library window's Options menu, choose Expand Folder.

   The folder's contents appear in the Library window (**Figure 6.11**).

To close one library folder:

1. In the Library window, select an open folder.

2. To close the folder, *do one of the following:*
   - ◆ Double-click the folder icon.
   - ◆ From the Library window's Options menu, choose Collapse Folder.

To sort library items:

- ◆ In the Library window, click the heading of the column you want to sort by.

  For example, to sort items by name, click the Name column header. Flash highlights the chosen column header and sorts the Library window by the items in that column.

✔ Tip

- ■ To change the sort order, click the Sort button, which toggles between alphanumeric and reverse alphanumeric order (**Figure 6.12**).

To move items between Library folders:

1. In the open Library window, select the item you want to move.

2. Drag the selected item over the icon of the destination folder.

   Flash highlights the target folder (**Figure 6.13**).

3. Release the mouse button.

   Flash moves the item into the new folder.

✔ Tips

- ■ To quickly move an item to a new folder, from the Library window's Options menu choose Move to New folder.

- ■ To open all library folders at the same time, from the Library window's Options menu, choose Expand All Folders. To close all folders, choose Collapse All Folders.

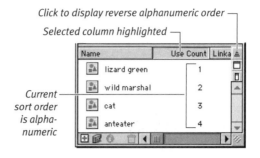
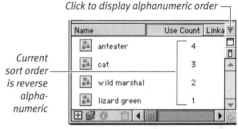

Click to display reverse alphanumeric order
Selected column highlighted
Current sort order is alpha-numeric

Click to display alphanumeric order
Current sort order is reverse alpha-numeric

Figure 6.12 Click the Sort button to sort library items by data in the selected column.

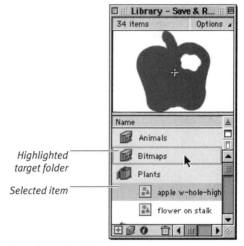

Highlighted target folder
Selected item

Figure 6.13 In the Library window you can simply drag items between folders.

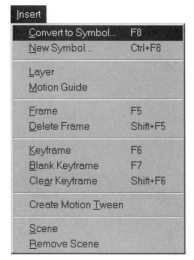

Figure 6.14 Choose Insert > Convert to Symbol to turn an existing graphic into a symbol.

Figure 6.15 The Symbol Properties dialog box lets you name your symbol and define its behavior.

Converting Graphics to Symbols

Not all graphics in a Flash movie are symbols; you need to take special steps to define the items you create as symbols. You can turn graphics you've already created into symbols, or you can create a symbol from scratch in the symbol editor. After you do, the symbol resides in the library of the document in which you created the symbol. You can copy a symbol from one document to another; the symbol then resides separately in each document's library. (You can also define shared symbols that reside in shared libraries; see "Creating Shared Libraries," later in this chapter.)

The standard library of a Flash document contains all the symbols used in that document; it can also contain unused symbols and pointers to symbols in shared libraries.

The following exercise covers creating static graphic symbols. But you can also turn graphics into symbols that are animations (see Chapter 11) or buttons (see Chapter 13).

To turn an existing graphic into a symbol:

1. On the Stage, select the graphic you want to convert to a symbol.

   Flash highlights the grahic.

2. From the Insert menu, choose Convert to Symbol (**Figure 6.14**), or press F8 on the keyboard.

   The Symbol Properties dialog box appears (**Figure 6.15**). Flash gives the symbol a default name—for example, Symbol 16—based on the number of symbols created for the library.

continues on next page

3. If you don't want to use the default, type a name for your symbol.

4. Choose Graphic as the behavior for your symbol.

5. Click OK.

Flash adds the symbol to the library. The graphic on the Stage becomes an instance of the symbol. The selection highlight no longer appears directly over the graphic itself but on the symbol's bounding box, and a crosshair indicating the center of the symbol appears within the box (**Figure 6.16**). You can no longer edit the item directly on the Stage—you must open it in symbol-editing mode.

Selected object

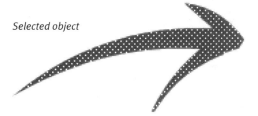

Converted to a symbol

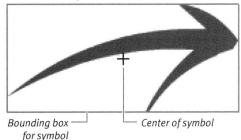

Bounding box ⎯⏋   ⎿⎯ Center of symbol
    for symbol

Figure 6.16 A selected graphic element on the Stage is highlighted with dots. When you convert the graphic to a symbol, the bounding box is the only item that gets highlighted. A crosshair indicates where the symbol's center is.

What Is Symbol Behavior?

In Flash, you must specify a behavior for each symbol. Symbols have three behaviors: graphic, button, and movie clip. Graphics are, as you might expect, graphic elements, but they can also be animated graphic elements. The feature that distinguishes one symbol behavior from another is the way the symbol interacts with the Timeline of the movie in which it appears. Graphic symbols operate in sync with the Timeline of the current movie. If you have a static graphic symbol, it takes up one frame of the movie in which you place it (just as any graphic element would). A three-frame animated graphic symbol takes up three frames of the movie (see Chapter 11). Buttons have their own four-frame Timeline; a button sits in a single frame of a movie but displays its four frames as a user's mouse interacts with it (see Chapter 13). Movie clips have their own multiframe Timeline that plays independently of the main movie's Timeline (see Chapter 11).

Figure 6.17 From the Library window's Options menu choose New Symbol to create a symbol from scratch.

New Symbol button

Figure 6.18 Click the Library window's New Symbol button to create a symbol from scratch.

Symbol being created — List of symbols —
Current scene — List of scenes —

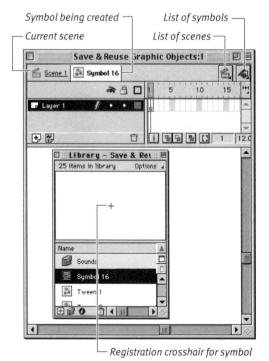

Registration crosshair for symbol

Figure 6.19 In symbol-editing mode, the name of the symbol being worked on appears at the top of the document window.

Creating New Symbols from Scratch

You can avoid the conversion process described in the preceding section by creating graphics directly in the symbol-editing mode. This makes all the tools, frames, and layers of the Flash editor available, but Flash defines the element you are creating as a symbol from the start.

To create a new symbol:

1. To enter symbol-editing mode, *do one of the following:*
   - From the Insert menu, choose New Symbol, or press ⌘-F8 (Mac) or Ctrl-F8 (Windows).
   - From the Library window's Options menu, choose New Symbol (**Figure 6.17**).
   - In the bottom-left corner of the Library window, click the New Symbol button (**Figure 6.18**).

   The Symbol Properties dialog box appears.

2. Type a name for your symbol.

3. Choose Graphic as the behavior for your symbol.

4. Click OK.

   Flash enters symbol-editing mode. Flash displays the name of the symbol you are creating at the top-left side of the document window and places a crosshair in the center of the Stage (**Figure 6.19**). The crosshair indicates the symbol's center and acts as a registration mark, aiding you in aligning the symbol when you use it in a movie.

   continues on next page

CREATING NEW SYMBOLS FROM SCRATCH

5. Create your graphic on the Stage of the symbol editor as you would in the regular editing environment.

6. Return to movie-editing mode, and *do one of the following:*

- ◆ From the Edit menu, choose Edit Movie. Flash returns you to the current scene.
- ◆ In the top-left corner of the document window, click the Current Scene button (**Figure 6.20**). Flash returns you to the current scene.
- ◆ From the Scene pop-up menu in the top-right corner of the document window, choose a scene (**Figure 6.21**). Flash takes you to that scene.

✔ Tips

- ■ When you enter symbol-editing mode, the central crosshair registration mark may be outside the current viewing area. To bring the registration mark to the center of your window, choose View > Magnification > Show Frame.

Current Scene button

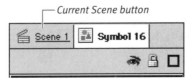

Figure 6.20 Click the Current Scene button to return to movie-editing mode.

Figure 6.21 Choose a scene from the scene pop-up menu to return to movie-editing mode.

Where Am I?

When you edit symbols, Flash simply switches the current window to symbol-editing mode. It's fairly easy to get confused about whether you're editing the main movie or a symbol. Learn to recognize the following subtle visual cues; they are the only indication that you are in symbol-editing mode.

In symbol-editing mode, Flash displays the name of the symbol you are editing near the top-left corner of the window, above the Timeline. Also, a small crosshair, which acts as a registration point for the symbol, appears on the Stage. Apart from these changes, the Timeline, the Stage, and the tools all appear and work just as they do in the Flash editor.

Using Symbol Instances

A symbol instance is a pointer to the full description of the symbol. This is a space-efficient way of reusing vector objects. If you converted a graphic on the stage to a symbol, you already have one symbol instance on the Stage. If you want to use the symbol again, or if you created your symbol from scratch in symbol-editing mode, you'll need to get a copy out of the library and onto the Stage.

Why Use Symbols?

Symbols help you keep file sizes small. You've already learned how Flash uses vectors to hold down file size: Each vector shape is really just a set of instructions, a recipe for creating the shape. So you could duplicate a vector graphic that you want to reuse, and it would be smaller than a bitmapped version of the same graphic. But symbols are even more efficient than duplicate vector shapes.

A symbol is a master recipe. Imagine a busy restaurant that serves three kinds of soup—chicken noodle, cream of chicken rice, and chicken with garden vegetables—and each pot of soup has its own cook. The head chef could go over with each cook all the steps required to make a chicken broth. But that would involve a lot of repetition and take a lot of time. If the restaurant has a master recipe for chicken broth, the chef can simply tell all the cooks to make a pot of chicken broth and then tell each cook just those additional steps that distinguish each dish—add noodles for chicken noodle; add rice and cream for cream of chicken rice; add potatoes, carrots, and peas for garden vegetable.

Symbols act the same way in your movie file. The full recipe is in the library. Each instance on the Stage contains just the instructions that say which recipe to start with and how to modify it—for example, use the recipe for the red rectangle but make it twice as large, change the color to blue, and rotate it 45 degrees clockwise. Because symbols can themselves contain other symbols, it really pays to break your graphic elements into their lowest-common-denominator parts, make each individual part a symbol, and then combine the parts into larger symbols or graphics.

To place a symbol instance in your movie:

1. In the Timeline, select the layer and keyframe where you want the graphic symbol to appear.

   Flash can place symbols only in keyframes. If you are currently in a blank frame, Flash places the symbol in the previous keyframe. (To learn more about keyframes, see Chapter 8.)

2. Open the library that contains the symbol you want to use.

3. In the Library window, navigate to the symbol you want to place on the Stage, and click it to select it.

   Flash highlights the chosen symbol and displays it in the preview window.

4. Position your pointer over the preview window.

5. Click and drag a copy of the symbol onto the Stage.

   Flash previews the symbol's location on the Stage with a rectangular outline (**Figure 6.22**).

6. Release the mouse button.

   Flash places the symbol on the Stage and selects it.

✔ Tip

- To quickly place a symbol instance, you can drag the symbol name directly from the Library window to the Stage without using the previewed image.

Preview location of symbol on the Stage

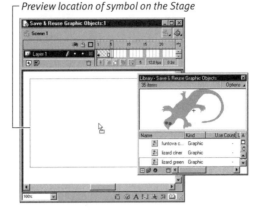

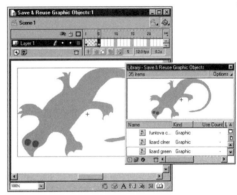

Figure 6.22 When you drag a symbol from the Library window to the stage (top), Flash places the symbol on the Stage, selects it, and updates that symbol's use count (bottom).

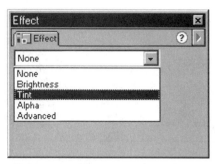

Figure 6.23 The Effect panel's Color Effect menu offers four choices for modifying the color of a symbol instance.

Figure 6.24 Use the Brightness settings in the Effect panel to change the intensity of a symbol instance.

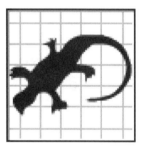

−100 percent brightness setting

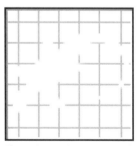

100 percent brightness setting

Figure 6.25 At its extremes, the Brightness setting lets you turn a symbol instance completely black or completely white.

Modifying Symbol Instances

You can change the appearance of each symbol instance without changing the symbol itself. You can scale and rotate a symbol instance just as you would any other element (see Chapter 3).

You can also change the color and transparency of a symbol in the Effect panel, where a pop-up menu lets you change the color, intensity, and transparency of a symbol. The effect panel also offers advanced color effects for simultaneously modifying a symbol's color and transparency.

To access the Effect panel:

◆ If the Effect panel is not currently open, from the Window menu, choose Panels > Effect.

The Effect panel opens or comes to the front if it's grouped in a window with other panels (Figure 6.23).

To change an instance's brightness:

1. On the Stage, select the symbol instance you want to modify.

2. From the Effect panel's Color Effect menu, choose Brightness.

   A field for entering a new brightness percentage appears (**Figure 6.24**).

3. Enter a value in the Brightness field.

   A value of -100 makes the symbol black; a value of 0 leaves the symbol at its original brightness; a value of 100 makes the symbol white (**Figure 6.25**).

4. Press Enter.

   Flash applies the color effect to the selected symbol on the Stage.

To change the instance's color:

1. On the Stage, select the symbol instance you want to modify.

2. From the Effect panel's Color Effect menu, choose Tint.

   Tint-modification parameters appear (**Figure 6.26**).

3. To choose a new color, *do one of the following:*

   ◆ Select a color with the crosshair in the color space.

   ◆ In the Red, Green, and Blue fields, enter new RGB values.

   ◆ Click the tint-color box, and choose a color from the swatch set that appears.

4. Type a percentage in the Tint Amount field.

   The tint percentage indicates how much of the new color to blend with the existing colors. Applying a tint of 100 percent changes all the lines and fills in the symbol to the new color. Applying a lesser percentage mixes some of the new color with the existing colors in the symbol. It's almost like placing a transparent film of the new color over the symbol.

5. Press Enter.

   Flash applies the color effect to the selected symbol on the Stage.

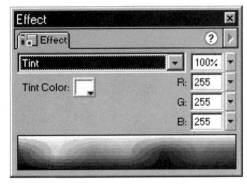

Figure 6.26 Use the Tint settings in the Effect panel to change the color of a symbol instance.

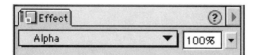

Figure 6.27 Use the Alpha settings in the Effect panel to change the transparency of a symbol instance.

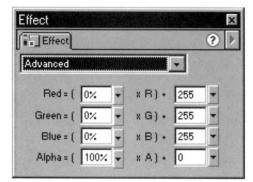

Figure 6.28 Use the Advanced settings in the Effect panel to change the color and transparency of a symbol instance simultaneously.

To change the instance's transparency:

1. On the Stage, select the symbol instance you want to modify.

2. From the Effect panel's Color Effect menu, choose Alpha (**Figure 6.27**).

3. Enter a new value in the Alpha field.

   A value of 0 makes the symbol completely transparent; a value of 100 makes the symbol completely opaque.

4. Press Enter.

   Flash applies the color effect to the selected symbol on the Stage.

To change the instance's tint and alpha simultaneously:

1. On the Stage, select the symbol instance you want to modify.

2. From the Effect panel's Color Effect menu, choose Advanced.

   Sliders and entry fields for changing Red, Green, Blue, and Alpha values appear (**Figure 6.28**).

continues on next page

MODIFYING SYMBOL INSTANCES

3. Adjust the values to fine-tune the color and transparency of the symbol instance.

The sliders on the left control what percentage of the RGB and alpha values that make up the colors in the original symbol will appear in the symbol instance. The sliders on the right modify the red, green, blue, and alpha values of the original colors. Imagine a symbol with three ovals. One is pure red, one is pure green, one is pure blue. The alpha setting is 50 percent. Changing the percentage of red (left slider) affects only the red oval. The green and blue ovals contain no red at all; halving or doubling the amount of red in a pure green doesn't change the green. Changing the right slider adds red to everything, including the green and blue ovals. These ovals now start to change color.

4. To apply the color effect, press Enter.

✔ Tips

■ For easy entry of new values, a slider accompanies each field in the Effects panel. Click the triangle to the right of an entry field to pop the slider open. Drag the lever to a new value; then press Enter.

■ To interactively preview new Effect values, click and drag the triangle to the right of an entry field. Flash updates the symbol on the Stage as you drag the slider lever. When you release the slider, Flash confirms the change; you don't need to press Enter.

■ Instead of pressing Enter to confirm a value you enter in one of the Effect panel's fields, you can just click a different entry field (if the current panel choice displays multiple fields) or click the Stage.

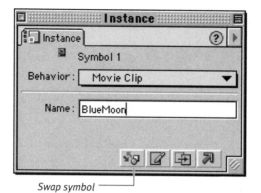

Swap symbol

Figure 6.29 The Instance panel is the gateway to modifying symbol instances.

Swapping One Symbol Instance for Another

The Instance panel allows you to replace one symbol with another while retaining all the modifications you've made in the symbol instance. If for example, you want to change the font of a logo in certain places in your site but not everywhere, you can create the new look as a separate symbol and swap it in as needed. (If you want to change the look for every instance, you could edit the symbol directly, as you learn to do in "Editing Symbols," later in the chapter).

To access the Instance panel:

Do one of the following:

◆ From the Window menu, choose Panels > Instance.

◆ In the Launcher bar, click the Show Instance button.

   The Instance panel opens or comes to the front if it's grouped in a window with other panels (Figure 6.29).

To switch symbols:

1. On the Stage, select the symbol instance you want to change.

2. In the Instance panel, click the Swap Symbol button

   The Swap Symbol dialog box appears, listing all the symbols in the current document's library. Flash highlights the name of the symbol you're modifying and places a bullet next to its name in the Symbol list.

continues on next page

3. From the Symbol list, select the replacement symbol.

The original symbol remains bulleted; Flash highlights the new symbol and places it in the preview window (**Figure 6.30**).

4. Click OK.

Flash places the new symbol on the Stage, locating the new object where the old one was located and applying any modifications you previously made to that instance (**Figure 6.31**).

✔ Tips

■ To quickly swap symbols, double-click the new symbol in the Swap Symbol dialog box. Flash replaces it and closes the dialog box.

■ To open all the panels related to modifying symbols, Option-double-click (Mac) or Alt-double-click (Windows) the symbol on the Stage.

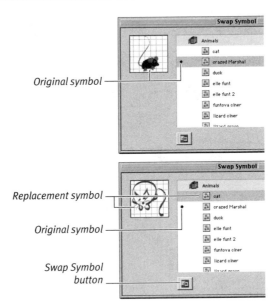

Original symbol

Replacement symbol

Original symbol

Swap Symbol button

Figure 6.30 In the Swap Symbol dialog box click the Swap Symbol button to replace one symbol with another.

Unmodified instance of mouse

Unmodified instance of cat

Instance of mouse scaled and rotated before swapping

After swapping: scaling and rotation applied to cat

Figure 6.31 When you swap symbols, any modifications you have made in the selected instance you're swapping apply to the replacement instance.

Figure 6.32 Edit > Edit Symbols takes you from movie-editing mode to symbol-editing mode. If the item you have selected on the Stage is a symbol, choosing Edit > Edit Selected also takes you to symbol-editing mode.

Figure 6.33 Choosing a symbol from this pop-up list takes you into symbol-editing mode.

Editing Symbols

After you create a symbol, you can refine and modify it in symbol-editing mode. Unlike modifying a symbol instance, which affects just one instance on the Stage and leaves the symbol in the library unchanged, making modifications in symbol-editing mode changes not only the symbol in the library but also all instances of it in your movie.

You can enter symbol-editing mode in several ways.

To enter symbol-editing mode from the Stage:

1. On the Stage, select the symbol you want to edit.

2. To open the symbol editor, *do one of the following:*

   ◆ From the Edit menu, choose Edit Symbols, or press ⌘-E (Mac) or Ctrl-E (Windows) (**Figure 6.32**).

   ◆ From the Edit menu, choose Edit Selected.

   ◆ From the pop-up list of symbols in the top-right corner of the document window, choose the symbol you want to edit (**Figure 6.33**).

   Flash opens the symbol editor in the current window.

✔ Tip

■ To enter symbol-editing mode quickly, double-click a symbol instance on the Stage.

To enter symbol-editing mode from the Library window:

1. In the Library window, select the symbol you want to edit.

2. To bring up the symbol editor, *do one of the following:*

   ◆ From the Options menu choose Edit.

   ◆ Double-click the icon next to the selected symbol name.

   ◆ Double-click the symbol in the preview window.

   Flash opens the symbol editor in the current window (**Figure 6.34**).

✔ Tips

■ After you've placed an instance of a symbol on the Stage, you may want to edit it in context with the items around it. The contextual menu for symbol instances allows you to edit a symbol in place on the Stage with all other items grayed out. To evoke the Edit in Place command, Control-click (Mac) or right-click (Windows) the symbol instance you want to edit. From the contextual menu that appears, choose Edit in Place.

■ You can also enter symbol-editing mode from within the Instance panel. Select the symbol you want to edit from the Symbol list. Click the Edit Symbol button (**Figure 6.35**). Flash takes you back to the Stage in symbol-editing mode.

■ You can edit a symbol in a separate window from your movie. Select an instance of the symbol on the Stage. Control-click (Mac) or right-click (Windows) to access the contextual menu. Choose Edit in New Window.

■ To evoke the Edit in Place command from the Instance panel, Option-click (Mac) or Alt-click (Windows) the Edit Symbol button

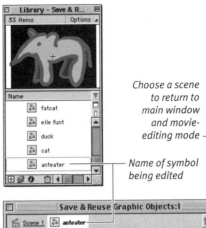

Choose a scene to return to main window and movie-editing mode

Name of symbol being edited

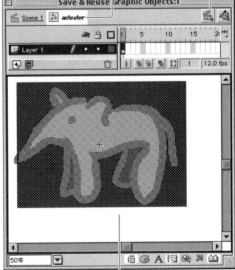

Symbol-editing window

Figure 6.34 Double-clicking a symbol in the Library window (top) brings up a separate window for editing that symbol (bottom).

Edit-symbol button

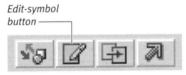

Figure 6.35 The Edit Symbol button in the Instance panel takes you directly to symbol-editing mode.

EDITING SYMBOLS

Figure 6.36 From the Library's Options pop-up menu, choose Duplicate to make a copy of the selected symbol.

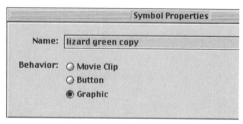

Figure 6.37 The default duplicate name for a symbol in the Symbol Properties dialog box.

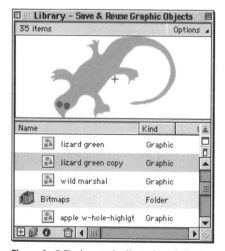

Figure 6.38 Flash puts duplicated symbols at the same library level as the original.

Copying Symbols

Although you can always modify the instances of a symbol on the Stage, if you need to use one variation of a symbol over and over you can make those changes to a duplicate of the original symbol.

To create a duplicate symbol:

1. In the Library window, select the symbol you want to duplicate.

2. From the Options menu, choose Duplicate (**Figure 6.36**).

   Flash opens the Symbol Properties dialog box, giving the duplicate symbol a default name (**Figure 6.37**).

3. If you want, type a new name for your symbol.

4. Choose Graphic as the behavior for your symbol.

5. Click OK.

   Flash adds the new symbol to the library at the same level in the hierarchy as the original (**Figure 6.38**). The duplicate doesn't link to the original symbol in any way. You can change the duplicate without changing the original and vice versa.

✔ Tip

- The Duplicate command is a good way to create a series of symbols with different behaviors. You might want a graphic that acts as a button—responding to a user's mouse clicks—only some of the time. You can create the button, duplicate it, and assign the duplicate Graphic behavior. In most instances, you'll place the graphic symbol in your movie. Use the button version only in places where you want a live button.

Converting Symbol Instances to Graphics

At times you'll want to break the link between a placed instance of a symbol and the original symbol in the library. For example, you may want to alter the shape in a specific instance but not in every instance. To convert a symbol back to an independent shape or set of shapes, break it apart, just as you break apart grouped shapes (see Chapter 4).

To break the symbol link:

1. On the Stage, select the symbol instance with the link you want to break.

2. From the Modify menu, choose Break Apart, or press ⌘-B (Mac) or Ctrl-B (Windows) (**Figure 6.39**).

   Flash breaks the link to the symbol in the library and selects the component shapes that made up the symbol. If you grouped any of the original components, they remain grouped after you break the link; ungrouped components stay ungrouped. You can now edit the shapes as you learned to do in previous chapters.

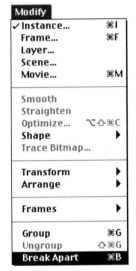

Figure 6.39 To break the link between an instance of a symbol on the Stage and the parent symbol in the library, choose Modify > Break Apart.

Figure 6.40
Choose Linkage from the Library window's Options menu to define a shared symbol.

Creating Shared Libraries

In earlier versions, Flash always stored all the symbols for a movie in a library stored with the movie's .fla and .swf files. That meant that even if you used the same company logo symbol in five movies on your site, you had to place that symbol in each of the five movie's libraries and users had to download it five separate times. Flash 5 lets you share library items among multiple movies.

To make it easier to see what's going on, for the following exercises, create two new movies. Name them for their functions—for example, ItemsToShare.fla and UsingSharedItems.fla. Store them both in the same folder, SharingTest.

To define a symbol as shared:

1. In the file ItemsToShare.fla create a symbol using the techniques described in the previous exercises.

2. Open the Library window (choose Windows > Library).

3. From the list of symbols, select the symbol to be shared.

4. From the Options menu in the top-right corner of the Library window, choose Linkage (**Figure 6.40**).

   The Symbol Linkage Properties dialog box appears.

continues on next page

Shared Library Basics

You can define any type of library asset—a symbol, movie clip, sound, bitmap, even font—as a *shared asset* by setting its Linkage property to Export (basically telling Flash that other movies can have access to this symbol and giving the symbol a unique name). The library in which you define the shared asset becomes a *shared library.*

To make shared assets available to other movies, you must also publish the movie containing the shared library. When you do so, Flash automatically creates links between the shared library's .swf file and the .swf files of any movies that incorporate the shared elements. You can specify the URL of the links yourself if you want to store the shared library in a different location.

5. Select Export this symbol (**Figure 6.41**). A blinking insertion point appears in the Identifier field.

6. Enter a name for this shared symbol. The identifier must not contain any spaces.

7. Click OK.

8. Repeat steps 1 through 6 for as many symbols as you want to share.

9. When you've created all the shared symbols you want for this session, be sure to save the file.

After creating and saving shared symbols in the Flash (.fla) file, you must create a Player (.swf) version of the file to make the shared items available for use in other movies.

To make shared symbols available to other movies:

1. Open the file containing the symbols that you defined as shared in the previous exercise (ItemsToShare.fla).

2. From the File menu, choose Publish Settings.
   The Publish Settings dialog box appears.

3. Click the Formats tab.

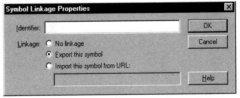

Figure 6.41 In the Symbol Linkage Properties dialog box, select Export this symbol to make a symbol available for sharing in other Flash movies. The name in the Identifier field allows Flash to locate and control the symbol. The name must not contain any spaces.

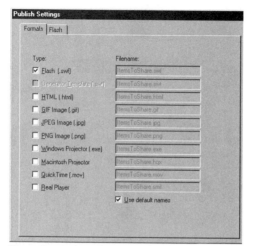

Figure 6.42 In the Publish Settings dialog box, check the flash (.swf) checkbox to publish a .swf file that contains the shared library items (to learn more about publishing movies, see Chapter 16).

4. Check the Flash (.swf) check box (**Figure 6.42**).

For the purpose of creating shared libraries, this is the only check box that must be checked. To learn more about the various publishing options and settings, see Chapter 16.

5. Click the Publish button.

Flash creates a Flash Player file (ItemsToShare.swf) that contains the shared library and puts it in the same folder as the original file (SharingTest).

✔ Tips

■ To create a Flash Player file quickly, without going through the publishing process, all you need to do is test your movie. Choose Control > Test Movie. Flash creates a Player file using default settings.

■ You don't have to keep a shared library .swf file where Flash places it, but you must tell Flash the URL where you plan to store the library. To do so, in the shared library's Library window, from the Options menu, choose Shared Library Properties. In the dialog box, enter the new URL.

CREATING SHARED LIBRARIES

To use a shared symbol in another movie:

1. Open the file (UsingSharedItems.fla) that will use the shared assets you defined in the previous exercises.

2. From the File menu, choose Open as Shared Library (**Figure 6.43**).

3. In the dialog box that appears, select the file that contains the symbols you've already defined as shared assets (ItemsToShare.fla).

4. Click Open.

   A new library window opens (Library—ItemsToShare). Its background is gray, and the options for adding, modifying, and removing symbols do not work, indicating it is not the library attached to the open Flash document (**Figure 6.44**).

5. Drag a shared symbol from the Library—ItemsToShare window to the Stage of the open Flash document (UsingSharedItems.fla).

   Flash adds the shared symbol to the current document's library.

✔ Tips

■ If you don't want to place the shared symbol on the Stage yet, drag the symbol name from the shared Library window to the list of symbol names in the Library window of the current Flash document.

■ To verify that the shared symbol made it into the document with the correct links, open the library for the current document, (choose Window > Library). From the current document's Options menu, choose Linkage. In the Symbol Linkage Properties dialog box, the symbol name should appear and Import This Symbol should be selected.

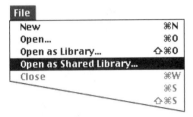

Figure 6. 43 Choose File > Open as Shared Library to access shared assets.

Figure 6.44 When you open a shared library, its background and modification buttons are grayed out. You can drag shared assets to the open Flash document, but you cannot alter the contents of the shared library's original document unless you open it too.

CREATING SHARED LIBRARIES

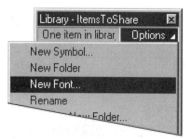

Figure 6.45 From the Library window of the file where you are defining shared assets, choose Options > New Font to create a new font symbol.

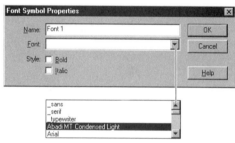

Figure 6.46 You name a font symbol and select a font for it in the Font Symbol Properties dialog box.

Using Font Symbols

Normally, Flash embeds the fonts you use within each published Flash movie. To avoid embedding the same font in multiple movies, you can create a special type of shared library element: the *font symbol.* Shared font symbols help you to keep movie files smaller and make download times faster for your users.

The first step in setting up a shared font is creating a font symbol in a library; you then set the symbol's Linkage properties just as you would for any other shared asset.

To create a font symbol:

1. Open the file containing symbols that you've defined as shared in the previous exercises (ItemsToShare.fla).

2. Open the file's Library window (choose Window > Library).

   The Library—ItemsToShare.fla window opens.

3. From the Options menu in the top-right corner of the Library window, choose New Font (**Figure 6.45**).

   The Font Symbol Properties dialog box appears. Flash gives the symbol a default name—for example, Font 1 (**Figure 6.46**).

4. Enter a new name for the font if you want.

5. In the Font field, enter the name of the font you want to be able to share.

6. Click the triangle to the right of the field to choose a font from a drop-down menu.

7. Click OK.

As with other shared library symbols, you define a font symbol as a shared asset by setting its linkage properties and by publishing the library in a .swf file.

To define a font symbol as a shared asset:

1. To set linkage properties for a font symbol, follow steps 2 through 9 in "To create shared symbols," earlier in this chapter, using the font symbol as your selected symbol.

2. To publish the library in a .swf file, follow the steps in "To make shared symbols available to other movies," earlier in this chapter.

To use a font symbol in another movie:

1. Open the movie in which you want to use the shared font.

2. Follow steps 2 through 5 in "To make a shared symbol in another movie," earlier in this chapter, using the font symbol as your selected symbol.

3. Open the Character panel.

4. From the Character panel's Font menu, choose the name of the shared font symbol (**Figure 6.47**).

   Font symbol names are always followed by an asterisk in font lists.

5. In the Toolbox, select the text tool, and create new text using the shared font.

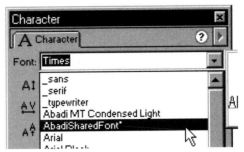

Figure 6.47 To use a font symbol, choose it from the Font menu in the Character panel. The asterisk following a name in the font list indicates that the is a font symbol.

USING NON-FLASH GRAPHICS

7

Macromedia Flash's drawing tools provide a lot of power, but that doesn't mean you have to abandon all other sources of graphic material. You may already be using another vector graphics program—Macromedia FreeHand or Adobe Illustrator, for example—and feel more comfortable with its tools or want to take advantage of some advanced features it offers. Or you may want to include scanned photos or other bitmaps in your Flash movie or use a body of artwork that you created outside Flash. Don't despair; you can import those graphics into Flash.

Importing Non-Flash Graphics

Flash imports vector art and bitmapped graphics either through the Clipboard or via the Import command. When you import graphics from FreeHand 7, 8, or 9, you can also drag and drop elements directly between files.

To import a FreeHand file:

1. From the File menu, choose Import.
   The import dialog box appears (**Figure 7.1**).

2. From the Show (Mac) or Files of Type (Windows) menu, choose the format of the file you want to import.

3. Navigate to the file on your system.

4. Select the file.
   On the Mac, you must also click the Add button to add the file to the list for import. You can import several files by adding them to the list in the import dialog box.

5. Click Import (Mac) or Open (Windows).
   The FreeHand Import dialog box appears (**Figure 7.2**).

6. In the Mapping section, to convert the FreeHand file's pages and layers to Flash format, *do one of the following:*

   ◆ To create a new scene from each FreeHand page, in the Pages section, choose Scenes.

   ◆ To create a new keyframe from each FreeHand page, in the Pages section, choose Keyframes.

   ◆ To create a new layer from each FreeHand layer, in the Layers section, choose Layers.

   ◆ To create a new keyframe from each FreeHand layer, in the Layers section, choose Keyframes.

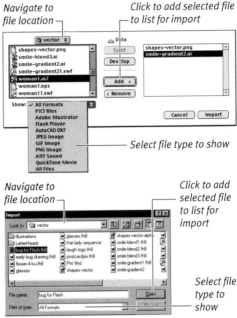

Navigate to file location — *Click to add selected file to list for import*

Select file type to show

Navigate to file location — *Click to add selected file to list for import*

Select file type to show

Figure 7.1 Bring graphics created in other applications into your Flash movie through the import dialog box (Mac version at top, Windows at bottom).

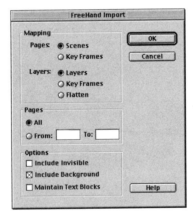

Figure 7.2 When you import files from FreeHand 7, 8, or 9, you have greater control of how the elements appear in the Flash document.

Layers added

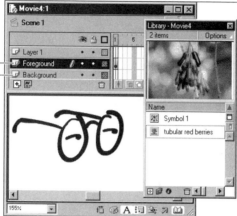

Figure 7.3 Flash imports FreeHand 7, 8, and 9 files according to the settings in the FreeHand Import dialog box. Here, the import options were set to include the background layer.

The Flash/FreeHand Partnership

Although not all features of other vector programs translate directly into Flash, Macromedia has strengthened the ties between Flash and Macromedia FreeHand 7, 8, and 9. You can import the full Free-Hand file, copy selected FreeHand content via the Clipboard and paste it on the Stage in Flash, and drag content from an open FreeHand file directly onto the Stage in Flash.

When you choose File > Import, the FreeHand Import dialog box appears, giving you a chance to control the way that content appears in the Flash document. In addition, if you are importing FreeHand 9 files that contain symbols, Flash automatically adds those symbols to the Flash document's library.

◆ To combine multiple FreeHand layers into one layer, in the Layers section, choose Flatten.

7. In the Pages section, to select the pages to import, *do one of the following:*

◆ To import the entire FreeHand file, choose All.

◆ To import a range of pages from the FreeHand file, choose From/To and then enter the first and last page number.

8. In the Options section, *do one of the following:*

◆ To import any hidden layers from the FreeHand file, choose Include Invisible.

◆ To import the background layer of the FreeHand file, choose Include Background.

◆ To have Flash create editable text blocks from any FreeHand text blocks, choose Maintain Text Blocks.

9. Click OK.

Flash imports the FreeHand graphics and arranges them according to the options you selected (**Figure 7.3**).

✔ Tips

■ If your FreeHand file contains a set of overlapping objects on a single layer, those elements will segment themselves, just as they would in Flash. To keep objects distinct, be sure to place them on multiple layers in FreeHand and choose Mapping: Layers: Layers in the FreeHand Import dialog box.

■ Flash supports only eight-color gradient fills. If you import FreeHand objects that have gradients with more colors, Flash adds clipping paths to simulate the gradient, which increases the file size. For best results, when creating FreeHand gradient fills, restrict yourself to eight color changes.

IMPORTING NON-FLASH GRAPHICS

To import other vector files:

◆ Follow steps 1 through 5 in the preceding exercise.

Flash imports the file and places the content of the file on the Stage as a grouped element. If you ungroup the element (choose Modify > Ungroup), you can work with the ungrouped shape (or any grouped shapes that were united in that group) as you would with any vector shape created in Flash. When you import files in Adobe Illustrator format, Flash re-creates the layers in the original file.

To import a bitmapped graphic:

◆ Follow steps 1 through 5 in the first exercise in this section.

Flash imports the bitmaps you selected into your document, storing them in the library and placing a copy on the Stage in the active layer (**Figure 7.4**).

If you use a program other than Flash to create a series of images that will be keyframes in a movie (a set of FreeHand files, for example), Flash can expedite the import process if the file names end in a series of sequential numbers. (To learn more about keyframe animation, see Chapter 8.)

To import a series of graphics files:

1. Follow steps 1 through 5 in the first exercise in this section.

A dialog box appears, asking whether you want to import what looks like a series of sequential images (**Figure 7.5**). Flash recognizes files that form a sequence if

Figure 7.4 Flash stores an imported bitmap in the library and places a copy on the Stage.

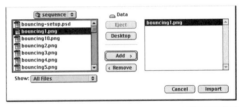

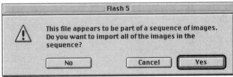

Figure 7.5 When you import one file in a series of numbered files (top), Flash asks whether you want to import the whole series (bottom).

Preview mode shows images in keyframes

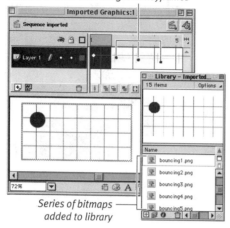

Series of bitmaps added to library

Figure 7.6 When Flash imports a numbered series of files, it places each one in a separate keyframe in the movie.

they are all within a single folder and have file names that differ only in the number at the end of the file name—for example, Bouncing 1, Bouncing 2, and Bouncing 3.

2. In the dialog box, click Yes.

Flash places each image in a separate keyframe on the active layer (**Figure 7.6**).

What Graphics Formats Does Flash Import?

Flash imports a variety of bitmapped and vector graphic file formats. For bitmaps, Flash accepts files in GIF, animated GIF, PNG, JPEG, and BMP (Windows) formats. For vector graphics, Flash accepts FreeHand 7, 8, and 9 files and files in Illustrator 88, 3.0, 5.0, and 6.0 format. Flash also accepts files in PICT (Mac) and in Metafile (WMF) and Enhanced Metafile (EMF) formats (Windows).

When Flash imports graphics in a format that includes transparency (such as GIF, PNG, or PICT), Flash preserves whatever transparency the items had originally. Transparent areas of a GIF image, for example, have an alpha value of 0 when imported into Flash. When it imports PICTs or PNGs with alpha channels, Flash correctly reads the transparency values of the alpha channel.

In addition to the standard bitmapped, vector, and metafile formats listed above, Flash can import AutoCAD DXF release 10 files.

Flash can work with Apple's QuickTime 4 (or a later version) to import additional file formats. Both Mac and Windows users who have the Flash 5/QuickTime 4 combination can import files in Photoshop, QuickTime Image, QuickTime Movie, Silicon Graphics, TGA, TIFF, and MacPaint formats. In addition, Windows users can import PICT files as bitmaps.

Using the Clipboard to Import Graphics

You can bring bitmaps and vector graphics into Flash via the Clipboard. The process is not always reliable, however. Vector graphics in particular may lose something in translation when they go through the Clipboard. If you have trouble using the Clipboard with a particular item, try saving the file that contains the graphic in one of the formats that Flash imports and then bringing the whole file in with the Import command. You can always delete any portions of the file you don't want to use in Flash.

To paste graphics through the Clipboard:

1. Open the application used to create the graphic you want to bring into Flash.

2. Open the file containing the graphic.

3. Select and copy the graphic, using the procedures appropriate to the creator application.

4. Open the Flash document in which you want to put the graphic.

5. From the Edit menu, choose Paste.

   If the graphic is a bitmap, Flash pastes it on the Stage as a group; Flash also places it in the library. If the graphic is a vector, Flash places it on the Stage as a grouped element. When you import multiple items, Flash brings each one in as a separate group (**Figure 7.7**). Flash does not add imported vectors to the library.

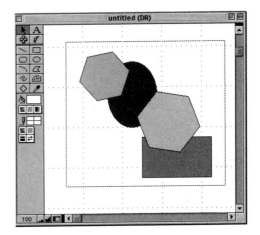

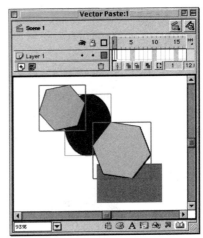

Figure 7.7 Select and copy non-Flash vector graphics (top). In Flash, choose File > Paste (middle). Flash brings each item onto the Stage as a separate group.

Options for export via Clipboard ⏤

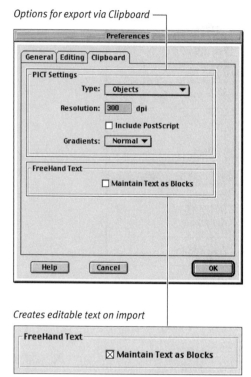

Creates editable text on import

┌─ **FreeHand Text** ─────────────────────┐
│   │
│   ⊠ **Maintain Text as Blocks** │
│   │
└──┘

Figure 7.8 The Clipboard preferences allow you to preserve editable text imported from FreeHand.

✔ Tip

■ Flash can preserve individual text boxes from FreeHand 7, 8, or 9 as editable text even if you import them through the Clipboard. Choose Edit > Preferences; in the Preferences dialog box, click the Clipboard tab; in the FreeHand Text section, choose Maintain Text as Blocks (**Figure 7.8**).

USING THE CLIPBOARD TO IMPORT GRAPHICS

Turning Bitmaps into Vector Graphics

After you've imported a bitmap into a Flash file, you can trace the bitmap to turn it into a set of vector shapes that look like the bitmap. Flash offers several parameters to help you strike a balance between accurate rendering of the various color areas in the bitmap and the creation of too many curves and small vectors within one object, which increases the file size.

To trace a bitmap:

1. Place a copy of the bitmap on the Stage.

2. Select the bitmap.

3. From the Modify menu, choose Trace Bitmap (**Figure 7.9**).

   The Trace Bitmap dialog box appears (**Figure 7.10**).

4. Enter values for the four parameters in the dialog box: Color Threshold, Minimum Area, Curve Fit, and Corner Threshold.

   The parameters in this dialog box control how closely the vector image matches the bitmapped image. Flash creates the vectors by examining the pixels that make up the bitmap, lumping together contiguous pixels that are the same color and making a vector object out of that clump.

   Color Threshold (a number between 1 and 500) tells Flash how to decide when one pixel is the same color as its neighbor. The higher the threshold, the broader the range of colors Flash lumps together. A sky made up of light and dark blue pixels in three slightly different shades, for example, might wind up as one vector object if you set a high enough threshold but might wind up as dozens of separate objects if you set a low threshold.

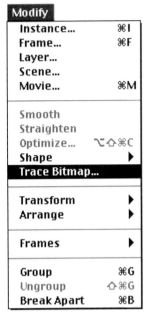

Figure 7.9 Choose Modify > Trace Bitmap to convert a bitmap to a vector shape.

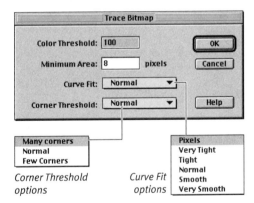

Figure 7.10 The Trace Bitmap dialog box controls how Flash converts bitmaps to vectors.

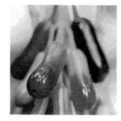

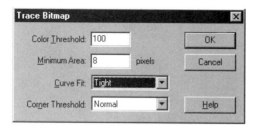

Minimum Area (a number between 1 and 1,000) determines how many neighbor pixels to include in calculating the color.

Curve Fit tells Flash how smoothly to draw the outlines around the vector shapes it creates.

Corner Threshold tells Flash whether to create sharp corners or smoother, more rounded ones.

5. Click OK.

The Trace Bitmap dialog box appears, with a progress bar and a Stop button. (To cancel the tracing process, click Stop.)

Flash replaces the bitmap with filled vector shapes that imitate the image (**Figure 7.11**).

✔ Tips

- For tracing bitmaps that are scans of photographs, Macromedia recommends settings of 10 for Color Threshold, 1 for Minimum Area, Pixels for Curve Fit, and Many Corners for Corner Threshold. These settings can, however, result in really huge files.

- Macintosh users who are working with bitmaps should be sure to increase the memory allocation for Flash by using the Finder's Get Info command. Tracing bitmaps and breaking them apart can take up large amounts of memory.

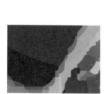

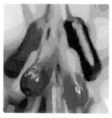

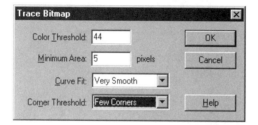

Figure 7.11 These tracings use different settings. The top one closely imitates the original bitmap; the bottom one has a posterized effect but ends up at a much smaller file size.

Using Bitmaps As Fills

Flash allows you to convert a bitmap image to a fill pattern. A bitmapped fill creates a repeating or tiling pattern within the area it fills. You can use bitmapped fills with any of the drawing tools that create fills: the oval, rectangle, paintbrush, and paint bucket tools.

To create a bitmapped fill graphic:

1. Create a new Flash document consisting of two layers.

The two layers keep the original bitmap separate from the shapes you will create and fill with the bitmap. You can name the layers Bitmap and Bitmapped Fills to distinguish the two as you work through the exercises in this section.

2. With Bitmap selected as the active layer, import a bitmapped graphic, following the steps described in the preceding section.

3. Select the bitmap.

4. From the Modify menu, choose Break Apart (**Figure 7.12**).

Flash converts the bitmap to a special type of graphic and selects it. Flash doesn't have a specific name for this type of graphic, but let's call it a bitmapped-fill graphic. A bitmapped fill graphic is no longer a collection of individual pixels, each with its own color value; neither is it a collection of tiny vector shapes.

A bitmap you've broken apart acts more or less like a single vector shape with a gradient fill. (Macromedia describes this state as a number of discrete color areas.) If you click any area of the image now, you select the entire image.

Try setting the paint bucket to solid red; click the image, and it becomes a red rectangle. Don't forget to undo your experiment.

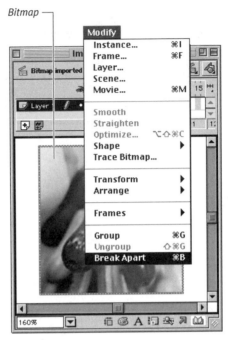

Bitmap

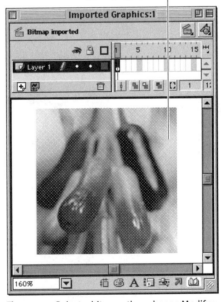

Converted to bitmapped-fill graphic

Figure 7.12 Select a bitmap; then choose Modify > Break Apart (top). Flash converts the bitmap to a bitmapped-fill graphic (bottom). This bitmapped-fill object acts like a gradient fill in that it's not a single color, but the various color areas are not vector shapes.

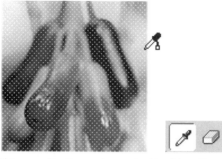

Figure 7.13 Use the eyedropper tool to pick up the bitmapped fill.

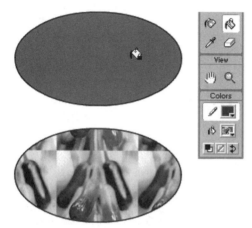

Figure 7.14 With the bitmapped fill selected as the Fill Color, click the item you want to fill with the bitmapped pattern (top). Flash fills the shape with repeating tiles of the bitmap.

To turn a bitmapped-fill graphic into a tiling bitmapped fill that you can apply to other shapes, you'll need the eyedropper tool.

To apply a bitmapped fill:

1. Create a bitmapped-fill graphic, following the steps in the preceding exercise.

2. On the Stage in the Bitmapped Fills layer, create a filled shape, using the oval, rectangle, or paintbrush tool.

3. To choose the bitmap as your fill color, in the Toolbox, select the eyedropper tool.

4. Position the eyedropper over the bitmapped-fill object (**Figure 7.13**).

5. Click the bitmapped fill graphic anywhere.

   In the Toolbox, Flash makes the bitmap the current fill selection and selects the paint bucket tool.

6. Position the paint bucket over the shape you created in step 1; then click.

   Flash fills your shape with a tiling pattern made from the bitmapped fill (**Figure 7.14**).

7. In the Toolbox, select the paintbrush tool, and use it to paint a shape on the Stage.

   The brushstrokes you create are filled with the tiling pattern. You can use the filled oval and rectangle tools this way, too.

✔ Tip

■ To load a bitmap fill directly into Flash's drawing tools, use the arrow tool to select a bitmapped fill graphic. Flash sets the current "color" in the fill-color box to the bitmap. The oval, rectangle, and brush tools are now ready to create objects with that bitmap fill.

Modifying Bitmapped Fills

You can modify—scale, rotate, and skew—bitmapped fills the same way you would modify gradient fills.

To move a bitmapped fill's center point:

1. In the Toolbox, select the paint bucket tool.

2. Choose the Transform Fill modifier, and make sure that Lock Fill is deselected (**Figure 7.15**).

   The pointer changes to the transform-fill arrow.

3. Position the pointer over the shape with the bitmapped fill you want to modify.

4. Click.

   Handles for manipulating the fill appear (**Figure 7.16**).

5. Drag the center-point handle to reposition the center point of the fill (**Figure 7.17**).

   Repositioning the center point changes the way the tiling pattern fits within your shape.

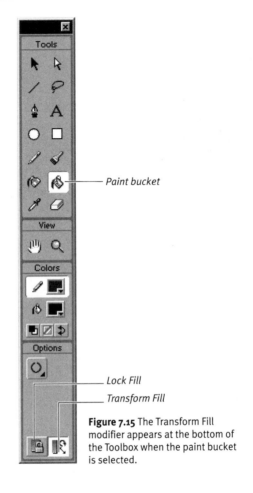

Paint bucket

Lock Fill

Transform Fill

Figure 7.15 The Transform Fill modifier appears at the bottom of the Toolbox when the paint bucket is selected.

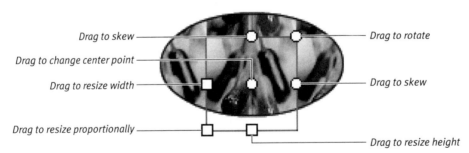

Drag to skew

Drag to rotate

Drag to change center point

Drag to resize width

Drag to skew

Drag to resize proportionally

Drag to resize height

Figure 7.16 Clicking the bitmapped fill pattern with the Transform Fill modifier brings up handles for modifying the tiles.

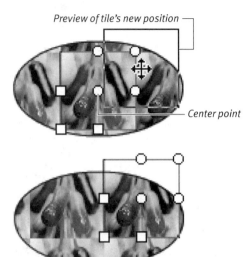

Preview of tile's new position

Center point

Arrangement of tiles with new center point

Figure 7.17 Drag the center point of the selected tile to change the way the tiling pattern fits within the object.

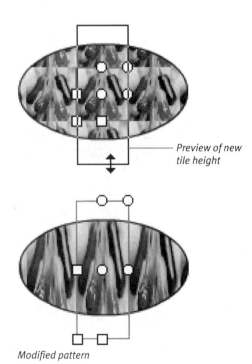

Preview of new tile height

Modified pattern

Figure 7.18 Drag the bottom handle to make the fill pattern taller or shorter.

To resize a bitmapped fill:

1. With the paint bucket in Transform Fill mode, click the shape whose bitmapped fill you want to modify.

   Modifier handles appear around one of the bitmapped tiles in your shape.

2. To change the height of the bitmapped tiles, drag the square handle at the bottom edge of the tile (**Figure 7.18**).

   The pointer changes to a double-headed arrow. Dragging toward the center of the tile makes all the tiles shorter; dragging away from the center of the tile makes all the tiles taller.

3. To change the width of the bitmapped tiles, drag the square handle on the left side of the tile.

   The pointer changes to a double-headed arrow. Dragging toward the center of the tile makes all the tiles narrower; dragging away from the center of the tile makes all the tiles wider.

4. To change the size of the bitmapped tiles proportionally, drag the square handle at the bottom-left corner of the tile.

   The pointer changes to a double-headed arrow. Dragging toward the center of the tile makes all the tiles smaller; dragging away from the center of the tile makes all the tiles larger.

MODIFYING BITMAPPED FILLS

To rotate and skew a bitmapped fill:

1. With the paint bucket in Transform Fill mode, click the shape whose bitmapped fill you want to modify.

2. To rotate the bitmapped fill, drag the round handle in the top-right corner (**Figure 7.19**).

The pointer changes to a circular arrow. You can rotate the tiles clockwise or counterclockwise.

3. To skew the bitmapped fill, drag the round handle on the right side or top (**Figure 7.20**).

The pointer changes to a double-headed arrow indicating the direction of the skew.

✔ Tip

■ If you skew and scale the original bitmapped-fill graphic (the bitmap you broke apart), instead of skewing and scaling the tiles within the filled shape, you can save your modifications for later use. Select the modified bitmapped fill graphic, and choose Insert > Convert to Symbol. When you need that fill again, drag an instance of the symbol to the Stage, break it apart, and sample it again with the eyedropper tool.

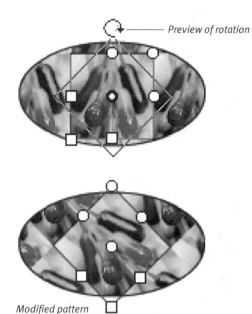

Preview of rotation

Modified pattern

Figure 7.19 Drag the round corner handle to rotate the fill pattern.

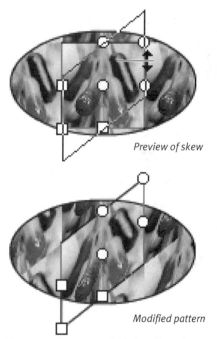

Preview of skew

Modified pattern

Figure 7.20 Drag a round side handle to skew the fill pattern.

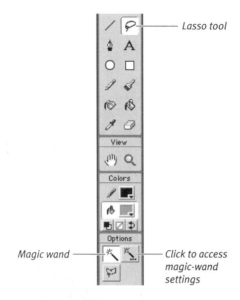

Lasso tool

Magic wand ——

—— Click to access magic-wand settings

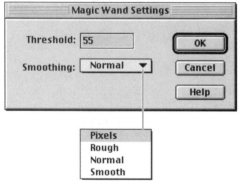

Figure 7.21 The magic wand modifier of the lasso tool allows you to select regions of color within a bitmapped-fill graphic.

Using the Magic Wand Tool

Using the magic wand tool, you can make selections by color within a bitmap you've broken apart. With the magic wand tool, clicking a pixel within the bitmapped-fill graphic selects that pixel and any pixels of the same color that touch it.

Like the Trace Bitmap command, the magic wand has a Threshold setting that determines how different two colors can be and still have Flash consider them to be the same color.

Use the paint bucket tool to fill your selection with a single color, and the filled region becomes an editable vector shape.

To make a selection within a bitmap you've broken apart:

1. Place a bitmap on the Stage, and break it apart to create a bitmapped-fill graphic, as described earlier in this chapter.

2. In the Toolbox, select the lasso tool.

3. Select the magic wand settings modifier (**Figure 7.21**).

   The Magic Wand Settings dialog box appears.

4. In the dialog box, enter the settings for Threshold and Smoothing.

   The Threshold setting works the same way as the Color Threshold setting in the Trace Bitmap dialog box (described earlier in this chapter). Smoothing works similarly to the Curve Fit setting of the Trace Bitmap dialog box; it determines how smooth a vector path Flash draws when the magic wand makes a selection.

5. Click OK.

continues on next page

6. On the Stage, position the pointer over the bitmapped-fill graphic.

The pointer changes to a magic-wand icon. The tool's hot spot is the transparent area in the center of the starburst (**Figure 7.22**).

7. Click a pixel in the region you want to select.

Flash selects that pixel and all the surrounding pixels that fall within the threshold you chose.

✔ Tip

■ If the magic wand fails to grab the full range of colors you wanted, change Threshold to a higher number and try again. You can also add to the selection by clicking (or Shift-clicking, depending on your Preferences setting) the missed pixels.

Magic-wand hot spot

Click to select

Selection with threshold of 10

Selection with threshold of 55

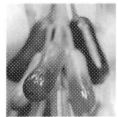

Selection with threshold of 155

Figure 7.22 Click with the magic wand's hot spot to select a region of color. The Threshold setting in the Magic Wand Settings dialog box determines how large a color range the magic wand grabs.

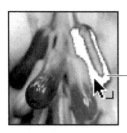

Selection filled with solid color

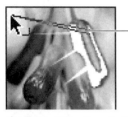

Editing the vector shape created

Figure 7.23 Filling the selection with the paint bucket tool reduces the full range of colors to a single color. This figure uses white, because it shows up well in this grayscale image. That part of the bitmapped-fill graphic then becomes an editable vector shape.

To create areas of solid color within a bitmapped-fill graphic:

1. Make a selection within the bitmapped-fill graphic.

   You can use any of the selection tools (arrow, lasso, or magic wand). The most precise way to select regions of the image is by color, using the magic wand as described earlier in this section.

2. In the Toolbox, select the paint bucket.

3. From the pop-up swatch set in the fill-color box, choose a color.

4. On the Stage, position the paint-bucket pointer over the selection and click.

   Flash fills the selection with the solid color. This solid-color shape is a vector shape, which you can edit just like any other shape in Flash (**Figure 7.23**).

✔ Tip

- You can use the magic wand to reduce the number of colors in a bitmapped fill. Keep selecting regions of similar colors and filling them with solid color until the entire bitmapped fill consists of vector shapes filled with solid colors. Use higher Threshold settings to gather more colors in each selection.

FRAME-BY-FRAME ANIMATIONS

Frame-by-frame animation was the traditional form of animation used before the days of computers. Live-action movies are really a form of frame-by-frame animation. The movie camera captures motion by snapping a picture every so often. Animation simulates motion by showing drawings of objects at several different stages of a motion.

Traditional animators, such as those who worked for the early Walt Disney or Warner Bros. studios from the 1930s through the 1960s, had to create hundreds of images, each one slightly different from the next, to achieve every movement of each character or element in the cartoon. To turn those drawings into animations, they captured the images on film, putting a different image in each frame of the movie.

Traditional animators painted individual characters (or parts of characters) and objects on transparent sheets called *cels*. They stacked the cels up to create the entire image for the frame. (Notice the similarity with how Flash works.) The cel technique allowed animators to save time by reusing parts of an image that stayed the same in more than one frame.

In Flash, you, too, can make frame-by-frame animations by placing different content in different frames. Flash calls the frames that hold new content *keyframes*.

Using the Timeline

In the Timeline, you have five size options for viewing frames and two options for previewing thumbnails of frame contents. A Flash movie may contain hundreds of frames; the Timeline's scroll bars enable you to access frames not currently visible in the Timeline window. You can also undock the Timeline so that it floats as a separate window and resize it to show more or fewer frames. Flash 5 gives you two options for viewing frames in the Timeline (see the sidebar "The Mystery of Timeline Display"). Except where noted, the pictures and descriptions in this book are for Flash's default frame-drawing style. **Figure 8.1** shows the Timeline for a movie with one layer and 15 frames.

To resize the Timeline's area:

1. From the File menu, choose New to open a new document.

   The default Timeline appears.

2. Click inside the gray bar at the top of the Timeline and drag away from the document window.

   A dotted line represents the Timeline palette's position.

3. With the Timeline in its new location, release the mouse button.

4. Drag the handle at the bottom-right corner of the Timeline window to resize it as you would any other window (**Figure 8.2**).

   You can make the Timeline wider than your open window showing the Stage to make more frames available without scrolling.

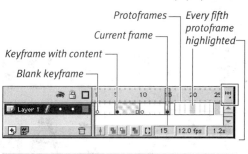

Frame View pop-up menu

Protoframes — Every fifth protoframe highlighted

Current frame

Keyframe with content

Blank keyframe

In-between frames do not have bullet

Frame rate

Current frame

Figure 8.1 Similar to an interactive outline, the Timeline represents each frame of your movie. Click any frame, and Flash displays its contents on the Stage. Flash 5 offers two style for drawing keyframes in the Timeline. The Flash 4 Frame Drawing style (top) gives visual cues for blank keyframes; Flash 5's default style (bottom) doesn't.

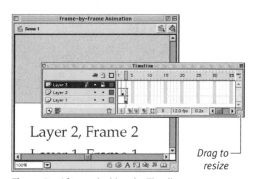

Drag to resize

Figure 8.2 After undocking the Timeline, you can resize it to show more frames.

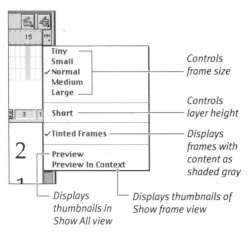

Controls frame size

Controls layer height

Displays frames with content as shaded gray

Displays thumbnails in Show All view

Displays thumbnails of Show frame view

Figure 8.3 The Timeline's Frame View pop-up menu lets you control the display of frames in the Timeline.

To view frames in the Timeline at various sizes:

◆ In the Timeline, from the Frame View menu, choose a display option (**Figure 8.3**).

Flash resizes the frame representations in the Timeline to reflect your choice (**Figure 8.4** shows some of the frame views available).

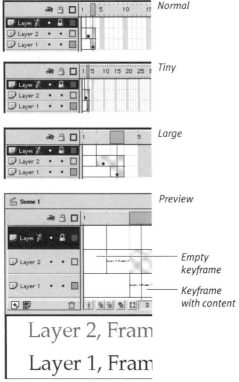

Normal

Tiny

Large

Preview

Empty keyframe

Keyframe with content

Figure 8.4 Flash can display the frames in the Timeline in a variety of sizes, from Tiny to Large. You can also preview the contents of each frame in the Timeline.

The Mystery of Timeline Display

When you create a new Flash document, the Timeline displays a single layer with hundreds of little boxes. The first box has a solid black outline; the rest of the boxes are gray. Every fifth box is solid gray; the others are outlines. The box with the black outline is a keyframe; the gray boxes are placeholder frames, or *protoframes*.

When you define a range of live frames by adding keyframes (see "Creating Keyframes" later in this chapter), the outline for the range of frames changes to black in the Timeline.

When a keyframe is blank (when it has no content) it can appear in the Timeline in one of two ways. In Flash 5's default frame-drawing style, the only visual cue for a blank keyframe is the frame's black outline in the Timeline. If you prefer more feedback, in the General tab of the Preferences dialog box (choose Edit > Preferences) you can set the Timeline Options to Flash 4 Frame Drawing. Then the Timeline displays a hollow bullet in each blank keyframe (**Figure 8.5**).

In both frame-drawing styles, Flash displays a solid bullet in the Timeline for a keyframe that has content. In the range between keyframes, when the initial keyframe has content, each subsequent in-between frame allows the contents of the preceding keyframe to appear on the Stage. In the Timeline, the last frame of an in-between range that has content displays a hollow square. If you've set Frame View to Tinted Frames (the default), the in-between range with content also has a tinted highlight.

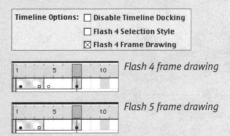

Figure 8.5 To have Flash display a hollow bullet in blank keyframes in the Timeline, check the Flash 4 Frame Drawing checkbox in the General tab of the Preferences dialog box (to open the dialog box, choose Edit > Preferences).

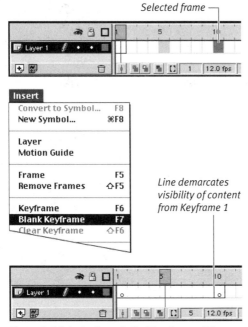

Selected frame

Insert

Convert to Symbol...	F8
New Symbol...	⌘F8
Layer	
Motion Guide	
Frame	F5
Remove Frames	⇧F5
Keyframe	F6
Blank Keyframe	**F7**
Clear Keyframe	⇧F6

Line demarcates visibility of content from Keyframe 1

Figure 8.6 Select a frame in the Timeline, and then choose Insert > Blank Keyframe to add a new blank keyframe.

Creating Keyframes

Flash offers two commands for creating keyframes. Insert Blank Keyframe defines a keyframe that's empty, and Insert Keyframe defines a keyframe that duplicates the content of the preceding keyframe in that layer. Use the Insert Blank Keyframe command when you want to change the contents of the Stage completely. Use Insert Keyframe when you want to duplicate the content of the preceding keyframe—when you will change the content in a minor way, for example.

✔ Tip

- The following tasks access frame-related commands from the main menu bar, but all the relevant commands for working with frames are available from the contextual frame menu. You can Control-click (Mac) or right-click (Windows) a frame in the Timeline to bring up the contextual frame menu.

To add a blank keyframe to the end of your movie:

1. Create a new Flash document.

   The new document by default has one layer and one blank keyframe at Frame 1.

2. In the Timeline, click the protoframe for Frame 10 to select it.

3. From the Insert menu, choose Blank Keyframe, or press F7 on the keyboard (**Figure 8.6**).

continues on next page

CREATING KEYFRAMES

Flash revises the Timeline to give you information about the frames you've defined. A black line now separates Frame 9 from Frame 10; the line indicates where the content for one keyframe ends and the content for the next keyframe begins. Frame 10 is a blank keyframe (when Flash 4 Frame Drawing is selected, a hollow bullet appears in this frame in the Timeline). There currently is nothing on the Stage in this frame. Flash replaces the gray bars separating Protoframes 2 through 9 with gray tick marks and removes the gray highlight that appeared in every fifth frame of the undefined frames.

To create a blank keyframe in the middle of your movie:

1. Follow the steps in the preceding section to create a single-layer, 10-frame movie.

2. In the Timeline, click Frame 1 to select it.

3. Place an object on the Stage (use the drawing tools to create something new, copy something from another document, or bring in an instance of a symbol from a library).

   Flash updates the Timeline, adding a solid bullet to Frame 1 (**Figure 8.7**).

   With Tinted Frames selected in the Frame View menu (Flash's default setting), Flash shades Frames 1 through 9 with gray. The shading indicates that there is content in Keyframe 1 that remains visible until Frame 10 in this layer. A hollow square appears in Frame 9, indicating the end of the range of frames that displays the content of Keyframe 1.

   Frame 10 is still white and blank, meaning that it has no content. (Try clicking Frame 10 to see that the Stage is completely blank.)

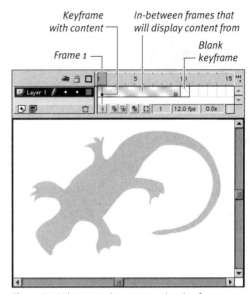

Figure 8.7 When you place content in a keyframe, Flash displays that frame in the Timeline with a solid bullet. The gray tint on the frames between keyframes indicates that content from the preceding keyframe appears during these frames. The hollow square indicates the end of the range of frames displaying the same content.

Display content from preceding keyframe —

Current frame —

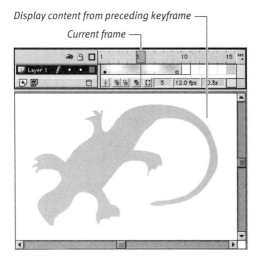

Stage is empty —

Blank keyframe inserted —

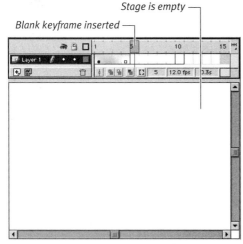

Figure 8.8 When you convert an in-between frame that displays content to a blank keyframe, Flash removes content from the Stage for that frame. Frames 6 through 9 are tinted when they display the content of Frame 1 (top). When you add a blank keyframe at Frame 5 (bottom), the tint disappears, because these frames now display the content of the most recent keyframe, Frame 5, which is empty.

4. In the Timeline, click the number 5 or drag the playhead to position it in Frame 5.

Flash displays Frame 5 on the Stage. Notice that this in-between frame continues to display the content of the preceding keyframe, Frame 1.

5. From the Insert menu, choose Blank Keyframe, or press F7 on the keyboard.

Flash converts the selected in-between frame to a keyframe and removes all content from the Stage in that frame (**Figure 8.8**).

To duplicate the contents of the preceding keyframe:

1. Follow the steps in the preceding exercise to create a single-layer, 10-frame movie with keyframes at 1, 5, and 10 and content only in Frame 1.

2. In the Timeline, position the playhead in Frame 3.

3. From the Insert menu, choose Keyframe, or press F6 on the keyboard.

   Flash creates a new keyframe, duplicates the contents of Frame 1 in Frame 3, and places a solid bullet in the Timeline at Frame 3 (**Figure 8.9**). The content of frames 1 and 3 is totally separate. Try selecting Frame 1 and making changes in its content—move the graphic or delete it entirely. Now select Frame 3 again; it remains unchanged.

✔ Tips

- The word *insert* in connection with keyframes is a bit misleading. When you use the Insert Keyframe command, Flash *adds* frames to your movie only if you've selected a protoframe. If you select an existing in-between frame, the Insert Keyframe command converts the selected frame to a keyframe and leaves the length of the movie as it was. The Insert Frame command, however, always adds frames to your movie.

- To create a series of keyframes quickly, select a range of protoframes (see "Selecting Frames" later in this chapter) and then choose Modify > Frames > Convert to Keyframes or Modify > Frames > Convert to Blank Keyframes. Convert to Keyframes creates a series of keyframes containing the same content as the keyframe to the left of your selection; Convert to Blank Keyframes creates a series of keyframes with no content.

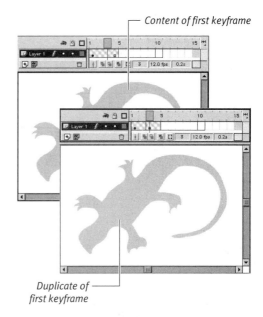

Content of first keyframe

Duplicate of first keyframe

Figure 8.9 The Insert > Keyframe command creates a keyframe that duplicates the contents of the preceding keyframe in that layer.

Keyframes

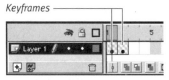

Movie before evoking Insert > Frame

In-between frame

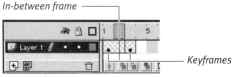

Keyframes

Movie after evoking Insert > Frame

End of keyframe unit

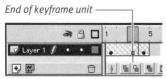

Movie after evoking Insert > Frame again

Figure 8.10 The Insert > Frame command adds an in-between frame after the selected frame. Unlike Insert > Keyframe and Insert > Blank Keyframe, which merely convert a selected frame to a keyframe, the Insert > Frame command actually adds a new frame to your movie. Note that the hollow square indicating the end of a range appears only in ranges of three frames or more.

Creating In-Between Frames

The frames that appear between keyframes are in a sense tied to the keyframe that precedes them. They display its content and allow you a space in which to create tweened animation (see Chapters 9 and 10). Flash 5 makes the connections between these frames clear by highlighting them and placing a hollow square at the end of any in-between range that's at least three frames long.

To add in-between frames:

1. Create a new Flash document with keyframes and content in Frame 1 and Frame 2.

2. In the Timeline, position the playhead in Frame 1.

3. From the Insert menu, choose Frame, or press F5 on the keyboard.

   Flash adds an in-between frame (**Figure 8.10**). Your movie now contains a keyframe at Frame 1, an in-between frame at Frame 2, and another keyframe at Frame 3.

✔ Tips

■ To insert several in-between frames in the middle of your movie, copy proto-frames from the end of your movie and paste them in the desired location. To insert four in-between frames between frames 2 and 4, for example, select five (yes, five) protoframes. Choose Edit > Copy Frames. Select Frame 3. Choose Edit > Paste Frames. Flash pastes the frames over the selected frame, in effect adding four new frames. (If the selected frame is the movie's initial keyframe, Flash leaves the content of the keyframe alone but still inserts only four frames.)

continues on next page

CREATING IN-BETWEEN FRAMES

■ If you have frames selected when you invoke the Insert > Frame command, Flash inserts as many new frames as you had selected. (The process is as though Flash copies and pastes the selected frames in a single step.) When you insert frames between back-to-back keyframes—if you select the frames you just inserted and press F5, for example—you double the number of in-between frames with a single command. You can continue the doubling procedure until you have as many in-between frames as you need.

What Are Keyframes and In-Between Frames?

In the early days of animation, it took veritable armies of artists to create the enormous number of drawings that frame-by-frame animation requires. To keep costs down, the studios broke the work into various categories based on the artistic skill required and the pay provided. The work might start with creating spec sheets for each character. Then came storyboards that outlined the action over the course of the animation. Eventually, individual artists drew and painted hundreds of cels, each slightly different, to bring the animation to life.

To make the process manageable, animators broke each movement into a series of the most crucial frames that define a movement, called *keyframes*, and frames that incorporate the incremental changes necessary to simulate the movement, called *in-between frames*.

Keyframes define a significant change to a character or object. Imagine a 25-frame sequence in which Bugs Bunny starts out facing the audience and then turns to his right to look at Daffy Duck. This scene requires two keyframes—Bugs in a face-on view and Bugs in profile—and 23 in-between frames.

In the early days, some artists specialized in creating keyframes. Other artists—usually, lower-paid ones—had the job of creating the frames that fell in between the keyframes. These in-betweeners (or tweeners, for short) copied the drawings in the keyframes, making just the slight adjustments necessary to create the intended movement in the desired number of frames while retaining the continuity of the character. In Chapters 9 and 10, you learn how to turn Flash into your own personal wage slave. The program takes on the drudgery of in-betweening for certain types of animation.

In Flash, you must use keyframes to define any change in the content or image, no matter how large or small the change. Flash doesn't use the term *in-between frames*; it simply uses the term *frame* for any frames that are not defined as keyframes. For clarity, the following exercises use the term *in-between frames* to refer to any defined frames that are not keyframes.

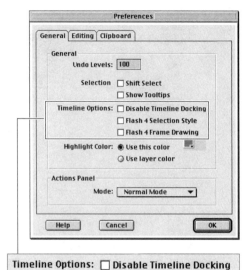

Figure 8.11 Choose the way selections work in the Timeline from the General tab of the Preferences dialog box.

Selecting Frames

Flash 5 offers two styles for selecting frames in the Timeline. The default Flash 5 Timeline creates a clear visual relation ship between a keyframe and any subsequent in-between frames that display that keyframe's content. The default selection style takes advantage of what I call *keyframe units* when you select frames. The Flash 4 style treats every frame as an individual. When you understand the way each style works, you can choose one style (or change between styles) to take advantage of the different selection capabilities.

Except where noted, the examples in this book use Flash 5's default selection style.

To choose a selection style:

1. From the Edit menu, choose Preferences. The Preferences dialog box appears.

2. Click the General tab (**Figure 8.11**).

3. In the Timeline Options section, *do one of the following:*
   - To manipulate frames individually, check the Flash 4 Selection Style checkbox.
   - To take advantage of Flash 5's unified keyframe units in manipulating frames in the Timeline, uncheck the Flash 4 Selection Style checkbox.

SELECTING FRAMES

To select frames the Flash 5 way:

In the Timeline, *do one of the following:*

◆ To select one protoframe, click it.

◆ To select two protoframes and all the frames between them, Shift-click the two protoframes.

◆ To select a keyframe, click it.

◆ To select the last frame in keyframe unit, click it.

◆ To select an entire keyframe unit, click a middle frame in the keyframe unit.

◆ To select an entire keyframe unit, Shift-click the first or last frame in a keyframe unit.

◆ To add other frames (or other keyframe units) to your selection, Shift-click the frames. The selection can include non-contiguous frames (**Figure 8.12**).

◆ To select a range of frames, Option-drag (Mac) or Alt-drag (Windows) through the frames.

To select frames the Flash 4 way:

In the Timeline, *do one of the following:*

◆ To select one protoframe, click it.

◆ To select two protoframes and all the frames between them, Shift-click the two protoframes.

◆ To select a keyframe, click it.

◆ To select the last frame in a keyframe unit, click it.

◆ To select just a middle frame in a keyframe unit, click that frame.

◆ To add frames to your selection, Shift-click the frames; Flash selects all the frames between the already-selected frames and the frame you Shift-click.

◆ To select a range of frames, click and drag through the frames.

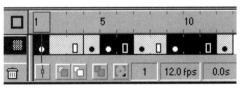

Figure 8.12 With Flash 5's default frame-selection style you can Shift-click to select frames that are not contiguous.

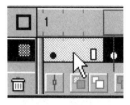

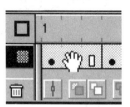

Figure 8.13
The pointer acts differently depending on which frame-selection style you use. The Flash 4 Selection Style (top) treats in-between frames as individual frames. Flash 5's default style (bottom) treats in-between frames as a unit.

✔ Tips

- Can't remember what selection style you've got set in Preferences? Here's an easy way to check. In the Timeline, the pointer usually appears as a hand but changes to an arrow when dealing with certain types of individual frames (**Figure 8.13**). Position the pointer over the middle frames of a keyframe unit. If the pointer changes to an arrow, Flash 4 Selection Style is active; clicking selects only the frame beneath the arrow. If the pointer remains a hand, Flash 5's default selection style is active; clicking grabs the whole keyframe unit.

- The contextual menu for frames contains one command not available in any other menu: Select all. Use this command to select all the frames in the current Timeline. Note that this command selects all frames on every layer in the Timeline.

Manipulating Frames in One Layer

You cannot copy or paste frames by using the standard Copy and Paste commands that you use for graphic elements. Flash's Edit menu provides special commands for copying and pasting frames. Flash also lets you drag selected frames to new locations in
the Timeline.

For the following exercises, open a new Flash document. Create a 10-frame movie with keyframes at frames 1, 3, 5, 7, and 9. Using the text tool, place a text box in each keyframe and enter the number of the frame in the text box; this makes it easy to tell what frame winds up where as you practice. Your document should look like **Figure 8.14.**

To copy and paste a single frame:

1. In the Timeline, select Frame 3.

2. From the Edit menu, choose Copy Frames, or press ⌘-Option-C (Mac) or Ctrl-Alt-C (Windows) (**Figure 8.15**).

   Flash copies the selected frame to the Clipboard.

3. In the Timeline, click Frame 4 to select it as the location for pasting the copied frame.

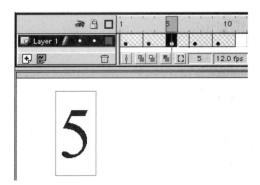

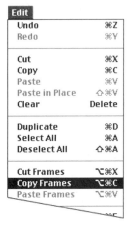

Figure 8.14 To practice moving frames around, create a document in which each keyframe contains a text box with the number of the frame.

Figure 8.15 Flash's Edit menu provides special commands for copying and pasting frames in the Timeline.

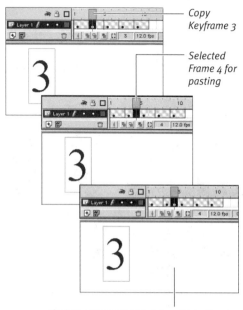

Copy
Keyframe 3

Selected
Frame 4 for
pasting

Flash pastes copied Keyframe 3 into Frame 4

Figure 8.16 When you paste a frame with new content into an in-between frame, Flash converts the frame to a keyframe.

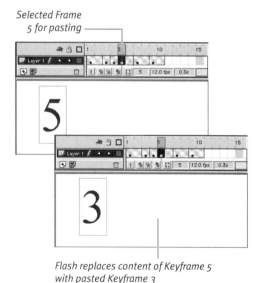

Selected Frame
5 for pasting

*Flash replaces content of Keyframe 5
with pasted Keyframe 3*

Figure 8.17 When you paste a frame with new content into a keyframe, Flash replaces the keyframe's content.

4. From the Edit menu, choose Paste Frames, or press ⌘-Option-V (Mac) or Ctrl-Alt-V (Windows).

Flash pastes the copied frame into Frame 4 (**Figure 8.16**).

5. Paste another copy into Frame 5 (**Figure 8.17**).

Flash replaces the contents of Keyframe 5 with the content of Keyframe 3.

6. Paste another copy into Protoframe 12.

Flash extends the movie to accommodate the pasted frame.

✔ Tips

■ You can copy and paste multiple frames; in step 1 of "To copy and paste a single frame," simply select a range of frames.

■ To copy and paste the content of a keyframe, simply copy an in-between frame that displays that content. When you paste, Flash creates a new keyframe.

■ Warning: Flash always replaces the content of the current frame with the pasted frame (or for multiple-frame pastes, with the first pasted frame). If you're not careful, you might accidentally eat up the content of keyframes you intended to keep. To be safe, always paste frames into in-between frames or blank keyframes. You can always delete an unwanted keyframe separately.

■ You cannot paste frames between back-to-back keyframes in a single step. You must first create an in-between frame (press F5) or a blank keyframe (press F7) between the two, select the new frame, and paste the copied frames into the new frame.

To move frames using drag and drop:

1. In the Timeline of your practice document, select frames 9 through 11.

2. Position the pointer over the selected frames.

   The pointer changes to a hand icon.

3. Click and drag the selected frames.

   Flash further highlights the selection with a rectangle of hatched lines. Flash uses this rectangle to preview the new location for the frames as you drag selected frames in the Timeline. (With the Flash 4 Selection Style active, the pointer changes to an arrow with a small rectangle as you drag frames.)

4. To move the selected frames to the end of your movie, drag the rectangle past the last defined frame and into the area of protoframes, and release the mouse button.

   Flash adds frames to the end of the movie and removes the content from frames 9 through 11 (**Figure 8.18**).

5. To move the selected frames to the beginning of your movie, drag the selected frames to Frame 1 and release the mouse button.

   The dragged frames replace the content of Frames 1 through 4.

✔ Tips

- To drag a copy of selected frames in the Timeline, hold down Option (Mac) or Alt (Windows) as you drag.

- In Flash 5's default selection style, you cannot always relocate individual keyframes where you want them (try dragging Frame 5 of your test file forward in the Timeline, for example). But if you switch to Flash 4 Selection Style, you can drag such frames anywhere in the Timeline.

Selected frames

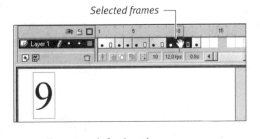

Frames ready for dragging

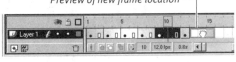

Preview of new frame location

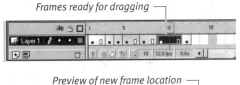

Frames in new location

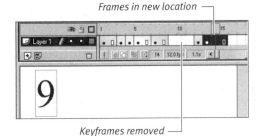

Keyframes removed

Figure 8.18 Flash 4 supports drag and drop of frames in the Timeline.

Content of selected
keyframe

Selected keyframe
is Frame 5

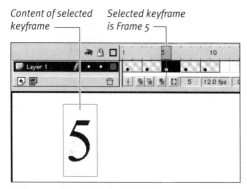

Before clearing the keyframe

Frame 5 displays the content
of the preceding keyframe

Frame 5 becomes an
in-between frame

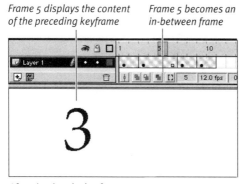

After clearing the keyframe

Figure 8.19 The Clear Keyframe command removes the contents of the selected keyframe from the movie and converts the keyframe to an in-between frame. The Clear Keyframe command doesn't change the overall length of the movie.

Removing Frames

Just as Flash has two kinds of frames and separate commands for creating each type, it has two commands for removing frames: Clear Keyframe and Remove Frames. The commands can be a little confusing at first. To choose the correct command, ask yourself in what sense you want to remove a frame. Do you want to eliminate it from the movie or just remove its status as a keyframe?

Flash's Clear Keyframe command removes keyframe status from a selected frame or range of frames. Clear Keyframe changes keyframes into in-between frames and deletes the keyframes' content from the movie. Clear Keyframe has no effect on the number of frames in the movie.

Remove Frames removes frames (and their content, if they are keyframes) from the movie. Remove Frames reduces the number of frames in the movie.

For the following exercises, use the same practice document you created for working with the exercises in the previous section, "Manipulating Frames in One Layer."

To remove keyframe status from a frame:

1. In the Timeline, select Keyframe 5.

2. From the Insert menu, choose Clear Keyframe, or press Shift-F6 on the keyboard.

   Flash removes the bullet from Frame 5 in the Timeline (indicating that the frame is no longer a keyframe) and removes the graphic element it contained. Frame 5 becomes an in-between frame, displaying the contents of the keyframe at Frame 3 (**Figure 8.19**). The total number of frames in the movie remains the same.

continues on next page

✔ Tip

- You cannot use the Clear Keyframe command to remove content from the first keyframe in a movie. To "clear" the keyframe manually, select it in the Timeline, choose Edit > Select All, and then press Backspace or Delete on the keyboard. Flash removes the graphical elements from the Stage and leaves a blank keyframe in Frame 1.

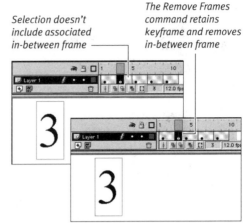

Selection doesn't include associated in-between frame

The Remove Frames command retains keyframe and removes in-between frame

Figure 8.20 The Remove Frames command won't delete a keyframe unless you've selected all of its associated in-between frames (the ones that display the keyframe's content).

The Indelible Keyframe

The Remove Frames command appears to go haywire sometimes. This happens if you try to delete a keyframe without deleting the in-between frames associated with it and if the content of that keyframe differs from the content of the preceding keyframe.

In-between frames don't really have content, but Flash gives them virtual content because they show the graphic elements of the preceding keyframe. Any change in content requires a keyframe. If you try to delete a keyframe without deleting its associated in-between frames, there seems to be a change in content because of the leftover in-between frame. Flash creates a keyframe with the virtual content, as though Flash refuses to get rid of the selected keyframe (**Figure 8.20**).

To avoid the problem, *do one of the following*:

- ◆ Select all associated in-between frames with any keyframes you want to delete.

- ◆ Delete the entire contents of the keyframe before using the Remove Frames command.

- ◆ Use the Clear Keyframe command and then the Remove Frames command to reduce the number of in-between frames.

Selected in-between frame

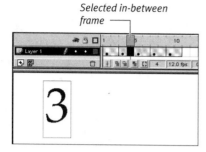

Content originally in
Frame 5 now in Frame 4 — After deleting

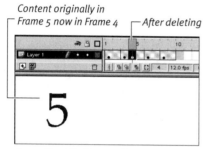

Figure 8.21 The Remove Frames command removes frames from the movie and reduces its length.

To delete a single frame from a movie:

1. With your practice file in its original state (keyframes at 1, 3, 5, 7, and 9), select Frame 4 in the Timeline.

   Frame 4 is an in-between frame associated with the keyframe in Frame 3.

2. From the Insert menu, choose Remove Frames, or press Shift-F5 on the keyboard.

   Flash deletes Frame 4, reducing the overall length of the movie by one frame (**Figure 8.21**).

3. Now select the keyframe at Frame 3 and choose Insert > Remove Frames again.

   Flash deletes the selected keyframe and its content, and reduces the length of the movie by one frame.

✔ Tip

■ Flash doesn't allow you to use Clear Keyframe to remove keyframe status from the first frame of a movie, but you can delete it. If you select all the frames in the movie and choose Insert > Remove Frames, Flash removes all the defined frames in the Timeline, leaving only protoframes. You must add back a keyframe at Frame 1 to place any content in the movie.

To delete a range of frames:

1. Using your practice file, in the Timeline, select frames 3 through 6.

2. From the Insert menu, choose Remove Frames.

Flash removes all the selected frames.

✔ Tips

■ When you have Flash 4 Selection Style active, you can copy the contents of one keyframe to another quickly. Select an in-between frame that displays the contents you want to copy. Drag that frame over the keyframe to which you want to copy the contents. Flash copies the contents of the displayed frame into the keyframe.

■ To avoid the multiple-step process of copying a series of frames, pasting them in a new location, and then deleting the originals, by cutting the frames. With frames selected, choose Edit > Cut Frames, or press ⌘-Option-X (Mac) or Ctrl-Alt-X (Windows). Flash removes the frames and copies them to the Clipboard, ready for pasting.

REMOVING FRAMES

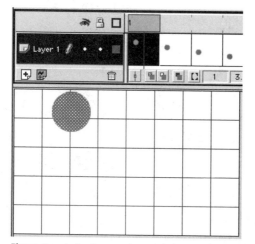

Figure 8.22 In Keyframe 1, draw a circle near the top of the Stage. This circle will become a bouncing ball.

Making a Simple Frame-by-Frame Animation

In traditional cel animation or flip-book animation, you create the illusion of movement by showing a series of images, each slightly different from the rest, simulating snapshots of the movement. When you create each of these drawings and place them in a series of keyframes, that's called *frame-by-frame animation*. When you create only the most crucial snapshots and allow Flash to interpolate the minor changes that take place between those changes, that's called *tweened animation*. You learn more about tweening in Chapters 9 and 10.

A classic example of frame-by-frame animation is a bouncing ball. You can create a crude bouncing ball in just three frames.

To set up the initial keyframe:

1. Create a new Flash document, and name it something like Frame-by-Frame Bounce.

Flash by default creates a document with one layer and a keyframe at Frame 1. Choose View > Grid > Show Grids to help you reposition your graphics in this exercise.

2. In the Timeline, select Frame 1.

Use the Frame View pop-up menu to set the Timeline to Preview in Context mode. This makes it easy to keep track of what you do in the example.

3. In the Toolbox, select the oval tool.

4. Set Stroke color to None.

5. Near the top of the Stage, draw a circle (**Figure 8.22**).

This circle will be your ball. Make it fairly large.

To create the second keyframe:

1. In the Timeline, select Frame 2.

2. Choose Insert > Keyframe.

Flash creates a keyframe in Frame 2 that duplicates your ball from Frame 1.

3. In Frame 2, select the ball and reposition it at the bottom of the Stage (**Figure 8.23**).

To create the third keyframe:

1. In the Timeline, select Frame 3.

2. Choose Insert > Keyframe.

Flash creates a keyframe in Frame 3 that duplicates your ball from Frame 2.

3. In Frame 3, select the ball and reposition it in the middle of the Stage (**Figure 8.24**).

That's it. Believe it or not, you have just created all the content you need to animate a bouncing ball. To see how it works, in the Timeline, click Frames 1, 2, and 3 in turn. As Flash changes the content of the Stage at each click, you see a very crude animation.

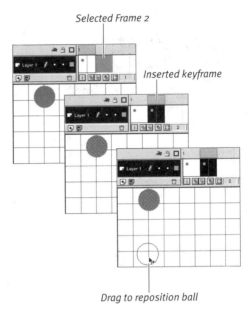

Selected Frame 2

Inserted keyframe

Drag to reposition ball

Figure 8.23 Use the Insert > Keyframe command to duplicate the ball from Frame 1 in Frame 2. You can then drag the ball to reposition it.

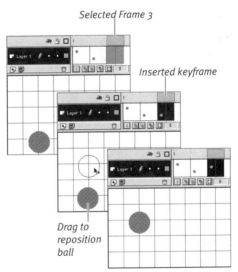

Selected Frame 3

Inserted keyframe

Drag to reposition ball

Figure 8.24 Use the Insert > Keyframe command to duplicate the ball from Frame 2 in Frame 3. Drag the ball to reposition it again.

MAKING A SIMPLE FRAME-BY-FRAME ANIMATION

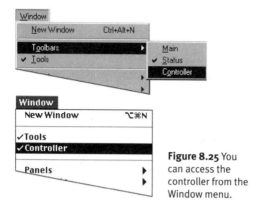

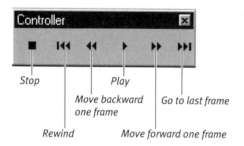

Figure 8.25 You can access the controller from the Window menu.

Stop

Play

Move backward one frame

Go to last frame

Rewind

Move forward one frame

Figure 8.26 The Controller window contains VCR-style buttons for controlling Flash movies.

Previewing the Action

Though you can click each frame to preview a movie, Flash provides more-sophisticated ways to see your animation. The Controller window offers VCR-style playback buttons. The Control menu has commands for playback. You can also have Flash export the file and open it for you in Flash Player via the Test Movie command.

To use the controller:

1. From the Window menu, choose Controller (Mac) or Toolbars > Controller (Windows) (**Figure 8.25**).

Flash opens a window containing standard VCR-style buttons.

2. In the Controller window, click the button for the command you want to use (**Figure 8.26**).

✔ Tip

■ The Control menu in the main menu bar duplicates most of the Controller's functions. The Controller window is the only place where you'll find the go-to-last-frame command, however.

PREVIEWING THE ACTION

To step sequentially through frames:

1. In the Timeline, select Frame 1.

2. From the Control menu (**Figure 8.27**), choose Step Forward, or press the greater-than key (>).
   Flash moves to the following frame.

3. From the Control menu, choose Step Backward, or press the less-than key (<).
   Flash moves to the preceding frame.

✔ Tip

■ You can *scrub* (scroll quickly back and forth) through the movie. Drag the play-head backward or forward through the frames in the Timeline. Flash displays the content of each frame as the playhead moves through it.

To play through all frames in the Flash editor:

◆ To play through the frames once, from the Control menu choose Play, or press Enter.
   Flash displays each frame in turn, starting with the current frame and running through the end of the movie. The Play command in the Control menu changes to a Stop command, which you can use to stop playback at any time.

✔ Tip

■ To play through the frames repeatedly, from the Control menu, choose Loop Playback. Now whenever you issue a Play command, Flash plays the movie repeat-edly until you issue a Stop command.

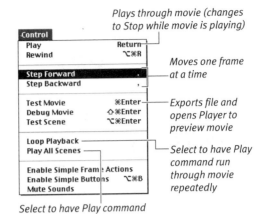

Plays through movie (changes to Stop while movie is playing)

Moves one frame at a time

Exports file and opens Player to preview movie

Select to have Play command run through movie repeatedly

Select to have Play command run through all scenes

Figure 8.27 The Control menu offers commands for previewing your Flash movie.

To play frames in Flash Player:

◆ Choose Control > Test Movie.

Flash exports your movie to a Flash Player (.swf) file and opens it in Flash Player. Flash stores the .swf file live at the same hierarchical level of your system as the original Flash file. The .swf file has the same name as the original, except that Flash appends the .swf extension to it.

✔ Tip

■ Warning: When you choose Control > Test Movie, Flash doesn't ask whether you want to replace an earlier version of the file that has the same name; it just replaces the file. The downside to that convention is that Flash may replace a file you don't intend it to. When you export a Flash movie yourself, it's tempting just to add the .swf extension to the original file name. Unfortunately, the Test Movie command will replace that file if it's in the same folder as the original movie. To be safe, always change the name of your movie when you export it yourself.

Smoothing the Animation by Adding Keyframes

The three-frame bouncing ball you created in the preceding exercise is crude. It's herky and jerky and much too fast. To smooth out the movement, you need to create more snapshots that define the ball's position in the air as it moves up and down. This means adding more keyframes and repositioning the ball slightly in each one.

In the preceding exercise, the ball moves from the top of the stage to the bottom in one step. In the following exercise, you expand that first bounce movement to three steps.

To add keyframes within an existing animation:

1. In the Timeline of the three-frame bouncing ball animation, select Frame 1.

2. Choose Insert > Frame; then choose Insert > Frame again.

   Flash creates new in-between frames at frames 2 and 3 and relocates the keyframes that show the ball at the bottom and middle of the stage to frames 4 and 5 (**Figure 8.28**).

3. In the Timeline, select frames 2 and 3.

4. Choose Modify > Frames > Convert to Key Frames.

   Flash converts the in-between frames to keyframes that duplicate the content of Keyframe 1 (**Figure 8.29**).

New in-between frames

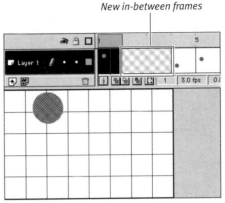

Figure 8.28 With Frame 1 selected, invoking the Insert Keyframe command twice inserts two new in-between frames after the first frame and pushes the original Keyframe 2 (the ball at the bottom of the Stage) to Frame 4.

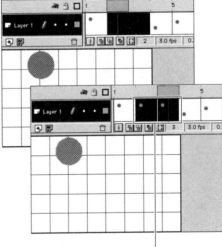

Duplicates of Keyframe 1

Figure 8.29 Modify > Frames > Convert to Keyframes changes the in-between frames to keyframes containing the content of the preceding keyframe.

Frames previewed in context

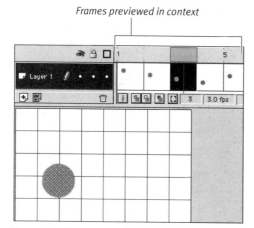

Figure 8.30 You can reposition the ball in Keyframes 2 and 3 to make the first bounce smoother.

4. In the Timeline, select Frame 2 and reposition the ball on the Stage.

You can use the grid line to help you visualize where to place the ball; you want to move it about a third of the distance between the top and bottom of the Stage.

5. In the Timeline, select Frame 3 and reposition the ball on the Stage (**Figure 8.30**).

Position the ball about two-thirds of the distance between the top and bottom of the Stage.

6. Preview the animation, using any of the methods described in the preceding section.

The initial bounce movement is smoother. You can repeat these steps to add even more frames with incremental movement to the first half of the bounce. You can also add frames to make the second half of the bounce smoother.

The Pitfall of Frame-by-Frame Animation

With frame-by-frame animation, the more frames you add, the smaller you can make the differences between frames and the smoother the action will be. Adding keyframes, however, also adds to your final movie's file size. Your goal is to strike a happy medium.

SMOOTHING THE ANIMATION BY ADDING KEYFRAMES

Using Onion Skinning

In the preceding section, you repositioned a circle to try to create smooth incremental movement for a bouncing ball. To make this task easier, Flash's onion-skinning feature lets you see the circle in context with the circles in surrounding frames.

Onion skinning displays dimmed or outline versions of the content on surrounding frames. You determine how many of the surrounding frames Flash displays. The buttons for turning on and off the various types of onion skinning appear at the bottom of the Timeline, in the Timeline's status bar.

To turn on onion skinning:

◆ In the status bar of the Timeline, click the Onion Skin button.

The content of all the frames included in the onion-skin markers appears in a dimmed form (**Figure 8.31**). You cannot edit the dimmed objects—only the full-color graphics on the current frame.

To turn on outline onion skinning:

◆ In the status bar of the Timeline, click the Onion Skin Outlines button.

The content of all the frames included in the onion-skin markers appears in outline form (**Figure 8.32**). You cannot edit the outline graphics —only the solid graphics that appear in the current frame.

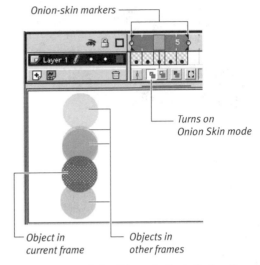

Onion-skin markers

Turns on Onion Skin mode

Object in current frame

Objects in other frames

Figure 8.31 In Onion Skin mode, Flash displays the content of multiple frames but dims everything that's not on the current frame. The onion-skin markers in the Timeline indicate how many frames appear at once.

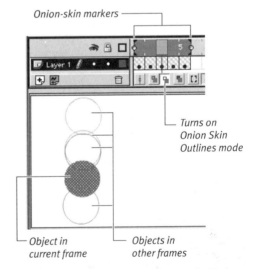

Onion-skin markers

Turns on Onion Skin Outlines mode

Object in current frame

Objects in other frames

Figure 8.32 In Onion Skin Outlines mode, Flash displays the content of multiple frames, but it uses outlines for everything that's not in the current frame. Notice that two of the outlines appear very close together in this example of the bouncing ball. Using that visual cue, you can reposition the ball in Frame 4 to make the spacing (and, thereby, the movement) more even.

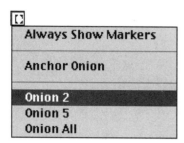

Figure 8.33 The Modify Onion Markers pop-up menu.

To adjust the number of frames included in onion skinning:

1. In the Timeline, click the Modify Onion Markers button.

A pop-up menu appears, containing commands for setting the way the onion-skin markers work (**Figure 8.33**).

2. To see frames on either side of the current frame, *do one of the following:*

◆ To see two frames on either side of the current frame, choose Onion 2.

◆ To see five frames on either side of the current frame, choose Onion 5.

◆ To see all the frames in the movie, choose Onion All.

Flash moves the onion-skin markers around in the Timeline as you move the playhead. Flash always includes onion skins (either solid or outline) for objects in the selected number of frames before the current frame and after it.

✔ Tip

■ Dragging an onion-skin marker in the Timeline header temporarily changes the number of frames visible as onion skins. When you move the playhead to a new frame, Flash resumes showing the number of frames that you had selected.

To display onion skins for a fixed set of frames:

◆ From the Modify Onion Markers menu, choose Anchor Onion.

Flash stops moving the onion-skin markers when you move the playhead and simply displays as onion skins the frames currently within the markers. As long as you keep the playhead inside the anchored range, that set of frames stays in the onion-skin mode. This feature lets you work on frames within the set without constantly repositioning the onion-skin markers.

Editing Multiple Frames

If you decide to change the location of an animated element, you must change the element's location in every keyframe in which it appears. Repositioning the items one frame at a time is not only tedious but also dangerous. You might forget one frame, and you could easily get the animated elements out of alignment. Flash solves this problem by letting you move elements in multiple frames simultaneously. The same markers that indicate the frames to include in onion skinning indicate the frames you are allowed to edit simultaneously in Edit Multiple Frames mode.

To relocate animated graphics on the Stage:

1. Open your frame-by-frame animation of a bouncing ball.

2. In the status bar, choose Edit Multiple Frames (**Figure 8.34**).

   Flash displays all graphics in all frames within the onion-skin markers and makes them editable.

3. From the Modify Onion Markers menu, choose Onion All.

   You can now see the ball at each stage of its bounce, and you can edit each of these stages.

4. In the Toolbox, select the arrow tool.

5. Draw a selection rectangle that includes all the visible balls on the Stage (**Figure 8.35**).

   Flash selects them all.

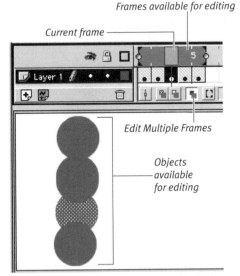

Frames available for editing

Current frame

Edit Multiple Frames

Objects available for editing

Figure 8.34 In Edit Multiple Frames mode, Flash displays and makes editable all the graphics in the frames that the onion-skin markers indicate. This features makes it possible to move an animated graphic to a new location in every keyframe at the same time.

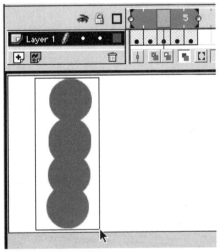

Figure 8.35 In Edit Multiple Frames mode, you can use a selection rectangle to select graphics in any of the frames enclosed in the onion-skin markers.

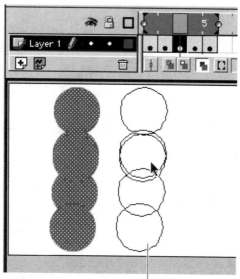

Outline previews new location —
    as you drag selected objects

Figure 8.36 In Edit Multiple Frames mode, you can relocate an animated graphic completely, moving it in every keyframe with one action.

Outline mode toggle

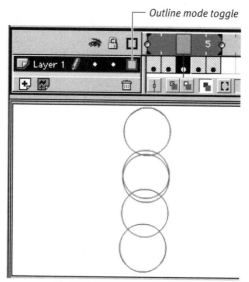

Figure 8.37 Select Outline mode to make it easier to work with graphics in multiple frames.

6. Drag the selection to the opposite side of the Stage (**Figure 8.36**).

With just a few steps, you've relocated the bouncing ball. (Imagine how much more work it would have been to select each frame separately, move the ball for that frame, select the next frame, line the balls up precisely in the new location, and so on.)

✔ Tip

■ When you select Edit Multiple Frames, Flash no longer displays onion skinning. If you find it confusing to view solid objects in multiple frames, turn on Outline view in the layer-properties section of the Timeline (**Figure 8.37**).

Understanding Frame Rate

The illusion of animation relies on the human brain's ability to fill in gaps in continuity. When we see a series of images in very quick succession, our brain perceives a continuous moving image. In animation, you must display the sequence of images fast enough to convince the brain that it's looking at a single image.

Frame rate controls how fast Flash delivers the images. If the images come too fast, the movie turns into a blur. Slow delivery too much, and your viewers start perceiving each frame as a separate image; then the movement seems jerky. In addition, when you're working in Flash, you're most likely planning to deliver the movie over the Web, and you may not be able to get the precise control you'd like to have to deliver a fast frame rate. The standard rate for film is 24 frames per second (fps). For animation that's going out over the Web, 12 fps is a good setting.

In Flash, you can set only one frame rate for the entire movie. You set the frame rate in the Movie Properties dialog box.

To set the frame rate:

1. To access the Movie Properties dialog box, *do one of the following:*
   - From the Modify menu, choose Movie, or press ⌘-M (Mac) or Ctrl-M (Windows).
   - In the Timeline's status bar, double-click the frame-rate box (**Figure 8.38**).

2. In the Movie Properties dialog box, enter a value in the Frame Rate field (**Figure 8.39**).

3. Click OK.

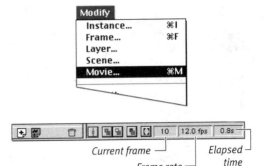

Current frame — Frame rate — Elapsed time

Figure 8.38 To call up the Movie Properties dialog box, choose Modify > Movie (top) or double-click the frame-rate box in the Timeline's status bar (bottom).

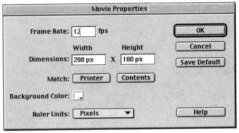

Figure 8.39 Enter a new value in the Frame Rate field. Flash's default frame rate is 12 fps.

Varying the Speed of Animations

Though the frame rate for a movie is constant, you can make any particular bit of animation go faster or slower by changing the number of frames it takes to complete the action. You can lengthen a portion of an animation by adding more keyframes or by adding in-between frames. In the bouncing-ball example, you might have the ball drop down slowly— say, over the space of five frames—but have it rebound more quickly—over the space of three frames, for example. To make the smoothest animation, each of those keyframes would show the ball in a slightly different position. Adding keyframes, however, increases file size. Sometimes, you can get away with simply adding in-between frames to slow the action. In-between frames add little to the exported movie's file size.

To add in-between frames:

1. Open (or create) a five-frame bouncing-ball movie.

   Frame 1 is a keyframe showing the ball at the top of the Stage, Frames 2 and 3 are keyframes showing the ball at two places in its descent, Frame 4 shows the ball at the bottom of the Stage, and Frame 5 shows the ball bouncing halfway back up. (For step-by-step instructions, see the exercises in "Smoothing the Animation by Adding Keyframes" earlier in this chapter.)

2. From the File menu, choose Save As, and make a copy of the file.

   Give the file a distinguishing name, such as Bounce Slower.

continues on next page

VARYING THE SPEED OF ANIMATIONS

3. In the copy's Timeline, select Frame 1.

4. From the Insert menu, choose Frame (or press F5 on the keyboard).

Flash inserts an in-between frame at Frame 2 and pushes the keyframe that was there to Frame 3 (**Figure 8.40**).

5. Repeat steps 3 and 4 for the second and third keyframes in the movie.

You wind up with keyframes in frames 1, 3, 5, 7, and 8 (**Figure 8.41**).

6. From the Control menu, choose Test Movie.

Flash exports the movie to a .swf file and opens it in Flash Player. You can see that the action in the movie with added in-between frames feels different from the action in the one in which one keyframe directly follows another.

✔ Tip

■ Keep in mind that this example serves to illustrate a process. In most animations, you would not want to overuse this technique. If you simply add many in-between frames, you'll slow the action too much and destroy the illusion of movement.

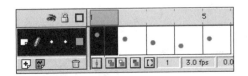

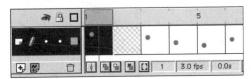

Figure 8.40 Select a frame and press F5 to insert an in-between frame directly after it (bottom).

Figure 8.41 With in-between frames separating the initial keyframes, the first part of the animation moves at a slower pace than the second.

ANIMATION WITH MOTION TWEENING

Frame-by-frame animation has two draw-backs: First, it's labor-intensive; second, it creates large files. Macromedia Flash offers a way to mitigate both problems with a process called *tweening*. In Chapter 8, you created a three-frame animation of a bouncing ball by changing the position of the ball graphic in each of the three keyframes. Then you learned how to stretch out the animation by adding in-between frames that simply repeated the contents of the preceding keyframe. With tweening, you create similar keyframes, but Flash breaks the keyframe changes into multiple steps and displays them in the in-between frames.

To tween a graphic, Flash creates a series of incremental changes to that graphic; these changes are simple enough that Flash can describe them mathematically. Flash performs two types of tweening: motion tweening and shape tweening. This chapter covers motion tweening; Chapter 10 covers shape tweening.

Both types of tweening follow the same basic pattern. You give Flash the beginning and end of the sequence by placing graphic elements in keyframes. You tell Flash to spread the change out over a certain number of steps by placing that number of in-between frames between the keyframes. Flash creates a series of images with incremental changes that accomplish the action in the desired number of frames.

Creating a Bouncing Ball with Motion Tweening

Flash provides a special command, Create Motion Tween, that helps you through the steps of making a motion tween. The Create Motion Tween command makes sure that you have symbols in your tweens and a keyframe at both the beginning and end of the tween sequence.

To use the Create Motion Tween command:

1. Create a new Flash document, and name it something like Motion Tween Bounce. By default, Flash creates a document with one layer and a keyframe at Frame 1.

2. In the Timeline, select Frame 1.

3. In the Toolbox, choose the oval tool and set the stroke to None.

4. Near the top of the Stage, draw a circle. This circle will be the ball. Make it fairly large.

Motion Tweening or Shape Tweening?

The key to deciding whether to use motion tweening or shape tweening is to ask yourself whether you could make this change via a dialog box or a panel. If the answer is yes, Flash can make the change with motion tweening. If the answer is no—if the change requires redrawing the shape of a vector object—Flash must use shape tweening.

Another important distinction between motion tweening and shape tweening is that motion tweening works only on groups and symbols and shape tweening works only on editable shapes. Sometimes, you can arrive at the same tweening effect with either a motion tween or a shape tween. (In fact, you'll do that with the bouncing-ball example in the following section and in the next chapter.)

If you want to tween a multipart graphic— say, a robot constructed of many shapes— and you don't want to tween each shape separately, you'll need to make that graphic a group or symbol. When the graphic is a symbol, you can tween it only with motion tweening. If you want to create morphing effects—transforming a pumpkin into a magic coach, for example—you must use shape tweening. In addition, if you want Flash to move a tweened graphic around the Stage along a curving path (as opposed to a straight line), you must use motion tweening.

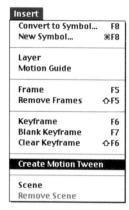

Figure 9.1 Choose Insert > Create Motion Tween menu to start the tweeing process.

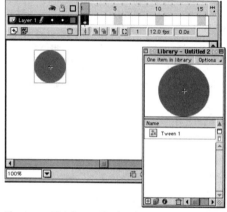

Figure 9.2 The Create Motion Tween command turns an editable shape on the Stage in the selected frame into a symbol and names the symbol Tween 1, Tween 2, and so on.

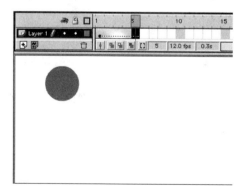

Figure 9.3 Adding frames to the motion tween results in a temporarily broken tween, indicated by the dashed line in the Timeline.

5. With Frame 1 still selected, from the Insert menu, choose Create Motion Tween (**Figure 9.1**).

Flash creates a symbol from the graphics on the Stage. Flash gives the symbol a default name based on the number of tweening graphics already created in the movie. In this case, Flash turns the ball into a symbol named Tween 1 (**Figure 9.2**). You can rename the symbol by using the techniques described in Chapter 6.

6. In the Timeline, select Frame 5.

7. Choose Insert > Frame.

Flash adds frames containing a dotted line (**Figure 9.3**). The dotted line indicates that these frames are set to contain a motion tween but something is wrong and Flash cannot complete the tween. In this case, the keyframe that describes where the ball should be at the end of this animation sequence is missing.

continues on next page

CREATING A BOUNCING BALL WITH MOTION TWEENING

8. In Frame 5, move the circle to the bottom of the Stage to create the downward bounce of the ball.

Flash creates a keyframe in Frame 5 with the symbol located at the bottom of the Stage. Flash then updates the Timeline to give you information about the tween. In the in-between frames that contain the motion tween (**Figure 9.4**), Flash replaces the dotted line with an arrow, indicating that tweening takes place in these frames. These in-between frames are still "empty," in the sense that they have no content on the Stage that you can edit. They no longer display the content of the preceding keyframe, but they display the incrementally changed content that Flash creates.

9. In the Timeline, select Frame 10.

10. Choose Insert > Frame.

Flash extends the motion-tween tinting to Frame 10. A dotted line indicating an incomplete tween appears in Frames 6 through 10.

11. In Frame 10, move the circle to the top of the Stage to create the upward bounce of the ball.

Flash creates a new keyframe to contain the changed content and puts the tweening arrow over the in-between frames (**Figure 9.5**).

12. From the Control menu, choose Play to preview the animation.

You've created another version of the simple bouncing ball. As in the frame-by-frame animation you created in Chapter 8, you created new content for just three frames, yet this tweened animation is much smoother than the three-keyframe animation you created with the frame-by-frame technique. That's because you've actually created a 10-frame animation;

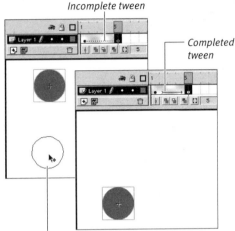

Incomplete tween

Completed tween

Change to content on a frame within the incomplete tween

Figure 9.4 After you create a motion tween over a range of frames, repositioning the content of a frame causes Flash to create a new keyframe in the current frame and complete the tween.

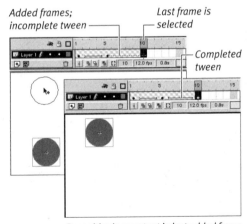

Added frames; incomplete tween

Last frame is selected

Completed tween

Repositioning content in last added frame

Figure 9.5 Adding frames to the end of a motion tween extends the tween. Repositioning the ball in the last frame of the tween completes the tween. Flash creates a new keyframe for the repositioned ball.

Range of frames being displayed as onion skins

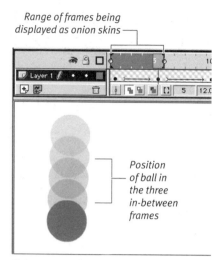

Position of ball in the three in-between frames

Figure 9.6 Turn on onion skinning to preview the positions of the tweened object on the Stage.

Which Frames Contain Tweening?

As your road map of the movie, the Timeline provides visual cues about which frames contain tweens. Flash draws an arrow across a series of frames to indicate that those frames contain a tween.

Flash color-codes frames in the Timeline to distinguish motion tweens from shape tweens. With Tinted Frames active (choose it from the Frame View pop-up menu at the end of the Timeline), Flash applies a light bluish-purple shade to the frames that contain a motion tween. If Tinted Frames is inactive, the frames are white, but Flash changes the keyframe bullets and the arrow that indicates the presence of a tween from black to red. Flash indicates shape tweens by tinting frames light green (if Tinted Frames is active) or by changing the keyframe bullets and tweening arrow to light green (if Tinted Frames is inactive).

you're just letting Flash do the work of repositioning the ball in the in-between frames.

✔ Tips

■ When you choose Preview or Preview in Context from the Frame View pop-up menu (at the end of the Timeline) you can't see the incremental steps Flash creates for the tween. But if you turn on onion skinning, you can see all the in-between frames in position on the Stage (**Figure 9.6**).

■ If you choose Insert > Keyframe in steps 7 and 10 of the preceding exercise, you will not see the broken tween line in the Timeline. That's because that command duplicates the content of the preceding keyframe and Flash considers the tween to be complete when there is an ending keyframe with content. Nevertheless, your tween will still seem to be broken until you go into the ending keyframe of the sequence and make a change to its content.

Setting the Tween Property

To have a working motion tween, you need three things: a beginning keyframe containing a group or a symbol, in-between frames defined as motion tweens, and an ending keyframe containing the same group or symbol to which you've made some kind of change.

The Create Motion Tween command helps ensure that you have all the ingredients in the correct places. You can also create motion tweens manually by setting up the beginning and ending keyframes and then defining the frame sequence as a motion tween in the Frame panel.

To access the Frame panel:

◆ If the Frame panel is not currently open, from the Window menu, choose Panels > Frame.

The Frame panel appears (**Figure 9.7**).

✔ Tip

■ If you place the Frame panel in its own window, you can access it quickly by double-clicking any frame in the Timeline.

You can use motion tweening to create the same bouncing ball as in the preceding exercise but in a slightly different way.

To define motion tweens via the Frame panel:

1. Create a new document with a ball near the top of the Stage in Frame 1.

   (For more detailed instructions, follow steps 1 through 4 in the preceding exercises.)

2. Select the ball, and from the Modify menu, choose Group.

   Flash can make motion tweens only from groups or symbols. The Create Motion Tween command creates a symbol if

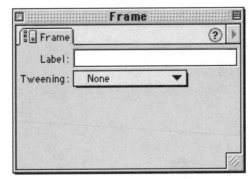

Figure 9.7 Choose Window > Panels > Frame to access the Frame panel.

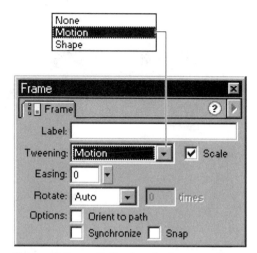

Figure 9.8 Choose Motion from the Frame panel's Tweening menu to access the parameters for motion tweens.

you use it on editable shapes. When you define the motion tween yourself, you must create the group or symbol yourself.

3. In the Timeline, select Frame 5, and choose Insert > Keyframe.

The Insert > Keyframe command makes a new keyframe that contains the same elements as the preceding keyframe.

4. Select Frame 10, and choose Insert > Keyframe.

5. Select Frame 5, and drag the ball to the bottom of the Stage.

You have just re-created the same keyframes you wound up with in the preceding exercise: In Frame 1, the ball is at the top of its bounce; in Frame 5, the ball is at the bottom of its bounce; and in Frame 10, the ball is back up at the top.

6. To define the motion tween for the first half of the ball's bounce, in the Timeline, select any of the frames in the first keyframe unit (frames 1, 2, 3, or 4).

Note that Flash automatically selects the ball graphic. When you define a motion tween, the graphic to be tweened must be selected.

7. From the Frame panel's Tweening menu, choose Motion.

The parameters for the motion tween appear (**Figure 9.8**). You learn more about using these parameters in the following exercises.

continues on next page

Flash defines frames 1 through 4 as a motion tween. The tweening arrow and color coding appear in the Timeline, just as they do when you use the Create Motion Tween command.

8. To define the motion tween for the second half of the ball's bounce, in the Timeline, select any of the frames in the second keyframe unit (frame 5, 6, 7, 8, or 9).

9. Repeat steps 6 and 7.

    Flash creates the second half of the ball's bounce with another motion tween (**Figure 9.9**). Note that in this exercise, you never see the broken line indicating an incomplete tween. That's because you already defined the changes to the ball in the three keyframes before you told Flash to do the tweening.

✔ Tips

■ You can access the Frame panel from the contextual menu for frames. Control-click (Mac) or right-click (Windows) a frame in the Timeline to bring up the contextual menu.

■ If you're having difficulty selecting the proper frames for defining a motion tween, position the playhead at the frame number you want; then use the arrow tool to select the object on the Stage. Flash selects the frame in the Timeline as well.

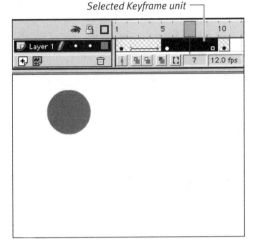

Selected Keyframe unit

Motion tween for frames 5 through 9

Ball in position for tweening the bounce

Figure 9.9 Defining a motion tween via the Frame panel for Frame 7 creates a motion tween that spans the entire Keyframe 5 unit (Frames 5 through 9).

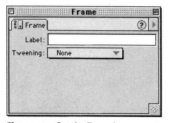

Figure 9.10 Set the Tweening property of a frame to None to end a series of tweens.

Ending a Motion Tween

When you use the Create Motion Tween command as described in the first exercise of this chapter, the final frame (Keyframe 10) has tween status. If you select that frame and check the Frame panel, you can see that the Tweening property is set to Motion. That property tells Flash to create a motion tween between Keyframe 10 and the next keyframe. If you add new frames after Keyframe 10, Flash defines the new frames as motion tweens, too. To end a motion-tween sequence, you must set Tweening to None in the Frame panel.

When you create a motion tween as described in the second exercise in this chapter, only the first keyframe and the in-between frames have tween status. The final keyframe has a Tweening property of None. Any frames you add to the end of that sequence will have the default Tweening property of None.

To remove tween status from a frame:

1. Create a new Flash document, and use the Create Motion Tween command to set up a series of tween sequences as you did in the first exercise in this chapter.

2. In the Timeline, select the last keyframe in the series of tweens.

   Flash tweens *from* one keyframe *up to* the next. Removing tween status from the final keyframe doesn't affect the tween. Removing tween status from any frame in the tweened keyframe unit, however, kills the tween.

3. From the Frame panel's Tweening menu, choose None (**Figure 9.10**).

   Flash removes the color coding that indicates tweening from the selected frame.

Adding Keyframes to Motion Tweens

After you create a motion tween (either with the Create Motion Tween command or via the Frame panel), Flash creates new keyframes for you when you reposition a tweened object in an in-between frame. You can also add new keyframes by using the Insert > Keyframe command.

To add new keyframes to a motion tween:

1. Create a 10-frame motion tween of a bouncing ball, following the steps in the one of the preceding two exercises.

2. In the Timeline, select Frame 3.

   On the Stage, you see the ball in one of the in-between positions Flash created.

3. In the Toolbox, select the arrow tool.

4. Drag the ball to a new position—slightly to the right of its current position, for example.

   Flash inserts a new keyframe at Frame 3 and splits the preceding five-frame tween into separate tweens (**Figure 9.11**).

In selected frame, ball appears in its tweened position

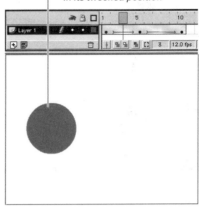

Repositioning the ball creates a new keyframe

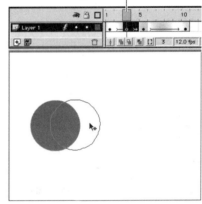

Turn on onion skinning

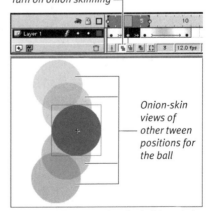

Onion-skin views of other tween positions for the ball

Figure 9.11 Repositioning the ball in an in-between frame that's part of a tween creates a new keyframe and a revision of the tweened frames.

Figure 9.12 You can change the color of a symbol rather than its position in a motion tween. Flash creates transitional colors for each in-between frame.

Animating Color Effects

Tweening is not just about changing the position of an item on the Stage. You can also tween changes to the color of symbol instances.

To change a symbol's color over time:

1. Create a new Flash document.

2. On the Stage, place a symbol in Frame 1.

3. In the Timeline, select Frame 5, and choose Insert > Keyframe.

   Flash duplicates the contents of Frame 1 in a new keyframe.

4. With Frame 5 as the current frame, select the symbol and change its color.

   (To change the color of a selected symbol, choose Modify > Instance or set new parameters in the Effect panel. For detailed instructions on editing symbols, see Chapter 6.)

5. Select any of the frames in the first keyframe unit (frames 1, 2, 3, or 4), and choose Insert > Create Motion Tween.

   Flash recolors the object in three transitional steps, one for each in-between frame (**Figure 9.12**).

✔ Tip

■ You can tween a change in an object's transparency to make that object appear to fade in or out.

Animating Graphics That Change Size

Flash can tween changes to the size of a graphic. To tween graphics that grow or shrink, you must check the Scale checkbox in the Frame panel.

To tween a growing and shrinking graphic:

1. Create a new Flash document.

2. On the Stage, create a new object in Frame 1.

3. With Frame 1 selected, choose Insert > Create Motion Tween.

    Flash turns your graphic into a symbol.

4. To create a keyframe that defines the end of a growing sequence, in the Timeline, select Frame 5 and choose Insert > Keyframe.

    Flash duplicates the symbol from Frame 1 in the new keyframe. The motion-tween arrow and color coding now appear in Frames 2 through 4.

5. With Frame 5 as the current frame, select your graphic and make it bigger.

    (For detailed instructions on resizing graphics, see Chapter 3.)

6. In the Timeline, select any of the frames in the first keyframe unit (Frame 1, 2, 3, or 4).

7. In the Frame panel, make sure that the Tweening property is set to Motion.

8. Check the Scale checkbox.

    Flash increases the size of your graphic in equal steps from Frame 1 to Frame 5 (**Figure 9.13**).

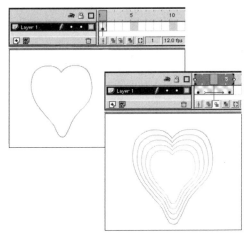

Figure 9.13 To tween a growing graphic, make the graphic in the end keyframe of the sequence larger than the graphic in the first keyframe of the sequence.

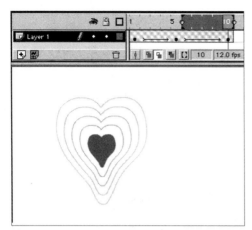

Figure 9.14 To tween a shrinking graphic, make it smaller in the end keyframe of the sequence. Turn on onion-skin mode to see the size of the graphic Flash creates for each in-between frame.

9. To add an ending keyframe for a shrinking sequence, in the Timeline, select Frame 10, and choose Insert > Keyframe.

Flash duplicates the symbol from Frame 5 in the new keyframe. The motion-tween arrow and color coding now appear in Frames 6 through 9. All the motion-tween parameters you set in the Frame panel continue in force.

10. With Frame 10 as the current frame, select your graphic and make it smaller.

Flash creates a tween that shrinks your graphic in five equal steps (**Figure 9.14**).

✔ Tip

■ As long as you don't change the settings in the Frame panel, the Scale checkbox remains checked, and Flash updates the tween any time you make changes to one of the keyframes in this series. You don't even have to have the Frame panel open to fine-tune the size of your scaling graphic.

Rotating and Spinning Graphics

You cannot create tweens of rotating and spinning graphics quite as simply as you create the types of tweens presented in the preceding exercises. That's because you can't describe rotation accurately with just two keyframes.

Imagine, for example, trying to rotate the pointer of a compass 180 degrees so that it turns from pointing north to pointing south. The initial keyframe contains the pointer pointing up; the ending keyframe contains the pointer pointing down. But how should the pointer move to reach that position?

Flash has three choices: rotate the pointer clockwise, rotate it counterclockwise, or simply flip it upside down. Trying to describe the pointer spinning all the way around the compass in just two keyframes would be even less informative, because the beginning and ending keyframes would be identical.

To clarify the motion, you could create a series of keyframes rotating the pointer a few degrees in each one. That method is tedious, however, and adds to the file size of the final exported movie. Fortunately, Flash's Frame panel lets you provide extra information about tweens so that Flash can create rotational tweens with just two keyframes.

To rotate a graphic less than 360 degrees:

1. Create a new Flash document.

2. On the Stage, in Frame 1, create a new graphic (or place a symbol instance).
   Be sure to use something that will look different at various stages of its rotation.

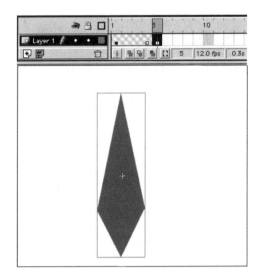

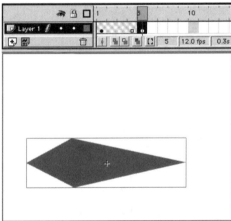

Figure 9.15 To prepare a rotational tween, rotate the item to be tweened.

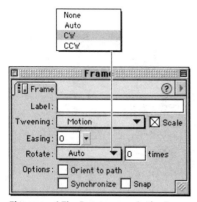

Figure 9.16 The Rotate menu in the Frame panel lets you tell Flash the direction in which to rotate a tweened object.

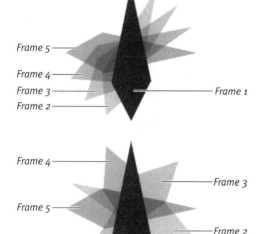

Figure 9.17 To create a tween that involves rotation, you can specify the direction of the rotation as clockwise or counterclockwise. You can also let Flash pick the direction that involves the smallest change, which allows Flash to create the smoothest motion. Compare the degree of change in each frame between rotating an arrow clockwise from 3 o'clock to 6 o'clock (top) versus rotating the arrow counterclockwise to reach the same position (bottom).

3. If you've created a new grahic, select it and then choose Modify > Group or Insert > Convert to Symbol.

Flash can create motion tweens only from grouped items or from symbols.

4. In the Timeline, select Frame 5, and choose Insert > Keyframe.

Flash duplicates the symbol from Frame 1 in the new keyframe.

5. On the Stage, in Frame 5, rotate your graphic 90 degrees in a clockwise direction (**Figure 9.15**).

(For detailed instructions on rotating objects, see Chapter 3.)

6. In the Timeline, select any of the frames in the first keyframe unit (Frame 1, 2, 3, or 4).

7. From the Frame panel's Tweening menu, choose Motion.

The parameters for motion tweening appear in the panel.

8. From the Rotate menu (**Figure 9.16**), *choose one of the following options:*

- ◆ To rotate the graphic in the direction that requires the smallest movement, choose Auto (**Figure 9.17**).
- ◆ To rotate the graphic clockwise, choose CW.
- ◆ To rotate the graphic counterclockwise, choose CCW.

Flash tweens the graphic so that it rotates around its center point. Each in-between frame shows the graphic rotated a little more.

ROTATING AND SPINNING GRAPHICS

To spin a graphic:

1. Follow steps 1 through 4 in the preceding exercise to create a five-frame movie with identical keyframes in Frame 1 and Frame 5.

   You don't need to reposition your graphic, because the beginning frame and end frame of a 360-degree spin should look exactly the same.

2. In the Timeline, select any of the frames in the first keyframe unit (Frame 1, 2, 3, or 4).

3. From the Frame panel's Tweening menu, choose Motion.

   The parameters for motion tweening appear in the panel.

4. From the Rotate menu, choose a direction of rotation.

5. In the Rotate field, to the right of the Rotate menu, enter the number of rotations that you want to use (**Figure 9.18**).

   The value that you enter in the Rotate field determines how Flash tweens the graphic. Flash creates new positions for the graphic to rotate it completely in the given number of in-between frames. Flash tweens the graphic differently depending on the number of rotations you choose (**Figure 9.19**).

   Flash tweens the item so that it spins the number of times you indicated over the span of frames that you defined as the motion tween.

Enter the number of rotations

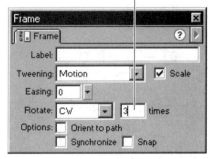

Figure 9.18 In the Frame panel, you can set the number of times a tweened item should spin.

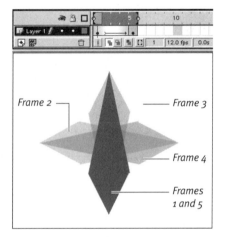

Frame 2

Frame 3

Frame 4

Frames 1 and 5

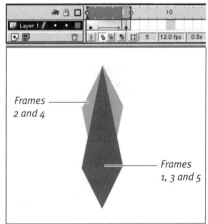

Frames 2 and 4

Frames 1, 3 and 5

Figure 9.19 Compare a single rotation (top) with a double rotation (bottom) in the same number of frames.

ROTATING AND SPINNING GRAPHICS

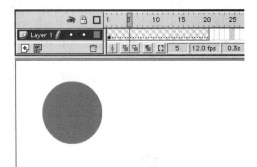

Figure 9.20 The broken line indicates that these 20 frames contain a motion tween.

Moving Graphics in Straight Lines

In the preceding exercises, you created an animation of a well-behaved bouncing ball, one that simply moves up and down. You can make that ball bounce all around the Stage like a crazy Ping-Pong ball, if you like. Simply add more keyframes and position the ball in a variety of locations. The ball moves in a straight line from one position to the next, but the effect can be one of much livelier movement.

If you move the ball a great distance and then tween the motion in a small number of in-between frames, you'll get frenetic bouncing. If you move the ball a short distance or use a larger number of in-between frames, you'll slow the action.

To move an item from point to point:

1. Create a new Flash document.

2. On the Stage, in Frame 1, use the oval tool to create a solid circle that represents the ball.

3. Select the ball, and choose Modify > Group or Insert > Convert to Symbol.

   Flash can create motion tweens only from grouped objects or from symbols.

4. In the Timeline, select Frame 20, and choose Insert > Frame.

   Flash creates 19 in-between frames.

5. In the Timeline, select Frame 1.
   select image to move

6. From the Insert menu, choose Create Motion Tween.

   Flash defines frames 1 through 20 as a motion tween but with a broken line, indicating that the tween is not yet complete (**Figure 9.20**). You need to create keyframes that describe the ball's motion.

continues on next page

MOVING GRAPHICS IN STRAIGHT LINES

7. In the Timeline, position the playhead in Frame 5.

8. On the Stage, drag the ball to a new position.

Try moving the ball a fair distance. Flash creates a new keyframe in Frame 5 and completes a tween for Frames 1 through 5.

9. In the Timeline, position the playhead in Frame 10.

10. On the Stage, drag the ball to a new position.

Flash creates a new keyframe in Frame 10 and completes a tween for Frames 5 through 10.

11. Repeat this repositioning process for Frames 15 and 20.

You now have a ball that bounces wildly around the Stage (**Figure 9.21**).

12. To add more frames, select Frame 30 or Frame 40 and then choose Insert > Frame.

Flash extends the motion tween, and you can add keyframes following the procedure described above. Just be sure to make the last frame in the series a keyframe.

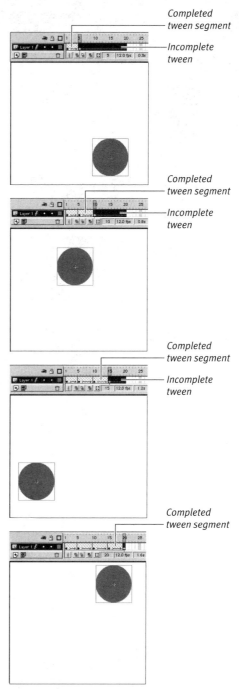

Completed tween segment

Incomplete tween

Completed tween segment

Incomplete tween

Completed tween segment

Incomplete tween

Completed tween segment

Figure 9.21 As you move the ball to new positions in different frames within the motion tween, Flash creates keyframes and completes the tween between one keyframe and the next.

Onion skinning

Edit Multiple
Frames

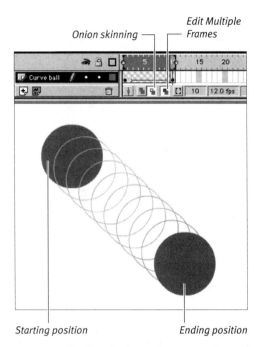

Starting position   Ending position

Figure 9.22 The first step in creating a tweened graphic that follows a path is defining a motion tween with the graphic in the beginning and ending positions you want to use. Here, the graphic moves from the beginning to the end in a straight line. (Onion skinning and Edit Multiple Frames are selected to show all the tween's components.)

Moving Graphics Along a Path

The preceding exercise showed how you can make graphics move all over the Stage in short, point-to-point hops. For a ball that bounces off the walls, ceiling, and floor, that's appropriate. But for other things, you want movements that are softer—trajectories that are arcs, not straight lines. You could achieve this effect by stringing together many point-to-point keyframes, but Flash offers a more efficient method: the motion guide.

A *motion guide* is a graphic you create on a special separate layer. The motion guide defines the path for a linked, tweened graphic to follow. One motion-guide layer can control items on several layers. The motion-guide layer governs any layers linked to it. The linked layers are defined as guided layers in the Layer Properties dialog box.

If you want different elements to follow different paths, you can create several motion-guide layers within a single Flash document. Each motion guide governs the actions of objects on its own set of linked layers.

To add a motion-guide layer:

1. Create a new Flash document containing a 10-frame motion tween.

   In the first frame, place a circle in the top-left corner of the Stage. In the last frame, place a circle in the bottom-right corner of the Stage. Your document should resemble **Figure 9.22**.

2. Select the layer that contains the tweened graphic you want to move along a path.

continues on next page

3. At the bottom of the Timeline, click the Add Guide Layer button.

Flash adds the motion-guide layer directly above the layer you selected and gives it a default name of Guide: followed by the name of the layer you selected (**Figure 9.23**). The motion-guide icon appears next to the layer name. Flash also indents the layer linked to the motion-guide layer.

4. With the motion-guide layer selected, use the pencil tool to draw a line on the Stage showing the path you want the graphic take (**Figure 9.24**).

5. In Frame 1, drag the circle to reposition its registration mark directly over the beginning of the motion path.

For Flash to move an item along a motion path, the center of the item must snap to the path.

6. In Frame 10, drag the circle to reposition its registration mark directly over the end of the motion path.

Flash redraws the in-between frames so that the circle follows the motion path (**Figure 9.25**). Flash centers the tweened item over the motion-guide path in each in-between frame. In the final movie, Flash hides the motion path.

✔ Tips

■ After you draw the motion path, lock the motion-guide layer to prevent yourself from editing the path accidentally as you snap the graphic to the guide line.

■ In the Frame panel, check the Snap checkbox to have Flash assist you in centering keyframe graphics over the end of the guide line.

■ You can use any of Flash's drawing tools—line, pencil, oval, rectangle, and brush—to create a motion path.

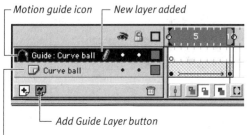

Motion guide icon   New layer added

Add Guide Layer button

Indentation indicates guided status

Figure 9.23 The Add Guide Layer button inserts a new layer, defined as a motion-guide layer, above the selected layer in the Timeline. The default name for the motion-guide layer includes the name of the layer selected when you created the motion-guide layer. The layer containing the tweened graphic is indented and linked to the motion-guide layer. Flash defines the linked layer as a *guided* layer.

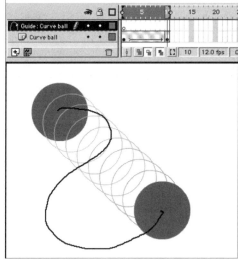

Figure 9.24 A line on a motion-guide layer acts as a path for the tweened graphic on a linked layer to follow.

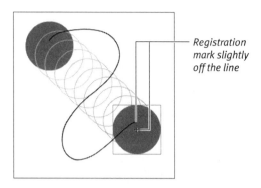

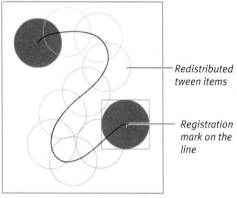

Registration mark slightly off the line

Redistributed tween items

Registration mark on the line

Figure 9.25 To follow the path, tweened items must have their center point (the crosshair registration mark) sitting directly on the line.

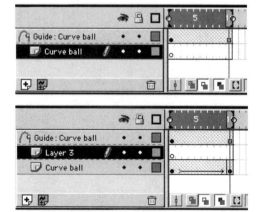

Figure 9.26 When a guided layer is selected, clicking the Add Guide Layer button creates another guided layer below the motion-guide layer.

If you want to have several items follow the same path, you need to put them on separate layers linked to the motion-guide layer.

To create a second guided layer:

1. In the Flash file you created in the preceding exercise, select the guided layer—the one containing the circle.

2. To add a new layer, *do one of the following*:
   - ◆ From the Insert menu, choose Layer.
   - ◆ In the Timeline, click the Add Layer button.

   Flash adds a new indented (guided) layer above the selected layer (**Figure 9.26**). Tweened items on this layer follow the motion guide when you position them correctly.

✔ Tip

■ To convert an existing layer to a guided layer quickly, drag it and position it below the motion-guide layer or any of its linked layers.

If you want to have items following different paths, you need to create multiple motion-guide layers, each with its own set of guided layers.

To add a second motion-guide layer:

1. In the Timeline, create or select a normal layer.

2. Click the Add Guide Layer button.

   Flash adds a motion-guide layer above the selected layer and links the selected layer to it. Follow the steps in the preceding exercises to draw the motion path and position the tweened item.

MOVING GRAPHICS ALONG A PATH

Orienting Graphics to a Motion Path

Imagine a waiter carrying a full tray through a crowded room, raising and lowering the tray to avoid various obstacles but always keeping the tray level so as not to spill anything. That's how the animation you created in the preceding exercise works. Flash moved the circle in each in-between frame to snap its center point to the motion guide, but it did not rotate the circle at all.

With a circle, that procedure results in a natural-looking motion, but with other objects, the result is very unnatural. Imagine animating a lizard following a path: If the lizard graphic snaps to different spots along the motion path, never changing the way that it's oriented in space, the lizard appears to be in the grip of some invisible force, not moving forward of its own volition.

To create more-natural movement, Flash gives you the option of forcing a tweened to orient itself parallel to the path in each frame of the tween.

To match a graphic's orientation to the path:

1. Create a 10-frame motion tween of an item that follows a motion guide, using the steps in the first exercise in "Moving Graphics Along a Path" earlier in this chapter.

    This time, however, don't use a circle; draw a small animal or create a simple noncircular graphic. An arrow or triangle works well.

2. Turn on onion skinning to see how the item moves along the path without orientation.

3. In the Timeline, select Frame 1.

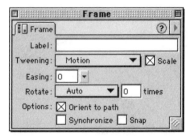

Figure 9.27 With Motion tweening selected in the Frame panel, check Orient to Path to make Flash rotate a tweened item to "face" the direction of movement.

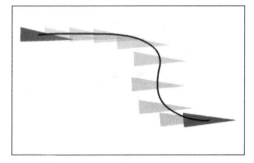

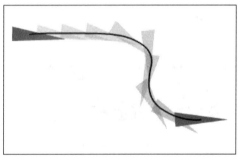

Figure 9.28 The arrow in the top tween is not oriented to the path; it stays parallel to the bottom of the Stage and moves to various points along the path. The bottom tween is oriented to the path. The arrow rotates to better align with the path.

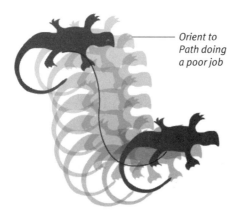

Orient to
Path doing
a poor job

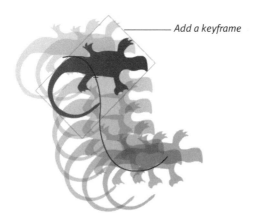

Add a keyframe

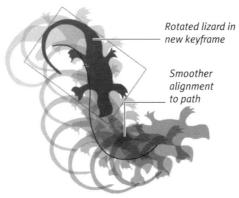

Rotated lizard in
new keyframe

Smoother
alignment
to path

Figure 9.29 Here, Flash is doing a poor job of aligning this lizard with the path (top). Creating a new keyframe and rotating the lizard manually in the second frame (middle) helps the Orient to Path feature do its job well (bottom).

4. In the Options section of the Frame panel, check the Orient to Path checkbox (**Figure 9.27**).

Flash redraws the tween. In the in-between frames, Flash rotates the tweened item to align it with the path more naturally (**Figure 9.28**).

✔ Tip

■ The Orient to Path option does not always create the most natural positions for your graphic. Step through the tween one frame at a time. When you get to a frame where Flash positions the graphic poorly, you can fix it. In the Timeline, select the in-between frame, and choose Insert > Keyframe. In the new keyframe Flash creates, select the graphic and rotate it manually to align it with the motion guide. Flash redraws the in-between frames (**Figure 9.29**).

ORIENTING GRAPHICS TO A MOTION PATH

Changing Tween Speed

In Chapter 8, you learned to make an animated item appear to move slowly or quickly by adjusting the number of in-between frames. When you create an animation with tweening, that method no longer works, because Flash distributes the motion evenly over however many in-between frames you create. You can, however, make an animation slower at the beginning or end of a tween sequence by setting an Easing value in the Frame panel.

You can use easing to create a more natural look in animations of objects that gravity affects. In an animation of a bouncing ball, for example, you might want the bouncing to start quickly but slow toward the end to simulate the way that entropy in the real world slows a bouncing ball.

To make the animation start slowly and accelerate (ease in):

1. Create a 10-frame motion tween of a graphic that follows a motion guide, using the steps in the first exercise in "Moving Graphics Along a Path" earlier in this chapter.

2. In the Timeline, select any of the frames in the keyframe unit (Frames 1 through 9).

3. In the Frame panel, enter a negative number in the Easing field (**Figure 9.30**).

   The word *In* appears next to the field. Easing in makes the animation start slow and speed up toward the end. The lower the Easing value, the greater the rate of acceleration.

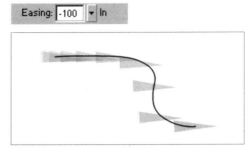

Figure 9.30 A negative easing value (top), makes changes in the initial frames of the tween smaller and changes toward the end larger (bottom). The animation seems to start slowly and then speed up.

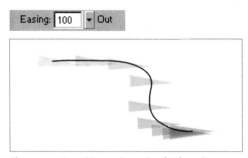

Figure 9.31 A positive easing value (top), makes changes at the end of the animation smaller and changes in the initial frames larger (bottom). The animation seems to start quickly and then slow down.

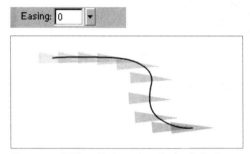

Figure 9.32 With an Easing value of 0 (top), Flash distributes the tweening changes evenly across the in-between frames (bottom). The effect is that of animation at a constant rate.

To make the animation start quickly and decelerate (ease out):

1. Follow steps 1 through 3 in the preceding exercise.

2. In the Frame panel, enter a positive number in the Easing field.

   The word *Out* appears next to the field. Easing out makes the animation start quickly and slow toward the end (**Figure 9.31**). The higher the Easing value, the greater the rate of deceleration.

✔ Tips

■ An Easing value of zero causes Flash to display the whole animation at a constant rate (**Figure 9.32**).

■ For easy entry of Easing values, click the triangle to the right of the Easing field. A slider pops open. Drag the slider's lever to choose a value between –100 and 100. Click away from the slider in the panel or on the Stage.

■ For even quicker changes, click and drag the slider triangle. When you release the slider's lever, Flash confirms the new easing value; you don't need to click anywhere.

ANIMATION WITH SHAPE TWEENING

10

In shape tweening, as in motion tweening, you define the beginning and ending graphics in keyframes. Macromedia Flash creates the in-between frames, redrawing the graphic with incremental changes that transform it. The important difference between motion tweening and shape tweening is that motion tweening works on groups and symbols and shape tweening requires editable graphics.

Shape tweening doesn't restrict you to changing the graphic's shape. You can change any of the graphic's properties—size, color, location, and so on—as you would in motion tweening. Though it's possible to shape-tween graphics that move in straight lines, the other automated-motion features are not available. You cannot instruct Flash to rotate a shape-tweened item, for example.

Flash can shape-tween more than one graphic on a layer, but the results can be unpredictable. When you have several shapes on a layer, there is no way to tell Flash which starting shape goes with which ending shape. By limiting yourself to a single shape tween on each layer, you tell Flash exactly what to change.

You define shape tweens by setting the tweening parameters in the Frame panel. For the exercises in this chapter, keep the Frame panel open on your desktop.

Creating a Bouncing Ball with Shape Tweening

To have a working shape tween, you need three things: a beginning keyframe containing one or more editable shapes, in-between frames defined as shape tweens, and an ending keyframe containing the new editable shape.

Although the Create Motion Tween command helps you combine those ingredients correctly for motion tweens, there is no equivalent command for shape tweens. You must create all shape tweens manually by setting up the beginning and ending keyframes and then defining the in-between frames as shape tweens in the Frame panel.

You'll mostly use shape tweens to transform one shape into another, but you start this chapter by using a shape tween to create another simple bouncing-ball animation. This exercise demonstrates the similarity between the two types of tweens and shows how you can achieve the same result by using different tween commands.

To define shape tweens via the Frame panel:

1. Create a new Flash document, and name it something like Shape Tween Bounce.

   Flash creates a document with one layer and a keyframe at Frame 1 by default.

2. In the Timeline, position the playhead in Frame 1.

3. In the Toolbox, choose the oval tool.

4. In the Toolbox or the Stroke panel, set the stroke to None.

5. Near the top of the Stage, draw a circle. This circle will be the ball. Make it fairly large.

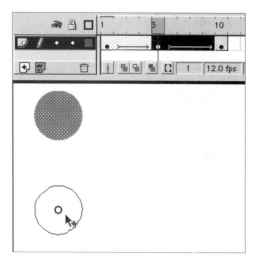

Figure 10.1 When you reposition an editable graphic, for the purposes of shape tweening Flash considers it a change in shape. In this figure, in the middle keyframe, you relocate the ball to create the bottom of the bounce.

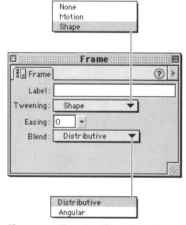

Figure 10.2 Choosing Shape from the Tweening menu in the Frame panel displays the shape-tween parameters.

6. In the Timeline, select Frame 5, and choose Insert > Keyframe.

The Insert > Keyframe command makes a new keyframe that contains the same elements as the preceding keyframe.

7. Select Frame 10, and choose Insert > Keyframe.

8. In Frame 5, select the ball and drag it to the bottom of the Stage (**Figure 10.1**).

You now have the keyframes necessary to make a simple bouncing ball like the one in the motion-tween exercise. In Frame 1, the ball is at the top of its bounce; in Frame 5, the ball is at the bottom of its bounce; and in Frame 10, the ball is back up at the top.

9. To define the shape tween for the first half of the ball's bounce, in the Timeline, select any of the frames in the first keyframe unit (frame 1, 2, 3, or 4).

Note that the ball is selected auto-mati-cally. When you define a motion tween, the element to be tweened must be selected.

10. From the Frame panel's Tweening menu, choose Shape.

The parameters for the shape tween appear (**Figure 10.2**).

Flash creates a shape tween in Frames 1 through 4 and color-codes those frames in the Timeline. With Tinted Frames active (choose it from the Frame View pop-up menu at the end of the Timeline), Flash applies a light green shade to the frames containing a shape tween. If Tinted Frames is inactive, the frames are white, but Flash changes the keyframe bullets and the arrow that indicates the presence of a tween from blue to green.

continues on next page

CREATING A BOUNCING BALL WITH SHAPE TWEENING

11. In the Easing field, *do one of the following:*

- ◆ To make the bounce start slowly and speed up, enter a negative value.
- ◆ To make the bounce start quickly and slow down, enter a positive value.
- ◆ To keep the bounce constant, enter 0.

12. From the Blend menu, *choose one of the following options:*

- ◆ To preserve sharp corners and straight lines as one shape transforms into another, choose Angular.
- ◆ To smooth out the in-between shapes, choose Distributive.

13. To define the motion tween for the second half of the ball's bounce, in the Timeline, ⌘-click (Mac) or Ctrl-click (Windows) any of the frames in the second keyframe unit (frame 5, 6, 7, 8, or 9).

In Flash 5's default frame-selection style, clicking an in-between frame selects not just the keyframe unit that contains that frame but also any contiguous keyframe units that contain the same symbol. Using the modifier key allows you to select a single frame and thereby apply your tween settings to just one keyframe unit.

14. Repeat steps 10 through 12.

Flash creates the second half of the ball's bounce with another shape tween (**Figure 10.3**).

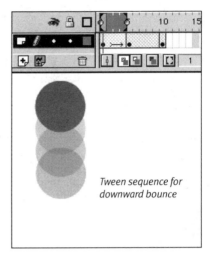

Tween sequence for downward bounce

Tween sequence for upward bounce

Figure 10.3 With onion skinning turned on, you can see the in-between frames Flash creates for the tween. In this case, because you changed only the position of the object, it looks just like the bouncing ball created with a motion tween.

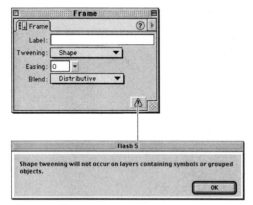

Figure 10.4 A warning button appears in the Frame panel when there are groups or symbols in frames you are defining as shape tweens (top). Click the button to see the warning dialog box (bottom).

✔ Tip

■ Flash doesn't prevent you from defining shape tweens for frames that contain grouped shapes or symbols. Flash 4 Frame Drawing selected (in the General tab of the Preferences dialog box) does warn you by placing the broken-tween dotted line in the relevant frames in the Timeline. When you select such frames, a warning button appears in the Frame panel (**Figure 10.4**). When you see these warnings, go back to the Stage and reevaluate what's there. If the item you want to tween is a group or symbol, you could use motion tweening. Or to use shape tweening, you could break the group or symbol apart (select the shape or symbol and then choose Modify > Break Apart). If there's an extra symbol or group on the same layer as the editable shape you want to tween, move the extra symbol or group to its own layer.

Morphing Simple Lines and Fills

In the bouncing-ball example, you worked with a fill shape but merely changed its location. The true work of a shape tween is to transform one shape into another. Flash can transform both fill shapes and lines. In this section, you try some truly shape-changing exercises with both types of shapes.

To transform an oval into a rectangle:

1. Create a new Flash document.

2. On the Stage, in Frame 1, draw an outline oval (**Figure 10.5**).

3. In the Timeline, select Frame 5, and choose Insert > Blank Keyframe.

   Flash creates a keyframe but removes all content from the Stage.

4. On the Stage, in Frame 5, draw an outline rectangle (**Figure 10.6**).

   Don't worry about placing the rectangle in exactly the same location on the Stage as the circle; you'll adjust the position later.

   In the Timeline, select any of the frames in the Keyframe 1 unit (frame 1, 2, 3, or 4).

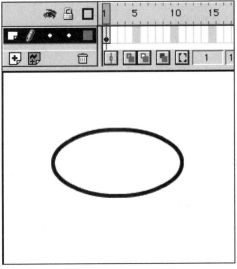

Figure 10.5 Draw an oval in the first keyframe of your shape tween.

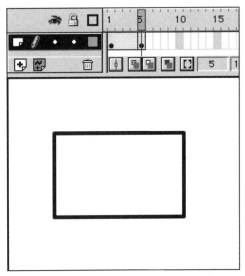

Figure 10.6 Draw a rectangle in the second keyframe of your shape tween.

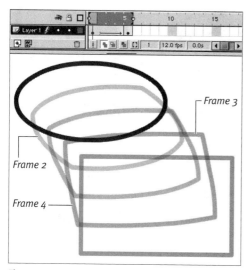

Figure 10.7 When you define frames 1 through 4 as shape tweens, Flash creates the three intermediate shapes that transform the oval into a square. Turn on onion skinning to see the shapes for the in-between frames.

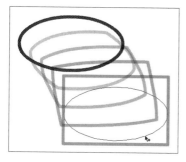

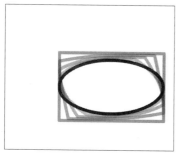

Figure 10.8 Use onion skinning to help you position your keyframe shapes. Here, with Frame 1 selected, you can drag the oval to center it within the rectangle. That makes the oval grow into a rectangle without moving anywhere else on the Stage.

5. From the Frame panel's Tweening menu, choose Shape.

   Flash transforms the oval into the rectangle in three equal steps, one for each in-between frame (**Figure 10.7**).

6. To align the oval and rectangle, in the Timeline status bar, click the Onion Skin or Onion Skin Outlines button.

   Flash displays all the in-between frames.

7. In the Timeline, position the playhead in Frame 1.

8. On the Stage, reposition the oval so that it aligns with the rectangle (**Figure 10.8**).

   The oval transforms into a rectangle, remaining in one spot on the Stage.

To transform a rectangle into a freeform shape:

1. Create a new Flash document.

2. On the Stage, in Frame 1, draw a rectangular fill.

3. In the Timeline, select Frame 5, and choose Insert > Blank Keyframe.

4. On the Stage, in Frame 5, use the brush tool to paint a freeform fill.

   Don't make it too complex, just a blob or brushstroke with gentle curves.

5. In the Timeline, select any of the frames in the Keyframe 1 unit (frame 1, 2, 3, or 4).

6. From the Frame panel's Tweening menu, choose Shape.

   Flash transforms the rectangle into the fill in three equal steps, one for each in-between frame (**Figure 10.9**).

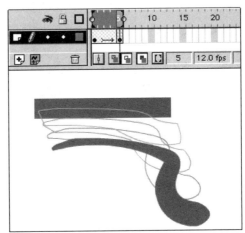

Figure 10.9 Flash transforms a rectangle into a freeform brushstroke with shape tweening.

All objects on one layer

All objects on one layer

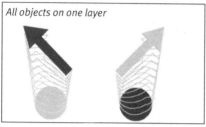

Light circle and arrow on one layer ⎯

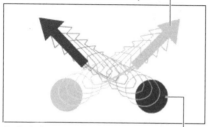

Dark circle and arrow on another layer ⎯

Figure 10.10 Tweening multiple shapes whose paths don't cross in a single layer works fine. In the top image, both objects are on the same layer, and the light circle transforms into the light arrow without a hitch. In the middle image, both objects are on the same layer, but Flash transforms the light circle into the dark arrow and the dark circle into the light arrow because that's the most direct path. If you want to create diagonal paths that cross, you must put each object on its own layer, as in the bottom image.

Shape-Tweening Multiple Shapes

In motion tweening, Flash limits you to one item per tween, meaning just one item per layer. In shape tweening, however, Flash can handle more than one shape on a layer. The drawback is that you may get some very strange results if you try to tween several shapes on a layer. The simpler and fewer the shapes, the more reliable your multishape tweens will be. For the most predictable results, limit yourself to one shape per layer.

You may want to keep both shapes on the same layer for a fill with an outline, however. As long as the transformation is not too complicated, Flash can handle the two together.

When Multiple Shape Tweens on a Single Layer Go Bad

If you are shape-tweening stationary objects, you probably can get away with having several on the same layer. But if the objects are in motion, Flash can get confused about which shape goes where. Though you may intend the paths of two shapes to cross, Flash creates the most direct route between the starting object and the ending object. **Figure 10.10** illustrates the problem.

To shape-tween fills with strokes (outlines):

1. Follow the steps in the preceding exercises to create a shape tween of an outline oval transforming into a rectangle.

2. Fill each shape with a different color.

   Flash tweens the fill and the stroke together and tweens the change in color (**Figure 10.11**).

3. In the Toolbox, choose the ink bottle, and select white for the stroke color.

4. In Frame 5, click the rectangle with the ink bottle tool.

   The rectangle's stroke changes to white (the same as the background).

   Flash tweens the shape, and the color changes as well, creating a "disappearing" stroke (**Figure 10.12**).

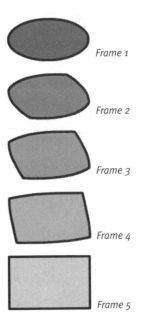

Figure 10.11 Flash transforms a shape with a stroke in five frames. The shape tween changes not only the graphic's shape but also its color (from dark to light).

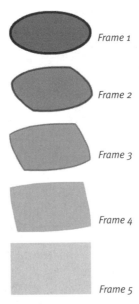

Figure 10.12 In this five-frame shape tween, the stroke color changes to match the movie's background, making the stroke disappear.

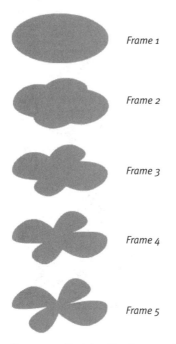

Frame 1

Frame 2

Frame 3

Frame 4

Frame 5

Figure 10.13 Flash handles the tween from an oval to a simple flower shape without requiring shape hints.

Transforming a Simple Shape into a Complex Shape

The more complex the shape you tween, the more difficult it is for Flash to create the expected result. That's because Flash changes the shapes by changing the mathematical description of the graphic. Flash does not understand how the forces of gravity, light, and so on affect the ways humans see; therefore, it doesn't always choose to make a change in a way that preserves the illusion you want. You can help Flash tween better by using *shape hints*—markers that allow you to identify points on the original shape's outline that correspond to points on the final shape's outline.

To shape-tween a more complex shape:

1. Create a new Flash document.

2. On the Stage, in Frame 1, draw an oval. Use different colors for the fill and the stroke.

3. In the Timeline, select Frame 5, and choose Insert > Keyframe.
   Flash duplicates the contents of Keyframe 1 in Keyframe 5.

4. In the Timeline, select any of the frames in the Keyframe 1 unit (frame 1, 2, 3, or 4).

5. From the Frame panel's Tweening menu, choose Shape.

6. In the Timeline, position the playhead in Frame 5.

continues on next page

TRANSFORMING A SIMPLE SHAPE INTO A COMPLEX SHAPE

7. Using the arrow tool or the pen and sub-selection tools, drag four corner points in toward the center of the oval to create a flower shape.

   For more detailed instructions on editing shapes, see Chapter 3.

8. Play the movie to see the shape tween. Flash handles the tweening for this change well (**Figure 10.13**). It's fairly obvious what points of the oval should move in to create the petal shapes.

   If you modify the shape further, however, it gets harder for Flash to know how to create the new shape. That's when you need to use shape hints.

To use shape hints:

1. Using the animation you created in the preceding exercise, in the Timeline, select Frame 10, and choose Insert > Keyframe.

   Flash duplicates the flower shape in a new keyframe.

2. In Frame 10, edit the flower to add a stem. Reshape the outline with the arrow tool or the pen and subselection tools, or add a stem with a brushstroke in the same color as the flower.

3. Define a shape tween for Frames 5 through 9.

4. Play the movie.

   The addition of the stem to the flower makes it hard for Flash to create a smooth tween that looks right (**Figure 10.14**).

5. To begin adding shape hints, position the playhead in Frame 5 (the initial keyframe of this tweening sequence).

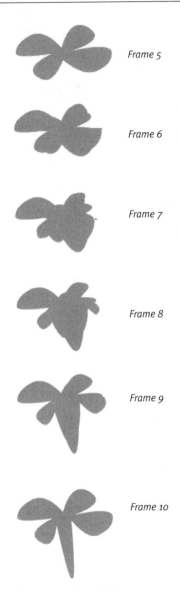

Frame 5

Frame 6

Frame 7

Frame 8

Frame 9

Frame 10

Figure 10.14 The addition of a stem to the flower overloads Flash's capability to create a smooth shape tween. Frames 7 and 8 are particularly bad.

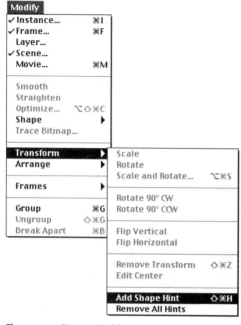

Figure 10.15 Choose Modify > Transform > Add Shape Hint to activate markers that help Flash make connections between the original shape and the final shape of the tween.

Areas of change

Figure 10.16 Start adding shape hints in the first keyframe of a tween sequence. Flash places the hints in the center of the tweened object (top). You must drag the hints into position (middle). Distribute the hints in alphabetical order around the outline of the object, placing them on crucial points of change (bottom). Here, the three points with hints a, b, and c define the points from which the stem of the flower will grow.

6. From the Modify menu, choose Transform > Add Shape Hint, or press ⌘-Shift-H (Mac) or Ctrl-Shift-H (Windows) (**Figure 10.15**).

   Flash places a shape hint—a small red circle labeled with a letter, starting with a—in the center of the object in the current frame. You need to reposition the shape hint to place it on a problem point on the shape's outline.

7. With the arrow tool, drag the shape hint to a problem point on the edge of the shape.

   Don't worry about getting the shape hint in exactly the right spot; you can fine-tune it later.

8. Repeat steps 6 and 7 until you have placed shape hints on all the problem points of your shape in Frame 5 (**Figure 10.16**).

   Each time you add a shape hint, you get another small red circle labeled with a letter. You cannot simply place the hints at random; you must place them so that they go in alphabetical order around the edge of the shape. (Flash does the best job when you place shape hints in counter-clockwise order, but you can also place them in clockwise order.)

9. In the Timeline, position the playhead in Frame 10.

   Flash has already added shape hints to this frame; they all stack up in the center of the shape.

   continues on next page

TRANSFORMING A SIMPLE SHAPE INTO A COMPLEX SHAPE

10. With the arrow tool, drag each shape hint to its position on the new shape. Keep them in the same order (counterclockwise or clockwise) you chose in step 8. (**Figure 10.17**).

11. To evaluate the improvement in tweening, play the movie.

12. To fine-tune the shape hints' positions, select one of the tween's keyframes and turn on onion skinning.

Where the onion skins reveal rough spots in the tween, you may need to better match the hint position from the first keyframe to the last one (**Figure 10.18**). Repositioning the shape hints changes the in-between frames. You may need to adjust the shape hints in both keyframes. If you still can't get a smooth tween, try adding more shape hints.

✔ Tips

■ To remove a single shape hint, make the initial keyframe the current frame. Select the shape hint you want to remove, and drag it completely off the Stage.

■ To remove all the hints at once, with the initial keyframe current, choose Modify > Transform > Remove All Hints.

■ Onion skins don't always update correctly when you reposition shape hints. Clicking a blank area of the Stage forces Flash to redraw them.

Figure 10.17 To complete placement of shape hints, you need to select the second keyframe of your tween sequence. Flash stacks up hints corresponding to the ones you placed in the preceding keyframe (top). You must drag them into the correct final position (bottom).

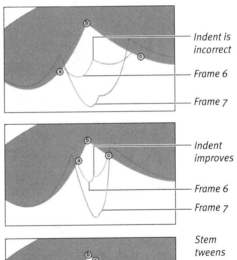

Figure 10.18 It can be difficult to match up points in the two keyframes exactly when you first place the shape hints. When you've positioned the hints in the beginning and ending keyframes of a sequence, turn on onion skinning to see where you need to adjust the placement of your hints. With the initial placement, Flash starts the stem growing with an indent at the bottom (top). Moving the points closer together improves the tween (middle). When the onion skins reveal a smooth tween, you're done (bottom).

Flash 5's default frame drawing

Flash 4 frame drawing

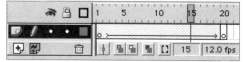

Figure 10.19 To save yourself numerous trips to the Frame panel's Tweening menu, you can assign the shape-tween property to a range of frames and add keyframes and shapes later. Flash defines a shape tween even though there's no content to tween yet. In Flash 5 frame-drawing style, tweening arrows appear in the Timeline only when there is content on the Stage.

Flash 5's default frame drawing

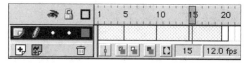

Flash 4 frame drawing

Figure 10.20 When you insert keyframes into a long tween sequence, Flash breaks it into smaller tween sequences.

Creating Shapes That Move As They Change

You cannot create shape tweens that follow a path, but you can move shapes around the Stage in straight lines. You simply reposition the elements on the Stage from one keyframe to the next.

To shape-tween a moving graphic:

1. Create a new Flash document.

2. On the Stage, select Frame 20, and choose Insert > Keyframe.

   Flash adds a blank keyframe at Frame 20 and blank in-between frames at Frames 2 through 19.

3. In the Timeline, select any frame from 1 to 19.

   Note that you must actually click the frame to select it—you cannot just position the playhead in the frame.

4. From the Frame panel's Tweening menu, choose Shape.

   Even though you have no shapes on the Stage to tween yet, Flash gives the frames the shape-tween property. In the Timeline, the frames have a green tint. If you have Flash 4 Frame Drawing selected in the General Tab of the Preferences dialog box, the tweening arrow appears as well (**Figure 10.19**). You can now add keyframes and shapes.

5. In the Timeline, insert a blank keyframe at Frames 5, 10, and 15.

   Flash creates four shape-tween sequences (**Figure 10.20**).

continues on next page

CREATING SHAPES THAT MOVE AS THEY CHANGE

6. In each keyframe, draw a different shape; place each one in a different corner of the Stage.

In Frame 1, for example, draw a circular fill in the bottom-left corner of the Stage. In Frame 5, draw a rectangular fill in the top-right corner of the Stage. In Frame 10, draw a flattened oval in the bottom-right corner of the Stage. In Frame 15, draw a star in the top-left corner of the Stage. And in Frame 20, duplicate Frame 1's circle in the bottom-left corner of the Stage. For extra variety, give each object a different color.

7. Play the movie.

You see a graphic that bounces around the Stage, morphing from one shape to the next (**Figure 10.21**).

✔ Tip

■ Although shape-tweened objects cannot follow a path the way motion-tweened objects can, you can make Flash do the work of creating the separate keyframes you need to animate shape tweens that move on curved paths. First, create your shape tween. In the Timeline, select the full range of frames in the tween sequence. From the Modify menu, choose Frames > Convert to Keyframes. Flash converts each in-between frame (with its transitional content) into a keyframe. You can now position each keyframe object anywhere you like. To simulate a motion guide, create a regular guide layer and draw the path you want your morphing shape to follow. Choose View > Guides > Snap to Guides. Reposition the shape in each keyframe. When you drag a shape object close to the line on the guide layer, Flash snaps the shape to the line.

Edit Multiple Frames

First half of the full tween sequence

Onion skinning on

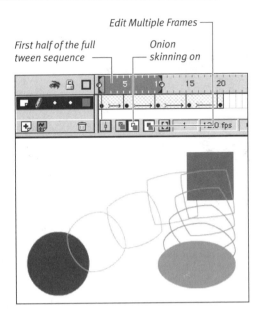

Second half of the full tween sequence

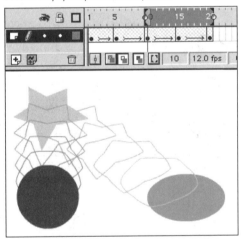

Figure 10.21 Place a different shape in a different location in each keyframe. Flash creates the intermediate steps necessary to transform the shapes and move them across the stage. Play through the movie, or turn on onion skinning to examine the motion and shape changes on the in-between frames. (Here, Edit Multiple Frames is also on, making it easy to see the keyframe shapes.)

MORE-COMPLEX ANIMATION TASKS

11

So far, you've learned to manipulate shapes and animate them one at a time, in a single layer. In many cases, those techniques are all you need, but Macromedia Flash is capable of handling much more complicated animation tasks. To create complex animated movies, you're going to need to work with multiple shapes, multiple layers, and even multiple scenes. In this chapter, you learn to work with multiple layers in the Timeline, stack animations on the various layers to create more-complex movement, and save animations as reusable elements for easy manipulation—either as animated graphic symbols or as movie-clip symbols. With these techniques, you can really start to bring your animations to life.

Understanding Scenes

In the metaphor of the Timeline being the table of contents for the "book" of your movie, scenes are the equivalent of chapters. Scenes help you organize the contents of a long movie. So far, you've worked with 5-, 10-, and 20-frame movies, but in real life, your movie may run to hundreds of frames. You can get pretty tired of scrolling around the Timeline, trying to keep track of where you are, if the movie has hundreds of frames. But you can break the animation into reasonable chunks and deal with each set of frames separately by creating scenes.

In your final published movie, Flash plays through the scenes in order unless you use the interactivity features to provide instructions for moving through the scenes in a different order. (To learn more about interactivity in Flash movies, see Chapters 12 and 13.)

Flash's Scene panel makes it easy to see what scenes exist in your movie, create new scenes, delete scenes, and reorganize them.

To access the Scene panel:

◆ If the Scene panel is not currently open, from the Window menu, choose Panels > Scene (**Figure 11.1**).

The Scene panel appears.

In a new Flash document, the Scene panel lists only the default Scene 1. When you add scenes to a movie, the Scene panel lists all the movie's scenes in order (**Figure 11.2**).

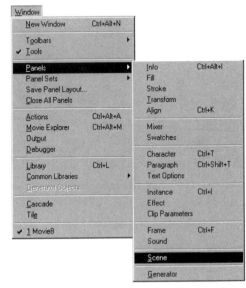

Figure 11.1 Choose Window > Panels > Scene to access the Scene panel.

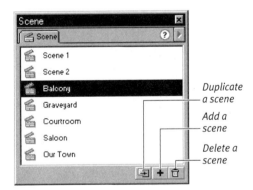

Figure 11.2 The Scene panel lists all the scenes in a movie. It also provides buttons for adding, duplicating, and deleting scenes.

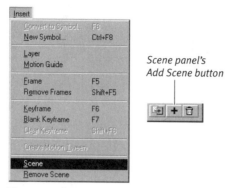

Figure 11.3 Choose Insert > Scene—or in the Scene panel, click the Add Scene button—to add a new scene to your Flash document.

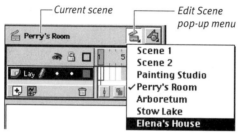

Figure 11.4 The Timeline displays the name of the current scene. Choose a scene from the Edit Scene pop-up menu to switch scenes quickly.

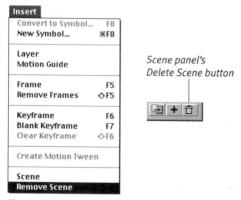

Figure 11.5 To delete a scene, choose Insert > Remove Scene (left) or click the Scene panel's Delete Scene button.

To add a scene:

Do one of the following:

◆ From the Insert menu, choose Scene (**Figure 11.3**).

◆ In the Scene panel, click the Add button.

Flash adds another scene, giving it the default name Scene 2.

✔ Tip

■ Flash bases default scene names on the number of scenes you have ever added, not on the number of scenes currently in the movie. If you add Scenes 2 and 3 and then delete Scene 2, Flash names the next scene you add Scene 4, even though the movie has only three scenes.

To select a scene to edit:

Do one of the following:

◆ From the Edit Scene pop-up menu in the Timeline, choose the scene that you want to edit.

◆ From the scrolling list in the Scene panel, select the scene that you want to edit.

Flash displays the selected scene on the Stage, putting its name in the current-scene box in the top-left corner of the window and placing a check next to that scene's name in the Edit Scene pop-up menu in the Timeline (**Figure 11.4**).

To delete a selected scene:

1. *Do one of the following:*

◆ From the Insert menu, choose Remove Scene (**Figure 11.5**).

◆ In the Scene panel, click the Delete button.

A dialog box appears, warning you that you can't undo this operation.

continues on next page

UNDERSTANDING SCENES

2. Click OK.

Flash deletes the scene, removing it from the Edit Scene pop-up menu in the Timeline as well as from the scrolling list in the Scene panel.

✔ Tip

■ If you don't want to see the warning dialog box each time you delete a scene, ⌘-click (Mac) or Ctrl-click (Windows) the Delete button in the Scene panel.

To change scene order:

◆ In the Scene panel, drag a selected scene name up or down in the list to reorder it.

The pointer changes to a dog-eared page and arrow. Flash previews the new location for the scene with a highlighted line (**Figure 11.6**).

To rename a scene:

1. In the Scene panel, double-click the name of the scene that you want to rename.

2. Type the new name in the Name field.

Preview of new scene location   *Reordered scenes*

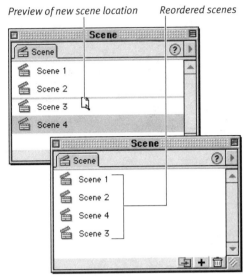

Figure 11.6 As you drag a selected scene, a highlighted bar previews the new location for the scene. When the bar is between the scenes where you want to place the selected scene, release the mouse button.

The Pitfalls of Using Scenes

In Flash, each scene is like a self-contained movie. The fact that each scene is, in a sense, a new beginning can make it difficult to keep the continuity of actions between scenes. For some types of movies—ones with interactivity that requires variables or preloading—scenes are inappropriate. In such cases, you may need to stick to a single long movie or use separate movies to organize your animation, stringing them together with interactivity features such as the Load Movie action.

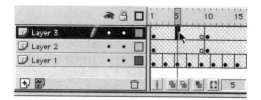

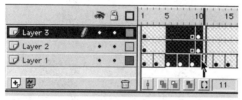

Figure 11.7 ⌘-click (Mac) or Ctrl-click (Windows) (top) and drag across frames and layers to select frames in those layers (bottom). (With Flash 4 frame-selection style, just click and drag to select multiple frames.)

Manipulating Frames in Multiple Layers

As your movie gets more complex, you may need to add layers. You can perform editing operations on selected frames and layers, for example, by copying, cutting, and pasting frames across multiple layers. You can also insert frames, keyframes, and blank keyframes into selected frames and layers.

To select and copy frames in several layers:

1. Open a new Flash document.

2. Add two layers—for a total of three layers in the movie—and insert 20 frames into each layer.

   Place content in the layers to help you see what's going on as you work with the various frames and layers. Use the text tool, for example, to place the frame number in every other frame of Layer 1 and to place a text block with the name of the layer in layers 2 and 3.

3. In the Timeline, in Layer 3, ⌘-click (Mac) or Ctrl-click (Windows) in Frame 5, and drag as though you were drawing a selection rectangle around frames 5 through 10 in all three layers.

   Flash highlights the selected frames (**Figure 11.7**).

   continues on next page

4. From the Edit menu, choose Copy Frames. Flash copies the frames and layer information to the Clipboard.

✔ Tip

■ To select a block of frames that spans several layers without dragging, ⌘-click (Mac) or Ctrl-click (Windows) a frame at one of the four corners of the block. Then ⌘-Shift-click (Mac) or Ctrl-Shift-click (Windows) the frame at the opposite corner. Flash selects all the frames in the rectangle that you've defined (**Figure 11.8**). (If you have Flash 4 Selection Style set in Preferences, just click and Shift-click to make your selection.)

To replace the content of frames with a multilayer selection:

1. Using the document that you created in the preceding exercise, select frames 15 through 20 on all three layers.

2. From the Edit menu, choose Paste Frames.

Flash pastes the copied frames 5 through 10 into frames 15 through 20 in each of the three layers. The numbers on the Stage in Layer 1 now start over with 5 at Frame 15, 7 at Frame 17, and 9 at Frame 19.

To paste a multiple-layer selection into blank frames:

1. Using the document that you created in the preceding exercise, select Frame 21 on all three layers.

2. From the Edit menu, choose Paste Frames.

Flash pastes the copied frames 5 through 10 into frames 21 through 26 in each of the three layers (**Figure 11.9**). Layer 1 now displays the number 5 at Frame 21, 7 at Frame 23, and 9 at Frame 25.

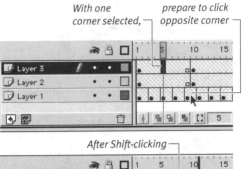

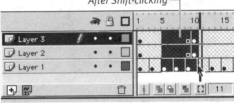

Figure 11.8 To select a block of frames, ⌘-click (Mac) or Ctrl-click (Windows) one corner of the block; then ⌘-Shift-click (Mac) or Ctrl-Shift-click (Windows) the opposite corner to define the block. (With Flash 4 frame-selection style, just click and Shift-click the corners of your selection block.)

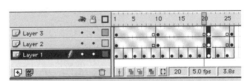

Figure 11.9 Pasting a multiple-layer, multiple-frame selection at the end of a movie extends the movie to accommodate the new frames and layers.

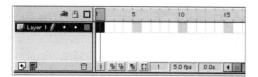

Figure 11.10 When you paste a multiple-layer, multiple-frame selection into a new scene, Flash creates new layers and frames to hold the contents of the Clipboard.

To paste a multiple-layer selection into a new scene:

1. Using the document that you created in the preceding exercise, insert a new scene, following the instructions in the first exercise in this chapter.

   By default, the new scene has one layer and one frame.

2. Select Frame 1.

3. From the Edit menu, choose Paste Frames.

   Flash pastes the copied selection from the first scene (frames 5 through 10 on layers 1 through 3) into the new scene. Flash adds layers 2 and 3 and creates frames 1 through 6 in each layer (**Figure 11.10**). Layer 1 now displays the number 5 at Frame 1, 7 at Frame 3, and 9 at Frame 5.

Animating Multiple Motion Tweens

As you learned in Chapter 9, Flash can motion-tween only one item per layer. You can tween multiple items simultaneously; you just have to put each one on a separate layer. You can use Onion Skin and Edit Multiple Frame modes to make sure that all the elements line up in the right place at the right time. To get a feel for tweening multiple items, try combining three simple motion tweens to create a game of Ping-Pong. One layer contains the ball; the other layers each contain a paddle.

To set up the three graphics in separate layers:

1. Open a new Flash document, and add two new layers.

   This arrangement gives you a total of three layers in the movie.

2. Rename the layers.

   Name the top layer Ball, the next layer 1st Paddle, and the bottom layer 2nd Paddle. Naming the layers helps you keep track of the elements and their locations.

3. Create the graphics.

   On the Stage, in the Ball layer, use the oval tool to create a circle; in the layer named 1st Paddle, use the rectangle tool to create a paddle; and then copy the paddle and paste the copy into the layer named 2nd Paddle. Give each shape a different color. Your file should look something like **Figure 11.11**.

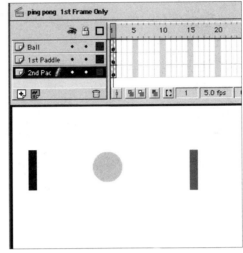

Figure 11.11 To have several graphics motion-tween simultaneously, you must place each one on a separate layer. Here, each item is on a separate layer. The descriptive layer names help you keep track of what goes where.

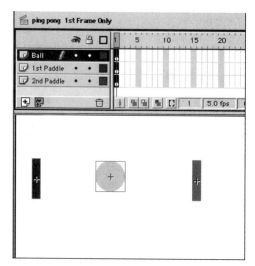

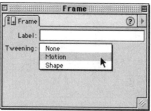

Figure 11.12 By using the Create Motion Tween command with frames selected on all three layers, you create three motion tweens with one command.

To set up the tween in all layers with one command:

1. Using the document that you created in the preceding task, in the Timeline, select Frame 1 in all three layers.

2. From the Insert menu, choose Create Motion Tween.

   Flash turns each shape into a symbol (naming the symbols Tween 1, Tween 2, and Tween 3) and gives all the frames the motion-tween property (**Figure 11.12**).

3. In the Timeline, select Frame 20 in all three layers.

4. From the Insert menu, choose Frame.

   Flash extends the motion tween through Frame 20 on all three layers, placing a dotted line across the frames to indicate that they are part of an incomplete motion tween. You need to reposition the symbols and create keyframes to complete the tweens.

ANIMATING MULTIPLE MOTION TWEENS

To adjust the positions of the tweened items:

1. Using the document that you created in the preceding task, in the Timeline, position the playhead in Frame 5.

2. On the Stage, drag the ball to the approximate location where it should connect with one of the paddles for the first hit.

   Flash makes Ball the active layer and creates a keyframe (in Frame 5) for the ball in its new location (**Figure 11.13**). Flash completes the motion tween between Frame 1 and Frame 5 of the Ball layer and leaves the broken-tween line in all the other frames.

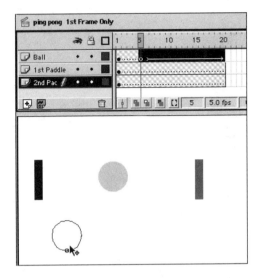

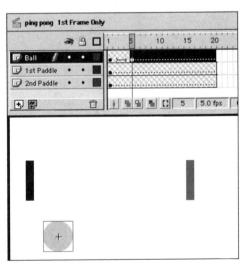

Figure 11.13 Moving a graphic in a frame that's defined as part of a motion tween causes Flash to make the layer containing the graphic the active layer. Flash creates a keyframe in that layer for the graphic's new position, completing one tween sequence.

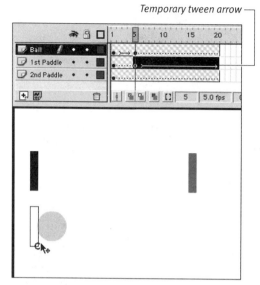

Temporary tween arrow

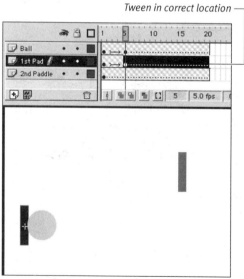

Tween in correct location

Figure 11.14 As you reposition the paddle, Flash appears to be putting the tween in the wrong set of frames (top), but when you release the mouse button, Flash correctly tweens frames 1 through 4 (bottom).

3. On the Stage, reposition the first paddle graphic so that the paddle connects with the ball for the first hit.

Flash makes 1st Paddle the active layer and creates a keyframe (in Frame 5) for the paddle in its new location (**Figure 11.14**).

4. In the Timeline, position the playhead in Frame 10.

5. On the Stage, drag the ball to the approximate location where you want it to connect with a paddle for the second hit.

Flash makes Ball the active layer and creates a keyframe (in Frame 10) for the ball in its new location. Flash completes the motion tween between Frame 5 and Frame 10 of the Ball layer.

continues on next page

ANIMATING MULTIPLE MOTION TWEENS

6. On the Stage, reposition the second paddle so that it connects with the ball for the second hit.

Flash makes 2nd Paddle the active layer and creates a keyframe (in Frame 10) for the paddle in its new location (**Figure 11.15**).

7. Repeat steps 1 through 6, using keyframes 15 and 20, to make the ball connect with each paddle one more time.

8. Play the movie to see the animation in action.

9. Select Onion Skin Outlines and Edit Multiple Frames, and reposition objects as necessary to fine-tune the motion (**Figure 11.16**).

✔ Tips

■ After you define a set of frames as tweens, any slight change in an object causes Flash to create a new keyframe. Even simply double-clicking an object causes Flash to insert a keyframe. So that you don't accidentally change objects' positions or create new keyframes, lock or hide the layers that you're not working on.

■ To position elements on the Stage with greater precision than dragging allows, use the Info panel to set the elements' x and y coordinates.

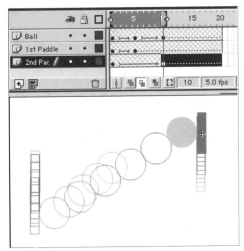

Figure 11.15 Moving an element in another frame creates another tween. Here, the paddle on the right side appears to move more slowly than the paddle on the left side, because Flash is creating a 10-frame tween for the right paddle while the left paddle tweens in five frames.

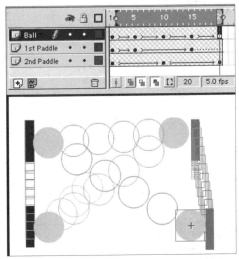

Figure 11.16 Selecting Onion Skin Outlines and Edit Multiple Frames makes fine-tuning the location of objects easier. Here, the paddle on the right doesn't move in a straight line. If you want it to do so, reposition the paddle so that one lies directly above the other; then reposition the ball so that it comes into contact with both paddles.

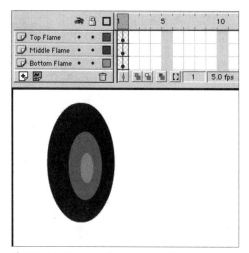

Figure 11.17 Create each part of a multiple-element shape tween on a separate layer. Name the layers to help you track what goes where.

Animating Shape Tweens in Multiple-Shape Graphics

An important thing to remember about complex shape tweens is that Flash deals most reliably with a single shape tween on a layer. In the following exercises, you create a multipart, multilayer graphic and shape-tween the whole package simultaneously.

To create shape tweens on separate layers:

1. Open a new Flash document, and add two new layers.

2. Rename the layers Top Flame, Middle Flame, and Bottom Flame.

Naming the layers helps you keep track of the objects and their locations.

3. Create the shapes.

On the Stage, use the oval tool to create three concentric oval shapes. In the Bottom Flame layer, create a large oval; in the Middle Flame layer, create a medium oval (center it over the first oval); in the Top Flame layer, create a small oval (center it over the medium oval). Give each oval a different color. Your file should look something like **Figure 11.17**.

continues on next page

When Should One Element Span Several Layers?

Often, an element that you think of as a single entity actually consists of several shapes in Flash. A candle flame is a good example. To simulate the flickering of a lighted candle, you might create a flame with three shades of orange and then animate changes in the flame shape and colors.

One natural way to do this is to draw each flame segment in the same layer so that you can immediately see the interaction of the shapes. Unfortunately, Flash has trouble tweening shapes that you create that way. You'll be better off creating a rough version of each segment in a separate layer and then fine-tuning that version. That way, Flash has to tween only one shape per layer, and the result will be cleaner.

4. Select Frame 5 in all three layers.

5. From the Insert menu, choose Keyframe. Flash creates a keyframe with the same content as Frame 1 for each layer.

6. In the Timeline, select any of the frames in the Keyframe 1 unit (frame 1, 2, 3, or 4) in all three layers.

7. From the Frame panel's Tweening menu, choose Shape.

    Flash gives the shape-tween property to frames 1 through 4 on all three layers (**Figure 11.18**). To create flickering flames, you need to reshape the ovals in Frame 5.

8. In the Timeline, position the playhead in Frame 5.

9. On the Stage, edit the ovals to create flame shapes.

10. Play the movie to see the animation in action.

    Flash handles the shape-tweening of each layer separately. For comparison, try creating the oval and flame shapes on a single layer and then shape-tweening them (**Figure 11.19**).

11. Select Onion Skin Outlines and Edit Multiple Frames; then reposition the flame objects as necessary to fine-tune the motion.

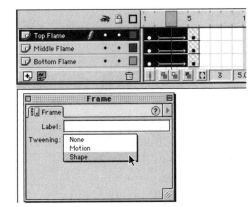

Figure 11.18 When you select multiple frames, you can set the tweening property for those frames simultaneously.

Figure 11.19 With the three colors of flames on separate layers (left), Flash does a reasonable job of tweening even when you don't add shape hints. With the three flame shapes on a single layer (right), Flash has great difficulty creating the tweens.

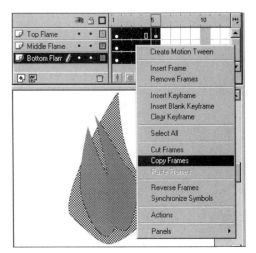

Figure 11.20 The contextual menu for frames lets you copy all currently selected frames with a single command.

Figure 11.21 After you paste the copied selection, the second tween sequence ends with the tall, flickering flame.

Reversing Frames

Sometimes, you can save work by creating just half the animation that you need and letting Flash do the rest of the work. Think of the candle flame that you created in the preceding section. You might want the flame to grow larger and then shrink back to its original size. The shrinking phase is really just the reverse of the growing phase. You can make a copy of the growing-flame animation and then have Flash reverse the order of the frames.

To reverse the order of frames:

1. Open the document that you created in the preceding section.

   This movie spans five frames on three layers. The first keyframe shows the flame as three concentric oval shapes; the final keyframe shows the flame in a taller, flickering configuration.

2. In the Timeline, select all five frames on all three layers.

3. In one of the selected frames, Control-click (Mac) or right-click (Windows) to access the contextual frame-editing menu; then choose Copy Frames (**Figure 11.20**).

4. In the Timeline, select Frame 6 in all three layers.

5. In one of the selected frames, Control-click (Mac) or right-click (Windows) to access the contextual frame-editing menu, and choose Paste Frames from that menu.

   Your movie now contains two back-to-back animation sequences of the growing flame (**Figure 11.21**).

   continues on next page

6. In the Timeline, select frames 6 through 10 on all three layers.

7. From the Modify menu, choose Frames > Reverse (**Figure 11.22**).

Flash reverses the tween in the second sequence so that the flame starts out tall and flickery and winds up in the final keyframe in its original oval configuration (**Figure 11.23**).

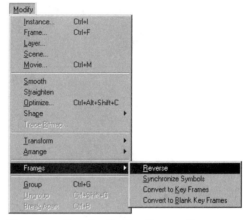

Figure 11.22 Choosing Modify > Frames > Reverse rearranges the order of selected frames. Use this command to make a selected tween go in "reverse."

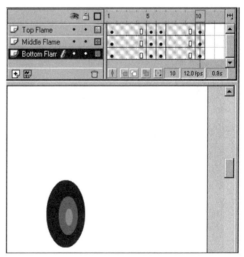

Figure 11.23 After you reverse the frames, the second tween sequence ends with the oval flame.

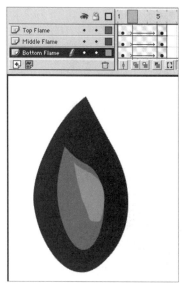

Figure 11.24 Flash's shape tween in Frame 2 leaves something to be desired.

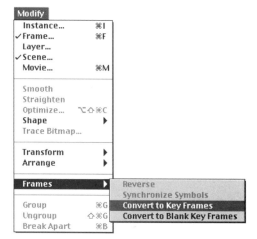

Figure 11. 25 Choose Modify > Frames > Convert to Key Frames to add a keyframe for adjusting your multilayer tween.

Combining Tweening with Frame-by-Frame Techniques

Especially with shape tweening, you cannot rely on Flash to create the in-between frames that capture the exact movement you want. You can combine Flash's tweening with your own frame-by-frame efforts, however, letting Flash do the work whenever it can. Or let Flash create the broad outlines of your animation and then add keyframes to refine the movement. Flash helps with the process by allowing you to convert those intangible in-between frames to keyframes that you can edit and refine yourself.

In the preceding section, you created a crude version of a flickering flame. In the following exercises, you refine it.

To convert in-between frames to keyframes:

1. Open the Flash document that you created in the preceding section.

2. In the Timeline, position the playhead in Frame 2.

The first step in this tween is not particularly effective: The central flame portion seems to be a bit too far to the side (**Figure 11.24**). Because Frame 2 is an in-between frame, however, you can't edit it. You can try to improve the motion by adding shape hints, or you can create a new keyframe to refine the animation.

3. To convert the in-between frame to a keyframe, in the Timeline, select Frame 2 in all three layers.

4. From the Modify menu, choose Frames > Convert to Key Frames (**Figure 11. 25**).

continues on next page

Flash converts Frame 2 from an in-between frame to a keyframe. You are now free to edit the contents to improve the tweening action (**Figure 11.26**). If you want to create a smoother motion, expand the tween between Keyframe 1 and Keyframe 2.

5. To add more in-between frames, position the playhead in Frame 1.

6. From the Insert menu, choose Frame.

   Flash adds new in-between frames in all layers. These frames inherit the shape-tween property that you defined for Frame 1. You can now examine Flash's tweening for the new frames and repeat the process of converting any awkward tween frames to keyframes and editing them.

✔ Tips

■ You can convert multiple in-between frames of a shape or motion tween by selecting them and then choosing Modify > Frames > Convert to Key Frames.

■ Flash limits you to one color change per tween sequence. To speed the process of making several color changes, set up one long tween (either motion or shape) that goes from the initial color to the final color. Then selectively convert in-between frames to keyframes so that you can make additional color changes.

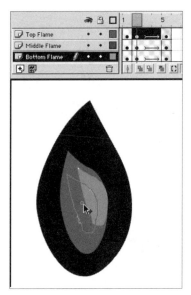

Figure 11.26 After you convert Frame 2 from an in-between frame (part of a tween) to a keyframe, you can edit the flame objects.

Figure 11.27 An easy way to create a rainbow object is to fill a circle with a multiple-color radial gradient and then delete the bottom half of the circle. Here, bisecting the circle by drawing a line through it (middle) makes deletion easy; just select the line and the bottom half of the circle (bottom) and press Delete.

Using Animated Masks

In Chapter 5, you learned about Flash's capability to create mask layers that hide and reveal objects on lower layers. Sometimes, the best way to create the illusion of movement is to animate a mask so that it gradually hides or reveals objects. You can use any of the three types of animation on a mask layer: frame-by-frame, motion tweening, or shape tweening.

Imagine a line that starts at the left edge of the Stage and goes all the way to the right edge. If you create a mask that reveals the line bit by bit, you create the illusion of a line that draws itself. Reverse the process, and you have a line that gradually erases itself.

Creating rotating and shape-tweened mask graphics can give you some interesting effects. For practice, try animating a mask that creates a growing rainbow. When you get the hang of the technique, you'll see when it's more efficient to animate elements on a mask layer than it is to animate the items that people will see in your movie.

To create an animated mask:

1. Open a new Flash document, and add a second layer.

2. In the Timeline, rename the bottom layer Rainbow, and rename the top layer Rotating Rectangle.

3. In Frame 1 of the Rainbow layer, on the Stage, use the oval tool to draw a perfect circle with a radial-gradient fill.

   To create a rainbow effect, use a gradient that has distinct bands of color.

4. Erase the bottom half of the circle (**Figure 11.27**).

continues on next page

This is your rainbow graphic. For safety, select the graphic and then choose Insert > Convert to Symbol so that you'll have a copy of the rainbow in case you accidentally delete the original.

5. In the Timeline, Control-click (Mac) or right-click (Windows) the Rotating Rectangle layer.

   The contextual menu for layers appears.

6. Choose Mask.

   Flash converts the layer to a mask, links the Rainbow layer to the mask, and locks both layers (**Figure 11.28**).

7. In the Timeline, click the padlock icons in the Rotating Rectangle and Rainbow layers to unlock them.

8. On the Stage, in Frame 1 of the Rotating Rectangle layer, use the rectangle tool to draw a rectangle just below the bottom of the rainbow (**Figure 11.29**).

   The rectangle is your mask. Any items that lie below the rectangle on a linked layer appear; everything else is hidden.

   Make the rectangle a bit larger than the rainbow so that the mask covers the whole rainbow. Using a transparent fill color lets you see the rainbow graphic through the mask graphic and helps you verify the mask's position. (To make the rectangle's fill color transparent, select it and then, in the Mixer panel, assign it a low Alpha percentage.)

9. Select the rectangle, and choose Insert > Convert to Symbol or Modify > Group.

   Because you want to create rotational animation, you must use a motion tween for the mask, which means that you must use a symbol or a grouped element.

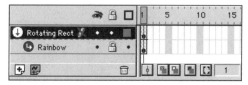

Figure 11.28 When you create a mask layer, Flash automatically links the layer directly below the mask layer in the Timeline and locks both layers.

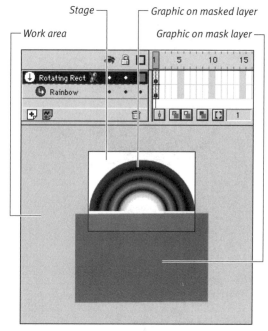

Figure 11.29 To create a mask that reveals the entire rainbow, draw a rectangle that's wider and taller than the rainbow graphic. Here, the rectangle is wider than the Stage, extending into the work area. Positioning the rectangle below the rainbow graphic hides the rainbow completely.

Figure 11.30 Choose Modify > Transform > Edit Center to reposition the point around which a symbol (or grouped item) rotates. Use the arrow tool to drag the crosshair that indicates the center point to a new position. A small circle previews the new center-point location.

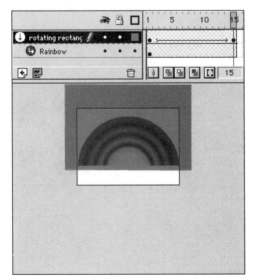

Figure 11.31 The final keyframe with the completed motion tween for the mask object. The mask rectangle has a transparent fill so that you can see the rainbow through it as you work. The transparency of objects on the mask layer doesn't appear in the final movie.

10. With the rectangle selected on the Stage, choose Modify > Transform > Edit Center, and reposition the crosshair that indicates the center of the object.

Use the arrow tool to move the crosshair straight up until it rests in the middle of the top edge of the rectangle (**Figure 11.30**). Then you can easily rotate the rectangle so that it swings up and over the rainbow.

11. In the Timeline, in the Rainbow layer, select Frame 15, and choose Insert > Frame.

12. In the Timeline, in the Rotating Rectangle layer, select Frame 15, and choose Insert > Keyframe.

13. In Frame 15, with the rectangle selected on the Stage, use the Rotate modifier of the arrow tool to reposition the rectangle. Click and drag the bottom-left corner of the rectangle and rotate it so that the rectangle completely covers the rainbow.

When you cover the rainbow, the mask graphic reveals the rainbow in the final movie.

14. In the Timeline, in the Rotating Rectangle layer, select any of the frames in the Keyframe 1 unit (frames 1 through 14).

15. From the Frame panel's Tweening menu, choose Motion.

16. From the Rotate menu, choose CW.

This step sets up the motion tween that rotates the rectangle, swinging it up and over the rainbow until it fully covers the rainbow (**Figure 11.31**).

continues on next page

17. To preview the animation, in the Timeline, lock both layers and play the movie.

If the rainbow is not fully revealed during the tween, you may need to enlarge or reposition the rectangle. Unlock both layers, and play the movie to see where the rectangle is in each in-between frame (**Figure 11.32**).

To make the rainbow appear to fade in gradually, create a keyframe for it in Frame 15 and tween a change in transparency for the rainbow graphic. If you made the rainbow object a symbol, select it in Frame 1 and assign it a low alpha value in the Effect panel.

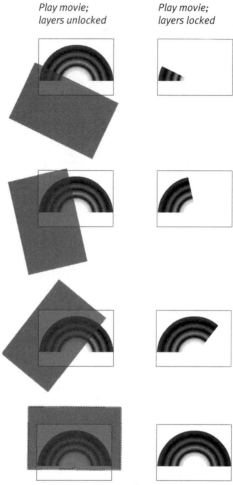

Play movie; layers unlocked　　　*Play movie; layers locked*

Figure 11.32 As you play the movie with the layers unlocked (left), you can see the in-between positions of the mask graphic. When you lock the layers (right), you see the masking as it will appear in the final exported movie.

Saving Animations As Graphic Symbols

One great thing about symbols is that they allow you to use the work you do over and over. In Chapter 6, you learned to save work and keep file sizes small by using symbols. Flash lets you do the same thing with entire multiple-frame, multiple-layer animation sequences. You can save such sequences either as an animated graphic symbol or as a movie-clip symbol. You can use these symbols repeatedly with a much smaller hit on file size than if you simply re-create the animation by using graphic-symbol instances within separate animations. Additionally, for complex animations, symbols help keep down the number of frames and layers that you have to deal with at any time.

In general, for tweened animations, you need to place each shape on a separate layer. To animate a character, for example, create separate layers for the head, the torso, each arm, and each leg. For complex motion, you might even create separate layers for eyes, mouth, fingers, and toes. Add some other elements to the character's environment, and you wind up dealing with many layers.

Turning an animation sequence into a symbol in effect collapses all those layers into one object. The process is a bit like grouping. On the Stage, the symbol exists on a single layer, but contained within that layer are all the layers of the original animation.

How Do Animated Graphic Symbols Differ From Movie-Clip Symbols?

Flash provides for two kinds of animated symbols: graphic symbols and movie clips. The difference is a bit subtle and hard to grasp at first. An animated graphic symbol is tied to the Timeline of any movie in which you place the symbol, whereas a movie-clip symbol runs on its own independent Timeline.

You can think of animated graphic symbols as being a slide show. Each frame of the symbol is a separate slide. When you move to the next frame in the animated graphic symbol, you must move to another frame in the hosting movie. Also, there's no sound track. Even if you have sounds or interactivity functions in a movie, when you convert it to a graphic symbol, you lose those features.

A movie-clip symbol is like a film loop. You can project all its frames one after another, over and over, in a single frame of the hosting movie. Movie clips do have a sound track and do retain their interactivity. (To learn more about interactivity, see Chapters 12 and 13.)

One more thing to know about the two symbol types is that movie clips, because they run on their own Timeline, do not appear as animations in the Flash editing environment. You see only the first frame of the movie as a static object on the Stage. Animated graphic symbols, which use the same Timeline as the main movie does, do display their animation in movie-editing mode.

To convert an animation to a graphic symbol:

1. Open the document that you created to make the Ping-Pong animation in "Animating Multiple Motion Tweens," earlier in this chapter, or create your own multiple-layer animation.

The Ping-Pong animation is a three-layer, 20-frame animation.

2. In the Timeline, select all 20 frames in all three layers.

3. From the Edit menu, choose Copy Frames.

4. From the Insert menu, choose New Symbol, or press ⌘-F8 (Mac) or Ctrl-F8 (Windows).

The Symbol Properties dialog box appears (**Figure 11.33**).

5. In the Symbol Properties dialog box, type a name for your symbol—for example, Ping Pong Animation.

6. Choose Graphic as the behavior type.

In Flash, a symbol's behavior identifies what kind of symbol it is: graphic, button, or movie clip. Movie Clip behavior is the default for all new symbols.

7. Click OK.

Flash creates a new symbol in the library and switches you to symbol-editing mode, with that symbol selected.

The name of your symbol appears in the top-left corner of the window. The default Timeline for your new symbol consists of just one layer and a blank keyframe at Frame 1.

continues on next page

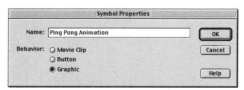

Figure 11.33 You set a new symbol's behavior in the Symbol Properties dialog box. Movie Clip is the default behavior for new symbols. Movie clips operate from their own, independent Timeline. Animated graphic symbols share a Timeline with the main movie that contains them. One frame of the main movie displays one frame of the symbol.

SAVING ANIMATIONS AS GRAPHIC SYMBOLS

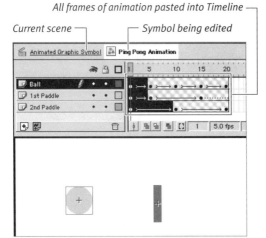

All frames of animation pasted into Timeline

Current scene

Symbol being edited

Figure 11.34 When you create a new symbol, Flash switches to symbol-editing mode, making the new symbol's Timeline available for editing. You must paste all the frames of your animation into the symbol's Timeline to create the animated symbol.

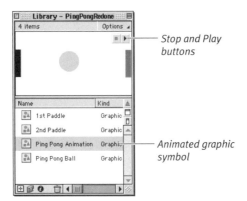

Stop and Play buttons

Animated graphic symbol

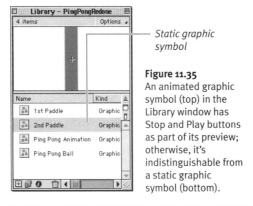

Static graphic symbol

Figure 11.35 An animated graphic symbol (top) in the Library window has Stop and Play buttons as part of its preview; otherwise, it's indistinguishable from a static graphic symbol (bottom).

8. In the symbol Timeline, select Frame 1, and choose Edit > Paste Frames.

Flash pastes the 20 frames and three layers that you copied from the original Ping-Pong movie into the Timeline for the Ping Pong Animation symbol (**Figure 11.34**). If you want to make any adjustments in the animation sequence, you can do so at this point.

9. To return to movie-editing mode, click the current scene name in the top-left corner of the window.

✔ Tips

■ In the list of symbols in the Library window, an animated graphic symbol looks the same as a static graphic; both have the same icon, and both are listed as Graphic in the Kind column (**Figure 11.35**). The animated graphic, however, has Play and Stop buttons in the top-right corner of the Library window; static graphics do not. You can preview an animated symbol by clicking the Play button.

■ When you copy frames on multiple layers and paste them into the Timeline of a new symbol, Flash doesn't copy the layer names. Be sure to rename your layers to help keep things organized.

SAVING ANIMATIONS AS GRAPHIC SYMBOLS

Using Animated Graphic Symbols

To put an animated graphic symbol to work, you must place an instance of it in your main movie. The layer containing the movie must have enough frames to display the frames of the symbol. You can use instances of an animated graphic symbol just as you would any other symbol—combine it with other graphics on a layer; motion-tween it; modify its color, size, and rotation; and so on.

To place an instance of an animated graphic symbol:

1. Using the movie and symbol that you created in the preceding section, from the Insert menu, choose Scene to create a new scene.

   Flash displays the new scene's Timeline—a single layer with a blank keyframe in Frame 1. The Stage is empty.

   Adding a new scene gives you a blank Stage to work with and makes it easy to compare the two animations: the original, created directly in the main movie; and the instance of the graphic symbol placed in the movie.

2. From the Window menu, choose Library.

3. In the Library window for your document, select the Ping Pong Animation symbol.

   The first frame of the animation appears in the preview window.

4. Drag a copy of the selected symbol to the Stage.

   Flash places the symbol in Keyframe 1. At this point, you can see only the first frame of the animation (**Figure 11.36**). The animation is 20 frames long, so you need to add least 20 frames to view the symbol in its entirety.

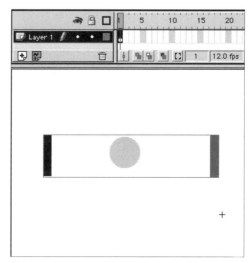

Figure 11.36 When you drag an instance of the animated graphic to the Stage, you see the symbol's first frame with its graphics selected. You must add frames to allow the full animation of the symbol to play in the main movie.

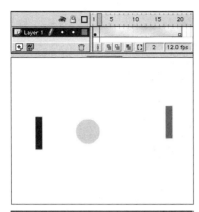

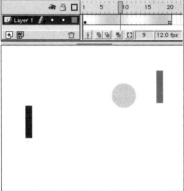

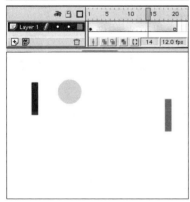

Figure 11.37 Frames 2 through 20 have a tweening property of None, but they still display animation. Flash displays the 20 tween frames of the graphic symbol that you placed in Keyframe 1. It's as though the symbol is a tray of slides, and Flash is projecting one image per frame in the main movie. If the main movie is longer than the slide show, Flash just starts the slide show over.

5. In the Timeline, select Frame 20, and choose Insert > Frame.

Flash adds in-between frames 2 through 20.

6. Play the movie.

Flash can now display each frame of the animated graphic symbol in a frame of the movie. Frame 2 of the symbol appears in Frame 2 of the movie, Frame 5 of the symbol appears in Frame 5 of the movie, and so on (**Figure 11.37**). If you place fewer than 20 frames in the movie, Flash truncates the symbol and displays only as many frames of the symbol as there are frames in the movie.

✔ Tip

■ To create complex motion, you can use animated graphic symbols in motion tweens in your main movie. You can create, for example, an animated graphic symbol of a bug whose legs move to simulate walking. Place an instance of the bug symbol in keyframes at frames 1 and 5. You can motion-tween the bug symbol in your main movie and add a motion layer to make the wiggly bug follow a path.

USING ANIMATED GRAPHIC SYMBOLS

Saving Animations As Movie-Clip Symbols

The procedure that you use to save an animation as a movie-clip symbol is the same as for saving an animated graphic symbol, except that you define the symbol as a movie clip in the Symbol Properties dialog box.

To convert an animation to a movie-clip symbol:

1. Open the document that you created to make the Ping-Pong animation in "Animating Multiple Motion Tweens" earlier in this chapter, or create your own multiple-layer animation.

   The Ping Pong animation is a 3-layer, 20-frame animation.

2. In the Timeline, select all 20 frames in all three layers.

3. From the Edit menu, choose Copy Frames.

4. From the Insert menu, choose New Symbol, or press ⌘-F8 (Mac) or Ctrl-F8 (Windows).

   The Symbol Properties dialog box appears.

5. In the Symbol Properties dialog box, type a name for your symbol—for example, Ping Pong Clip.

   As the default behavior, Movie Clip is already selected for your symbol (**Figure 11.38**).

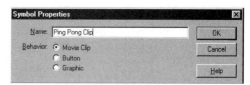

Figure 11.38 Selecting Movie Clip in the Behavior section of the Symbol Properties dialog box defines a symbol that has an independent Timeline. The entire movie-clip symbol runs in a single frame in the main movie that contains that symbol.

Current scene   *Name of symbol being edited*

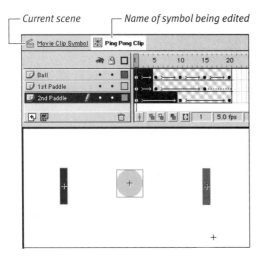

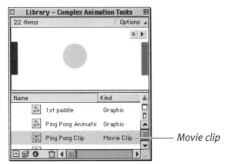

Movie clip

Figure 11.39 After you name the symbol and define its behavior in the Symbol Properties dialog box, Flash switches to symbol-editing mode. The movie-clip icon precedes the name of the symbol. You can now paste the animation frames into the symbol's Timeline.

6. Click OK.

Flash creates a new symbol in the Library window and switches you to symbol-editing mode, with that symbol selected.

The name of your symbol appears in the top-left corner of the window. The default Timeline for your new symbol consists of just one layer and a blank keyframe at Frame 1.

7. In the symbol Timeline, select Frame 1, and choose Edit > Paste Frames.

Flash pastes all the 20 frames and three layers that you copied from the original Ping-Pong movie into the Timeline for the Ping Pong Animation symbol (**Figure 11.39**). If you want to make any adjustments in the animation sequence, you can do so at this point.

8. To return to movie-editing mode, click the current scene name in the top-left corner of the window.

✔ Tip

■ If as in the preceding exercise, you want to make a movie clip that contains exactly the same frames as an existing animated graphic symbol, you can duplicate the symbol and change its behavior. Select the animated graphic symbol in the Library window. From the Library window's Options menu, choose Duplicate. The Symbol Properties dialog box appears, allowing you to rename the symbol and give it Movie Clip behavior.

Using Movie-Clip Symbols

You put movie-clip symbols to work by placing an instance of the symbol on the Stage in your Flash document. Unlike animated graphic symbols, movie-clip symbols have their own Timeline. A movie clip plays continuously—like a little film loop—in a single frame of the main movie. As long as the movie contains no other instructions that stop the clip from playing—a blank keyframe in the Timeline for the layer containing the movie clip, for example—the clip continues to loop.

As you work on your Flash document, you can see only the first frame of a movie clip. To view the animation of the movie-clip symbol in context with all the other elements of your movie, you must export the movie (by choosing one of the test modes, for example). You can preview the animation of the movie-clip symbol by itself in the Library window.

To place an instance of a movie clip:

1. With the movie that you created in the preceding exercises open, in the Scene panel, click the Add Scene button.

   Flash creates a new scene and displays in its Timeline a single layer with a blank keyframe in Frame 1. The Stage is empty.

2. Access the Library window (if it's not open, choose Window > Library).

3. Select the Ping Pong Clip symbol.

   The first frame of the animation appears in the preview window.

4. Drag a copy of the selected symbol to the Stage.

   Flash places the symbol in Keyframe 1 (**Figure 11.40**). You don't need to add any more frames to accommodate the anima-tion, but you must export the movie to see the animation.

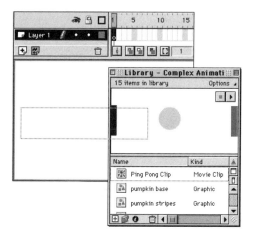

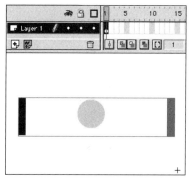

Figure 11.40 Drag an instance of your movie clip from the Library window to the Stage (top). Flash places the instance in Keyframe 1 (bottom).

Figure 11.41 Choose Control > Test Scene to preview the animation of just one scene in a movie.

Figure 11.42 The Exporting Flash Player dialog box contains a progress bar and a button for canceling the export.

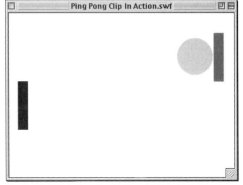

Figure 11.43 The Flash Player displays your movie in a regular window. To exit the Player, close the window.

To view movie-clip animation in a movie:

1. Using the movie that you created in the preceding exercise, from the Control menu, choose Test Scene (**Figure 11.41**).

   Flash exports the movie to a Flash Player format file, adding the .swf extension to the file name and using the current publishing settings for all the export options. (For more information on using the Publish Settings dialog box, see Chapter 16.) During export, Flash displays the Exporting Flash Player dialog box, which contains a progress bar and a Stop (Mac) or Cancel (Windows) button for canceling the operation (**Figure 11.42**).

   When it finishes exporting the movie, Flash opens the .swf file in Flash Player so that you can see the movie in action (**Figure 11.43**).

2. When you have seen enough of the movie in test mode, click the movie window's Close box to exit Flash Player.

   Flash returns you to the editing environment.

USING MOVIE-CLIP SYMBOLS

INTERACTIVITY WITH SIMPLE FRAME ACTIONS

12

By default, Macromedia Flash plays the scenes and frames of a movie sequentially. The movie opens with Scene 1, plays all those frames in order, moves to Scene 2, plays all those frames, and so on. Sometimes, that's appropriate. But you can also instruct Flash to jump around in a movie, playing scenes and frames in any order you choose.

You tell Flash what to do by assigning *actions* to frames, buttons, and movie clips in a movie. Actions are a set of commands, or *statements,* that you can string together to make Flash perform certain...well, actions, such as replaying Scene 2 at the end of every other scene or repeatedly displaying the first five frames of a movie until all the other frames in the movie have loaded onto the viewer's computer. Actions can add efficiency and a degree of intelligence or interactivity to your movie.

Flash 5 provides a full-fledged scripting language called ActionScript for adding actions to movies. You create ActionScripts in the Actions panel, which provides various levels of scripting assistance.

In this chapter, you learn about the Actions panel by assigning some simple actions to frames, using Flash's most-assisted scripting mode: Normal. To learn about creating buttons and attaching actions to buttons and movie clips, see Chapter 13. To learn about more-complex actions, see Chapter 15.

Using the Actions Panel

You construct ActionScripts in a window in the Actions panel, called the Actions List. You basically have two ways to get actions into the list. In Normal mode, you choose English-like statements from a menu or list. Flash helps you fill in any parameters appropriate to the statements and translates them into ActionScript. In Expert mode, you can choose statements from a list, enter ActionScript statements into the Actions List directly or import them from a text editor. The statements available in the Normal and Expert modes are the same; in Expert mode, however, you must always script any parameters yourself.

You can set the ActionScript mode as a preference so that Flash automatically opens the Actions panel in your preferred mode. You can also switch modes from the Actions panel itself. For the following exercises, keep the Frame Actions panel set to Normal mode.

Two Types of Actions

Flash can attach actions to frames and to objects (buttons and movie clips). Flash calls actions attached to a frame *frame actions*. Frame actions require no input from the person watching your movie. In the final exported movie, when the playhead reaches a frame that contains an action, Flash carries out the instruction.

Flash calls actions attached to buttons and movie clips *object actions*. Actions attached to buttons require input from someone who is viewing the movie. In a text-heavy frame, for example, you could make Flash pause the movie until the user clicks a button.

Actions attached to movie clips can respond to user input. If your text-heavy frame also contains a movie clip, for example, you could attach an action to the movie clip that pauses playback until the user clicks anywhere in the same frame. Movie-clip actions can also be triggered without user intervention. You might, for example, have Flash stop playing all sounds when a movie clip first appears. Attaching that action to the movie clip instead of the frame containing the movie clip lets you tie the soundtrack more precisely to the movie clip's appearance.

Figure 12.1
With a frame selected in the Timeline, choose Window > Actions (top) or click the Show Actions button in the Launcher bar (bottom) to access the Frame Actions panel.

To access the Actions panel:

If the Actions panel is not currently active, *do one of the following:*

◆ From the Window menu, choose Actions or press ⌘-Option-A (Mac) or Ctrl-Alt-A (Windows).

◆ In the Launcher bar at the bottom of the Stage, click the Show Actions button (**Figure 12.1**).

The Frame Actions panel opens or comes to the front if it's grouped in a window with other panels.

The Actions panel is quite large. You resize the panel as you would any other window. You also have several options for hiding and showing certain portions of the panel.

To customize the Actions panel display:

With the Actions panel open, *do one of the following:*

◆ To hide the Toolbox List and display the Actions List full width, click the triangle between the Toolbox List window and the Actions List window.

◆ When the Toolbox List is hidden, to show it, click the triangle to the left of the Actions List window.

continues on next page

USING THE ACTIONS PANEL

- ◆ To hide/show the Parameters pane, click the triangle in the bottom-right corner of the Frame Actions panel.
- ◆ To reveal the Options menu, click the triangle in the top-right corner of the Frame Actions panel (**Figure 12.2**).

✔ Tips

- ■ Double-clicking a frame in the Timeline opens the Frame Actions panel and—in the default panel set—a window containing the Sound and Frame panels, with the Sound panel foremost. If you put the Sound and Frame panels in separate windows, you can make all Frame-related panels available with that double-click.

- ■ If you happened to click the Stage or work area, the name of the open panel changes from Frame Actions to Object Actions. To return to the Frame Actions panel, click the Timeline. You learn about the Object Actions panel in Chapter 13.

To choose Normal mode for ActionScripting:

- ◆ In the Actions panel, from the Options menu in the top-right corner, choose Normal Mode.

✔ Tips

- ■ The Options menu in the Frame Actions panel lists keyboard shortcuts for switching between Normal and Expert modes. These shortcuts are available only when you have actually selected something in the Toolbox List.

- ■ Normal mode is Flash's default setting for ActionScripting. If you prefer to have Flash open the Actions panel with Expert mode selected, choose Edit > Preferences > General and then in the Actions Panel section, choose Expert from the Mode menu.

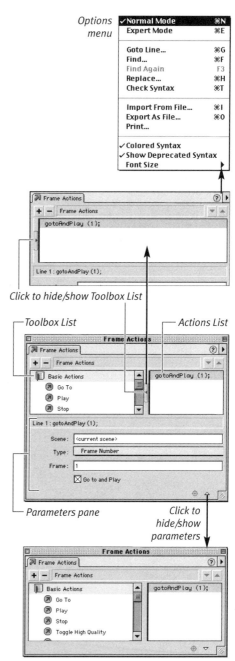

Figure 12.2 The Frame Actions panel in Normal mode has three main areas: the Toolbox List, where you choose actions; the Actions List, where Flash assembles the ActionScript; and the Parameters pane, where you identify items to be acted upon. You can resize these areas to view just what you need.

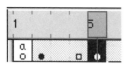

Figure 12.3 Keyframes that contain actions display the letter *a* in the Timeline.

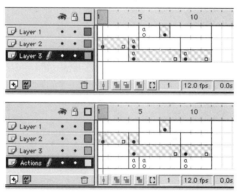

Figure 12.4 When you assign actions to many layers (top), it's harder to find them, and you might accidentally assign actions to the same frame number on different layers. Adding a separate layer just for actions (bottom) makes it easy to find them all and to see whether a certain frame does contain an action.

The Pitfall of Placing Actions on Multiple Layers

At each point in the Timeline, Flash implements the actions in the highest-level frame that contains an action. Imagine a three-layer movie. Frame 2 of the top layer contains no actions. In Frame 2 of the middle layer, an action tells Flash to skip to Frame 5. In Frame 2 of the bottom layer, an action tells Flash to skip to Frame 10. When you play this movie and the playhead hits Frame 2, Flash looks in the top layer for actions and finds none. Flash moves to the next layer down. There, it finds an instruction and follows it. Flash whisks you away to Frame 5; it never has a chance to get to the instruction in the bottom layer. But if you reorder the layers so that the bottom layer is on top, Flash whisks you to Frame 10 instead of Frame 5! This situation could cause havoc with your movie.

Organizing Actions

Flash identifies each frame that has attached actions by putting a little letter *a* in that frame in the Timeline (**Figure 12.3**). But can you imagine scrolling through dozens—or hundreds—of layers, looking for little letter *a*'s when you want to edit a movie's actions? That's a recipe for eyestrain. Create a layer just for actions, so that you'll know exactly where the actions are at any point in the Timeline. Also, with a separate layer for actions, you won't accidentally assign actions to two different layers at the same point in the Timeline, which could cause problems if you reorder the layers.

To create a separate layer for actions:

1. Add a new layer.

   (For more detailed instructions on adding layers, see Chapter 5.)

2. Rename the layer Actions.

3. Drag the layer to the top or bottom of the Timeline.

   With a separate Actions layer as the top or bottom layer, you'll always know where to find the frames that contain actions when you need to modify or add to them (**Figure 12.4**).

✔ Tip

- To prevent yourself from accidentally adding any graphics to the Actions layer, lock it. Locking keeps you from making changes in the elements on the Stage for that layer, but it doesn't prevent you from adding actions to frames.

ORGANIZING ACTIONS

Choosing Actions

In Normal mode, the Actions panel provides two ways for you to select action statements to include in an ActionScript: You can choose items from a drop-down hierarchical menu, or you can choose items from a scrolling hierarchical list.

To use the Add Statement menu:

1. In the Frame Actions panel, click the Add Statement button (the one with a plus sign).

A menu of action-statement categories appears.

2. Choose a category.

A submenu of action statements appears (**Figure 12.5**).

3. Choose a statement.

Flash adds the chosen statement to the Actions list: the window in the top-right section of the Actions panel.

✔ Tip

■ The Add Statement menu is always available. Use it to create ActionScripts when you've configured the Actions panel to hide the Toolbox List.

Figure 12.5 The hierarchical Add Statement pop-up menu lists actions to choose from.

The Mystery of ActionScript Spelling

What's the difference between Toggle High Quality and `toggleHighQuality`? Spaces and capitalization.

ActionScript statements often consist of several words or word fragments. Just smashing the words together makes them hard to read, but the ActionScript language reserves the space character to act as a separator between statements. Adding internal capitalization makes the multiword statements easier to decipher.

What looks like English in the Basic Actions category of the Toolbox List, Stop All Sounds, for example, winds up in the Actions List as `stopAllSounds`.

In the other categories in the Toolbox List, action statements appear in their ActionScript-code form. Throughout this book, when referring to an action you choose from Basic Actions, we'll use the English-like form. When referring to actions in other categories or statements that appear in the ActionScript List, we'll use the coded form.

The Mystery of Action Categories

In Flash 4, you put together ActionScripts by choosing statements from a single menu. With Flash 5's expanded ActionScript language, scrolling through one monster list of statements would be impractical; Flash organizes statements hierarchically. Expert mode offers five action categories: Actions, Operators, Functions, Properties, and Objects. Normal mode includes those five and adds one more: Basic Actions. Here's a breakdown of what's in each category.

◆ **Basic Actions** includes the actions that are available in Flash 4. They are the basic instructions for navigating and controlling movies. You can use the items in Basic Actions to create ActionScripts that stop and start playback of a movie, jump to specific frames or scenes, load and unload new movies, and respond to viewers' mouse movements or keyboard input.

◆ **Actions** expands on the basic set. Using statements from this category, you can create more sophisticated, subtle controls. You can create ActionScripts that do such things as test whether certain conditions are true, manipulate movie clips, and work with variables and expressions.

◆ **Operators** are tools for working with variables and expressions. You might think of operators as being mathematical symbols. You can use the + operator for adding a series of numbers, for example. There's more to operators than that, however; sometimes, you perform the "math" on text elements—for example, "adding" a series of words to form a message.

◆ **Functions** are predefined chunks of ActionScript. Just as macros in a word processor encapsulate the necessary code for repetitive typing, formatting, and so on, functions in ActionScripts encapsulate bits of ActionScript that perform frequently used operations.

◆ **Properties** are the characteristics of objects. You include properties statements in ActionScripts that control objects—for example, setting the transparency (_alpha) or screen position (_x and _y) of a movie-clip instance.

◆ **Objects** are collections of predefined properties. Many of the statements for objects are *methods*—sets of instructions for carrying out operations involving the object. The Movie Clip object, for example, includes the methods prevFrame, nextFrame, play, and stop.

CHOOSING ACTIONS

To use the Toolbox List:

1. In the Toolbox List window on the top-left side of the Frame Actions panel, click a category button.

   A sublist of action statements appears.

2. To add a statement to the Actions List, *do one of the following:*

   ◆ Double-click the statement.

   ◆ Drag the statement from the Toolbox List to the Actions List (**Figure 12.6**).

   Flash places the appropriate text in the Actions List and displays any parameters associated with the statement in the Parameters pane (the bottom portion of the Actions panel) (**Figure 12.7**).

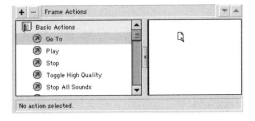

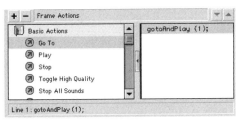

Figure 12.6 You can drag a statement from the Toolbox List (top) to the Actions List to add it to your ActionScript (bottom).

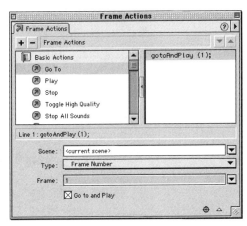

Figure 12.7 When you add a statement to the Actions List, any parameters that define the action appear at the bottom of the Actions panel.

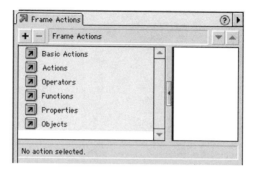

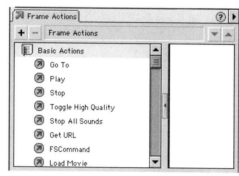

Figure 12.8 Click a category icon (top) to reveal individual action statements in the Toolbox List (bottom).

Adding Actions to a Frame

You can assign actions to only one frame at a time, but each frame can contain multiple actions. Flash executes the actions in the order in which they appear in the Actions List. To change a selected action's place in the list, click the Up and Down buttons. To get a feel for working with the Actions panel, practice adding, moving, and deleting actions that have no parameters. You learn more about how the actions and parameters operate in later exercises.

For the following exercises, create a Flash movie that has two scenes, each of which consists of two layers. To help keep track of what goes in which layer, name the bottom layer in each scene Actions; name the top layer Content. In each Content layer, insert keyframes into Frames 1 through 5. Use the text tool to place identifying text on the Stage for each frame—Scene 1·Frame 1, Scene 1·Frame 2, and so on.

To add a single action to a frame:

1. In the Timeline for Scene 1, in the Actions layer, select Frame 1.

2. In the Frame Actions panel, in the Toolbox List, click the Basic Actions icon.

   A list of basic actions opens in the scrolling window (**Figure 12.8**).

continues on next page

3. Double-click the statement Stop All Sounds.

Flash adds the action `stopAllSounds ();` to the Actions List for Frame 1.

The message No Parameters appears in the Parameters pane (**Figure 12.9**). If an action has parameters, those parameters appear at the bottom of the Frame Actions panel when you select the action in the Actions List.

(The `stopAllSounds ();` action turns off any event sounds that were initiated by earlier frames and that are still playing. To learn more about sounds, see Chapter 14.)

4. In the Timeline, deselect Frame 1.

A small letter *a* now appears in Frame 1 of the Actions layer, indicating that this frame contains actions (**Figure 12.10**).

To add multiple actions to a frame:

1. Using the file that you created in the preceding exercise—with an action in Scene 1, Frame 1 in the Actions layer—in the Timeline, select Frame 1.

2. In the Frame Actions panel in the Actions List, select `stopAllSounds ();`.

3. From the Frame Actions panel's Add Statement menu, choose Basic Actions > Toggle High Quality.

Flash adds `toggleHighQuality ();` to the list, below `stopAllSounds ();`. The message No Parameters appears in the Parameters pane.

(The `toggleHighQuality ();` action turns antialiasing on and off. Turning off antialiasing makes each frame of your movie redraw faster so that the whole movie plays faster.)

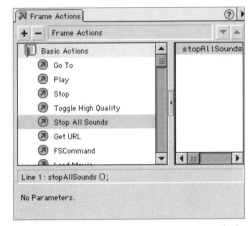

Figure 12.9 When an action has no parameters, Flash tells you so.

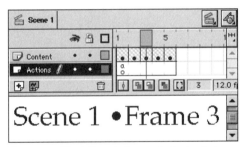

Figure 12.10 The letter *a* in Frame 1 indicates that actions are assigned to that frame.

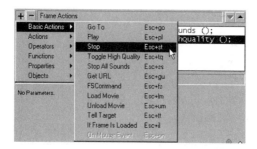

Figure 12.11 As you choose additional actions from the Toolbox List or from the Add Statement menu (top), Flash adds them below whatever action was selected in the Actions List for that frame (bottom).

Figure 12.12 When you drag an action from the Toolbox List, you can scroll the Actions List and position the action where you want it.

4. With `toggleHighQuality();` selected in the Actions List, from the Add Statement menu, choose Basic Actions > Stop.

Flash adds `stop();` to the Actions List, below the `toggleHighQuality` action. The message No Parameters appears in the Parameters pane (**Figure 12.11**).

(The Stop action makes the movie pause in the current frame until another instruction tells Flash to resume playback.)

✔ Tip

■ If you want to add an action to a particular spot in the Actions List, drag the action from the Toolbox List to the Actions List. You get the dog-eared page icon, and a highlighted line indicates where in the list the new action will go (**Figure 12.12**). If the Actions List is too long to fit in the current window, this drag technique lets you scroll up and down the list to find the spot you want.

ADDING ACTIONS TO A FRAME

Editing the Actions List

Flash plays the actions for a frame in the order in which they appear in the Actions List. The Up and Down buttons let you change the order of the actions that you've selected. The Delete Statement button lets you remove actions from the list.

For these exercises, use the file that you created in the preceding exercise. Your movie should contain two scenes, each of which contains a bottom layer named Actions and a top layer named Content. Each Content layer contains keyframes in Frames 1 through 5. The Actions layer of Frame 1 of Scene 1 contains the following actions:
stopAllSounds ();
toggleHighQuality ();
stop ();

To change the order of actions:

1. In the Timeline, select Frame 1.

2. In the Frame Actions panel's Actions List, choose stopAllSounds ();.

3. To send the action down one level in the Actions List, click the Down button.
   The stopAllSounds (); action is now the second of three actions.

4. To send the action down another level in the Actions List, click the Down button again.
   The stopAllSounds (); action is now the last of the three actions (**Figure 12.13**).

✔ Tip

■ To reorder items in the Actions List quickly, click the item you want to reposition to select it and then click and drag the item. The dog-eared page pointer appears, and you can scroll the list to find the spot where you want the item to be.

Moves selected action up one level
Moves selected action down one level

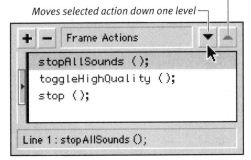

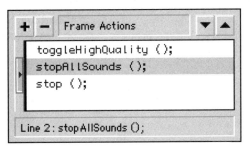

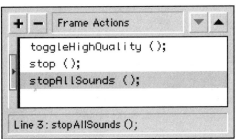

Figure 12.13 The Up and Down buttons let you change the order of the actions in the list. Select an action and then click the Down button (top) to move the action down one level (middle). Click the Down button again to move the selected action again (bottom).

Deletes selected action

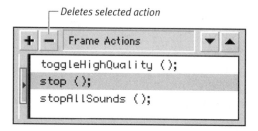

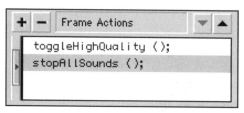

Figure 12.14 Click the Delete Statement button (top) to delete the selected action from the list (bottom).

To remove an action from the list:

1. Continuing with the file that you created in the preceding exercises, in the Timeline, select Frame 1.

2. In the Frame Actions panel, in the Actions List, select the stop (); action.

3. To remove the action from the Actions List, *do one of the following:*

    ◆ Click the Delete Statement button (the one with the minus sign).

    ◆ Press Delete.

    The Actions List now contains only two actions (**Figure 12.14**).

Using Frame Labels and Comments

Some actions call for you to specify a frame of your movie—when you want Flash to jump to a new location or to get information from a frame, for example. You can always refer to frames by number, but it's often safer to refer to them by label. That way, if you later add or subtract frames or move them around, you won't have to respecify the frame number; Flash will always find the frame by its label name. For frames that are not the target of an action, it may be more useful to add a comment that describes what's going on at this point in the movie. You can label a frame or attach a comment to it but not both. You add labels and comments through the Frame panel.

To label a frame:

1. In the Timeline, select the frame that you want to label.

2. Access the Frame panel.

3. In the Label field, type a name for this frame (**Figure 12.15**).

   Do not include spaces in frame labels.

4. In the Timeline, deselect the frame.

   In the Timeline, a little red flag appears in the labeled frame. If there's room before the next keyframe, the text of the label appears as well (**Figure 12.16**).

Figure 12.15 Enter text in the Label field of the Frame panel to label a selected frame.

Figure 12.16 A red flag in the Timeline indicates a frame that has a label. Flash prints as much of the label as fits in the keyframe unit.

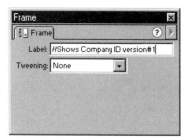

Figure 12.17 You enter comments in the Frame panel's Label field. Start the label with two slashes. Flash interprets the text as a comment.

Figure 12.18 Two green slashes identify a frame with comments. Flash displays as much comment text as fits in the keyframe unit.

To add comments to a frame:

1. In the Timeline, select the frame to which you want to add a comment.

2. Access the Frame panel.

3. In the Label field, type two slashes, followed by the comment for this frame (**Figure 12.17**).

   Two slashes tell Flash to interpret this text as a comment instead of a label.

4. In the Timeline, deselect the frame.

   In the Timeline, two green slashes appear in the frame that has a comment. If there's room before the next keyframe, the text of the comment appears as well (**Figure 12.18**).

✔ Tips

- If you see a red flag or green slashes in the Timeline but the label or comment is cut off by the next frame or because it's the end of the movie, turn on Tooltips (choose File > Preferences and check the Tooltips box). When you position the mouse pointer over a frame, the Tooltip window displays as many as 82 characters of that frame's label or comment.

- Frame labels are important parts of a movie's interactivity, and frame-label text gets exported with the other movie data when you publish a Flash Player file. Keeping frame labels short helps keep file sizes small. Comments do not get exported with the final movie, so they can be as long as you like.

Using Stop Actions

You can think of the Stop action as being like the Pause button on a VCR remote control. When you export a movie (covered in Chapter 16) as a Flash Player (.swf) file or as a projector, Flash is set to play the movie as soon as your viewer opens it. You can override that default by placing a Stop action in the first frame of your movie.

To set the movie to pause at startup:

1. Open the Flash file for the movie that you want to pause.

   If the movie doesn't already have a separate layer for actions, add a layer, name it Actions, and drag it to the bottom of the layers list so that you can always find it easily.

2. In the Actions layer, select Frame 1.

3. In the Frame Actions panel, in the Toolbox List, click the Basic Actions button.

4. In the list of basic actions, double-click Stop.

   Flash adds stop (); to the Actions List for Frame 1. There are no additional parameters for the Stop action (**Figure 12.19**).

5. In the Timeline, deselect Frame 1.

   A small letter *a* now appears in Frame 1 of the Actions layer, indicating that this frame has actions. When you export the movie to a Flash Player file (or create a stand-alone projector) and open the movie, it will not play until it receives further instructions that tell it to do so.

Figure 12.19 In the Toolbox List's Basic Actions category, double-clicking Stop adds a stop (); action to the current frame's Actions List.

✔ Tips

- You can add a Stop action to any frame of a movie. You might, for example, want a movie to pause in a frame where you expect the user to make choices or enter text.

- When a movie is stopped, you cannot use a frame action to start it again. Frame actions trigger only when the playhead enters a frame. You must assign a Play action to a button or movie clip so that the viewer can trigger the action with a mouse or keyboard action. (For more information about controlling movie playback at various points, see Chapter 13)

Using Go To Actions

A Go To action has parameters that you must fill in to make the action work. The parameters identify a specific scene and frame in your movie and tell Flash either to pause there or start playback from there. Playing around with Go To is a good way to familiarize yourself with the way that parameters work in the Actions panel.

Although you could use the Go To action alone (simply as a way to organize the order in which things play back in your movie), Go To works best in combination with object actions or other frame actions. You learn more about these complex forms of interactivity in Chapters 13 and 15.

For this exercises, create a file similar to the ones that you used in the preceding exercises. The file should contain two scenes, each with a bottom layer named Actions and a top layer named Content. Each content layer contains keyframes in Frames 1 through 5. Use the text tool to place identifying text on the Stage for each frame—Scene 1·Frame 1, Scene 1·Frame 2, and so on. This text makes it easy to see how Flash moves around in the movie when you play it.

To use actions to jump to a new location:

1. In the Timeline in the Actions layer for Scene 1, select the frame where you want to stop the movie's sequential playback and make Flash jump to a new location in the Timeline.

2. In the Frame Actions panel, in the Toolbox List, click the Basic Actions button.

continues on next page

3. In the list of basic actions, double-click Go To.

Flash adds the action `gotoAndPlay(1);` to the Actions List and displays parameters that direct Flash to a particular frame (**Figure 12.20**). By default, the parameters for Go To tell Flash to start playing the new frame immediately.

The default target scene is the current scene, and the target frame is Frame 1. In other words, the default parameters direct Flash to the first frame of the scene that you're in right now. You must change these parameters to make Flash go somewhere else.

4. To make Flash pause after switching to a new location, uncheck the Go To and Play checkbox in the Parameters pane (**Figure 12.21**).

5. To tell Flash which scene to jump to, *do one of the following:*

- ◆ In the Scene field, type the name of the scene (Scene 2, for example).

- ◆ From the Scene pop-up menu, choose the scene.

Flash lists all the current scenes by name in this pop-up menu, along with the descriptive choices <next scene> and <previous scene> (**Figure 12.22**).

6. To specify the frame that Flash should jump to in the finished movie, *do one of the following:*

- ◆ From the Type pop-up menu, choose Number, and type the target frame number in the Frame field.

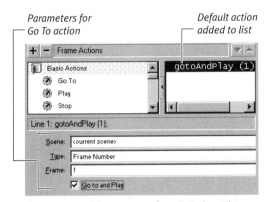

Parameters for Go To action — *Default action added to list*

Figure 12.20 Adding `goto` to a frame's Actions List brings up the parameters needed to describe the target frame.

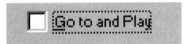

Figure 12.21 The default Go To action starts playback immediately after switching to a new location in the Timeline. To have Flash pause in the new location, uncheck Go To and Play.

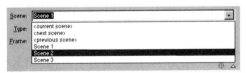

Figure 12.22 You define the target scene by typing its name or choosing it from the list of scenes in the current movie.

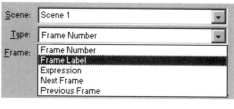

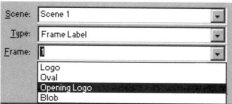

Figure 12.23 You define a target frame by choosing one of the frame types (top). When specifying a frame by label, you can type the label name or choose it from the pop-up menu (bottom).

- ◆ From the Type pop-up menu, choose Frame Label, and enter the target frame's label in the Frame field. Flash lists all existing labels in a pop-up menu to the right of the Frame field for quick and accurate input (**Figure 12.23**).

- ◆ From the Type pop-up menu, choose Expression, and enter the expression that describes the target frame in the Frame field.

- ◆ From the Type pop-up menu, choose Next Frame.

- ◆ From the Type pop-up menu, choose Previous Frame.

7. Play the movie.

When the playhead reaches the frame containing the Go To action, it jumps to whatever scene and frame you specified.

✔ Tips

- ■ When you resize the Actions panel to make it narrower, the triangles indicating pop-up menus for the Scene, Type, and Frame fields may disappear. To access these menus, resize the window and make it wider.

- ■ You can enter the name of a scene or frame as the target even if that scene or frame doesn't exist yet. If you have created a storyboard or outline for your movie and you know for sure what you will name crucial scenes and frames that will be targeted by actions, you can go ahead and type the names as you create the actions. When Flash encounters an action that tells it to go to a frame or scene that doesn't exist, Flash simply ignores the Go To action.

What Are Expressions?

One of the frame-type Choices—Expression —may be mysterious to anyone not used to scripting. *Expressions* are formulas that allow Flash to calculate numeric values or enter text strings based on external information, such as information that users type in text boxes. Expressions can also test whether certain conditions are true, such as whether the playhead is currently in Frame 5. (To learn more about expressions and variables, see Chapter 15.)

Previewing Actions in Action

As you can imagine, it would be difficult to work in the Flash editor if the actions that you add to frames were continually sending you to new locations in the Timeline. The default movie-editing mode disables frame actions. To see frame actions at work when you play your movie in the Flash editor, you must enable them via the Enable Simple Frame Actions command.

To enable frame actions:

1. Open the Flash file whose actions you want to preview.

2. From the Control menu, choose Enable Simple Frame Actions.

   Flash places a check next to the Enable Simple Frame Actions command in the menu to indicate that frame actions are enabled (**Figure 12.24**). When you play the movie now, Flash follows the instructions in the Action List.

To disable frame actions:

1. Open the Flash file that has frame actions enabled.

2. From the Control menu, choose the checked Enable Simple Frame Actions command (**Figure 12.25**).

   Flash removes the check next to the Enable Simple Frame Actions command in the menu to indicate that frame actions are disabled. When you play the movie now, Flash ignores any instructions in the Action List and plays the movie frames sequentially.

✔ Tip

■ You can also preview your actions by playing the movie in a test mode. From the Control menu, choose Test Scene or Test Movie. Frame actions are always enabled in these test modes.

Figure 12.24 When no check precedes the Enable Simple Frame Actions command in the Control menu, frame actions are disabled.

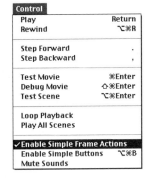

Figure 12.25 When a check precedes the Enable Simple Frame Actions command in the Control menu, frame actions are enabled.

INTERACTIVITY WITH OBJECTS

As you learned in the preceding chapter, Macromedia Flash's frame actions give you control over a movie's playback, but object actions let you put viewers in the driver's seat, giving them the power to interact directly with a Flash movie. You can create ActionScripts for two kinds of objects: buttons and movie clips.

Buttons can be simple, displaying static graphics that change slightly as you roll over them and click them. Or buttons can be wild and animated, using movie clips and sounds.

In Flash 5, movie clips themselves have become vehicles for controlling interactivity. Movie clips can respond to user input, Timeline-related cues, and input from variables, making them highly flexible for advanced ActionScripters.

In this chapter, you learn to create buttons and attach simple ActionScripts to buttons and movie clips. To get a taste of more complex interactivity, check out Chapter 15.

Creating a Basic Rollover Button

Flash labels the four frames of a button's Timeline Up, Over, Down, and Hit. In the Up state, you create a graphic that looks like a static, unused button. This graphic appears whenever the pointer lies outside the active area of the button. In the Over state, create the graphic as it should look when the pointer rolls over the button. Usually, you want some kind of visual change to alert your viewer that the pointer is now on a live button. In the Down state, create the graphic as it should look when someone clicks the button.

In the fourth frame, which is called the Hit frame, create a graphic that defines the boundary of the button. Any solid graphic area in this frame becomes the place where mouse movements trigger the button in the final movie.

To create the most basic button, choose a simple geometric shape and use it throughout the button states; just change the color or internal elements of the button.

To create a button symbol:

1. Open a new Flash document, or open an existing Flash document to which you want to add buttons.

2. From the Insert menu, choose New Symbol, or press ⌘-F8 (Mac) or Ctrl-F8 (Windows) (**Figure 13.1**).

    The Symbol Properties dialog box appears.

Figure 13.1
Choose Insert > New Symbol as the first step in creating a button.

The Mystery of Buttons

In Flash, you create a button by creating a symbol and then assigning it button behavior. Buttons are actually short—four frames, to be precise—interactive movies. When you select button behavior for a symbol, Flash sets up a Timeline with four keyframes. The first three keyframes display the three ways a button can look; the fourth keyframe (never shown to the viewer) defines the active area of the button.

Any changes you make in the appearance of the graphic elements in the keyframes create the illusion of movement. In other Flash animation sequences, changes occur over time as the playhead moves through the frames. In Flash buttons, however, changes occur when the user moves the pointer over a specific area of the screen.

You can include movie clips within each frame of a button, to create buttons that are fully animated, and you can attach actions to buttons to give your viewers more control of the movie.

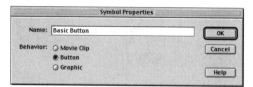

Figure 13.2 To make a button, you must create a new symbol and assign it button behavior in the Symbol Properties dialog box. You can also name the button.

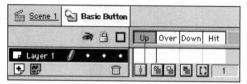

Figure 13.3 The Timeline for every button symbol contains just four frames: Up, Over, Down, and Hit. Flash automatically puts a keyframe in the Up frame of a new button symbol.

Registration crosshair marks
center of symbol's Stage

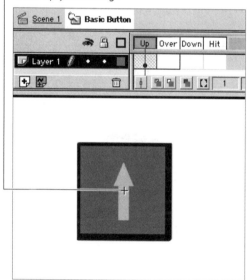

Figure 13.4 When a button is waiting for your viewer to notice and interact with it, Flash displays the contents of the Up frame.

3. Type a name in the Name field, choose Button Behavior, and click OK (**Figure 13.2**).

Flash creates a new symbol in the Library window and returns you to the Timeline and Stage in symbol-editing mode. The Timeline for a button symbol contains the four frames that you need to define the button: Up, Over, Down, and Hit.

By default, the Up frame contains a keyframe (**Figure 13.3**). You must add keyframes to the Over, Down, and Hit frames and place the graphics in each frame of the button. To give users feedback about the button—so that they can tell when they're on a live button and sense the difference when they actually click it—use a different graphic in each frame.

To create the Up state:

1. Using the file from the preceding exercise, in the Timeline, select the Up frame.

2. On the Stage, create a new graphic or place a graphic symbol (**Figure 13.4**).

This graphic element becomes the button as it's just sitting onstage in your movie, waiting for someone to click it. In symbol-editing mode, the crosshair in the middle of the Stage serves as the central point for registering your graphic symbols.

CREATING A BASIC ROLLOVER BUTTON

To create the Over state:

1. Using the file from the preceding exercise, in the Timeline, select the Over frame.

2. From the Insert menu, choose Keyframe.

   Flash inserts a keyframe that duplicates the contents of the Up keyframe. You can now make minor changes in the Up graphic to convert it to an Over graphic. You might enlarge an element within the button, for example (**Figure 13.5**). Duplicating the preceding keyframe makes it easy to align all your button elements so that they don't appear to jump around as they change states.

To create the Down state:

1. Using the file from the preceding exercise, in the Timeline, select the Down frame.

2. From the Insert menu, choose Keyframe.

   Flash inserts a keyframe that duplicates the contents of the Over keyframe. You can now make minor changes to convert the Over graphic to a Down graphic. You might change the button color, for example, and reverse the shadow effect so that the button looks indented (**Figure 13.6**).

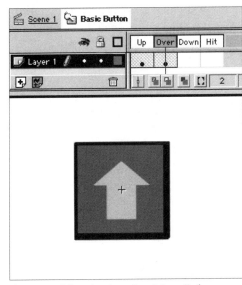

Figure 13.5 When the viewer's pointer rolls (or pauses) over the button, Flash displays the contents of the Over frame.

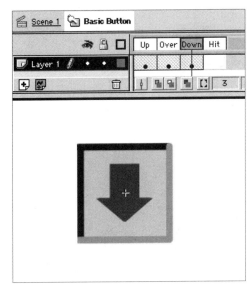

Figure 13.6 When the viewer clicks the button, Flash displays the contents of the Down frame.

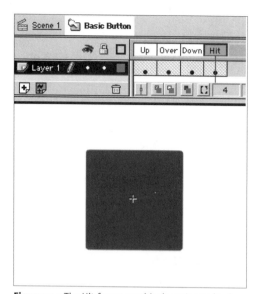

Figure 13.7 The Hit-frame graphic doesn't need to be a fully detailed image of the button in any state; it just needs to be a silhouette of the button shape. Flash uses that shape to define the active button area. This Hit frame contains a copy of the Down frame that has been filled with dark gray.

After you create graphics for the three states of your button, you need to define the active area of the button.

To create the Hit state:

1. Using the file from the preceding exercise, in the Timeline, select the Hit frame.

2. From the Insert menu, choose Keyframe to duplicate the contents of the Down keyframe.

   When you use a graphic with the same shape and size for all three phases of your button, you can safely use a copy of any previous frame as the Hit-frame graphic.

3. If you want, using the paint-bucket tool, fill the Hit-frame graphic with a single color (**Figure 13.7**).

   This step is not required, but it helps remind you that this graphic is not one that viewers of your movie will actually see.

   When you've completed all four frames, your button is ready to use. Return to movie-editing mode, and drag a copy of the button symbol from the Library window to the Stage.

To return to movie-editing mode:

◆ From the Edit menu, choose Edit Movie.

Flash returns you to the main Timeline. You can now use the button symbol in your movie just as you would use any other symbol. Drag an instance of the button from the Library window to the Stage. You can modify an instance to change its size, rotation, and color. (For more information on using symbols, see Chapter 6.)

✔ Tips

■ To create a consistent look on a Web site, you might want to use a set of buttons over and over. You can even reuse buttons in several projects with only slight changes. To save time, try devoting one whole document to buttons, and always create your button symbols there. You can then copy a button from this master button file to your current Flash movie file and tweak the button in that file. You can also create a shared library of buttons (see Chapter 6).

■ Always fill your Hit-frame silhouette with the same color—say, light gray or neon blue. That way, the silhouette becomes another visual cue that you are in the Hit frame of a button, in symbol-editing mode.

The Mystery of Hit-Frame Graphics

Though it never appears in a Flash movie, the Hit frame's graphic content is vital to a button's operation. The sole purpose of the Hit-frame graphic is to define the button's boundaries. This graphic doesn't need to be detailed; it's just a silhouette that defines the button shape. Any painted area in the Hit frame becomes an active part of the button. In the final movie, when the viewer moves the pointer into that area, the Over frame of the button appears; when the user clicks that area, the Down frame appears.

For the clearest, most user-friendly buttons, make sure that your Hit-frame graphic is large enough to cover all the graphics in the first three frames of the button. To be safe, make your Hit-frame graphic a little larger than the other graphics.

If your button is something delicate, such as a piece of type or a line drawing, make your Hit-frame graphic a geometric shape—say, a filled rectangle or oval—that completely covers the Up, Over, and Down graphics. That way, your viewers will have no trouble finding and clicking the button.

Control	
Play	Return
Rewind	⌥⌘R
Step Forward	.
Step Backward	,
Test Movie	⌘Enter
Debug Movie	⇧⌘Enter
Test Scene	⌥⌘Enter
Loop Playback	
Play All Scenes	
Enable Simple Frame Actions	
Enable Simple Buttons	⌥⌘B
Mute Sounds	

Figure 13.8
Choose Control >
Enable Simple
Buttons to test
rollover buttons
in Flash's movie-
editing mode.

Previewing Buttons in Movie-Editing Mode

By default, Flash disables the rollover capabilities of buttons in movie-editing mode. If buttons were always active, you could never reposition them or work with them on the Stage. Every time you tried to grab the button, it would simply display its Over and Down frames. To view a button's operation in movie-editing mode, you must enable buttons.

To enable buttons on the Stage:

◆ Using the file from the preceding exercise, from the Control menu, choose Enable Simple Buttons (**Figure 13.8**).

Any buttons on the Stage now act live. As you move the mouse over a button, Flash displays the Over frame; when you click within the button's active area, Flash displays the Down frame.

✔ Tips

■ You can preview the Up, Down, and Over frames of a button by selecting the button in the Library window and then clicking the Play button in the preview window. Flash displays each frame in turn.

■ The Enable Simple Buttons command allows you to see only the most basic button actions in movie-editing mode. If your enabled buttons behave unexpectedly in movie-editing mode, try viewing them in test mode to verify all their functionality. (Choose Control > Test Movie or Control > Test Scene to enter test mode.)

Creating Buttons That Change Shape

You can use Flash to create buttons more exotic than the simple geometric shapes you'd find on a telephone or calculator. Button graphics can emulate real-world switches or toggles. You can disguise buttons as part of a movie's scenery—making the blinking eye of a character a button, for example. That situation often happens in games; finding the hot spots or buttons is part of the fun. When the exterior shape of the button changes in Up, Over, and Down modes, however, creating an effective Hit-frame graphic can be a bit tricky.

To create Up, Over, and Down states with various graphics:

1. Open a new Flash document, or open an existing Flash document to which you want to add buttons.

2. From the Insert menu, choose New Symbol. The Symbol Properties dialog box appears.

3. Enter a name in the Name field, choose Button in the Behavior section, and click OK.

   Flash creates a new symbol in the Library window and returns you to the Timeline and Stage in symbol-editing mode. The Timeline for a button symbol contains the four frames necessary for defining the button: Up, Over, Down, and Hit.

4. In the Timeline, select the Over, Down, and Hit frames.

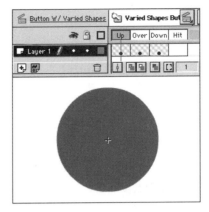

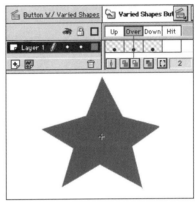

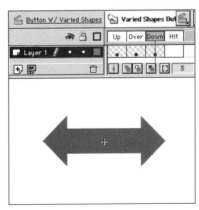

Figure 13.9 You can create fanciful buttons that change shape when a user rolls over or clicks them. In this example, the inactive button is a simple circle (top). When the pointer rolls over the button, the circle changes to a star (middle). When the user clicks the button, it changes to a double-headed arrow.

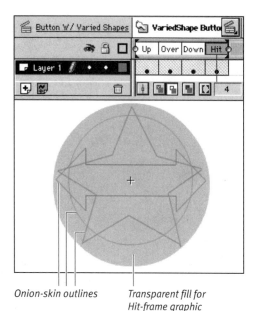

Onion-skin outlines   Transparent fill for
Hit-frame graphic

Figure 13.10 The Hit-frame silhouette needs to encompass all possible button areas in all three button modes. If for example, you duplicate only the circle as your Hit frame for this button, you exclude the tips of the star. A user who clicked those tips in the Over phase would be unable to activate the button. If you duplicate only the star, the user could roll over several areas of the circle and never discover that it's a button.

5. From the Modify menu, choose Frames > Convert to Key Frames.

   You now have a blank keyframe in every frame of your button, and you're ready to place various graphics in each frame.

6. With the Up frame selected in the Timeline, on the Stage, create a new graphic, or place the graphic symbol that you want to use for the button's Up state.

7. Repeat step 6 for the Over and Down frames.

   For this exercise, use graphics that have different shapes—a circle, a star, and a double-headed arrow, for example (**Figure 13.9**).

When the Up, Over, and Down frames of your button contain graphics of different shapes and sizes, you need to create a graphic for the Hit state that covers all of them.

To create the Hit state for graphics of various shapes:

1. Using the file that you created in the preceding exercise, in the Timeline, select the Hit frame.

2. To create the Hit-frame graphic, *do one of the following:*

   ◆ Draw a simple geometric shape large enough to cover all areas of the button. Turn on onion skinning so that you can see exactly what you need to cover (**Figure 13.10**).

continues on next page

- ◆ Use Flash's Edit > Copy and Edit > Paste in Place commands to copy the graphic elements from the first three frames of the button and paste them into the Hit frame of the button one by one.

The graphics stack up in the Hit frame, occupying the exact area needed to cover the button in any phase of its operation (**Figure 13.11**).

✔ Tips

- ■ When you use the copy-and-paste-in-place technique to create your Hit-frame graphic, it's a good idea to expand the resulting graphic slightly—by using the Modify > Shape > Expand Fill command, for example. Making the Hit graphic slop over the edges of the active button areas ensures that your viewers will activate the button as soon as they get the mouse near the graphic.

- ■ Use a transparent color (one with an alpha value less than 100 percent) for your Hit-frame graphic. The other graphics will show through the Hit-frame graphic in onion-skin mode, making it easy to see how to position or size the Hit-frame graphic to cover the graphics in the other frames.

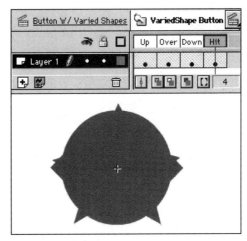

Figure 13.11 By copying the graphic in each of the button modes and using the Paste in Place command to place them in the Hit frame, you wind up with a perfectly positioned silhouette that incorporates all the possible button areas.

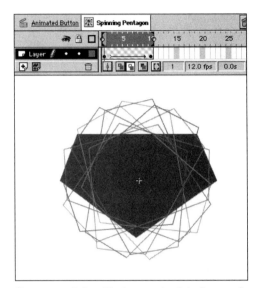

Figure 13.12 Onion skinning reveals all the frames of the spinning pentagon (a motion tween) that appear when the fully animated button is in the Up state.

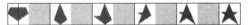

Figure 13.13 The Preview mode of the Timeline shows the animation of the clip that appears when the pointer rolls or rests over the button area.

Creating a Fully Animated Button

The buttons that you created in the preceding exercises are animated in the sense that they change as the user interacts with them. Flash also allows you to create buttons that are fully animated—a glowing light bulb, for example, or a little ladybug that jumps up and down, saying, "Click me!" The trick to making fully animated buttons is placing movie clips in the frames of your button. Because the movie clips play in their own Timeline, animated buttons remain animated even when you pause the movie.

To animate a rollover button:

1. Create a new Flash document, or open an existing Flash document to which you want to add buttons.

2. Choose Insert > New Symbol.
   The Symbol Properties dialog box appears.

3. Choose Button in the Behavior section, name your button, and click OK.

4. In the Timeline, select the Over, Down, and Hit frames of the button, and choose Modify > Frames > Convert to Key Frames.
   Flash creates blank keyframes for the button's Over, Down, and Hit frames.

5. In the Timeline, select the Up frame, and create a movie-clip symbol or import one from an existing movie.
   For this example, the Up-frame clip contains a spinning pentagon (**Figure 13.12**).

6. In the Timeline, select the Over frame, and create a movie-clip symbol or import one from an existing movie.
   In this example, the Over-frame clip contains a pentagon that turns into a star (**Figure 13.13**).

continues on next page

7. In the Timeline, select the Down frame, and create a movie-clip symbol or import one from an existing movie.

For this example, the Down-frame clip contains a star that flies apart (**Figure 13.14**).

8. In the Timeline, select the Hit frame, and create a graphic that covers all the button areas for the three button states (Up, Over, and Down).

A large oval works well for this purpose (**Figure 13.15**). This graphic creates an active button area that's larger than the spinning pentagon. As your viewer's pointer nears the spinning graphic in the final movie, the button switches to Over mode. In Over mode, the oval is big enough to encompass all points of the star, and in Down mode, the user can let the pointer drift a fair amount and still be within the confines of the button.

9. Return to movie-editing mode by clicking the current scene name in the top-left corner of the window.

10. Drag a copy of your button from the Library window to the Stage.

✔ Tips

■ You can place a movie clip in the Hit frame of your button, but only the visible graphic from the clip's first frame determines the hit area.

■ With buttons enabled, in movie-editing mode, Flash previews the Up, Over, and Down frames of your button but not its complete animation. For each frame, you see only the first frame of the movie clip. To view the fully animated button, you must export the movie and view it in Flash Player (by choosing Control > Test Movie, for example).

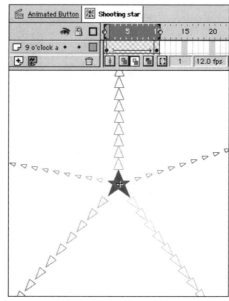

Figure 13.14 Onion skinning reveals the animation of the clip that appears when the viewer clicks inside the button area.

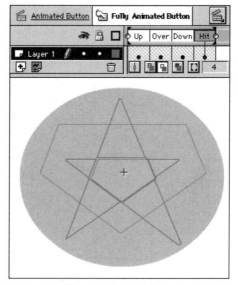

Figure 13.15 When creating a Hit-frame graphic, use onion skinning to see the first frame of the movie clip in each button frame. Here, the Hit-frame graphic is a transparent fill, which also helps you position the graphic to cover the graphics in the other frames.

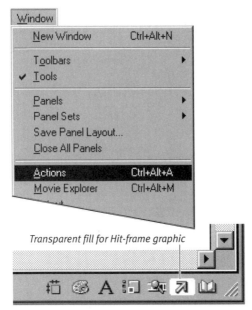

Transparent fill for Hit-frame graphic

Figure 13.16 When the Stage has focus (when the dark border appears around the Stage) choose Window > Actions (top) or click the Show Actions button in the Launcher bar (bottom) to access the Object Actions panel. To set focus on the Stage, click it or select items on it.

Adding Actions to Buttons

All Flash buttons have certain actions built in. By default, when you move the mouse into the button area, Flash jumps to the Over frame; when you click the button, Flash takes you to the Down frame. To create more interactivity or to refine the way a button responds to a user's mouse movements, you attach ActionScripts to an instance of a button. The process is similar to adding frame actions (see Chapter 12), except that you create your scripts in the Object Actions panel.

To access the Object Actions panel:

1. Click the Stage, or select an object (a button or a movie-clip symbol) on the Stage.

2. If the Object Actions panel is not currently active, *do one of the following:*

    ◆ From the Window menu, choose Actions.

    ◆ In the Launcher bar at the bottom of the Stage, click the Show Actions button (**Figure 13.16**).

    The Object Actions panel opens or comes to the front if it's grouped in a window with other panels.

To add an action to a button instance:

1. Open a new Flash document, and place keyframes in frames 1 and 2.

2. Use the text tool to add text that identifies each frame (Scene 1·Frame 1 and Scene 1·Frame 2).

3. Add a Stop action to each frame so that the movie doesn't loop through the frames on playback.

    (For more-detailed instructions on adding actions to frames, see Chapter 12.)

4. In the Timeline, select Frame 1.

continues on next page

5. Create a button symbol, or copy one from an existing movie.

6. Place an instance of the button symbol on the Stage, and select the button.

7. Access the Object Actions panel.

8. From the Add Statement menu, choose an action (choose Basic Actions > Go To, for example).

Flash adds the button handler and appropriate statements for the action to the Actions List (**Figure 13.17**).

9. In the Parameters pane of the Object Actions panel, define any parameters necessary for the action that you chose.

In the Frame section for the Go To action, for example, in the Scene field enter <current scene>, in the Type field enter Frame Number, and in the Frame field enter 2 (**Figure 13.18**).

10. From the Control menu, choose Enable Simple Buttons, and test the action of your button.

ADDING ACTIONS TO BUTTONS

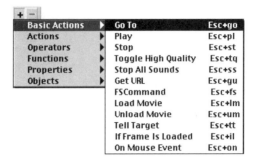

Figure 13.17 In Normal mode, when you select an action for a button (top), Flash embeds that action in a button handler (bottom). The default handler makes your action take place when the user clicks and releases the mouse button within the active area of your button.

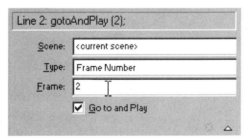

Figure 13.18 In the Parameters pane of the Object Actions panel, set any parameters required for your actions. For goto, for example, define the destination frame by entering a scene, frame type, and frame.

The Mystery of ActionScript Terminology

Learning to script means learning to use a whole new language—a task beyond the scope of this book. Still, the following definitions introduce some important ActionScript terms and concepts.

ActionScript is an *object-oriented scripting language*. The name of the object-oriented game is organization. You want to assemble and organize pieces of code for efficiency. When you write documents in English, you use containers and tools to help make your writing fast and efficient. You can create files and folders, templates and boilerplate text, macros and mail merges, to name a few such tools.

In writing scripts, you also use a variety of containers and tools for storing and reusing pieces of code. By nesting containers within containers and stringing them together, you wind up with a whole set of building blocks for creating interactivity in Flash documents.

The largest ActionScript container is a *class*, a group of items that are similar in some way. The items themselves are referred to as *objects* or *instances* of the class. Objects can be either concrete graphical elements (buttons and movie clips) or abstract containers that merely hold data and never appear on the Stage (*variables*).

Objects have two aspects: form and function. In scripting, the two aspects are called *properties* and *methods*. (You could also think of these two aspects as *characteristics* and *behaviors*.)

Consider a concrete example. Imagine Ball, a class of items defined as spherical things. One particular *object* in this class is a movie clip called MyBall. MyBall's *properties* (its form/characteristics) might be the color red, a bumpy surface, and a 2-inch diameter; its *methods* (functions/behaviors) might be bounce, roll, and spin.

Each property and method is defined by *actions* (also called *statements*). Statements are pieces of code that tell Flash how to draw and manipulate the element at any point in your movie.

The Mystery of Button Handlers

The Basic Actions set contains one action that is available only for buttons: On Mouse Event. That action is called a *handler* because it handles the decisions about when and how to run a button's ActionScript.

The button handler must be present at the beginning of all ActionScripts attached to buttons. In Normal mode, whenever you choose an action from the Toolbox List, Flash checks to make sure there is a handler in the Actions List. If there is no handler, Flash embeds your action in the default handler (**Figure 13.19**).

on indicates the start of the handler.

(release) indicates the condition under which the handler tells the button's script to run the script. The statement inside the parentheses is called an *event*. You can choose new events from the Actions panel's Parameters pane.

{ indicates the beginning of the list of actions that are to be triggered by the specified mouse event.

} indicates the end of the list of the actions that are to be triggered by the specified mouse event.

All actions between the two braces take place when the triggering mouse event occurs.

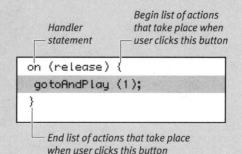

Figure 13.19 The default button handler, on (release), tells Flash to run the ActionScript after the user has clicked inside a button and released the mouse button. The rest of the ActionScript—the part that tells the button what to do—goes between the opening and closing curly-brace symbols in the ActionScript List.

Preparing to add stopAllSounds

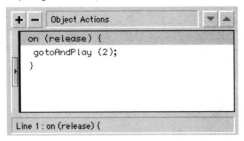

Preparing to add toggleHighQuality

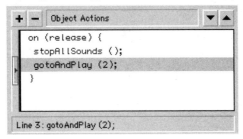

Final script

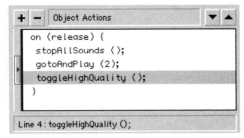

Figure 13.20 You can add multiple actions within one set of curly braces. Flash adds new actions directly below the selected line in the Actions List. In the bottom script, releasing the mouse button stops all sounds, sends the movie to Frame 2, and turns off antialiasing. One mouse event triggers all the actions.

To add multiple actions to a button instance:

1. Using the file that you created in the preceding exercise, with the button selected, access the Object Actions panel.

   The Actions List contains the button handler and the gotoAndPlay () action.

2. To add more actions to the list, *do one of the following:*

   ◆ To add an action before the gotoAndPlay (2) action, select on (release) in the Actions List and then choose another action from the Add Statement menu (or double-click an action in the Toolbox List).

   Flash adds the new action to the Actions List and displays the action's parameters.

   ◆ To add an action after the gotoAndPlay (2) action, select gotoAndPlay (2) in the Actions List and then choose another action from the Add Statement menu (or double-click an action in the Toolbox List).

   Flash adds the new action to the Actions List (**Figure 13.20**) and displays the action's parameters.

✔ Tip

■ When you choose actions from the Add Statement menu (or double-click actions in the Toolbox List), Flash adds the new action directly below whatever action is selected in the Actions List. You can also drag actions directly from the Toolbox List and place them where you want in the Actions List.

Using On Mouse Event

When you click a basic Flash button, the press of the mouse button actually triggers Flash to display the Down frame. When you attach an ActionScript to a button, however, the default button handler adds on (release) to the Actions List. That code makes releasing the mouse button the event that triggers the actions. You can change that behavior by selecting a different Event parameter for the button's handler.

To choose the triggering mouse events:

1. Create a new Flash document with keyframes in frames 1 and 2.

2. Use the text tool to add text that identifies each frame (Scene 1·Frame 1 and Scene 1·Frame 2).

3. Add a stop action to each frame so that the movie doesn't loop through the frames on playback.

4. Place a single button instance in Frame 1, and select the button.

5. Access the Object Actions panel.

6. From the Add Statement menu, choose Basic Actions > On Mouse Event (**Figure 13.21**).

   Flash adds the button handler— on (release) and a pair of curly braces— to the Actions List. The parameters governing mouse events appear in the Parameters pane. These parameters specify the exact mouse event that will trigger any actions that you add between the handler's curly braces.

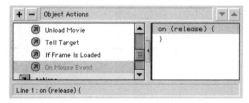

Figure 13.21 Choose On Mouse Event from the Toolbox List or the Add Statement menu to define a button's triggering mouse event.

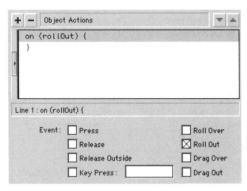

Figure 13.22 With the mouse-event action selected in the Actions List, you can select one or more triggering mouse events for a button in the Parameters pane.

7. In the Event section of the Parameters pane, uncheck the Release checkbox.

8. Check one or more of the other Event check boxes (Roll Out, for example).

Flash updates the Actions List, adding the specified mouse events within the parentheses. To set multiple parameters for a mouse event—such as making the button respond to a click within the button area as well as to the user's rolling the pointer out of the button area—check more than one box (**Figure 13.22**).

continues on next page

Mouse Event Parameters

The On Mouse Event action has eight mouse events that you can choose.

Press refers to the downward part of a click when the pointer is located within the hit area of a button.

Release refers to the upward part of a click (the user presses and then releases the mouse button) when the pointer is located within the hit area of a button. A Release event lets users click and then change their minds—and avoid activating the button—by dragging away before releasing the mouse button.

Release Outside happens when the user clicks inside the button area, holds down the mouse button, and moves the mouse outside the active button area before releasing the mouse button.

Key Press happens any time the user presses the specified keyboard key while

the Flash button is present. The user doesn't have to use the mouse to interact with the button for this event to trigger an action.

Roll Over occurs any time the pointer rolls into the button's hit area.

Roll Out happens any time the pointer rolls out of the button's hit area.

Drag Over works in a slightly unexpected way. A Drag Over event occurs when the user holds down the mouse button within the button's hit area, rolls the pointer outside the hit area, and then rolls the pointer back into the hit area.

Drag Out happens when the user clicks within the button's hit area, holds down the mouse button, and rolls the pointer out of the hit area.

9. With on (press, rollOut) { selected in the Actions List, from the Add Statement menu, choose Basic Actions > Go To.

10. From the Parameters pane's Type menu, choose Next Frame.

    The Go To and Play checkbox is grayed out. The button will take you to the next frame and then stop playback.

    Flash adds nextFrame (); to the Actions List between the curly braces (**Figure 13.23**).

    You're ready to see the button in action.

11. Choose Control > Test Movie.

    Flash exports the movie and opens it in Flash Player. The button responds to the pointer's rolling into and then out of the button area by taking you to Frame 2 of the movie. Flash also responds to a click within the button area by taking you to Frame 2.

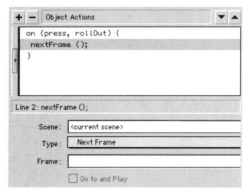

Figure 13.23 When Press and Roll Out are selected as On Mouse Event parameters, your viewers can trigger the nextFrame action in two ways: by clicking inside the button area or by rolling the pointer into and then out of the active button area.

Creating Buttons That Respond to Mouse Events

You can make a single button respond differently to different mouse events by placing several handlers in the button's ActionScript. You could, for example, create one action set that jumps Flash to the next scene when the user clicks and then releases the mouse button within the active button area. You could create a second action set that opens a new movie with help information in a separate window if the user clicks within the button area but then drags the pointer out of the button area before releasing the mouse button. And you could deliver yet another action if the user presses a key on the keyboard, such as jumping to a frame that displays the message "You must click the button to move to the next question."

To vary a button's response to different mouse events:

1. Create a new Flash document with keyframes in the first three frames.

2. Use the text tool to add text that identifies each frame (Scene 1·Frame 1, Scene 1·Frame 2, and Scene 1·Frame 3).

3. Add a `stop` action to each frame so that the movie doesn't loop through the frames on playback.

4. Place a single button instance in Frame 1, and select the button.

5. Access the Object Actions panel.

6. From the Add Statement menu, choose Basic Actions > On Mouse Event.

7. In the Event section of the Parameters pane, uncheck the Release checkbox and check the Roll Out checkbox.

continues on next page

8. From the Add Statement menu, choose Basic Actions > Go To.

9. From the Parameters pane's Type menu, choose Frame Number, and enter 2 in the Frame field.

Flash adds `gotoAndPlay(2);` to the Actions List between the braces of the button handler (**Figure 13.24**).

10. In the Actions List, select the closing curly brace.

11. Repeat steps 6 and 7, this time choosing the mouse event Press.

Flash adds a second handler—`on (press)` and a second set of curly braces—to the bottom of the Actions List (**Figure 13.25**).

12. With `on (press)` selected, from the Add Statement menu, choose Basic Actions > Go To.

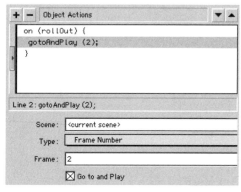

Figure 13.24 This set of actions tells Flash to jump to Frame 2 if the user rolls the pointer into and then out of the active button area.

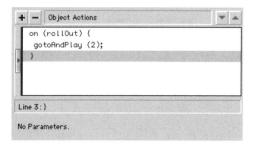

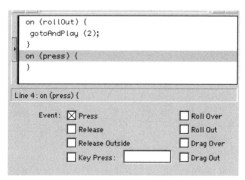

Figure 13.25 To add a second set of actions with a different mouse-event trigger, in the Actions List, select the closing curly brace of the first handler (top). From the Add Statement menu, choose On Mouse Event and select a new event (bottom).

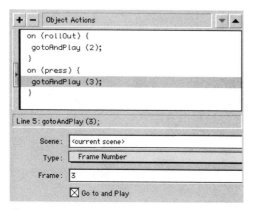

Figure 13.26 The second set of actions in the Actions List tells Flash to jump to Frame 3 if the user clicks within the active button area.

13. From the Parameters pane's Type menu, choose Frame Number, and enter 3 in the Frame field.

Flash adds gotoAndPlay (3) to the Actions List between the second set of curly braces (**Figure 13.26**).

You're ready to see the button in action.

14. Choose Control > Test Movie.

Flash exports the movie and opens it in Flash Player. If you move the mouse so that the pointer rolls into and then out of the active button area, Flash jumps to Frame 2. If you click within the active button area, Flash immediately jumps to Frame 3, even before you release the mouse button.

Triggering Button Actions from the Keyboard

The On Press mouse event allows viewers to trigger actions from the keyboard by pressing a specified key. Although you assign it to a button, on (press) affects the entire range of frames in which it resides. The button's Hit-frame graphic need not cover the whole Stage, and the user need not position the pointer over the button before pressing the specified key. Whenever the button is in the currently displayed frame, pressing the specified key triggers the assigned actions.

To set up an action triggered by a key press:

1. Create a new Flash document with keyframes in the first two frames.

2. Use the text tool to add text that identifies each frame (Scene 1·Frame 1 and Scene 1·Frame 2).

3. Add a stop action to each frame so that the movie doesn't loop through the frames on playback.

4. Place a single button instance in Frame 1, and select the button.

5. Access the Object Actions panel.

6. From the Add Statement menu, choose Basic Actions > On Mouse Event.

7. In the Event section of the Parameters pane, uncheck the Release checkbox.

8. Check the Key Press checkbox, and type the letter A in the text field (**Figure 13.27**).

   Flash adds on (keyPress "A"). In the final movie, pressing the letter *A* on the keyboard triggers whatever actions you specify in this action sequence.

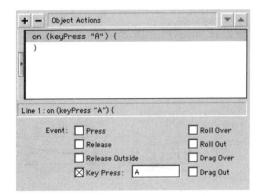

Figure 13.27 When you select Key Press from the Event parameters for an On Mouse Event action, you must specify the triggering key by typing it in the text field.

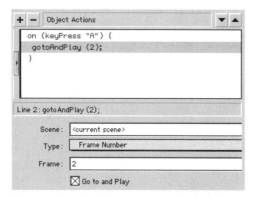

Figure 13.28 This action sequence makes Flash jump to Frame 2 when the user presses A on the keyboard at a time when this button is present in the movie.

9. With on (keyPress "A") selected in the Actions List, from the Add Statement menu, choose Basic Actions > Go To.

10. From the Parameters pane's Type menu choose Frame Number, and enter 2 in the Frame field.

    Flash adds gotoAndPlay (2); to the Actions List between the curly braces (**Figure 13.28**).

    You're ready to see the button in action.

11. Choose Control > Test Movie.

    Flash exports the movie and opens it in Flash Player. No matter where the pointer is, when the button is on-screen and you press *A* on the keyboard, Flash jumps to Frame 2 of the movie.

✔ Tip

■ In some cases, assigned key-press actions fail to work in a published movie. (Browsers, for example, often intercept all key presses, assuming that the user wants to enter a new URL.) When a user clicks a button in a Flash movie, Flash sets the key-press focus—the ability to intercept all key presses. To ensure that your key-press actions always work, include a button for users to click before they can enter a part of the movie that uses key presses.

Creating an Invisible Button

You don't actually have to place a graphic in every frame of a button. The only frame that must have content is the Hit frame, because it describes the active button area. Buttons without content in the Up frame are invisible in the final movie. A common use for an invisible button is to resume playback of a movie that pauses on a frame that contains lots of text. Make an invisible button with a Hit-frame graphic that covers the whole Stage, and give the button a `play` action; then place the button in the paused movie frame. When viewers finish reading your text, they can click anywhere in the frame to resume playback of the movie.

To create an invisible button:

1. Create a new Flash document with keyframes in the first two frames.

2. Using the text tool, place a long text block in Frame 1; place identifying text in Frame 2 (**Figure 13.29**).

3. Put a `stop` action in each frame so that the movie doesn't loop through the frames on playback.

4. With Frame 1 selected, choose Insert > New Symbol.
   The Symbol Properties dialog box appears.

5. Choose Button in the Behavior section, type a name for your button, and click OK.

6. In symbol-editing mode, in the Timeline for your button, select the Hit frame.

7. Choose Insert > Blank Keyframe.

8. Use the rectangle tool to create a filled rectangle large enough to cover the entire Stage (**Figure 13.30**).

There's really too much text here. You won't be able to read it in the few seconds allowed by the speeding movie playback. So we've paused the movie for you. Just click anywhere on the screen when you are ready to move on to the next frame.

Figure 13.29 Your practice file should look something like this: a two-frame movie with lots of text in the first frame and a `stop` action in each frame.

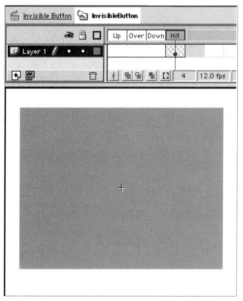

Figure 13.30 To make an invisible button, create a button symbol that has nothing in the Up, Over, and Down frames. Here, the Hit frame contains a filled rectangle large enough to cover the Stage.

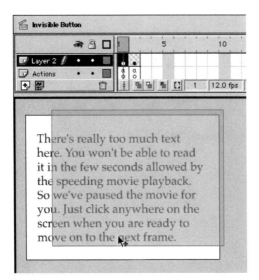

Figure 13.31 When the Up frame of a symbol is empty, Flash displays a transparent version of the Hit-frame graphic to help you position your invisible button in movie-editing mode.

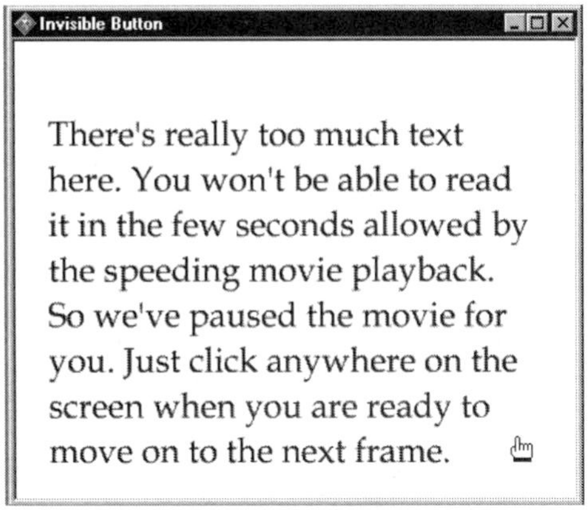

There's really too much text here. You won't be able to read it in the few seconds allowed by the speeding movie playback. So we've paused the movie for you. Just click anywhere on the screen when you are ready to move on to the next frame.

Figure 13.32 This movie is paused on a frame with a stop action and an invisible button that covers the entire frame. The index-finger pointer indicates the presence of the button. Clicking takes the user to the second frame.

This solid rectangle turns the whole Stage into an active button, but because no graphics are associated with the button, it will be invisible to the user.

9. Return to movie-editing mode, and drag a copy of your button to the Stage.

    Flash shows a transparent object that previews the hot-spot area. If necessary, you can reposition (or resize) the button so that it fully covers the Stage (**Figure 13.31**).

10. On the Stage, select the hot-spot preview.

11. Access the Object Actions panel.

12. Assign a `play` action to your button instance (as described in "Adding Actions to Buttons" earlier in this chapter).

    You're ready to see the button in action.

13. Choose Control > Test Movie.

    Flash exports the movie and opens it in Flash Player. Playback pauses on Frame 1—the one with lots of text (**Figure 13.32**). But as soon as you click within the current frame in the Player window, Flash moves on to Frame 2.

✔ Tips

■ In symbol-editing mode, the Stage is a fixed size (10 inches by 10 inches), and it's not necessarily the same size as the Stage in your current movie. To make sure that your Hit-frame rectangle covers the whole Stage in the movie, select the rectangle and access the Info panel. Enter values in the width and height fields that are slightly larger than the dimensions of your movie.

■ For frames that contain movie clips, you can skip creating an invisible button and attach to the movie clip itself an ActionScript that responds to mouse events (see "Adding Actions to Movie Clips" later in this chapter).

Creating a Button with Multiple Hot Spots

Part of the fun of buttons is that you can use them for anything. You don't have to simulate buttons or switches. Flash buttons are versatile in part because each frame of a button can have quite different content. The Hit-frame graphic, for example, need not coincide with any of the graphics of the previous frames: It can be a separate graphic that creates hot spots in various areas of the Stage.

Imagine an animated shell game in which your viewer must determine which cup is hiding a bean. You could create a separate button that displays the message "Nope, try again" for each empty cup, or you could create one button that displays the message and put a graphic for each empty cup in the Hit frame of that button.

To create multiple hot spots for a single button:

1. Create a new Flash document with a simple illustration of five cups in Frame 1 (**Figure 13.33**).

2. On the Stage, use the arrow tool to select four of the cups, and choose Edit > Copy (**Figure 13.34**).

3. Choose Insert > New Symbol.
   The Symbol Properties dialog box appears.

4. Choose Button in the Behavior section, type a name, and click OK.

5. In symbol-editing mode, in the Timeline for your button, select the Hit frame.

6. Choose Insert > Blank Keyframe.

7. Choose Edit > Paste.

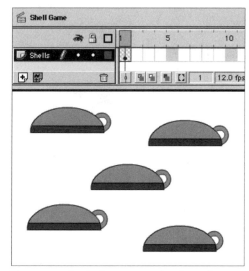

Figure 13.33 On the Stage, create the picture for which you want to activate multiple hot spots. Here, five cups are part of a shell game. One cup hides an item; the others are empty. You can use one button with multiple hot spots to display the same message when the user clicks any of the empty cups.

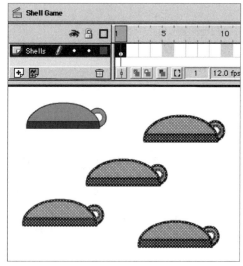

Figure 13.34 Copy the empty cups on the Stage.

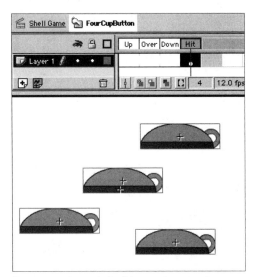

Figure 13.35 In symbol-editing mode, paste the Clipboard contents (the empty cups) into the Hit frame of your invisible button.

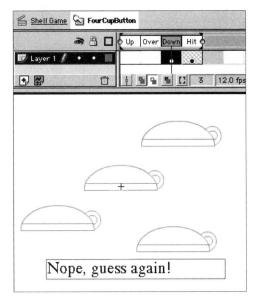

Figure 13.36 Whatever you place in the Down frame appears whenever someone clicks one of the hot-spot areas that you created for the Hit-frame graphic.

Flash pastes copies of the four cup graphics in the center of the Stage (**Figure 13.35**). You can fill these graphics with a solid color if you want to remind yourself that users will not see them.

8. In the Timeline, select the Down frame.

9. Choose Insert > Blank Keyframe.

10. On the Stage, create the message that you want people to see when they click an empty cup (**Figure 13.36**).

11. Return to movie-editing mode, and drag a copy of your button to the Stage.

Flash shows transparent previews of the hot-spot area.

continues on next page

CREATING A BUTTON WITH MULTIPLE HOT SPOTS

12. Use the arrow tool or the arrow keys to reposition the hot-spot cups to coincide with the cups in Frame 1 of your movie (**Figure 13.37**).

You're ready to see the button in action.

13. Choose Control > Test Movie.

Flash exports the movie and opens it in Flash Player. When you click one of the four empty cups, Flash displays the message that you created for the Down frame of your button.

✔ Tip

■ If you were creating a real game, you'd want to create another, separate button to place over the fifth cup so that the pointer would consistently change to the pointing finger so as not to give the game away.

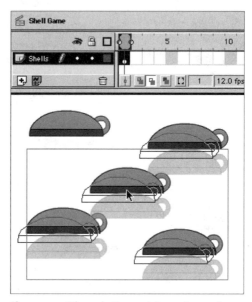

Figure 13.37 When a button contains no images in the Up frame, Flash displays a transparent version of the Hit-frame graphic. You can use the arrow tool or the arrow keys to position the button so that the preview graphics precisely cover the graphic elements on the Stage.

Adding Actions to Movie Clips

Just as you can attach ActionScripts to button instances, you can attach ActionScripts to movie-clip instances. Movie clip ActionScripts require a specific handler (`onClipEvent`) that encompasses its own set of event parameters. Movie clips can respond to mouse events (such as pressing the mouse button or moving the mouse), keyboard activity (such as pressing a certain key), the activity of the movie clip itself (such as loading into the main Timeline), and the receipt of data (from variables).

The Mystery of Deprecated Actions

As any language evolves, new words and expressions become standard and old terms fall out of everyday use. You can continue to speak and write with the older words, but as time passes those antiquated words become unintelligible to modern speakers. The same is true for scripting languages, where the term *deprecated* is used to designate "words," pieces of code, that still work but are superceded by more recent code.

ActionScript in Flash 5 is a much fuller language than its Flash 4 counterpart, and several Flash 4 actions are now deprecated. Flash 5 continues to support the deprecated actions, and they are compliant with ECMA-262—a set of specifications for the JavaScript language developed by the European Computers Manufacturers Association (ECMA). A day may come, however, when that's no longer true. So it makes sense to switch to the new actions as soon as you can.

To see which actions are deprecated, in the Publish Settings dialog box, set Flash to export version 5. (For more information on publishing Flash movies, see Chapter 16.) In the Actions panel, open the Actions, Operators, Functions, or Properties categories in the Toolbox List. Flash highlights the deprecated actions in green.

Flash does not highlight deprecated actions in the Basic Actions set, but that set does contain three deprecated actions in the Actions List: Toggle High Quality, If Frame Is Loaded, and Tell Target. Because the Basic Actions set offers more assistance to beginning scripters, it can be useful to start scripting with these actions, even though they are deprecated. As you get more familiar with scripting, you can switch to the newer actions for accomplishing the same things.

To add an action to a movie-clip instance:

1. Open a new Flash document.

2. In Frame 1, use the oval tool to draw a long, narrow oval outline; give it a fairly heavy stroke.

3. In Frame 1, place an instance of a movie clip on the Stage next to the oval.

   You can create your own movie clip or choose Window > Common Libraries > Movie Clips to open the library of clips that comes with Flash and then drag one of those clips to the Stage (**Figure 13.38**).

4. Select the movie clip.

5. Access the Object Actions panel.

6. From the Add Statement menu, choose Basic Actions > Toggle High Quality.

   Flash adds the default movie-clip handler onClipEvent (load) and the toggleHighQuality action to the Actions List (**Figure 13.39**).

   The default handler tells Flash to implement the ActionScript as soon as the movie clip loads into Frame 1 during playback of the movie.

7. To make the handler respond to a different event, in the Actions List, select the handler.

   The event parameters for the onClipEvent action appear in the Parameters pane.

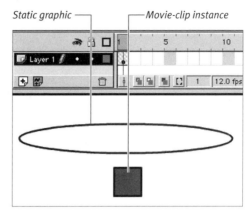

Static graphic — Movie-clip instance

Figure 13.38 To test adding the Toggle High Quality action, place an outline shape on the Stage with a movie-clip instance. A long, narrow oval is a good shape for demonstrating the difference between aliased and antialiased modes.

movie-clip handler

```
Object Actions
onClipEvent (load) {
    toggleHighQuality ();
}
Line 2: toggleHighQuality ();
No Parameters.
```

Figure 13.39 With a movie clip selected on the Stage, when you choose Basic Actions > Toggle High Quality from the Object Actions panel's Add Statement menu, Flash adds the movie-clip handler and the toggleHighQuality action to the Actions List.

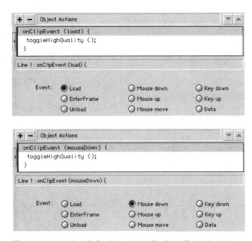

Figure 13.40 The default movie-clip handler triggers when the clip loads (top). Selecting Mouse Down as the triggering event changes the ActionScript (bottom).

8. Click the Mouse Down radio button.

    The first line of code in the Actions List updates to reflect the new event parameter (**Figure 13.40**). You're ready to test the script.

9. From the Control menu, choose Test Movie.

    The move opens in Flash Player. When you click the movie clip, Flash switches between antialiased and aliased modes. In antialiased mode, the oval appears smooth but a bit blurry where Flash adds lighter-colored pixels to fill out the oval form; in aliased mode, you see all the jaggies clearly.

Clip Event Parameters

The onClipEvent action has nine parameters. The parameters tell Flash when to run the ActionScript that falls within the curly braces of the movie-clip handler statement. Some parameters are pairs of opposite events, such as Load and Unload. Some require further scripting to create a precise event trigger. If you want to trigger an ActionScript with a particular key, for example, you must add to the Key Press statement other actions that test to see what key the user has pressed.

Load triggers the ActionScript when the playhead reaches the first frame in the Timeline containing that movie clip and the clip appears; Unload triggers when the playhead reaches the first frame that no longer contains that movie clip.

Enter Frame triggers the ActionScript when each new frame of the movie clip appears.

Mouse Down/Mouse Up triggers the ActionScript when the user presses and releases the mouse button anywhere in a frame that contains the movie clip.

Mouse Move triggers the ActionScript when the user moves the mouse anywhere in a frame that contains the movie clip.

Key Down/Key Up triggers the ActionScript when the user presses/releases a key on the keyboard while a frame that contains the movie clip appears.

Data triggers the ActionScript when the script of another object or movie passes variables to the current movie.

Previewing Button and Movie-Clip Actions in Test Mode

Test mode is the only place where you can check the full interactivity of your buttons and movie clips: the feedback of the button's rollover capabilities, the button actions, any movie-clip animation that you've placed in your button, and any actions that you've attached to movie-clip instances in your movie. Buttons, movie clips, and their attached actions are fully enabled in test mode.

To test the fully enabled button:

1. Open a Flash movie containing buttons (or movie clip actions) that you want to try.

2. From the Control menu, choose Test Scene or Test Movie (**Figure 13.41**).

    Flash exports the scene or movie to a Flash Player file, adding the .swf extension to the file name and using the parameters currently assigned in the Publish Settings dialog box. (For more information on Publish Settings, see Chapter 16.) During export, Flash displays the Exporting Flash Player dialog box, which contains a progress bar and a button for canceling the operation (**Figure 13.42**).

    When it finishes exporting the movie, Flash opens the SWF file in Flash Player so that you see the movie in action. The buttons and movie clips in the test window are all live, so you can see how they interact with mouse actions by the viewer.

3. When you finish testing your buttons, click the movie window's close box to exit the player.

    Flash returns you to the movie-editing environment.

Figure 13.41 To test the full animation and interactivity of buttons, you must export your movie. To export only the current scene, choose Control > Test Scene.

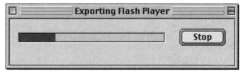

Figure 13.42 The Exporting Flash Player dialog box appears during export.

✔ Tip

- Warning: When you choose Control > Test Movie, Flash does not ask whether you want to replace earlier versions of the file with the same name; it just assumes that you do. The down side of that convention, however, is that Flash may replace a file that you don't intend to replace. When you export a Flash movie yourself, it's tempting to use the file name and just add the .swf extension to differentiate your original Flash file from your exported SWF file. Unfortunately, Flash can't tell the difference between SWF files that you create and SWF files that it creates in test mode. As a result, the Test Movie command replaces your file. To be safe, always change the name of your movie somewhat when you export it yourself.

ADDING SOUND TO YOUR MOVIES

14

It's amazing how much a classic silent film conveys with just moving pictures and text, but that era is history. Audio is a vital feature of today's Web sites. In Macromedia Flash, movies can incorporate sound, either as an ongoing background element or as a synchronized element that matches a particular piece of action—say, a slapping sound that accompanies a pair of hands clapping.

Flash deals only with sampled sounds—those that have been recorded digitally or converted to digital format. Flash imports AIFF-format files for Mac OS, WAV-format files for Windows, and MP3-format files for both platforms. In addition, with the combination of Flash 5 and QuickTime 4, users on both platforms can import QuickTime movies containing sounds and Sun AU files. Mac users can also import WAV, Sound Designer II, and System 7 sounds. Any sounds you import or copy into a movie reside in the movie file's library.

Flash offers a limited form of sound editing. You can clip the ends off a sound and adjust its volume, but you must do other kinds of sound editing outside Flash.

When you publish your finished movie, pay attention to the sampling rate and compression of sounds to balance sound quality with the file size of your finished movie. You learn more about these considerations in Chapter 16.

Using Sounds in Flash

To add sound to Flash movies, you must attach sound clips to keyframes. You access sounds and control synchronization of sounds via the Sound panel. You can also call up Flash's simple sound-editing tools through the Sound panel.

To access the Sound panel:

◆ If the Sound panel is not currently active, from the Window menu, choose Panels > Sound (**Figure 14.1**).

The Sound panel opens or comes to the front if you've grouped it with other panels (**Figure 14.2**).

✔ Tip

■ The Sound panel also appears (together with the Frame and Actions panels) when you double-click a frame in the Timeline.

Figure 14.1 To access the Sound panel, choose Window > Panels > Sound (top) or click the Show Instance button in the Launcher bar (bottom).

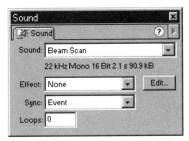

Figure 14.2 Using the Sound panel, you can attach sounds to keyframes, set synchronization, and perform simple sound-editing operations.

Independent Sounds Versus Synchronized Sounds

Unsynchronized sound clips play independently of the frames in a movie and can even continue playing after the movie ends. Flash starts these *event sounds* at a specific frame, but thereafter, event sounds play without relation to specific frames. On one viewer's computer, the sound may take 10 frames to play; on another slower setup, the sound may finish when only 5 frames have appeared.

Flash can also synchronize entire sound clips with specific frames. Flash breaks these *streaming sounds* into smaller pieces and attaches each piece to a specific frame. For streaming sounds, Flash forces the animation to keep up with the sounds. On slower setups, Flash draws fewer frames so that important actions and sounds stay together.

Figure 14.3
Choose File > Import to bring sounds into your Flash file.

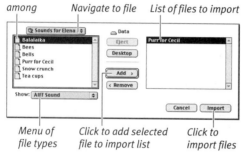

Files to choose among — *Navigate to file* — *List of files to import*

Menu of file types — *Click to add selected file to import list* — *Click to import files*

Files to choose among — *Navigate to file*

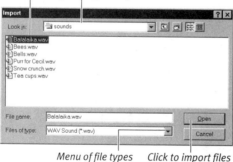

Menu of file types — *Click to import files*

Figure 14.4 The Import dialog box (Mac, top; Windows, bottom) allows you to import sound files into Flash. Choose the sound-file type that is appropriate for your platform—AIFF (Mac) or WAV (Windows)—from the pop-up file-types menu.

Importing Sounds

The procedure for importing sounds is just like the procedure for importing bitmaps or other artwork: You use the File > Import command. Flash brings the sound file into the library for the current movie, and you drag a copy of the sound from the Library window into that movie.

To import a sound file:

1. From the File menu, choose Import (**Figure 14.3**).

The standard file-import dialog box appears (**Figure 14.4**).

2. From the Show menu (Mac) or the Files of Type menu (Windows), choose the format of the sound file that you want to import.

Flash imports AIFF files for the Mac, WAV files for Windows, and MP3 files for both platforms.

3. Navigate to the sound file on your system.

4. Select the file.

(On the Mac, you must also click the Add button to add the file to the list for import. You can import several sound files by adding them to the import list.)

continues on next page

5. Click Import (Mac) or Open (Windows).
Flash imports the sound file that you
selected, placing it in the library. Flash
displays the waveform of the sound in the
Library preview window (**Figure 14.5**).

✔ Tips

■ You can hear a sound without placing
it in a movie. Select the sound in the
Library window. Flash displays the waveform in the preview window. To hear the
sound, click the Play button in the preview window.

■ When QuickTime 4 is installed on your
system, you can import AIFF and WAV
files regardless of what platform you
are using.

Play button

Figure 14.5 Flash keeps sound files in the
library, giving them a separate sound-file icon.
You can see the waveform for a selected sound
in the preview window. Click the Play button to
hear the sound.

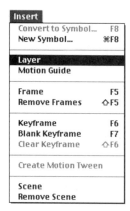

Figure 14.6 It's best to keep sounds in separate layers from the graphics and actions in your movie. To add a new layer, choose Insert > Layer.

Organizing Sounds in Separate Layers

Nothing prevents you from adding sounds in layers that contain other content, but your movie will be easier to handle—and sounds will be easier to find for updating and editing—if you always put sounds in separate layers reserved just for your soundtrack. Flash can handle multiple sound layers.

To add a layer for sound:

1. Open a new Flash document, or open an existing one to which you want to add sound.

2. In the Timeline, select a layer.

3. *Do one of the following:*
   - From the Insert menu, choose Layer (**Figure 14.6**).
   - In the Timeline, click the Add Layer button.

   Flash always adds the new layer directly above the selected layer. If you want to add a layer below the current bottom layer, you'll need to create it and then reposition it at the bottom of the stack.

4. Drag the layer to the desired position in the layer stacking order.

   The position in the stacking order of layers has no effect on the playback of sounds in the movie, but you may find it helpful to place all your sound layers at either the bottom of the layers or at the top so that you can find them easily.

   continues on next page

ORGANIZING SOUNDS IN SEPARATE LAYERS

5. To rename the layer, double-click the layer name.

Flash activates the text field containing the name, and you can type a new name to identify this sound layer.

6. To exit the text field, press Enter or click outside the text field.

✔ Tips

■ After you've placed sounds in a layer, you can lock the layer—to prevent yourself from accidentally adding graphics to it—by clicking the bullet in the column below the padlock icon.

■ Flash lacks a way to organize layers hierarchically in the Timeline—to link all sound layers below one main soundtrack layer, for example. You can fake a hierarchy by using the mask layer, though. Create a mask layer, and name it Soundtrack. Drag every sound layer on top of the Soundtrack layer, and Flash will indent it in the Timeline below the mask named Soundtracks. No masking is involved, but the indentation lends a visual aid to your movie's organization (**Figure 14.7**).

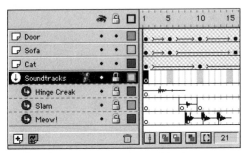

Figure 14.7 You can put Flash's masking layers to an unexpected use: hierarchical organization of the Timeline. Because sound layers have no graphics, you don't need to worry that they will be hidden by the mask layer, and you can group them below the heading Soundtracks.

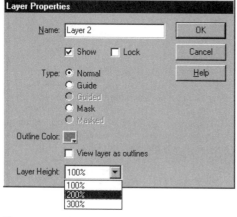

Figure 14.8
Choose Modify > Layer to access the Layer Properties dialog box, where you can change a layer's height.

Figure 14.9 In the Layer Properties dialog box, choose 200% or 300% from the Layer Height pop-up menu to enlarge the layer view in the Timeline and make any sound wave attached to the layer easier to view.

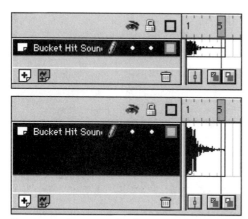

Figure 14.10 Compare a five-frame sound wave at normal layer height (top) with the same sound wave in a 300 percent layer (bottom).

Adjusting Sound-Layer Height

As a default, Flash displays layers at 100 percent, but you can bump the layer display up to 200 or 300 percent. It can be helpful to make the sound layers larger so that you can see the waveform (a graphic image of the sound) for that layer better. You change layer size in the Layer Properties dialog box.

To adjust the layer height for sound:

1. In the Timeline, select the sound layer that you want to enlarge.

2. To access the Layer Properties dialog box, *do one of the following:*

   ◆ From the Modify menu, choose Layer (**Figure 14.8**).

   ◆ Double-click the layer icon of the selected layer.

   The Layer Properties dialog box appears.

3. From the Layer Height pop-up menu, choose the desired percentage (**Figure 14.9**).

   Choose 200% or 300% to make the layer taller.

4. Click OK.

   Flash returns you to the Timeline. The selected layer is now taller, and the waveform in it is larger and shows a bit more detail (**Figure 14.10**).

Adding Sounds to Frames

You can assign a sound to a keyframe the same way that you place a symbol or bitmap: by selecting the keyframe and then dragging a copy of the sound from an open Library window (either that movie's or another's) to the Stage. You can also assign any sound that resides in the movie's library to a selected keyframe by choosing the sound from the Sound menu in the Sound panel.

To assign a sound to a keyframe:

1. Open a Flash file to which you want to add sound.

   The Ping-Pong animation that you created in Chapter 11 makes a good practice file. The movie contains four keyframes, in which a ball connects with a paddle. Adding sound can heighten the reality of that contact: You can make the sound realistic (say, a small *thwock*) or make it humorous, if the sound is unexpected (a wolf's howl, for example).

2. Add a new layer for the sounds in your movie.

   (For more detailed instructions, follow the steps in "Organizing Sounds in Separate Layers" earlier in this chapter.)

3. Name the layer Sound.

4. In the Timeline, select your new Sound layer, and add keyframes at frames 5, 10, 15, and 20.

   These four keyframes match the keyframes in the animation in which the ball hits one of the paddles (**Figure 14.11**).

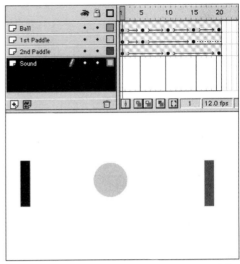

Figure 14.11 Create a separate layer for the sounds in your movie. In that layer, add a separate keyframe at each place where you want a sound to occur. Here, the keyframes correspond to the keyframes in which the ball makes contact with a paddle.

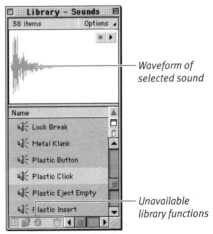

Waveform of selected sound

Unavailable library functions

Figure 14.12 Flash comes with a library of sounds for you to use in your movies. Choosing Window > Common Libraries > Sounds opens the Sounds Library without opening its parent movie. This makes sounds available for copying to other movies but prevents you from accidentally changing them in the original movie. Plastic Click makes a good Ping-Pong-ball sound.

Highlighted Stage   *Sound-symbol outline*

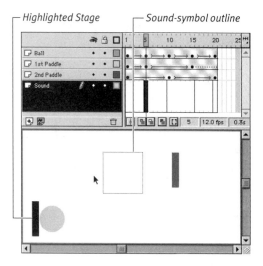

Waveform of sound assigned to Keyframe 5

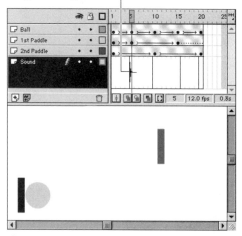

Figure 14.13 When you drag a sound from the Library window to the Stage, you see the symbol outline and Flash highlights the Stage just as it does when you drag a graphic symbol or button (top). A sound has no visible presence on the Stage, but Flash displays the sound's waveform in the Timeline (bottom).

5. From the Window menu, choose Common Libraries > Sounds.

The Library - Sounds window opens (it's one of the libraries that Macromedia provides with Flash). The library's background and editing functions are grayed out because you haven't opened the Sound.fla file—just its library. But you can drag sounds to your own Flash file.

6. In the Library - Sounds window, choose the sound named Plastic Click (**Figure 14.12**).

Its waveform appears in the preview window.

7. In the Timeline, select Keyframe 5 of the Sound layer.

This is the first frame in which the ball and paddle connect.

8. Drag a copy of the Plastic Click sound from the Library window to the Stage of your movie.

Although sounds have no visible presence on the Stage, you must drag the sound copy to the Stage. On Mac and Windows, you see the outline of a box on the Stage. In addition, on the Mac, Flash highlights the Stage with a thick gray outline. When you release the mouse button, Flash puts the sound in the selected keyframe and displays the waveform in that keyframe and any in-between frames associated with it (**Figure 14.13**).

9. In the Timeline, select Keyframe 10 of the Sound layer.

This is the second frame in which the ball and paddle connect.

continues on next page

ADDING SOUNDS TO FRAMES

10. Access the Sound panel.

11. From the pop-up Sound menu, choose the sound named Plastic Click.

All the sounds in the movie's library are available from the Sound panel's Sound menu (**Figure 14.14**). You don't have to drag a copy of the sound to the Stage each time you want to turn that sound on in a keyframe.

For now, leave the other settings in the Sound panel alone. You learn more about them in later tasks.

12. Repeat steps 7 and 8 (or 9 and 10) for keyframes 15 and 20.

Now you are ready to play the movie and check out the sounds. As each paddle strikes the ball, Flash plays the Plastic Click sound, adding a level of realism to your simple Ping-Pong animation.

✔ Tip

■ Can't remember what sound that little squiggly waveform is? With Tooltips active (choose it in the General tab of the Preferences dialog box), let the mouse pointer hover over the waveform in the Timeline. Flash displays the name of the sound.

Figure 14.14 In the Sound panel, the Sound pop-up menu lists all the sounds that are in the movie. From this menu, choose a sound that you want to assign to the keyframe that's currently selected in the Timeline.

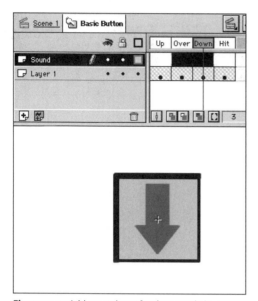

Figure 14.15 Add a new layer for the sounds in a button, and insert keyframes into frames where you plan to assign sounds.

Adding Sounds to Buttons

Auditory feedback helps people who view your movie interact with buttons correctly. For buttons that look like real-world buttons, adding a click sound to the Down frame provides a more realistic feel. For more fanciful buttons or ones disguised as part of the scenery of your movie, adding sound to the Over frame alerts users that they've discovered a hot spot.

To enhance buttons with auditory feedback:

1. Open a Flash file containing a button to which you want to add sound.

   (To learn how to create buttons, see Chapter 13.)

2. Open the file's Library window (choose Window > Library), and select the button symbol that you want to modify.

3. From the Options menu, choose Edit.

   Flash opens the button in symbol-editing mode.

4. In the Timeline, add a new layer (click the Add Layer button), and name it Sound.

5. In the Sound layer, select the Over and Down frames, and choose Insert > Blank Keyframe (**Figure 14.15**).

continues on next page

6. Using the techniques described in "Adding Sounds to Frames" earlier in this chapter, assign a sound to the Over frame and a different sound to the Down frame.

Flash displays as much of the waveform as possible in each frame. When you add sounds to buttons, it makes sense to increase the height of the layer that contains sounds (**Figure 14.16**).

7. Return to movie-editing mode.

Every instance of the button in the movie now has sounds attached.

8. To hear the buttons in action, choose Control > Enable Simple Buttons.

When you move the pointer over the button, Flash plays the sound that you assigned to the Over frame. When you click the button, you hear the sound that you assigned to the Down frame.

✔ Tip

■ The most common frames to use for button feedback are the Over and Down frames, but you can add sounds to any of the button frames. Sounds added to the Up frame play when the pointer rolls out of the active button area. Sounds added to the Hit frame play when you release the mouse button within the active button area.

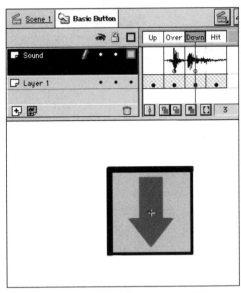

Figure 14.16 Flash displays the waveform of the assigned sound in the keyframe. Unlike movie Timelines, button Timelines have no in-between frames that can contain part of the waveform. Increasing the layer height for a button's sound layer enlarges any waveforms in the button's frames, letting you see more detail.

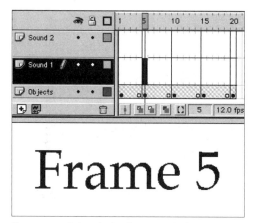

Figure 14.17 Select the keyframe to which you want to assign a sound. Settings you create in the Sound panel get applied to the selected keyframe.

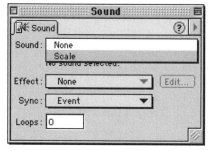

Figure 14.18 In the Sound panel, choose a sound from the Sound pop-up menu.

Using Event Sounds

One of the parameters available in the Sound panel is Sync. The Sync setting determines the way that Flash synchronizes the sounds in your movie. There are four settings for Sync: Event, Start, Stop, and Stream. The default is Event.

Event sounds play in their own Timeline. Flash synchronizes the beginning of an event sound with a specific keyframe in a movie, but then the event sound plays until Flash reaches the end of the sound clip or encounters an instruction to stop playing either that specific sound or all sounds. If it's long enough, an event sound continues to play after the movie ends. If your movie loops, every time the playhead passes a frame containing an event sound, Flash starts another instance of that sound playing.

To make an assigned sound an event sound:

1. Create a 20-frame, 3-layer Flash movie.

2. Label the layers Objects, Sound 1, and Sound 2.

3. In all layers, insert keyframes into frames 1, 5, 10, 15, and 20.

4. In the Object layer, place identifying text on the Stage for each keyframe.

5. Import into the movie whatever sound you want to use.

   This example uses a 15.8-second sound clip of a musical-scale passage.

6. In the Timeline, select Frame 5 of the Sound 1 layer (**Figure 14.17**).

7. In the Sound panel, from the Sound pop-up menu, choose the sound named Scale (**Figure 14.18**).

continues on next page

USING EVENT SOUNDS

8. From the Sync pop-up menu, choose Event (**Figure 14.19**).

The Scale sound is now assigned to Keyframe 5 of the Sound 1 layer.

9. Play your movie one time.

In a movie that has a standard frame rate of 12 fps, the 15.8-second Scale sound continues to play after the end of the movie.

✔ Tip

■ To better understand how Flash handles event sounds, choose Control > Loop Playback. Now play the movie again, and let it loop through a couple of times. Each time the movie reaches Frame 5, Flash starts another instance of the Scale sound, and you start to hear not one set of notes going up the scale but a cacophony of bad harmonies. When you stop the playback, each sound instance plays out until its end—an effect sort of like people singing a round.

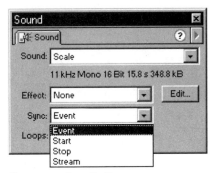

Figure 14.19 From the Sync pop-up menu, choose Event to make the assigned sound start in the selected keyframe and play to the end of the sound, without synchronizing with any subsequent frames of the movie.

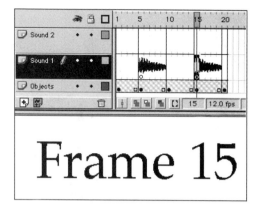

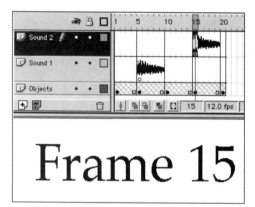

Figure 14.20 You can add a second instance of your sound and make it play on top of the first. Event sounds play in their own Timeline, so you're free to add the second sound to the same layer as the first (top). Alternatively, you can add the second sound to its own layer (bottom).

To play overlapping instances of the same sound:

1. Using the file that you created in the preceding exercise, to assign a sound to a later point in the movie's Timeline, *do one of the following*:

    ◆ Select Frame 15 of the Sound 1 layer.

    ◆ Select Frame 15 of the Sound 2 layer.

    Because Flash starts a new instance of an event sound, even if that sound is already playing, you have the choice of adding a second instance to the same layer as the first or adding it to a different layer.

2. In the Sound panel, from the Sound pop-up menu, choose the sound named Scale.

3. From the Sync pop-up menu, choose Event.

    The Scale sound is now assigned to Keyframe 15 of whichever layer you chose (**Figure 14.20**).

4. Play your movie one time.

    When the playhead reaches Frame 5, the Scale sound starts. When the playhead reaches Frame 15, another instance of the Scale sound starts, and the two sounds play together (you hear two voices). When the first instance ends, you again hear only one voice.

Each frame of a Flash movie can contain just one sound. To make Flash play multiple sounds at the same point in a movie, you must create multiple layers to contain the sounds.

To start different sounds simultaneously:

1. Open the file that you created in "To make an assigned sound an event sound" earlier in this chapter.

   Keyframe 5 of the Sound 1 layer contains the Scale sound, with Sync set to Event.

2. In the Timeline, select Frame 5 of the Sound 2 layer.

3. In the Sound panel, from the Sound pop-up menu, choose a different sound.

   You might choose, for example, the Bucket Hit sound from Flash's Sounds Library.

4. From the Sync pop-up menu, choose Event.

   Flash places the waveform for the second sound in Keyframe 5 of the Sound 2 layer (**Figure 14.21**).

5. Play your movie one time.

   When the playhead reaches Frame 5, Flash starts playing the Scale sound and the Bucket Hit sound simultaneously.

✔ Tip

■ All the information required to play an event sound lives in the keyframe to which you assigned that sound. When you play the movie, Flash pauses at that keyframe until all the information has downloaded. It's best to reserve Event Syncing for short sound clips; otherwise, your movie may be interrupted by long pauses for downloading sounds.

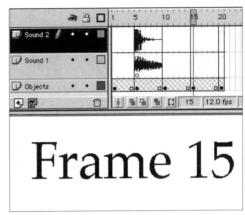

Figure 14.21 To make two different sounds begin playing simultaneously, you must put each sound in a different layer.

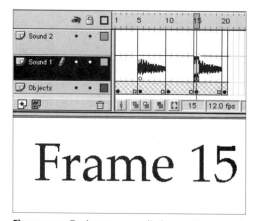

Figure 14.22 To change a sound's Sync setting, select the frame that contains the sound. From the Sound panel's Sync menu, choose a new setting.

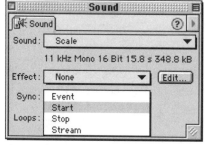

Figure 14.23 To prevent Flash from playing another instance of the sound, if that sound is already playing, choose Start from the Sound panel's Sync menu.

Using Start Sounds

Start sounds behave just like event sounds, with one important difference: Flash does not play a new instance of a start sound if that sound is already playing.

To set an assigned sound's Sync to Start:

1. Open the file that you created in "To play overlapping instances of the same sound" earlier in this chapter.

   You should have one instance of the Scale sound in Keyframe 5 and another in Keyframe 15. The second instance is in the Sound 1 or Sound 2 layer, depending on what you did in the earlier exercise.

2. In the Timeline, select the Keyframe 15 that contains the Scale sound (**Figure 14.22**).

3. In the Sound panel, from the Sync pop-up menu, choose Start (**Figure 14.23**).

4. Play your movie one time.

   When the playhead reaches Frame 5, the Scale sound starts. When the playhead reaches Frame 15, nothing changes; you continue to hear just one voice as the Scale sound continues playing. When a sound is playing and Flash encounters another instance of the same sound, the Sync setting determines whether Flash plays that sound. When Sync is set to Start, Flash doesn't play another instance of the sound.

✔ Tip

- In movies that loop, the playback of event sounds can get confusing if they're long, because they can stack up on each loop. To avoid playing multiple instances of a sound, set the sound's Sync to Start. If the sound is still playing when Flash starts the movie again, Flash lets it play and adds nothing new. If the sound has finished playing by, say, the time Flash starts the movie on its third loop, Flash plays the sound again.

Using Streaming Sounds

Streaming sounds are specifically geared for playback over the Web. When Sync is set to Stream, Flash breaks a sound into smaller sound clips. Flash synchronizes these sub-clips with specific frames of the movie—as many frames as are required to play the sound. Flash stops streaming sounds when playback reaches a new keyframe or an instruction to stop playing either that specific sound or all sounds. Unlike event sounds, which must download fully before they can play, streaming sounds can start playing after a few frames have downloaded. This makes streaming the best choice for long sounds, especially if you'll be delivering your movie over the Web.

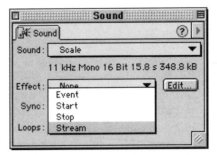

Figure 14.24 To make Flash force a sound to synchronize with specific frames of your movie, choose Stream from the Sound panel's Sync menu.

To make an assigned sound a streaming sound:

1. Create a new 15-frame Flash movie.

2. Insert a blank keyframe at Frame 5, add text to identify the keyframes, and import the sound that you'd like to stream.

   This example uses the 15.8-second Scale sound again.

3. In the Timeline, select Frame 5.

4. In the Sound panel, from the Sound pop-up menu, choose Scale.

5. From the Sync pop-up menu, choose Stream (**Figure 14.24**).

The Mystery of Streaming Sound

When you choose Stream as the Sync setting for a sound, Flash divides that sound clip into smaller subclips and embeds them in individual frames. The movie's frame rate determines the subclips' size. In a movie with a frame rate of 10 frames per second (fps), for example, Flash divides streaming sounds into subclips that are a tenth of a second long. For every 10 frames, Flash plays 1 second of the sound.

Flash synchronizes the start of each subclip with a specific frame of the movie. If the sound plays back faster than the computer can draw frames, Flash sacrifices some visuals (doesn't draw some frames of the animation) so that sound and images match up as closely as possible. Streaming sound ensures, for example, that you hear the door slam when you see it swing shut—not a few seconds before. If the discrepancy between sound-playback speed and frame-drawing speed gets big enough, however, those dropped frames make the movie look jerky, just as it would if you set a low frame rate to begin with.

Sound will stop playing here

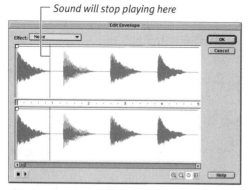

Figure 14.25 When you set a sound's Sync to Stream, you can check how much of the sound will play, given the number of in-between frames your movie has for the sound to play in. Click the Sound panel's Edit button to open the Edit Envelope window. This window displays a sound's full waveform in relation to time or to frame numbers.

Figure 14.26 There is time enough in these 15 frames to play only the first note of the Scale sound. Flash displays just that much of the full 15.8-second waveform in the Timeline.

6. To see how the sound fits into the available time in your movie, click the Sound panel's Edit button.

   The Edit Envelope window appears.

   At 15.8 seconds, the Scale sound is too long to play completely in 10 frames. When Sync is set to Stream, Flash plays only as much of the sound as can fit in the frames that are available to it—in this case, slightly less than a second. In the Edit Envelope window, a vertical line indicates where Flash truncates this instance of the sound (**Figure 14.25**).

7. To close the Edit Envelope window, click OK or Cancel.

   The truncated waveform appears in frames 5 through 15 (**Figure 14.26**).

8. Play your movie to hear the sound in action.

   When the playhead reaches Frame 5, the Scale sound starts. When the playhead reaches Frame 15, the movie ends and Flash stops playback of the Scale sound.

9. Choose Control > Test Movie to hear the sound in looping mode.

   Flash simply repeats the same snippet of sound, stopping it each time the movie ends.

   continues on next page

✔ Tips

- You can hear streaming sounds play as you drag the playhead through the Timeline (a technique called *scrubbing* in audio circles). As the playhead moves over the waveform, you can see how the images and sounds fit together. You can then add or delete frames to better synchronize the sounds with the images on-screen.

- Shift-click the Timeline to take the playhead to a particular frame (or Shift-drag the playhead to that frame). As long as you hold down the mouse button, Flash repeats the portion of sound that synchronizes with that frame.

- If you find that your streaming sound is getting cut off too soon, switch the units of measure in the Edit Envelope window to see how many frames you need to add to accommodate the sound (**Figure 14.27**).

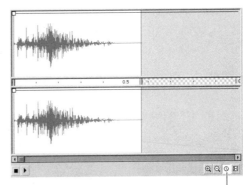

Set scale to seconds ⌐
Set scale to frames ⌐

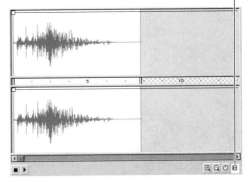

Figure 14.27 The scale for the waveform in the Edit Envelope window can be set to seconds (top) or frames (bottom). If you set the scale to frames, you can see exactly how many frames the movie needs to provide enough time for the major parts of the sound to finish. Usually, you want to make room for the segments of the wave that have the greatest amplitude.

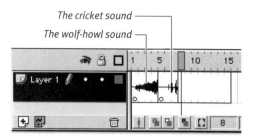

The cricket sound
The wolf-howl sound

Figure 14.28 Inserting a new keyframe cuts off your view of the preceding sound's waveform in the Timeline. If the sound is an event sound, however, it continues playing through the keyframe.

Stopping Sounds

Although event sounds normally play to the end, you can force them to stop at a specific keyframe. To issue an instruction to stop a specific sound, you must set that sound's Sync parameter to Stop.

To stop playback of a sound:

1. Create a new 15-frame Flash movie with two fairly long event sounds (at least 3 seconds); place one sound in Frame 1 and the other in Frame 5.

   (For more detailed instructions, see "Adding Sounds to Frames" earlier in this chapter.) In this example, Frame 1 contains the sound Sound-wolf_howl and Frame 2 contains the sound Sound-Cricket. (Both sounds are from Flash's Sound lesson. To use these sounds yourself, open the Sound lesson movie's library and drag a copy of each sound to your movie.)

2. In the Timeline, insert a new blank keyframe at Frame 8 (**Figure 14.28**).

   Flash cuts off the waveform at Frame 8 because of the keyframe, but on playback, the event sounds continue to play after Frame 8.

3. Select Keyframe 8.

4. In the Sound panel, from the Sound pop-up menu, choose Sound-wolf_howl.

continues on next page

5. From the Sync pop-up menu, choose Stop (**Figure 14.29**).

Flash uses this instruction to stop playback of the wolf-howl sound at Frame 8.

Flash places a small square in the middle of Frame 8 in the Timeline to indicate that the frame contains a stop-sound instruction (**Figure 14.30**).

6. Play your movie to hear the sounds in action.

The wolf howl starts immediately; the crickets kick in at Frame 5. When the playhead reaches Frame 8, the wolf cuts out but the cricket continues playing even after the playhead reaches the end of the movie.

✔ Tips

- The Stop setting and the sound that it stops can be in different layers. The Stop setting stops playback of all instances of the specified sound that are currently playing in any layer.

- If you want to stop only one instance of a sound, set the Sync parameter of that instance to Stream; then put a blank keyframe in the frame and layer where you want that instance of the sound to stop.

- You can stop all sounds at the same time by adding the frame action Stop All Sounds to your movie. For detailed instructions, see Chapter 12.

Figure 14.29 To stop a sound's playback at a specific point in a movie, select the keyframe where the sound should stop. From the Sound panel's Sound menu, choose the sound you want to stop. From the Sync menu, choose Stop. Here, the Stop instruction refers to the Sound-wolf_howl sound.

Sync is set to Stop for this keyframe

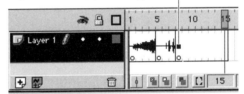

Figure 14.30 In the Timeline, a small square in the middle of a keyframe indicates the presence of the stop-sound instruction.

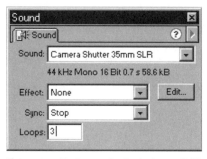

Figure 14.31 Typing a value in the Loops field tells Flash how many times to play the sound.

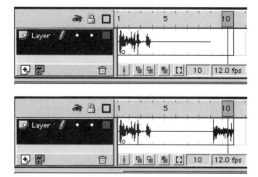

Figure 14.32 When Loops is set to 0, Flash displays just the original waveform in the Timeline (top). When Loops is set to 3, Flash displays as much of the repeated waveform as there is room for (bottom).

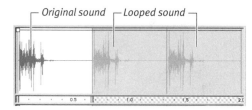

Figure 14.33 You can see a precise waveform for the repeated loops graphed against seconds or frames of your movie in the Edit Envelope window. The grayed-out waveforms are the looped portion of the sound.

Looping Sounds

Flash's sound-looping parameter allows you to repeat sounds without adding another instance of the sound to a frame. Type a value in the Loops text box in the Sound panel. Flash plays the sound the specified number of times. You can loop event sounds and streaming sounds. The sound's Sync parameter applies to the whole set of repeated sounds.

To set a Loop value:

1. Create a 10-frame movie with a short sound in Frame 1.

   This exercise uses the sound called Camera Shutter 35mm SLR from Flash's common library named Sounds.

2. In the Timeline, select Frame 1.

3. In the Sound panel, enter 3 in the Loops field (**Figure 14.31**).

   Flash extends the sound's waveform by stringing together three copies of it. In the Timeline, Flash displays as much of the extended waveform as will fit in the available frames (**Figure 14.32**).

✔ Tips

- To see the extended waveform graphed against seconds or frames, in the Sound panel, click Edit. The full sound appears in the Edit Envelope window (**Figure 14.33**).

- Because Flash links the repeated sounds and displays them as a single sound in the Edit Envelope window, you can edit the looping sound. You can change the volume so that the sound gets louder with each repetition, for example. You learn about editing sounds in the following section of this chapter.

Editing Sounds

Flash allows you to make limited changes in each instance of a sound in the Edit Envelope window. You can change the start and end point of the sound (that is, cut a piece off the beginning or end of the waveform) and adjust the sound's volume.

Flash offers six predefined volume edits: Left Channel, Right Channel, Fade Left to Right, Fade Right to Left, Fade In, and Fade Out. These sound-editing templates create common sound effects, such as making a sound grow gradually louder (Fade In) or softer (Fade Out), or for stereo sounds, making the sound move from one speaker channel to the other.

To assign packaged volume effects:

1. Open the movie that you created in the preceding exercise.

   This is a 10-frame movie with a sound that loops three times in Frame 1.

2. In the Timeline, select Frame 1.

3. In the Sound panel, click the Edit button.

   The Edit Envelope window appears (**Figure 14.34**).

4. From the Effect pop-up menu, choose Fade In (**Figure 14.35**).

   Flash adjusts the sound envelope (**Figure 14.36**). When the envelope line is at the top of the window, Flash plays 100 percent of the available sound. When the envelope line is at the bottom of the window, Flash plays 0 percent of the available sound.

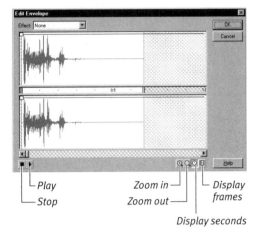

Play — Stop *Zoom in — Zoom out* *Display frames*
Display seconds

Figure 14.34 Flash lets you perform simple sound editing—for length and volume—in the Edit Envelope window.

Figure 14.35 The Effect pop-up menu in the Edit Envelope window offers six templates for common sound effects that deal with volume. You can also choose Custom to create your own effect.

0 percent   *100 percent*

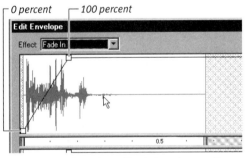

Figure 14.36 The Fade In effect brings the sound's envelope down to 0 percent (the bottom of the sound-editing window) at the start of the sound and quickly raises it to 100 percent (the top of the sound-editing window).

EDITING SOUNDS

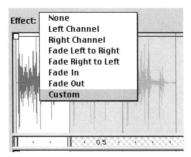

Figure 14.37 To edit the volume of a sound yourself, from the Effect pop-up menu in the Edit Envelope window, choose Custom.

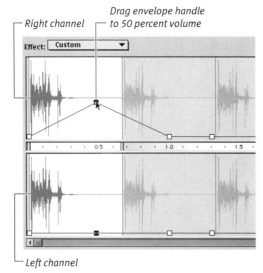

Figure 14.38 Click the waveform in the sound-editing window to add a handle. Drag the handle to adjust the sound envelope. You can make the sound envelope the same or different for both channels. For monaural sounds, both waveforms are identical.

5. Click the Play button to hear the sound with its fade-in effect.

The first iteration of the sound starts soft and grows louder. The repetitions play at full volume.

6. Click OK.

Flash returns you to movie-editing mode.

✔ Tip

■ If you don't need to look at your sound's waveform, you can bypass the Edit Envelope window. Just choose an effect from the Effect menu in the Sound panel.

To customize volume effects:

1. Using the movie that you created in the preceding exercise, select Frame 1.

2. To access the Edit Envelope window, in the Sound panel, click the Edit button.

3. From the Effect menu, choose Custom (**Figure 14.37**).

4. In the Edit Envelope window, drag the square envelope handles that appear at the 0-second mark in both channels down to 0 percent.

5. In the right channel (the top section of the window), click the waveform at the 0.5-, 1.0-, and 1.3-second marks.

Flash adds new envelope handles to both channels.

6. In the right-channel window, at the 0.5 second mark, drag the handle up to the 50 percent volume level (**Figure 14.38**).

7. Repeat step 6 for the left channel.

continues on next page

EDITING SOUNDS

8. In both channels, drag the 1.0-second mark handles to the 50 percent level and the 1.3-second mark handles to the 100 percent level (**Figure 14.39**).

You can add as many as eight handles to create a variety of volume changes within one sound.

9. Click the Play button to hear the sound with its fade-in effect.

Flash fades in the first iteration of the sound, plays the second iteration at half volume, and plays the third iteration at full volume.

10. Click OK.

✔ Tips

■ To remove unwanted envelope handles, drag them out of the sound-editing window.

■ When you add a handle to one channel, Flash automatically adds another to the same location in the other channel. To create different volumes from the two channels, however, you can drag the handle to a different level in each channel.

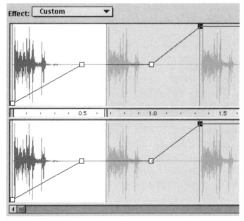

Figure 14.39 You can use eight handles to shape a sound's envelope. By using the zoom tools to view more of the sound in the Edit Envelope window, you can see the sound envelope for all three iterations of the sound. The first fades in, the second plays at 50 percent volume, and the third plays at full volume.

Time-in control   Dead air   Time-out control

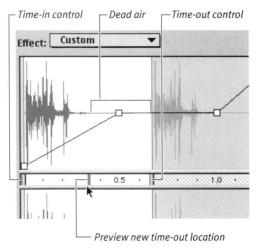

Preview new time-out location

Figure 14.40 Flash lets you trim the beginning and end of a sound in the Edit Envelope window. Here, dragging the time-out control clips off the end of the sound (which is just very soft sound or silence).

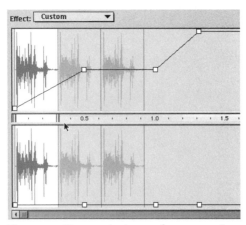

Figure 14.41 The new, shorter waveform appears in the Edit Envelope window.

Third loop
Second loop
Original sound

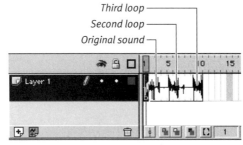

Figure 14.42 After you shorten the sound, all three iterations fit into the 10-frame movie.

In addition to changing a sound's volume, you can make a sound shorter by instructing Flash to omit some of it at the beginning, the end, or both. The Camera Shutter 35mm SLR sound has a lot of dead air (recorded silence) at the end that you can cut.

To edit sounds for length:

1. Using the movie that you created in the preceding exercise, select Frame 1.

2. To access the Edit Envelope window, in the Sound panel, click the Edit button.

3. In the Edit Envelope window, drag the time-out control to the 0.3-second mark (**Figure 14.40**).

   Flash shortens the sound in both channels (**Figure 14.41**).

4. Click OK.

   Flash returns you to movie-editing mode. Now all three iterations of the looping sound are visible in the Timeline (**Figure 14.42**).

✔ Tip

■ Although you can change the start and end points of a sound in Flash, you still have the whole sound taking up room in your movie file. If you find yourself trimming many sounds in Flash, you should consider investing in a sound-editing program that allows you to leave the excess on the cutting-room floor rather than behind the curtains in Flash.

EDITING SOUNDS

INTRODUCING COMPLEX INTERACTIVITY

15

In Chapters 12 and 13, you created scripts using Basic Actions statements and simple parameters. As you explore the full Actions set, you begin to work with more complex parameters. These complex actions allow you to manipulate objects within the main movie; test for the truth of certain conditions; retrieve information from user input, other movies, and other types of files; and control the programs that display your movies.

Key to this kind of scripting is working with *variables*—containers for storing information—and *expressions*—formulas for manipulating that information. With these items, you can create sites that respond more directly and individually to users.

The ways in which you can combine the elements of a movie with actions are too varied and advanced to cover in this book. But to get you started, this chapter takes you through some basic concepts that you need to create complex actions.

Using Expressions and Variables

Suppose that you want to create a lucky-number generator, and you define the lucky number as a person's age plus today's date. You could make up a formula to figure out this number: age + day + month + year. That formula is called an *expression*. Each word in the formula is a *variable*, a container for temporarily holding a series of numbers or letters.

Variables can be concrete—text fields in which users type information or where information generated by ActionScripts gets output. Variables can also be abstract—containers that live only in Macromedia Flash's electronic brain.

You set up concrete variables by creating two types of editable text fields: Dynamic Text and Input Text. The contents of these variables appear in your movie. You create abstract variables by using the `set variable` action. Flash can then add to the variable or change its contents according to your instructions, even though you never see the contents in your movie.

A good way to get a feel for variables is to play around with expressions that manipulate the contents of Input and Dynamic text boxes.

To create a variable from an input-text field:

1. Open a new Flash file.

2. In the Toolbox, select the text tool.

3. Access the Text Options panel. (If it's not open, choose Window > Panels > Text Options.)

4. From the Text Type menu, choose Input Text.

    The panel displays the parameters for text boxes that allow users to enter text (**Figure 15.1**).

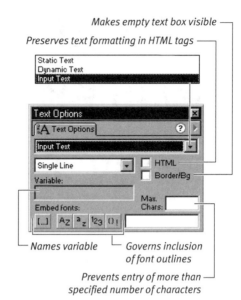

Makes empty text box visible

Preserves text formatting in HTML tags

Names variable *Governs inclusion of font outlines*

Prevents entry of more than specified number of characters

Figure 15.1 To access the parameters for creating text boxes that accept input from your movie's viewers, choose Input from the Text Type menu. The input parameters control the field's appearance and function—giving the text field a border and background, for example, so that the field is visible in the final movie even if it's empty.

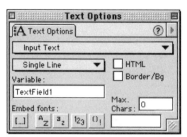

Figure 15.2 When you create input text boxes, Flash gives them default variable names.

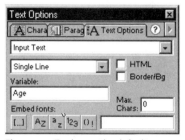

Figure 15.3 To change the default variable name for a text box, enter the new name in the Variable field.

The Mystery of Expressions and Variables

Expressions and variables go hand in hand. If creating ActionScripts were like cooking, expressions would be the recipes, and variables would be the bowls, cups, pans, and other containers that you use in cooking. The values would be the ingredients that you place in the containers.

The recipe/expression might say, "Combine the contents of the red bowl and the green bowl, and put it in the blue pan." If you put eggs in the red bowl and milk in the green bowl, you'll get one dish. If you put tomatoes in the red bowl and pasta in the green bowl, you'll get quite another. Although the containers are the same, and although the instructions for combining their contents are the same, the variety of the contents makes for different results.

5. On the Stage, in Keyframe 1, create a text field that contains the word *Age*.

    Flash enters a default variable name for your text box in the Text Options panel (**Figure 15.2**).

6. To assign the variable a new name, in the Variable field, enter Age (**Figure 15.3**).

    You will be able to use this variable name when you write expressions. Flash will then retrieve whatever data your movie viewers enter in this field.

7. To make your text field visible in the movie even when the field contains no text, check the Border/Bg checkbox.

8. To restrict the length of the text field, in the Max. Chars field, enter 3.

    This setting prevents users from inadvertently typing an impossible age.

9. To preserve the formatting of your text box with HTML tags, check the HTML checkbox.

10. To include outlines for rendering all (or part) of the font used in your text box, click the Embed Font buttons at the bottom of the Text Options panel.

11. Leave all other options at their default settings.

12. Repeat steps 5 through 11 to create text fields and variables for Day, Month, and Year.

    If you want, restrict the text length of Day, Month, and Year.

✔ Tip

■ You can print the contents of the Actions list. In the Actions panel, from the Options menu in the top-right corner, choose Print.

To create a variable from a dynamic-text field:

1. Using the file you created in the preceding exercise, with the text tool, create a text box that contains the words *Lucky Number.*

2. With the text box still active, access the Text Options panel.

More Mysteries of ActionScript Syntax

ActionScript has it own rules, which are analogous to the rules of grammar and spelling in English. These rules, called *syntax*, govern such things as word order, capitalization, and punctuation of action statements. When you set the Actions panel to operate in Normal mode, Flash enters the statements you choose and handles most of the details of syntax for you. The following list briefly describes common ActionScript punctuation marks.

Dot (.) ActionScript uses *dot syntax*, meaning that the periods on the keyboard act as links between objects and the *properties* (characteristics) and *methods* (behaviors) applied to them. In the statement

`cloneMC._duplicateMovieClip`

the dot (the period) links the movie clip named cloneMC with the method that creates a copy.

The dot also indicates the hierarchy of files and folders in path names, similar to the way that a slash does in HTML syntax. (Note that Flash 4 used slashes to indicate path names. Flash 5 still recognizes this *slash syntax*, but Macromedia recommends using dot syntax, and that's what you'll find in this book.)

Semicolon (;) A semicolon indicates the end of a statement. The semicolon is not required: Flash interprets the end of the line of statements correctly without it, but including it is good scripting practice.

Braces ({}) Braces set off ActionScript statements that belong together. A set of actions that take place after on (release), for example, must be set off by braces.

Note that the action statements within braces can require their own beginning and ending braces. The opening and closing braces must pair up evenly. When you use Normal mode and Basic Actions, Flash enters the pairs of braces for you. You still need to pay attention to where you are adding scripts within the Actions list, however, to ensure that you group the actions as you intend.

Parentheses () Parentheses group the arguments that apply to a particular statement—defining the scene and frame in a goto action, for example. Parentheses also allow you to group operations, such as mathematical calculations, so that they take place in the right order.

Prevents selecting text-field contents —

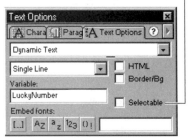

Figure 15.4 The Dynamic parameters are similar to the Input parameters. In dynamic text fields, however, you restrict users from selecting text in the field instead of restricting the number of characters the field will accept.

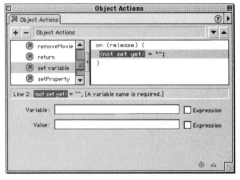

Figure 15.5 The highlighted code in the Actions List indicates a problem in the script. Flash further describes the problem in the Parameters pane of the Actions panel.

3. From the Text Type menu, choose Dynamic Text.

The panel displays the parameters for dynamic text (**Figure 15.4**).

4. In the Variable field, enter LuckyNumber.

5. To prevent viewers from typing in this field accidentally, uncheck the Selectable checkbox.

6. Leave all other options at their default settings.

To script a button action that manipulates variables:

1. Continuing with the file you created in the preceding exercises, on the Stage, in Keyframe 1, place an instance of a button.

2. Select the button.

3. Access the Object Actions panel.

4. In the Toolbox list, click the Actions category.

A list of action statements appears.

5. Double-click set variable.

Flash updates the Actions list to look like **Figure 15.5**.

Flash highlights the words <not set yet> in red to indicate that you must define the parameters of this action.

6. In the Variable field, enter the variable name LuckyNumber.

This field directs Flash where to put the result of the expression that you are about to write. In this case, output goes to the text field named LuckyNumber.

7. In the Value field, enter the following:

Number (Age) + Number (Day) + Number (Month) + Number (Year)

continues on next page

USING EXPRESSIONS AND VARIABLES

This code tells Flash to add four numbers: the numbers contained in each of the four variables. The word *number* (called a *function* in ActionScript terminology) tells Flash to treat the content of the variable in the following parentheses as a number (not a letter). The script takes whatever the viewers type in the Age, Day, Month, and Year text fields and adds them as numbers (mathematically). If you entered only Age + Day + Month + Year, the script would *concatenate* the numbers (join them in one long text string, 422692000, for example). Try entering the code both ways to see what happens.

8. Check the Expression checkbox to the right of the Value field.

   You've now defined a formula that adds the contents of the Age, Day, Month, and Year fields (**Figure 15.6**).

9. From the Control menu, choose Test Movie to try out your LuckyNumber generator.

10. Type numbers in the editable text fields named Age, Day, Month, and Year.

11. Click the button.

   Flash adds the numbers that you typed and displays the total in the text field named LuckyNumber (**Figure 15.7**).

✔ Tip

■ You can use the various categories in the Toolbox list to help you enter expressions in the Actions List. Click the Functions category, for example, and then double-click Number. Flash enters the word *number,* followed by parentheses, in the Actions List and in the Value field of the Parameters pane. Click the Operators category and then double-click the plus sign to have Flash enter the addition operator.

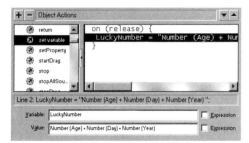

Figure 15.6 To create a variable without an editable text field, use the set variable action and fill in the variable name and value.

Figure 15.7 The value of the LuckyNumber variable is an expression that adds the numbers of the other text-field variables in the movie.

USING EXPRESSIONS AND VARIABLES

Using Conditional Actions

Conditional actions allow you to ask certain questions (or test whether a condition has been met) and make Flash carry out another action if the answer is true (or the condition has been met). You could ask Flash to determine, for example, whether the number that is currently in the variable Age is greater than 59. If it is, you could instruct Flash to jump to a scene that describes discounts for senior citizens.

In Flash 5, the set of Basic Actions contains one conditional action: If Frame Is Loaded. This action comes with a built-in condition to test, which makes it a good action with which to start learning about conditional actions. The If Frame Is Loaded action is often used to create a teaser animation that tells your viewers there will be a wait to download information.

To test for download of a frame:

1. Create a 100-frame Flash file.

2. In the first 20 frames, created a simple animation that will play while the user waits for the entire file to download.

   For example, create a 20-frame animation of a ball moving around a rectangle containing the message "One moment while I get that for you ..." Add keyframes containing identifying text to every tenth frame; add a couple of bitmapped graphics and plenty of sounds to ensure that the file is large. The larger the file the longer it takes to download, and the more time you'll have to check your preload message.

3. In the Timeline, create a new layer to contain your actions, and label it Actions.

4. Select Keyframe 1 in the Actions layer.

continues on next page

When Do You Need a Preloader?

If your site contains large or complex animations, you might want to download much or all of the data to the user's computer before allowing the user to explore the site. Waiting until all the data is available locally ensures the smoothest possible playback. To keep users amused (and informed) during the download process, you might create a teaser animation with a small number of frames and fast-loading content (often referred to as a *preloader*) that loops until the last frame of your animation has downloaded to the user's computer.

The If Frame Is Loaded action checks the user's computer to see whether the data for a certain frame already exists on that computer. If the data is there, Flash follows whatever instruction you include in the If Frame Is Loaded action. If the data isn't there, Flash plays the next frame of the movie (or completes the next action, if there is one).

5. In the Frame Actions panel, from the Add Statement menu, choose Basic Actions > If Frame Is Loaded (**Figure 15.8**).

Flash updates the Actions List with the following code:

```
ifFrameLoaded(){
}
```

6. In the Parameters pane, *set the following parameters:*

- In the Scene field, enter <current scene>.
- From the Type menu, choose Frame Number.
- In the text field, enter 100.

Flash updates the Actions List to reflect the parameters that you chose (**Figure 15.9**). This action tells Flash to check for the presence of Frame 100.

7. With ifFrameLoaded(){ selected in the Actions List, from the Add Statement menu, choose Basic Actions > Go To.

Flash adds gotoAndPlay(1); to the Actions List.

8. In the Parameters pane, *set the following parameters:*

- In the Scene field, enter <current scene>.
- From the Type menu, choose Frame Number.
- In the text field, enter 21.

Flash updates the Actions List to read as follows:

```
ifFrameLoaded(100){
    gotoAndPlay(21);
}
```

This action tells Flash to jump to Frame 21 if Frame 100 has already downloaded (**Figure 15.10**).

In the published movie, Flash checks for Frame 100 before starting to play the movie. If Frame 100 is present on the Viewer's

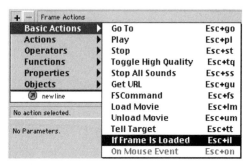

Figure 15.8 To create an ActionScript that checks when a frame is loaded, from the Add Statement menu of the Actions panel, choose Basic Actions > If Frame Is Loaded.

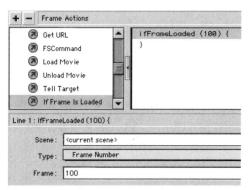

Figure 15.9 Set the parameters for the ifFrameLoaded statement in the Parameters pane. From the Scene menu, choose <current scene>; from the Frame Type menu, choose Frame; for Frame Number, enter 100. In the published movie, Flash tests whether Frame 100 is available on the user's computer yet.

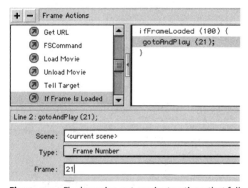

Figure 15.10 Flash carries out any instructions that fall between the curly braces. Adding gotoAndPlay(21) instructs Flash to jump to Frame 21 when Frame 100 is available.

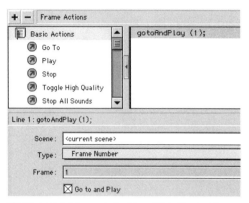

Figure 15.11 Adding gotoAndPlay (1) to the last frame of your teaser animation tells Flash to jump to Frame 1 and start over. This action creates a loop that repeatedly tests to see whether Frame 100 has arrived. If not, Flash plays the teaser again.

The Pitfalls of Conditional Actions

In the following ActionScript, Flash carries out the action between the opening and closing curly braces only when the test result is true:

```
ifFrameLoaded (100){
    stopAllSounds;
}
gotoAndPlay (21)
```

When an action comes after the ending brace, Flash carries it out whether the result is true or false. Make sure that all the actions that should take place when the test result is true are placed *inside* the curly braces.

If you want Flash to carry out one action when the condition is true and a different action when the condition is false, you need to create a *branching condition*. The Basic Action set contains no branching actions; you must use the if, else, and else if actions, which you can find in the

---

computer, Flash jumps to Frame 21 and starts playing from there. If Frame 100 is absent, Flash moves on to Frame 2 of the movie and continues playing the movie.

To make the movie repeat the teaser until Frame 100 arrives, you need to tell Flash to go back to Frame 1 at the end of the teaser animation.

To loop the teaser animation:

1. Using the file that you created in the preceding exercise, in the Actions layer, insert a keyframe at Frame 20 (the last frame of the teaser animation).

2. In the Timeline, select Keyframe 20.

3. In the Frame Actions panel, from the Add Statement menu, choose Go To.

   Flash adds gotoAndPlay (); to the Actions List.

4. With gotoAndPlay (); selected in the Actions List, in the Parameters pane, *set the following parameters:*
   - In the Scene field, enter <current scene>.
   - From the Type menu, choose Frame Number.
   - In the text field, enter 1.

   Flash updates the Actions List with the statement gotoAndPlay (1) (**Figure 15.11**).

   When the playhead reaches Frame 20, Flash jumps back to Frame 1. There, the frame actions that you set up in the preceding exercise test for the presence of Frame 100 all over again. You can't test the If Frame Is Loaded action in the movie-editing environment. To see the actions work, choose Control > Test Scene or Control > Test Movie.

To preview If Frame Is Loaded:

1. In the file that you created in the preceding exercise, from the Control menu, choose Test Scene.

Flash exports the movie and opens it in Flash Player.

2. From Flash Player's View menu, choose Show Streaming (**Figure 15.12**).

Flash now simulates the way that your movie will stream over the Internet. (For more details on simulated streaming, see Chapter 16.) As a result, Frame 100 will not be available for a while, and you'll have a chance to see your teaser animation repeat.

Figure 15.12 When you are in Flash Player and choose Control > Test Movie, menus offer several commands other than the ones that are available in movie-editing mode. Choose View > Show Streaming to see how ifFrameLoaded works as your movie streams over the Internet.

✔ Tips

■ Using If Frame Is Loaded in a practice file can be tricky unless you have a movie that you know will take several seconds to load. If your downloading message doesn't appear or appears too briefly for you to check it, add more sounds or bitmaps to frames 21 through 100 of your movie to increase the file size and download time. In a real-world situation, if you have that "problem," you may not need a downloading message at all.

■ To ensure that your viewers get to the heart of your movie as soon as possible after the last frame loads, put an If Frame Is Loaded test in every frame of the teaser animation.

Conditionals for Error Checking

In the tasks in "Using Expressions and Variables" earlier in this chapter, you restricted the length and selectability of some text fields to help ensure that users enter data correctly. As you get more comfortable with scripting, you can use conditional actions (if, else, if else) to test for common user errors. The following script is similar to the one you created, but adds an if action to see whether someone accidentally enters letters in fields that should be numbers. The predefined function isNaN returns a value of true when the tested item contains letters. When users enter letters, a message appears in the Lucky Number field reminding them to use numbers.

```
on (release) {
    LuckyNumber = Number (Age) + Number
    (Day) + Number (Month) + Number (Year);
    if (isNaN(LuckyNumber)) {
        LuckyNumber = "Use Numerals Only";
    }
}
```

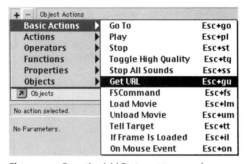

Figure 15.13 From the Add Statement menu, choose Basic Actions >Get URL to make Flash open another file in the browser.

Loading New Files

Flash provides two ways to load new files into your movie or Web site. The Get URL action allows you to find other files and display them in a browser window when you run your movie in a browser. These files might be Flash Player files (with the extension .swf) or HTML pages. You can display the new file in the current browser window or in a new window. If your HTML page uses frames, you can target any frame to display the new file.

The Load Movie action lets you display new movie files within the current movie window. The loaded movie can replace the current movie or stack up on top of the current movie as though it were simply another layer of animation. (An advanced application for the Load Movie and Get URL actions is to pass variables from one file to another file.)

To use Get URL to open a separate browser window:

1. Create a new Flash document.

2. Place an instance of a button symbol in Keyframe 1 of your movie.

   (For more details on using symbols and buttons, see chapters 6 and 13.)

3. On the Stage, select the button.

4. In the Actions panel, from the Add Statement menu, choose Basic Actions > Get URL (**Figure 15.13**).

   Flash updates the Actions List to read as follows:

```
on (release) {
    getURL ("");
}
```

continues on next page

5. In the Parameters pane of the Actions panel, in the URL field, enter the name or path of the file that you want to appear in a separate window (**Figure 15.14**).

For testing this exercise, enter a relative URL for a file on your computer, such as a file located in the same folder as the Flash file that you created. (Make sure that the Expression checkbox is unchecked. You want Flash to treat the URL as a text string, not a variable or expression.) You can also use an absolute URL in this field, but in that case, you must have an Internet connection open to test the action.

6. From the Window pop-up menu, choose _blank (**Figure 15.15**).

The _blank parameter tells Flash to open the new file in a new window in the browser. The three other predefined choices are _self (which opens the new file in the current browser window), _parent (which opens the new file in the parent of the current frame), and _top (which opens the new file in the top-level frame in the current browser window). Again, leave the Expression checkbox unchecked. You can also type the name of the window or frame that you want to display the new URL.

7. From the File menu, choose Publish Preview > HTML (**Figure 15.16**).

Flash exports your movie to a .swf file, creates an HTML file that plays the file, and opens that file in whatever browser you have available. (For more details on using Flash's publishing features, see Chapter 16.)

8. In the movie playing in the browser window, click the button that you just created.

Flash opens a new browser window and displays the file that you specified in the Get URL action.

Uncheck when URL is a string ⌐

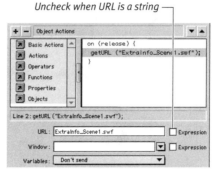

Figure 15.14 For testing on your computer without opening an Internet connection, enter a relative URL in the Actions panel's Parameters pane. The file you specify as the URL must be in the same folder as the main movie file. To make Flash interpret the URL as an actual file name (a *string*), uncheck the Expression checkbox.

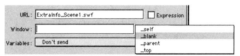

Figure 15.15 Choose _blank from the Window pop-up menu to make Flash open the new URL in a separate browser window.

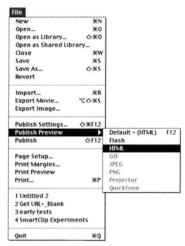

Figure 15.16 Choose File > Publish > HTML to test the getURL action in your browser.

LOADING NEW FILES

Figure 15.17 To open a new movie that plays in a different level of your movie, from the Actions panel's Add Statement menu, choose Basic Actions > Load Movie.

✔ Tip

■ You can create a text box that links directly to a URL. Using the text tool, create a text box, and enter the text that you want to be a hot link. With that text selected, in the Character panel's URL field, enter the URL of the page to link to.

To use Load Movie:

1. Follow steps 1 through 3 of the preceding exercise.

2. In the Object Actions panel, from the Add Statement menu, choose Basic Actions > Load Movie (**Figure 15.17**). Flash updates the Actions List with the following code:
   ```
   on (release){
       loadMovieNum ("",0);
   }
   ```

3. With `loadMovieNum ("",0);` selected in the Actions List, in the Parameters pane's URL field, enter the name of the Flash Player (.swf) file that you want to load.

continues on next page

4. From the Location menu, choose Level and enter 1 in the text field (**Figure 15.18**).

The elements of movies loaded in higher levels obscure elements in movies at lower levels, just as graphics on higher layers of a movie obscure graphics in the lower layers.

5. From the Control menu, choose Test Movie to try out the Load Movie action.

When you click the button, Flash loads the second movie on top of the movie that contains the button (**Figure 15.19**).

✔ Tip

- You can also use actions to unload movies that you've previously loaded. The process is similar to the preceding exercise, except that in Step 2, you choose Basic Actions > Unload Movie and you can skip Step 3. In Step 4, you enter the level number from which Flash should remove a previously loaded movie.

Figure 15.18 Defining the Location parameter as Level, with a number greater than 0, tells Flash to display the loaded movie on top of the current movie. A Level of 0 tells Flash to replace the current movie with the loaded movie. (You can also choose to load a movie's variables without displaying or playing any of the movie.)

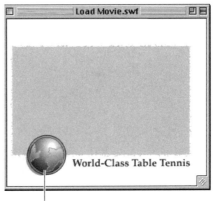

Button with Load Movie action

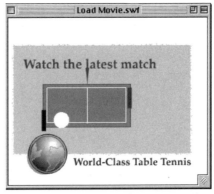

Figure 15.19 The main movie (Load Movie.swf) is playing in Level 0 (top). When you click the globe button, Flash loads another movie (Extra Info.swf) into Level 1. The movie in Level 1 plays as though it were an additional layer of animation sitting on top of the original movie (bottom).

The Mystery of Movie Levels

When you add movie clips to a Flash file, or start loading other movies, the independent Timelines start stacking up. To control them with ActionScripts, you need to tell Flash which Timeline you're trying to control. You do this with the target path name, which makes the hierarchical relationships of the nested Timelines clear.

Imagine three family members having lunch: a grandparent, a parent, and child. If you restrict the conversation to the people at the table, the grandparent can talk about "my child," the parent can talk about "my child," and everybody can talk about "my family." The same word can refer to different people because the context is clear; the person saying the word has a known relationship to the person being referred to.

There's a similar phenomenon in creating target paths in ActionScript. Imagine you have a Flash file named Grandma, which contains a movie clip named Mom; the Mom clip contains another movie clip named Kid. A script attached to a frame or object inside the Kid clip can control the Mom clip's Timeline by using the target path _parent. But if you attach a script using the path name _parent to an object in the Mom clip, you'll be controlling the Timeline in the Grandma movie. In other words, which Timeline _parent refers to depends on where the script containing it resides. A path name that always refers to the "founding parent" movie in a set of nested Timelines is _root. No matter where a script lives (in the Kid clip, the Mom clip, or the Grandma movie) when it uses the path name _root it controls the main movie Timeline—in this example, Grandma.

In addition to having Timelines that stack up within an individual Flash file, in the Flash Player, you can stack up several movies on separate levels. You target these separate movies with the pathname _level plus the number of the level containing the movie (_level1, _level2, and so on). To refer to the main movie Timeline in the bottom-most level, use the path name _level0. You determine which level contains which movie when you use the Load Movie action. You can replace the current movie by entering 0 for the Level parameter. If you type a higher number, Flash stacks the loaded movie on top of the current movie.

LOADING NEW FILES

Controlling Nested Timelines

One way to create highly complex interactions is to use actions to manipulate movie clips (and loaded movies). The item that you want to manipulate is called the *target*. You point Flash to the target by identifying its *target path* (its address).

As you learned in Chapter 11, movie clips are miniature movies playing within other Flash movies. Each movie clip has its own Timeline. The ActionScript language provides two actions—Tell Target and `with`—that can send instructions from the main movie to a movie clip within that movie (or vice versa). These actions allow you to do such things as start or stop playback or jump to a certain frame of a target's timeline. (You can also control the Timeline of a movie that you loaded into the current movie by using the Load Movie action.)

Tell Target Versus with Action

Tell Target is a deprecated action (for more information, see the sidebar, "The Mystery of Deprecated Actions," in Chapter 13). Anyone who scripted actions in Flash 4 and is familiar with Tell Target can continue to use it to create ActionScript. But the actions you can carry out with Tell Target—controlling the Timelines of movie clips—are so important that it's worth the effort to start learning the new action right away. The action `with` complies with ECMA-262, performs the same work as Tell Target, and is not much harder to use for simple Timeline controls.

Compare the following scripts, each one of which enables a button to control a movie clip's playback.

Using Tell Target
```
on (release) {
    tellTarget ("/Pong") {
        stop ();
    }
}
```

Using Tell with
```
on (release) {
    with (_root.Pong) {
        stop ();
    }
}
```

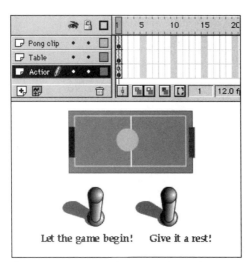

Figure 15.20 You can assign with actions to buttons so that anyone who views your movie can start and stop a clip inside the movie, such as the Ping-Pong clip that you created in Chapter 11.

Figure 15.21 To make buttons identifiable to Flash as targets for with actions, you must name the button instance in the Instance panel.

To control a movie clip by using with:

1. Create a new Flash document that contains a movie clip and two buttons in Keyframe 1.

   This example uses the Ping-Pong clip that you created in Chapter 11, plus two buttons that look like switches (**Figure 15.20**). In this exercise, you set one of the buttons to stop the action of the Ping-Pong game and the other to start it again. (Add text to identify the button functions, if you want.)

2. On the Stage, select the Ping-Pong movie clip.

3. Access the Instance panel.

4. To identify the movie clip as the target of your instruction, in the Name field, enter a unique name. Do not include spaces in this name.

   For this exercise, call this instance of the clip Pong (**Figure 15.21**).

5. On the Stage, select the button that you want to use to stop the action.

6. Access the Object Actions panel.

continues on next page

7. From the Add Statement menu, choose Actions > with (**Figure 15.22**).

Flash updates the Actions List to read as follows:

```
on (release) {
    with (<not set yet>){
    }
}
```

8. To get assistance with entering the correct path to your target movie clip, in the Object field, in the Parameters pane, click the Insert Target Path button (**Figure 15.23**).

9. In the Insert Target Path window that appears, *do the following:*

  ◆ In the hierarchical list of movie elements, click the icon for the movie clip you want to control.

  ◆ To use dot syntax in writing the path name, in the Notation section, choose Dots.

  ◆ To use an absolute URL in writing the path name, in the Mode section, choose Absolute.

10. Click OK.

Flash enters the path name in the Object Actions panel's Object field and updates the Actions List to read as follows:

```
on (release) {
  with (_root.Pong) {
  }
}
```

11. In the Actions List, select

```
with (_root.Pong) {.
```

Figure 15.22 To begin creating an ActionScript that controls a movie-clip Timeline, select the object that will do the controlling. In the Actions panel, from the Add Statement menu, choose Actions > with.

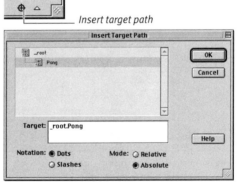

Figure 15.23 In the bottom-right corner of the Actions panel, click the Insert Target Path button (top) to open a window that lists possible movie-clip targets (bottom). Click one of the movie-clip icons to enter its name in the path field.

CONTROLLING NESTED TIMELINES

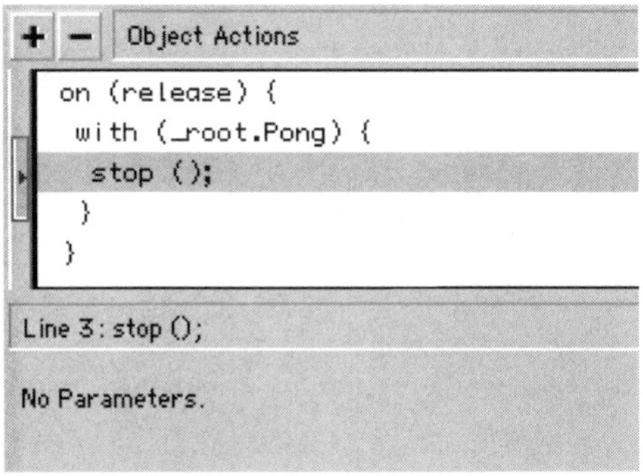

```
+ -   Object Actions
  on (release) {
   with (_root.Pong) {
    stop ();
   }
  }
Line 3 : stop ();

No Parameters.
```

Figure 15.24 The full ActionScript for the button that stops the movie clip named Pong.

12. From the Add Statements menu, choose Actions > stop.

Flash updates the Actions List (**Figure 15.24**).

13. On the Stage, select the second button (the one that starts the action again), and repeat steps 6 through 12.

This time, in Step 12, choose play.

14. To see your buttons in action, from the Control menu, choose Test Movie.

When you click the Stop button, Flash stops playback of the Ping-Pong clip. When you click the Start button, Flash resumes playback of the movie clip.

✔ Tip

■ The with action doesn't control just the timeline of movie clips; it can also control the properties of movie clips. Use this action to change a clip's transparency, visibility, position on the Stage, and so on. You can select the appropriate properties from the Properties category of the Actions panel's Toolbox List.

In addition to controlling the Timeline of nested movie clips by using the `with` action, you can control the main Timeline of your movie.

To control the main Timeline by using with:

1. Create a new Flash document with keyframes in frames 1 and 5, a stop action in Frame 1, and some identifying text in Frame 5.

2. In Frame 1, place an instance of a movie clip on the Stage.

3. With the movie clip selected, access the Object Actions panel.

4. From the Add Statement menu, choose Actions > with.

   Flash adds a movie-clip handler to the Actions List.

5. In the Actions List, select the first line of code, and choose Mouse Up from the Parameters pane (**Figure 15.25**).

6. In the Actions List, select the line of code containing <not set yet>.

7. In the Parameters pane, in the Object field, enter `_level0.gotoAndStop (5)`.

   This statement tells Flash, "In the main movie's Timeline, jump to Frame 5, and wait for further instructions." Flash updates the Actions List to look like **Figure 15.26**.

8. From the Control menu, choose Test Movie.

   You can click the Stage anywhere while the movie clip is playing, and Flash jumps to Frame 5.

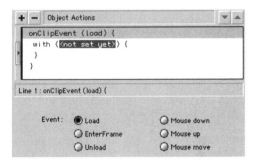

Figure 15.25 To change the default movie-clip handler, select it in the Actions List and then click the radio button for the event you want.

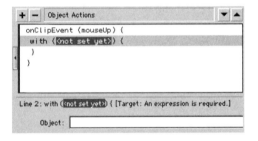

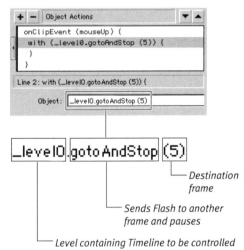

Figure 15.26 Flash highlights incomplete action statements in the Actions List (top). Here, the full action directs Flash to control the movie in Level 0: the main Timeline.

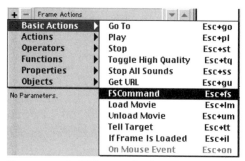

Figure 15.27 The FS Command action allows you to communicate with the program that's running Flash Player, such as your browser or a stand-alone projector.

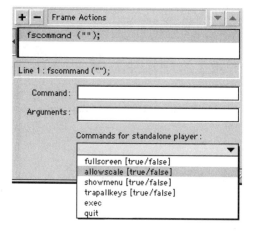

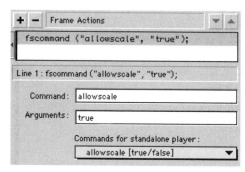

Figure 15.28 Choose allowscale to make your movie's graphics scale proportionately when viewers resize a projector window.

Using FSCommand

The preceding exercises taught you how to control various movie Timelines within Flash. The FS Command action allows you to communicate with and control the program that is running your published movie, such as a browser or a stand-alone projector. (For details about publishing movies, see Chapter 16.) In a movie published as a stand-alone projector, for example, you can set an FS Command action's parameters to make the movie fill the screen, to hide and show the menu bar, and to allow graphics to scale (or prevent them from scaling) when viewers resize the movie's window.

To allow graphics to scale in a projector window:

1. Create a new Flash document.

2. Select Frame 1, and place some graphics on the Stage.

3. With Frame 1 selected, access the Frame Actions panel.

4. From the Add Statement menu, choose Basic Actions > FSCommand (**Figure 15.27**).

5. In the Parameters pane, from the Commands for Stand-Alone Player menu, choose allowscale [true/false].

   Flash enters allowscale in the Command field, enters true in the Arguments field, and updates the Actions List (**Figure 15.28**).

6. From the File menu, choose Publish Settings.

continues on next page

USING FSCOMMAND

7. In the Formats tab of the Publish Settings dialog box, check the projector checkbox for the platforms you are working on, and uncheck all other checkboxes (**Figure 15.29**).

8. Click the Publish button.

    Flash creates a projector, using the default name and settings, and places it in the same location as the Flash file from which it derives. (To learn more about publishing, see Chapter 16.)

9. To close the dialog box, click OK or Cancel.

10. To play the movie, navigate to the projector file on your system and double-click the projector icon.

    The stand-alone projector opens in window. When you resize the window, the graphics scale proportionally to fit within the new window (**Figure 15.30**).

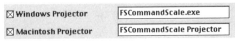

Figure 15.29 To create a projector, check the checkbox for your platform in the Formats tab of the Publish Settings dialog box.

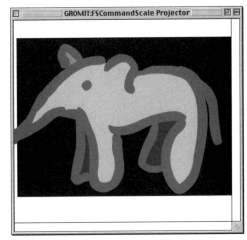

Original window

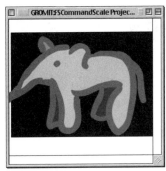

Resized window

Figure 15.30 With allowscale set to true, graphics shrink when viewers make the projector window smaller.

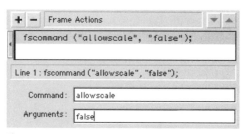

Figure 15.31 Set allowscale to false to keep graphics at a constant size when viewers resize the projector window.

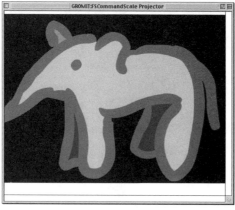

Original window

Resized window

Figure 15.32 With allowscale set to false, graphics remain the same size when viewers make the projector window smaller.

To prevent graphics from scaling in a projector window:

1. Open the Flash document you created in the preceding exercise, and select Frame 1.

2. In the Frame Actions panel, in the Actions List, select the line of code containing the fscommand action.

3. In the Parameters pane, in the Arguments field, enter false.

Flash updates the Actions List (**Figure 15.31**).

4. Repeat steps 6 through 10 in the preceding exercise.

Now when you resize the projector window, the graphic remains the same size. If you make the window smaller, parts of the graphic may be hidden (**Figure 15.32**).

USING FSCOMMAND

The Mystery of URLs

The acronym *URL* stands for *Uniform Resource Locator,* which is a standardized way of handling the addresses of files so that they can be found on the Internet. The conventions of the URL make it possible to decipher the hierarchical structure of the server (or local computer) on which a file is stored, allowing you to maneuver through all the directories, folders, and layers to the specific file that you want.

There are two forms of URLs: absolute URLs and relative URLs.

An *absolute URL* is a complete address that specifies the protocol your browser should use to open the file (HTTP, or Hypertext Transfer Protocol, is one used to transfer the text and graphics of Web sites), the name of the server on which the file resides, the path name (the nested hierarchy of directories, volumes, folders, and so on), and the name of the file itself.

A *relative URL* is a shorthand version of the full address that lets you describe one file's location in relation to another. In essence, you tell Flash to move up and down the hierarchy of nested files, folders, and directories, starting from the file where you give Flash the Get URL instruction. It's like saying. "Look in the folder you're in right now for a file called Fabulous.fla," or "Look in the folder you're in right now for another folder called Other Junk; then look inside that folder for the file Fabulous.fla," or "Go up a level to the folder that contains the folder that contains the file you're in right now. In that higher-level folder, look for another folder called This Junk. Look in This Junk for a file called Abysmal.fla."

Using relative URLs in actions has the advantage of allowing you to test your movies on your computer without opening an Internet connection. Additionally, provided that you keep your files in the same relative positions in the hierarchy, you won't need to rename the files when you transfer them from your local computer to the server where you'll make them available to your viewers.

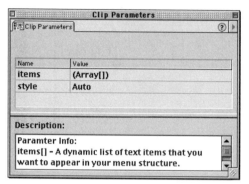

Figure 15.33 The Clip Parameters panel shows the customizable features of a SmartClip selected on the Stage. For the Menu SmartClip double-click the word (Array[]) to open a window containing a list of values for the menu items.

Using SmartClips

ActionScripting is complex and labor-intensive. Flash 5 provides a way to preserve the complex programming that you do with ActionScript in reusable, customizable movie clips. This special form of movie clip is called a *SmartClip*.

The task of defining a SmartClip's capabilities is beyond the scope of this book. But Flash provides three SmartClip objects in its SmartClips common library that you can play with to get the idea: a checkbox, a radio button, and a drop-down menu. You customize the SmartClip's features—the text label for each menu choice, for example—via the Clip Parameters panel.

To access the Clip Parameters panel:

◆ If the panel is not currently open, from the Window menu, choose Panels > Clip Parameters.

To customize an instance of the menu SmartClip:

1. Open a Flash document to which you want to add a menu.

2. From the Window menu, choose Common Libraries > SmartClips. The Smart Clips Library opens.

3. Drag an instance of the movie clip named Menu to the Stage in Keyframe 1.

   Notice that the SmartClip's icon is slightly different than that of a regular movie-clip symbol.

4. With the SmartClip instance selected on the Stage, access the Clip Parameters panel.

   The customizable features of the menu appear in the panel (**Figure 15.33**).

continues on next page

5. In the first line of parameters, under the heading Value, double-click the word (Array[]).

The Values window opens (**Figure 15.34**). The values listed are the default names of the various menu choices. You can edit them to create menu lists with your own choices.

6. To edit the name of the first value, double-click the name defaultValue1 and enter new text (**Figure 15.35**).

7. Repeat the preceding step for as many menu items as you want to create.

For this exercise create three menu items: Glinka, Borodin, and Shostakovich.

8. Click OK.

Flash sets the parameters, but the menu-clip instance on the Stage looks the same as it did before.

9. To view your new menu, choose Control > Test movie.

The menu items you created appear in a drop-down menu. On the Mac, when you open the menu, a check appears next to the currently selected item.

Figure 15.34 In SmartClips, values are elements that you can customize. Each defaultValue line in this Values window represents a menu item.

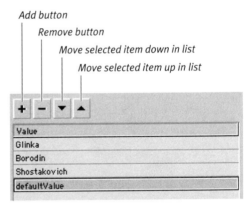

Figure 15.35 Double-click a value to edit it, and give it a new label. To add menu items, click the Add (+) button; to remove menu items, click the Remove (-) button. Use the up and down triangles to change a selected menu item's place in the list.

USING SMARTCLIPS

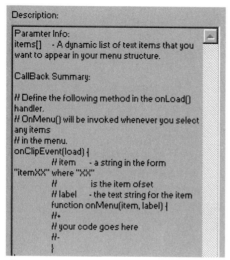

```
Description:

Paramter Info:
items[]   - A dynamic list of text items that you
want to appear in your menu structure.

CallBack Summary:

// Define the following method in the onLoad()
handler.
// OnMenu() will be invoked whenever you select
any items
// in the menu.
onClipEvent(load) {
        // item      - a string in the form
"itemXX" where "XX"
        //          is the item ofset
        // label    - the text string for the item
        function onMenu(item, label) {
        //+
        // your code goes here
        //-
        }
```

Figure 15.36 This cryptic description tells you to activate the menu with a clip handler. The first action within the handler must be a function that checks to see what menu item your viewer selects. After that, you can add actions to do whatever you want.

```
+  -   Object Actions                    ▼ ▲

onClipEvent (load) {
   function <not set yet> () {
   }
}


Line 2: function <not set yet> () { [You must enter a function

     Name: [                              ]

Parameters: [                            ]
```

```
+  -   Object Actions                    ▼ ▲

onClipEvent (load) {
   function onMenu (item, label) {
   }
}


Line 2: function onMenu (item, label) {

     Name: [onMenu                        ]

Parameters: [item, label                 ]
```

Figure 15.37 To create the onMenu function that allows the menu SmartClip to work, in the Actions List, add function (top). Enter the name and parameters outlined in the SmartClip's description (bottom).

At this point, of course, your menu doesn't actually do anything. To make a working menu, you must assign actions to it. A good SmartClip developer will add comments that appear in the Clip Parameters panel to guide users in using the SmartClip.

To assign actions to a menu SmartClip:

1. Open the file you created in the preceding exercise.

2. In Frame 1, on the Stage, select the menu SmartClip.

3. Access the Clip Parameters panel, and resize the window to view the notes in the Description window (**Figure 15.36**).

   Creators of SmartClips should include instructions about how to work with the SmartClip.

   The menu SmartClip requires you to activate the menu with a movie-clip handler and then create a special function to read the menu choices.

4. To add a clip handler and start setting up the function, in the Object Actions panel, from the Add Statement menu, choose Actions > function.

   Flash updates the Actions list to look like **Figure 15.37**.

5. To name your function, with <not set yet> selected, in the Name field, enter onMenu.

6. In the Parameters field, enter item, label.

   Flash updates the Actions List with the proper syntax:
   function onMenu (item, label).

   continues on next page

7. With the second line of code selected in the Actions List, from the Add Statement menu, choose another action—Actions > trace, for example.

The trace action displays a message of your devising in a separate window named Output. The Output window and trace action are for use solely during the process of developing a script. They provide a quick way to test that everything up to a certain point in a script is working correctly.

8. In the Message field, enter a text string or expression (**Figure 15.38**).

For this exercise, enter "My favorite composer is" + label. This formula adds the label name of a selected menu item to the end of the text string.

9. Check the Expression box.

10. To see your menu in action, choose Control > Test Movie.

When you select a menu item, Flash opens the Output window, and your message text appears. To make the menu fully functional, continue adding whatever actions you want. You probably would want to add actions that test which menu choices people make, for example, and deal with them accordingly.

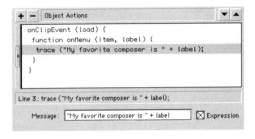

Figure 15.38 The trace action (top) allows you to check your ActionScript at various points for debugging. The trace comments appear in the Output window (bottom) whenever you use the Test Movie or Test Scene command. Here, the trace action attached to the menu SmartClip adds a different message each time you select a new menu item.

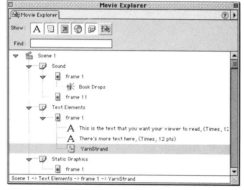

Figure 15.39 To access the Movie Explorer panel, choose Window > Movie Explorer.

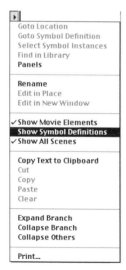

Figure 15.40 The Movie Explorer panel's Options menu lets you choose what elements of your movie appear in the panel's display list and offers commands for editing elements that you've selected in the display list.

Using the Movie Explorer

As you add text, graphic symbols, buttons, movie clips, and actions to your movies, the job of tracking where each element resides increases dramatically. The Movie Explorer is a powerful tool for tracking, finding, and modifying the elements in your movies. It also gives you an overview of the whole movie.

The Movie Explorer window displays the various movie elements hierarchically in a *display list*. You determine which types of elements appear in the list. You can expand and collapse the list levels, similar to the way that you expand and collapse folders as you navigate your hard drive.

To access the Movie Explorer panel:

If the Movie Explorer panel is not currently open, *do one of the following:*

- ◆ From the Window menu, choose Movie Explorer (**Figure 15.39**).
- ◆ In the launcher bar, click the Show Movie explorer button.

To determine overall content of the display list:

From the Options menu in the Movie Explorer panel's top-right corner (**Figure 15.40**), *choose any of the following:*

- ◆ To display all the elements in the movie, choose Show Movie Elements.
- ◆ To display a list of all the symbols used in the movie (including a display list for the elements that make up each movie clip), choose Show Symbol Definitions.
- ◆ To display the contents of all the scenes of a movie, not just the current scene, choose Show All Scenes.

USING THE MOVIE EXPLORER

To determine which types of elements appear in the display list:

In the Show section of the Movie Explorer panel, *do any of the following:*

◆ To display text elements, click the first button (**Figure 15.41**).

◆ To display buttons, movie clips, and graphic elements, click the second button.

◆ To display ActionScripts, click the third button.

◆ To display video clips and bitmapped graphics, click the fourth button.

◆ To display frame and layer information, click the fifth button.

◆ To create a custom set of elements to display, click the sixth button and select elements in the window that appears.

To find an element:

In the Find field of the Movie Explorer panel, enter text that identifies the element you want to find (**Figure 15.42**), as in the following examples:

◆ To find an instance of a symbol, enter the instance name; to find all instances of a symbol, enter the symbol name.

◆ To find all text boxes that use a certain font, enter the font name.

✔ Tips

■ You don't need to press Enter after typing in the Find field; Flash starts searching as soon as you enter any characters.

■ The Movie Explorer panel puts a big drain on your system, because it constantly checks for changes. Even when the panel is just sitting open on your desktop as you work on a file, Flash can slow to a crawl. Keep this panel closed until you're ready to use it.

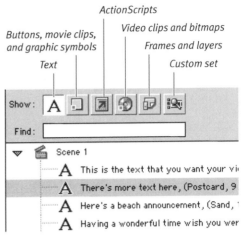

ActionScripts

Buttons, movie clips, and graphic symbols

Video clips and bitmaps

Frames and layers

Text

Custom set

Figure 15.41 Click the buttons in the Show section of the Movie Explorer panel to specify which movie elements to display.

Figure 15.42 To find all instances of a movie-clip symbol, enter the symbol name in the Find field.

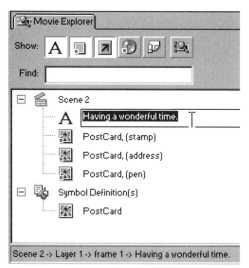

Figure 15.43 Double-click a text item to edit it directly in the Movie Explorer panel.

To modify elements from the Movie Explorer panel:

1. In the display list, select the element you want to modify.

2. From the Options menu, *choose one of the following options:*

   ◆ To select the object on the Stage, choose Goto Location.

   ◆ To make changes in the element's properties, choose Panels.

   The panels relevant to the selected element open. Any changes you make in the related panels modify the element selected in the Movie Explorer panel.

   ◆ To rename an element, choose Rename.

   ◆ To edit a symbol, choose Edit in Place or Edit in New Window.

✔ Tip

■ Double-click an element to modify it quickly. Double-click a scene or a text box, for example, to change the scene's name or change the contents of the text box directly in the Movie Explorer window (**Figure 15.43**). Double-click a symbol to open it in symbol-editing mode. Double-click an ActionScript to open the Actions panel, where you can update the selected script.

To print a display list:

1. Set the display list to show the hierarchy levels and contents you want to print.

2. From the Options menu, choose Print.

DELIVERING MOVIES TO YOUR AUDIENCE

16

When you finish creating graphics, animation, and interactivity in Macromedia Flash, it's time to deliver the goods to your audience. To do that, you must export the Flash movie file to another format for playback. You can choose among several formats. The one that guarantees viewers will see all your animations and take part in all your movie's interactivity is the Flash Player format. Player files end with the extension .swf.

Installing Flash also installs the Player application—Flash Player (Mac) or FlashPla.exe (Windows). The Player lets Flash users view SWF files by running Flash Player on their computers. Other programs, such as Web browsers, can control Flash Player, too.

You can export movies as a series of images in either bitmap format (.GIF or .PNG files, for example) or vector format (such as Adobe Illustrator files). Another option for movie delivery is a self-playing file called a *projector*. Users double-click the projector file to open and play the movie. And you can print your entire movie or individual frames, should you want to give someone a hard-copy version of the movie (for storyboarding, for example). Flash 5 also lets you control viewers' ability to print selected frames, or all frames, from Flash Player's contextual menu. (In previous versions of Flash, viewers could print from the browser but not from the movie itself.)

Preparing Your Movie for Optimal Playback

When you create movies to show over the Web, you must face the issue of quality versus quantity. Higher quality (smoother animation and better sounds) increases file size. The larger the file, the longer the download time and the slower your movie will be. Things that add to your file's size include lots of bitmaps (especially animated bitmaps), sounds, lots of keyframes instead of tweening, multiple areas of animation at one time, embedded fonts, gradients, and separate graphic elements instead of symbols and groups. To help you find out where your movie is bogging down, Flash offers simulated streaming. The Size Report and Bandwidth Profiler reveal which frames will cause hang-ups. You can then rethink or optimize the problem areas.

To use Bandwidth Profiler:

1. Open the Flash document that you want to test for playback over the Web.

2. From the Control menu, choose Test Movie (or Test Scene).

   Flash exports the movie and opens it in Flash Player.

3. From Flash Player's Debug menu, choose the download speed that you want to test.

   The menu lists six speeds, all of which are customizable. To change them, choose Debug > Customize (**Figure 16.1**). By default, Flash lists three common modem speeds—14.4 Kbps, 28.8 Kbps, and 56 Kbps—set to simulate real-world data-transfer rates (**Figure 16.2**).

Figure 16.1 To create a custom connection speed for simulating playback over the Web, from the test environment's Debug menu, choose Customize.

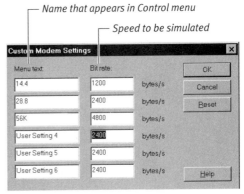

Figure 16.2 At its default setting, Flash offers choices for simulating three standard modem speeds. To more accurately imitate the real world, Flash simulates a data-transfer rate of 1.2 KBps for a 14.4 Kbps modem (not the theoretically possible rate of 1.7 Kbps). Flash simulates 28.8 Kbps and 56 Kbps modems at 2.3 KBps and 4.7 KBps, respectively. You can change the test names and rates in the Custom Modem Settings dialog box.

Figure 16.3 To view a graph of the amount of data in each frame, choose View > Bandwidth Profiler when a Flash Player window is open.

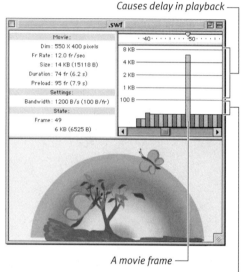

Causes delay in playback

A movie frame

Downloads within set frame rate

Figure 16.4 The Bandwidth Profile graph at the top of the Flash Player window shows you how much data each movie frame contains and where the movie will pause to download data. Each bar represents a frame of the movie.

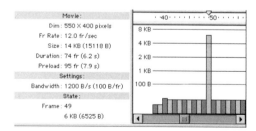

Figure 16.5 In Frame by Frame Graph mode, the height of each bar indicates how much data the frame holds. If the frame extends above the bottom line of the graph, the movie must pause to download the frame. In this movie, Frame 49 will cause a pause in playback.

4. From Flash Player's View menu, choose Bandwidth Profiler (**Figure 16.3**).

At the top of the Test Movie window, Flash graphs the amount of data that is being transmitted against the movie's Timeline (**Figure 16.4**). The bars represent the number of bytes of data per frame. The bottom line (highlighted in red) represents the amount of data that will safely download fast enough to keep up with the movie's frame rate. Any frame that contains a greater amount of data forces the movie to pause while the data downloads.

Flash offers you two ways to view the bandwidth graph.

To view the contents of each frame separately:

1. From the View menu, choose Frame by Frame Graph, or press ⌘-F (Mac) or Ctrl-F (Windows).

Flash presents a single bar for each frame in the Bandwidth Profiler graph. The numbers along the top of the graph represent frames (**Figure 16.5**). The height of the bar represents the amount of data in that frame.

2. Select a bar.

Specifics about that frame and the movie in general appear in the profile window.

PREPARING YOUR MOVIE FOR OPTIMAL PLAYBACK

To see how frames stream:

1. From the View menu, choose Streaming Graph, or press ⌘-G (Mac) or Ctrl-G (Windows).

Flash displays the frames as alternating bars of light and dark gray, sized to reflect the time each one takes to download (**Figure 16.6**). The numbers along the top of the streaming graph represent frames as a unit of time based on the frame rate. (In a 12-fps movie, for example, each number represents 1/12 second.) For frames that contain very little data, you might see several bars in a single time unit in the graph. Frames that have lots of data stretch out over several time units.

2. Select a bar.

Specifics about that frame and the movie in general appear in the left profile window.

In either type of graph, you have Flash simulate the actual time it takes your movie to load.

To display a download-progress bar:

◆ From Flash Player's Control menu, choose Show Streaming, or press ⌘-Enter (Mac) or Ctrl-Enter (Windows).

As the animation plays in the test window, Flash highlights the numbers of the Timeline in green to show where you are in the download progress.

To exit Bandwidth Profiler:

◆ From Flash Player's View menu, choose Bandwidth Profiler again.

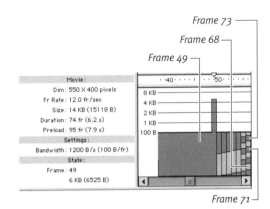

Figure 16.6 In Streaming Graph mode, the width of each bar indicates how long the frame takes to download at the given connection speed and frame rate. In this movie, Frame 49 contains 6KB of data and takes roughly 5 seconds to download at a frame rate of 12 fps over a 14.4 Kbps modem. Each number along the top of the graph is a frame, and at 12 fps, this equals 1/12 second.

✔ Tips

■ After you set up a test environment incorporating the Bandwidth Profiler, you can open any SWF file directly in test mode. Choose File > Open, navigate to the file that you want to test, and then click Open. Flash opens the movie in a Flash Player window, using the bandwidth profile and other viewing options that you selected.

■ You can get a printed version of the information about the amount of data in each frame. Choose the Generate Size Report option in the Export Flash Player dialog box or the Flash tab of the Publish Settings dialog box (for more information, see "Publishing and Exporting," later in this chapter). During the export or publishing process, Flash simultaneously creates a text file documenting how many bytes of information each frame of the movie contains.

PREPARING YOUR MOVIE FOR OPTIMAL PLAYBACK

Figure 16.7 To access the settings for publishing a movie, choose File > Publish Settings.

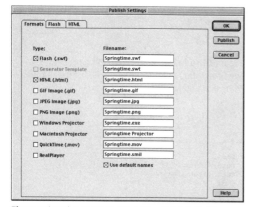

Figure 16.8 The Formats tab of the Publish Settings dialog box allows you to publish your Flash movie in as many as eight formats at the same time. You also can create an HTML document for displaying the published files in a browser.

Publishing and Exporting

Flash's Publish function is geared toward presenting animation on the Web. The Publish command can create the Flash Player (.swf) file and an HTML document that puts your Flash Player file in a browser window. The Publish command can also create alternative file formats—GIF, JPEG, PNG, QuickTime, and RealPlayer—and the HTML needed to display them in the browser window. Alternative formats let you make some of the animation and interactivity of your site available even to viewers who lack the Flash plug-in.

Flash's Export Movie command exports a movie directly into a single format. In general, the options for exporting from Flash—GIF, JPEG, PNG, QuickTime, and RealPlayer—are the same as those for publishing to those formats. The arrangement of some options differs between the export and publish dialog boxes, and some formats have more options in the Publish Settings dialog box. In the Publish Settings dialog box, for example, you have the choice to remove gradients from GIFs (to keep the file size small), whereas in the Export GIF dialog box, you don't have that option. Another difference between publishing and exporting is that Flash stores the publish settings with the movie file for reuse.

To set a movie's publishing format:

1. Open the Flash document that you want to publish.

2. From the File menu, choose Publish Settings, or press ⌘-Shift-F12 (Mac) or Ctrl-Shift-F12 (Windows) (**Figure 16.7**). The Publish Settings dialog box appears.

3. Click the Formats tab (**Figure 16.8**).

continues on next page

4. Choose one of the nine format options.

The formats available are Flash (.swf), HTML (.html), GIF Image (.gif), JPEG Image (.jpg), PNG Image (.png), Windows Projector, Macintosh Projector, QuickTime (.mov), and RealPlayer. (Users who also have Generator installed get a tenth option: Generator Template.) Choosing HTML automatically selects Flash as well.

5. To set the options for a selected format, choose the tab associated with that format (as outlined in separate exercises later in this chapter).

6. To save these settings with the current file, click OK.

Flash uses these settings each time you choose the Publish or Publish Preview command. Flash also uses a file's current publish settings when you enter test mode (by choosing Control > Test Movie or Control > Test Scene).

To publish a movie:

1. Open the movie that you want to publish.

2. To issue the Publish command, *do one of the following:*

◆ From the File menu, choose Publish Settings. The Publish Settings dialog box appears. You can follow the steps in the preceding exercise to set new format options or accept the current settings. Click the Publish button.

◆ From the File menu, choose Publish, or press Shift-F12 (**Figure 16.9**). The Publishing dialog box appears, displaying a progress bar and a button for canceling the procedure (**Figure 16.10**). Flash uses the publish settings that are currently stored with your Flash movie.

Figure 16.9
Choose File > Publish to publish the files.

Figure 16.10 To cancel the publishing process, click the Stop (Mac) or Cancel (Windows) button in the Publishing dialog box.

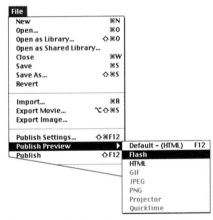

Figure 16.11 The File > Publish Preview menu displays all the formats that are currently selected in the Publish Settings dialog box. Flash publishes your movie in the selected format and opens it in your browser.

☒ **Use default names**

Figure 16.12 To enter your own file names, first deselect Use Default Names in the Filename section of the Publish Settings dialog box.

Who Plays Flash Player

The Web-browser option for playing Flash animation is a common choice. Many users already have Flash Player, because it comes with their browser or system software. Programs that can install Flash Player for you include Macintosh OS 8.1 and later; Windows 95, 98, and ME (when the OS comes preinstalled); Corel Linux, Stromix Linux, Mandrake, and Caledra Systems; Netscape Navigator and Communicator; Microsoft Internet Explorer 4, 5.0 (Mac), 5.5 (Windows); America Online; Prodigy; RealPlayer; QuickTime; @Home; Intel Web Outfitters CD/Web; Web TV/Liberate; and NeoPlanet.

Macromedia's SWF format is an open standard, so the number of programs that support Flash Player may grow. But at the time when this book was written (in the fall of 2000), the following programs could control Flash Player: a Web browser (by means of the Flash Player plug-in), Macromedia Director and Authorware (by means of the Flash Xtra), any program that supports the Flash Active X control (for example, Microsoft Office), and QuickTime.

Flash creates a new file for each format that is currently selected in the Publish Settings dialog box. By default, Flash places the published files in the same location as the original Flash file.

✔ Tips

■ You can open your browser and preview a movie in one step. Choose File > Publish Preview. Flash offers a menu that contains all the formats currently selected in the Publish Settings dialog box (**Figure 16.11**). Choose a format. Flash publishes the file in that format, using the current settings, and opens the movie in a browser window.

■ Flash makes one of the formats the default for Publish Preview. To publish in the default format, press F12. If you want to do lots of testing in a format other than SWF (if you want to test your animated GIF versions, for example), set your publish settings in only that format. Then that format will be the default, and you can choose it quickly by pressing F12.

■ By default, Flash names the published files by adding the appropriate extension to the current file name, adding .gif for a GIF file or .png for a PNG file, for example. To create your own file names, deselect the Use Default Names option in the Filename section of the Publish Settings dialog box (**Figure 16.12**).

■ The Publish and Publish Preview commands do not give you a chance to name the published files; they take the names directly from the Publish Settings dialog box. If you want to publish multiple versions of a movie, each with different settings, you must make sure that you don't overwrite the published file. Rename the published file, move that file to a new location, or type a different name in the Formats tab of the Publish Settings dialog box.

Working with Flash Player Settings

The stand-alone Flash Player is an application file that installs with Flash. The Player opens when you double-click the icon of a file that has the .swf extension. (From within Flash Player, you can use the File > Open command to open and play SWF files.) To prepare a Flash movie for playing in the stand-alone Player, choose either the Export or Publish command in the Flash editor. The options are the same for both commands.

To publish a Flash Player (.swf) file:

1. In the Flash editor, open the Flash file that you want to publish.

2. From the File menu, choose Publish Settings.
   The Publish Settings dialog box appears.

3. Click the Formats tab.

4. In the Type section, select Flash (.swf). To enter a file name other than the default, deselect Use Default Names as the Filename option and type a name for your Flash Player. (Be sure to include the .swf extension.)

5. Select the Flash tab (**Figure 16.13**).

6. Set Flash options as described in the following exercises.

7. Click Publish.

To control how Flash draws the movie's first frame:

◆ From the Load Order pop-up menu, choose the order in which Flash loads a movie's layers for displaying the first frame of your movie (**Figure 16.14**).
   When playback over the Web is slow, Flash starts displaying individual layers as they download. The Top Down setting tells

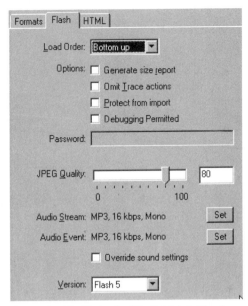

Figure 16.13 The Flash tab of the Publish Settings dialog box offers options for publishing your Flash movie as a Flash Player (.swf) file.

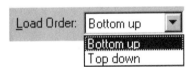

Figure 16.14 The Load Order pop-up menu determines the order in which Flash draws the layers of the first frame of your movie.

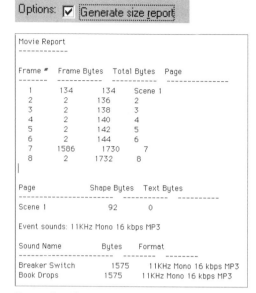

Figure 16.15 Choose Generate size report (top) to have Flash create a text file that lists the amount of data in your movie (bottom).

Flash to send (and display) the top layer first and then work its way to the bottom layer. Bottom Up does just the opposite.

To list the amount of data in the movie by frame:

◆ Check the Generate size report checkbox (**Figure 16.15**).

Flash creates a separate text file listing the frames of the movie and how much data each frame contains. This report helps you find frames that bog down the movie's playback. You can then optimize or elimi-nate some of the content in those frames.

To remove Trace action comments:

◆ Check the Omit Trace Actions checkbox.

If you make extensive use of Trace actions when you create ActionScripts, those comments can add to the size of your published movie file. Get rid of them.

To protect your work:

◆ Check the Protect from Import checkbox.

This setting prevents viewers from obtaining the .swf file and converting it back to a Flash movie.

To debug ActionScripts remotely:

◆ Check the Debugging Permitted checkbox.

This option allows you or others to debug a Flash Player (.swf) file as it plays over the Internet.

✔ Tip

■ When the Debugging Permitted option is selected, you can enter text in the Password field of the Formats tab of the Publish Settings dialog box. When a pass-word has been set, you must enter the password to access the .swf file for debug-ging remotely.

To control compression of bitmaps:

To set JPEG compression, do *one of the following:*

◆ Adjust the JPEG Quality slider.

◆ Enter a specific value in the JPEG Quality field (**Figure 16.16**).

This setting controls how Flash applies JPEG compression as it exports the bitmaps in your movie. A setting of 0 provides the most compression (and the lowest quality, because that compression leads to loss of data).

Figure 16.16 To set JPEG compression for any bitmaps in your movie, enter a value in the JPEG Quality field or use the slider. A setting of 0 results in the most compression (worst quality); 100 results in the least compression (best quality).

✔ Tip

■ Flash doesn't apply JPEG compression to GIF images that you've imported into your movie, because Flash defaults to using lossless compression for GIFs.

To control compression and sample rate for all movie sounds:

Flash divides sounds into two types: streaming and event (for more details, see Chapter 14). You must set the compression for each type separately, but the process and options are the same for both.

1. In the Audio Stream section (or the Audio Event section) of the Publish Settings dialog box, click the Set button (**Figure 16.17**).

   The Sound Settings dialog box appears.

2. To set compression parameters, from the Compression pop-up menu (**Figure 16.18**), *choose one of the following:*

   ◆ When you have mostly short event sounds, such as handclaps or button clicks, choose ADPCM. (Generally, you'll use this setting in the Audio Event section.) The ADPCM options appear. From the ADPCM Bits pop-up menu, choose 2-Bit for the greatest degree of compression (resulting in the

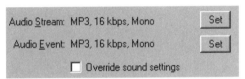

Figure 16.17 You must set the sample rate and compression options for streaming sounds and event sounds separately. Click the Set button to access the options for each type of sound.

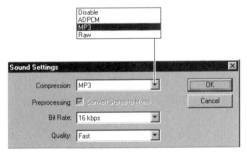

Figure 16.18 Choose a compression method from the Compression pop-up menu. Other options appropriate to the selected method appear. Choose Disable to turn off sound.

Sample-Rate Rule of Thumb

Sample rates are measured in kHz or frequency. Recording for music CDs is done at 44 kHz. For multimedia CD-ROMs, 22 kHz is a standard rate. For music clips in Flash movies played on the Web, 11 kHz is often sufficient. For shorter sounds, including spoken words, you may be able to get away with even lower sampling rates.

lowest-quality sound); choose 5-Bit for the least com-pression (resulting in the highest-quality sound). With the ADPCM setting, you can also set a sample rate and convert stereo sound to mono sound.

◆ To make Flash omit sound from the published file, choose Disable.

◆ When you mostly have longer streaming sounds, choose MP3. (Generally, you'll use this setting in the Audio Stream section.) The MP3 options appear. From the Bit Rate pop-up menu, choose one of 12 bit rates for the published sounds. At Bit Rate settings of less than 20 Kbps, Flash converts sounds from stereo to mono; at settings of 20 Kbps and above, you can publish stereo sounds or convert them to mono sounds. From the Quality pop-up menu, choose Fast for movies that will play back over the Web; Medium and Best provide better quality.

◆ To omit sound compression, choose Raw. Raw does allow you to control file size by choosing a sample rate and converting stereo sound to mono.

To choose a Flash version:

◆ From the Version pop-up menu, choose one of the five Flash versions.

Your options are Flash 1 (formerly known as FutureSplash Animator), 2, 3, 4, and 5. If you publish your file as an earlier Flash version, you lose some features specific to Flash 5.

✔ Tip

■ Before you start creating any ActionScripts, set the Flash export options in the Publish Settings dialog box to the lowest version of Flash to which you plan to export. Any Flash 5 actions that won't work in that version appear with yellow highlighting in the Actions panel's Toolbox list.

Advanced Sound Handling

An advanced method of dealing with sound compression is setting compression options and sample rates for sounds individually. Assigning the highest quality to selected sounds helps you keep file size reasonable but still have high-quality sound where you need it. You set compression options for individual sounds via the Sound Properties dialog box. In the movie's Library window, Control-click (Mac) or right-click (Windows) the sound name. Choose properties from the contextual menu that appears. The Sound Properties dialog box appears, offering the same sound-export settings as the Flash tab of the Publish Settings dialog box.

If some sounds in a movie have individual sound-export settings, Flash uses those settings for those sounds when you choose Publish. Flash uses the sound options that you set in the Publish Settings dialog box for all other sounds in that movie.

If you've used individual compression methods for some sounds in your movie, you can force Flash to ignore them and publish all sounds by using the sound options in the Publish Settings dialog box. In the Flash tab of the Publish Settings dialog box, choose Override Sound Settings. You might use this feature to make a lower-quality Web version of a movie that you created for CD-ROM.

Publishing HTML for Flash Player Files

An HTML document is the master set of instructions that tells a browser how to display Web content. The Publish function of Flash creates an HTML document that tells the browser how to display the files that Flash creates when you click the Publish button (in Flash, GIF, JPEG, QuickTime, or RealPlayer format).

The Publish command creates the required HTML by filling in blanks in one of the templates provided with Flash or by using a template that you create. The templates included with Flash contain the basic HTML coding needed to display the formats that are available with the Publish command.

To publish HTML for displaying a Flash file:

1. Open the Flash document that you want to publish for the Web.

2. From the File menu, choose Publish Settings.
   The Publish Setting dialog box appears.

3. Click the Formats tab.

4. In the Type section, choose HTML (.html).
   When you choose HTML, Flash automatically selects Flash (.swf) as well. To use a file name other than the default, deselect Use Default Names as the Filename option and type the appropriate name for your Flash and HTML files. (Be sure to include the correct file extension.)

Digitally Recorded Sounds

As motion pictures are to movement, digital recordings are to sound. Both media capture slices of a continuous event. By playing the captured slices back in order, you re-create the event. In a movie, the slices are frames of film; in a digital recording, they're slices of sound.

You can think of the recording process as capturing a sound wave by laying a grid over it and copying a piece of the wave at each intersection on the grid. The lines across the horizontal axis are the *sample rate*—how often you capture the sound. The lines up and down the vertical axis are the *bit rate*—how much of the sound wave's amplitude you capture. The greater the frequency and bit rate (the finer the mesh of your recording grid), the greater the realism of your recording during playback. Unfortunately, greater realism translates into larger files.

The sound options in the Publish Settings dialog box give you the flexibility to create different versions of your movie with different sample rates and bit rates without actually changing the sounds embedded in the movie. You might allow yourself larger file sizes and higher-quality sounds for a version being delivered on CD-ROM than for a version being distributed on the Web. As you try different sound options, be sure to actually listen to your published sounds to determine the best balance between sound quality and file size.

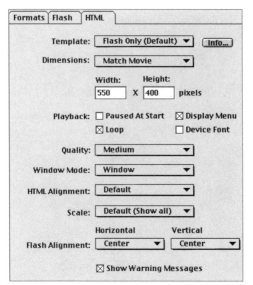

Figure 16.19 The HTML tab of the Publish Settings dialog box displays options for displaying your Flash file in the browser window.

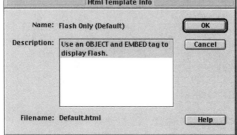

Figure 16.20 Choose Flash Only (Default) as the template when you want to create HTML for displaying only a Flash movie, with no other options for alternative images (top). Click the Info button to see a description of what the template does (bottom).

5. Select the HTML tab (**Figure 16.19**).

Flash displays the options for displaying your Flash file in the browser window (see "Publishing HTML for Flash Player Files," later in this chapter). When you publish the current movie, Flash feeds your choices into the appropriate HTML tags and parameters in the template of your choice.

To choose an HTML template for Flash only:

◆ From the Template pop-up menu, choose Flash Only (Default) (**Figure 16.20**).

This template is the simplest one. It uses the OBJECT and EMBED tags to display your Flash movie for viewers who are properly equipped with the Flash 5 Player. Other viewers will be unable to see your movie. (Other template choices create HTML that displays alternative images when the viewer lacks the proper plug-in.)

To choose an HTML template that detects the Flash 5 Player:

◆ From the Template pop-up menu, choose User Choice.

This template uses JavaScript to check whether the Flash 5 Player is installed on a viewer's machine. If it's not, the user can choose to get the Player or view a GIF or JPEG version of your site.

✔ Tip

■ If you can't remember what one of the included HTML templates does, click the Info button next to the Template pop-up menu in the HTML tab of the Publish Settings dialog box. Flash displays a brief description, including instructions about which formats to choose.

The Mystery of HTML Templates

The HTML codes (called tags) required for displaying a SWF file in a browser window are OBJECT for Internet Explorer (Windows) and EMBED for Netscape Navigator (Mac and Windows) and Internet Explorer (Mac). (In addition, Flash can use the IMG tag to display a file in another format, such as a JPEG image or an animated GIF.)

Flash's Publish command works hand in hand with HTML templates—which are fill-in-the-blank recipes—to define the parameters of those tags. These parameters include the width and height of the movie window, the quality of the images (the amount of antialiasing to provide), and the way the movie window aligns with the browser window.

Each option and parameter in the HTML tab of the Publish Settings dialog box has an equivalent template variable. The template variable is a code word that starts with the dollar sign ($). When you choose an option in the Publish Settings dialog box, Flash enters your choice as an HTML tag that replaces the variable in the template document. If you set the width of your movie as 500 pixels in the Publish Settings dialog box for HTML, for example, Flash replaces the template variable for width ($WI) with the proper coding to display the movie in a window 500 pixels wide.

Flash's HTML templates contain coding not only for displaying your Flash movie but also for showing the JPEG, GIF, or PNG versions of your movie that you want to make available to viewers who don't have the proper browser player to view Flash.

During the publishing process, Flash saves a copy of the HTML template for your movie, giving it the name of your movie file and adding whatever extension the template file has. (The template files that come with Flash 5 use the extension .html, for example.) You can go into a template file as you would any other text file and modify the HTML coding.

You can extend the Publish command's capability to create HTML documents by setting up your own HTML templates. To be available to Flash's template menu, the HTML file must include a title (use the code $TT). The HTML file must be inside the HTML folder within the Flash application folder on your system.

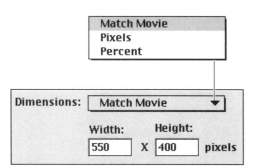

Figure 16.21 Choose a method for sizing the movie-display window (the window in which a browser displays your Flash movie).

Scale:	Default (Show all)
	No border
	Exact fit

Figure 16.22 The Scale method tells Flash how to fit the Flash movie inside the movie-display window that you define. You need to set the scale only if you define a movie-display window with different dimensions from those of the movie itself—as a percentage of the browser width and height, for example.

Controlling Movie Placement in the Browser

When you publish HTML for displaying movies in a Web page, you need to think in terms of three windows:

◆ The *browser window* contains the entire Web page.

◆ Within the browser window is a *movie-display* window (created by the OBJECT, EMBED, and IMG tags), where the Flash plug-in displays a Flash movie.

◆ Inside the movie-display window is the actual *movie window*.

Each of the three windows has its own dimensions, and you need to tell Flash where to put the windows and how to handle them if their aspect ratios differ, for example, or when a user resizes the browser window.

You instruct browsers on how to deal with these three windows by choosing settings in the HTML tab of the Publish Settings dialog box.

To set the dimensions of the movie-display window:

To set the width and height of the rectangle created by the OBJECT and EMBED tags for displaying your movie in the browser, from the Dimensions pop-up menu in the HTML tab of the Publish Settings dialog box (**Figure 16.21**), *choose one of the following:*

◆ To use the movie's dimensions (specified in the Movie Properties dialog box), choose Match Movie.

◆ To specify the dimensions as a percentage of the browser window's dimensions, choose Percent, and type a value between 1 and 100 in the Width and Height fields.

continues on next page

◆ To specify new dimensions, choose Pixels, and type the new values in the Width and Height fields.

When you define a movie-display window with a different width or height from the original Flash movie, you must tell Flash how to scale the movie to fit in that window.

To scale the movie to fit a movie-display window:

From the Scale pop-up menu (**Figure 16.22**), *choose one of the following:*

◆ To keep the movie's original aspect ratio (width to height) and resize the movie so that it fits completely within the newly specified rectangle, choose Default (Show All) (**Figure 16.23**). (Be aware that the resized movie may not fill the new rectangle: Gaps may appear on the sides or at the top and bottom.)

◆ To keep the movie's original aspect ratio and resize the movie so that the whole new rectangle is filled with the movie, choose No Border. (Some of the movie may slop over the edges and be cropped.)

◆ To change the movie's height and width to the new specifications, even if it involves changing the aspect ratio and distorting the image, choose Exact Fit.

✔ Tip

■ If you define the movie-display window as 100 percent of the width and height of the browser window, no matter how large your viewer makes the browser window, a scroll bar always appears. Set the Width and Height to 96 percent (or lower) to allow viewers to enlarge the browser window enough to eliminate the scroll bar.

Dimensions: Match Movie. Scale: NA

Dimensions: 100 by 50 pixels. Scale: No Border

Dimensions: 100 by 50 pixels. Scale: Exact Fit

Dimensions: 100 by 50 pixels. Scale: Default

Dimensions: % of Window. Scale: Default

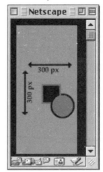

Figure 16.23 This 300-by-300 pixel movie looks quite different in the different dimension-and-scale combinations. The movie-display window's dimensions and the scale setting are identified in the examples above.

Horizontal: left. Vertical: center.

Horizontal: right. Vertical: center.

Figure 16.24 The Flash Alignment section's Horizontal and Vertical pop-up menus allow you to position your movie within the movie-display window when the dimensions of the movie-display window differ from those of the movie. Compare the results of two different settings for this 300-by-300-pixel movie set inside a 200-by-100-pixel display window. The light-gray rectangle is the display window.

To control placement of the movie window in the movie-display window:

To align the movie window within the movie-display window, in the Flash Alignment section of the HTML tab of the Publish Settings dialog box, *do one of the following:*

◆ From the Horizontal pop-up menu, choose Left, Center, or Right.

◆ From the Vertical pop-up menu, choose Top, Center, or Bottom.

Flash positions the movie within the movie-display window (**Figure 16.24**).

To set playback options:

In the Playback section of the HTML tab of the Publish Settings dialog box, *choose any of the following options:*

◆ To make users begin the movie manually (by clicking a button or by choosing Play from the contextual menu), choose Paused At Start.

◆ To create a contextual menu with playback options that are available to users, choose Display Menu.

◆ To make the movie start over when it reaches the last frame, choose Loop.

◆ To speed playback on Windows systems, choose Device Font. The Device Font option allows Windows systems to substitute aliased system fonts any time a movie uses fonts installed on the user's system.

For the best viewing experience, you need to balance the image quality and playback speed of your published movie.

To control antialiasing and smoothing:

From the Quality pop-up menu in the HTML tab of the Publish Settings dialog box (**Figure 16.25**), *choose one of the following options:*

- ◆ **Low.** Flash keeps antialiasing off.

- ◆ **Autolow.** Flash starts playback with antialiasing off, but if it finds that the viewer's computer and connection can handle antialiasing while keeping the movie's specified frame rate, Flash turns antialiasing on.

- ◆ **Autohigh.** Flash turns antialiasing on to start with and turns it off if playback drops below the movie's specified frame rate.

- ◆ **Medium.** Taking the middle ground, Flash forgoes bitmap smoothing but does do some antialiasing.

- ◆ **High.** Flash uses antialiasing on everything except animation that contains bitmaps.

- ◆ **Best.** Flash keeps antialiasing on.

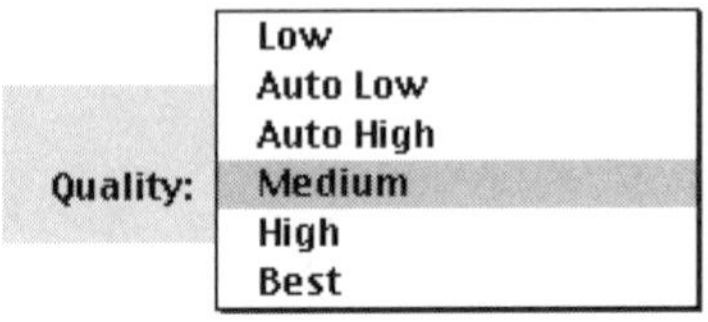

Figure 16.25 The Quality setting for publishing HTML balances image quality against playback speed in a published movie.

Figure 16.26 For viewers of your movie who use Internet Explorer on the Windows platform, you can create a transparency effect that reveals Web page elements beneath any transparent areas of your Flash movie. In the HTML tab of the Publish Settings dialog box, set Window Mode to Transparent Windowless.

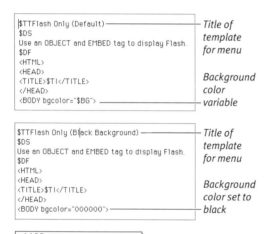

Figure 16.27 The default HTML template picks up the movie's background color as the Web page's background color. You can modify a copy of the template (top). Change the Title tag and set a specific background color (bottom). The new title appears in the Template menu in the HTML tab of the Publish Settings dialog box.

On Windows computers running Internet Explorer 4 or later, Flash movies can have transparent backgrounds.

To control transparency (for Windows only):

From the Window Mode pop-up menu, *choose one of the following options:*

◆ To play the movie in its own window within the Web page, choose Window.

◆ To make the transparent areas of your movie block out the background and other elements of the Web page that lie below the Flash movie, choose Opaque Windowless.

◆ To allow those elements to show through in any transparent areas of your movie, choose Transparent Windowless (**Figure 16.26**).

To alert users to problems with HTML:

◆ Choose Show Warning Message if you want Flash to display error messages when it finds problems with your HTML tags.

✔ Tip

■ The default HTML template automatically sets the background color of your Web page to the background color of your movie. If you want to use a different color, try creating a modified template (**Figure 16.27**). Open the default template, and save a copy with a new name. In the first line of code—$TTFlash Only (Default)— change the title to something like $TTFlash Only (MyBackground), so that Flash recognizes and adds the template to the Template menu. In the tag <BODY bgcolor="$BG">, replace $BG with the HTML code for a specific hex color (000000 for a black background, for example). Be sure to place the new template in Flash's HTML folder.

Using HTML for Alternative Images

Although most of your viewers will have access to the plug-ins that they need to view your Flash movies, some may not. You can make at least some of your site available to them by providing alternative image files for their browsers to display. If you're using Flash animations for a simple Web banner, for example, you could use an animated GIF to re-create that banner for viewers who lack the Flash plug-in. The other alternative files types are JPEG, PNG, QuickTime, and RealPlayer.

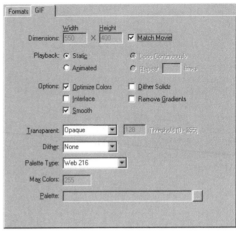

Figure 16.28 Click the GIF tab of the Publish Settings dialog box to access the options for creating a static or animated GIF for your alternative image.

To publish HTML for displaying an animated GIF:

1. Open the Flash document for which you want to create an alternative GIF image.

2. Choose File > Publish Settings.
   The Publish Setting dialog box appears.

3. Choose the Formats tab.

4. Choose GIF Image (.gif) and HTML (.html).

5. Set the options for Flash as described in "Working with Flash Player Settings" earlier in this chapter.

6. Choose the HTML tab.

7. From the Template pop-up menu, choose User Choice.
   This template allows Flash to create an HTML document that uses JavaScript to check the viewer's browser for the Flash 5 plug-in. If the plug-in is not available, the HTML calls for a display of the animated GIF that you're about to set up and publish.

8. Set the other HTML options as described in "Publishing HTML for Flash Player Files" earlier in this chapter.

9. Choose the GIF tab (**Figure 16.28**).

USING HTML FOR ALTERNATIVE IMAGES

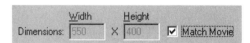

Figure 16.29 Choose Match Movie to enter the Flash movie's dimensions as the dimensions of your GIF image.

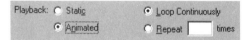

Figure 16.30 To preserve the motion of your Flash movie (though not the sound or interactivity) for viewers who lack the Flash plug-in, choose Animated.

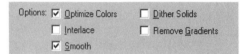

Figure 16.31 The settings in the Options section of the GIF tab help you limit the amount of time that your viewers will spend looking at a blank screen, waiting for an image to appear. (The Remove Gradients option is available only in the Publish Settings dialog box, not in the Export GIF dialog box.)

10. Set GIF options as described in the following exercises.

11. Click Publish.

To set the dimensions of the GIF image:

1. In the Dimensions section of the GIF tab of the Publish Settings dialog box, uncheck Match Movie and type values in the Width and Height boxes.

Flash uses those dimensions for the published GIF image.

2. To keep the GIF images the same size as the original Flash movie, choose Match Movie (**Figure 16.29**).

To make an animated GIF:

1. In the Playback section of the GIF tab of the Publish Settings dialog box, choose Animated (**Figure 16.30**).

The animation settings become active.

2. Choose Loop Continuously.

You can also limit the number of times that the animation loops by choosing Repeat and typing a number. (Choosing Static makes Flash export only the first frame of the movie as a single GIF image.)

To balance size, download speed, and appearance:

In the Options section of the GIF tab of the Publish Settings dialog box (**Figure 16.31**), *do one of the following:*

◆ To remove any unused colors from the GIF file's color table, choose Optimize Colors.

◆ Deselect Interlace. (This option is for static GIFs, making them appear quickly at a low resolution and come into focus as the download continues.)

continues on next page

USING HTML FOR ALTERNATIVE IMAGES

- To reduce the size of the file, deselect Smooth. (Select it if you want Flash to create smoothed bitmaps for your animated GIF.)

- To apply the dither method to solids as well as gradients and bitmapped images, choose Dither Solids (see "To control colors that are not in the current color palette," later in this chapter).

- To reduce file size by converting gradient fills to solid fills, choose Remove Gradients. (Flash uses the first color in the gradient as the solid fill color.)

To set a GIF's background transparency:

From the Transparent pop-up menu of the GIF tab of the Publish Settings dialog box (**Figure 16.32**), *choose one of the following options:*

- To make background areas of the Flash movie opaque in the published GIF, choose Opaque.

- To make the background areas of the Flash movie transparent in the published GIF, choose Transparent.

The Alpha and Threshold settings control not only the background of your movie but also any shapes with transparent fills within the movie.

To control transparency of Flash fill colors in GIFs:

- From the Transparent pop-up menu in the GIF tab of the Publish Settings dialog box, choose Alpha.

  The Alpha setting makes the GIF's background transparent and allows you to set a threshold below which partially transparent fills in Flash convert to full transparency in the published GIF. The threshold settings are values from 0 to 255 (the number of possible colors in a

Figure 16.32 The Transparent setting (top) determines how the background of a published GIF appears. Choose Opaque to make the background a solid color (middle); choose Transparent to make the background invisible (bottom).

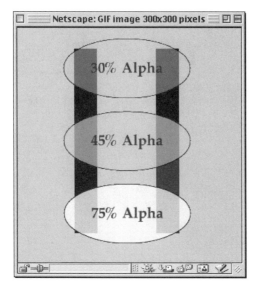

Figure 16.33 When you publish a movie as a GIF, you can make partially transparent graphic elements sitting on the background of the Flash movie look fully transparent in a browser window. Each oval here has the same color fill but a different Alpha value. For this GIF, the Transparent option is set to Alpha with a threshold of 128 (equal to 50 percent Alpha in Flash). The 30 percent and 45 percent ovals are fully transparent where only background lies below them. Where those ovals overlap other graphic elements, however, they are 30 percent and 40 percent transparent, respectively. The 75 percent oval (above the threshold value) retains its partial transparency even over the background.

Figure 16.34 The GIF format has three options for dithering the colors that are not included in the current color table.

Figure 16.35 Choose a palette that optimizes colors for the published GIF image. You can create custom palettes or use the Web-safe or adaptive palettes provided by Flash.

GIF image). The default threshold value is 128 (corresponding to an Alpha value of 50 percent in Flash).

✔ Tip

- The GIF Alpha transparency setting can have unexpected results, especially in animated GIFs. Full GIF transparency appears only where a filled graphic element sits directly on the background of the Flash movie. Wherever the graphic element overlaps (or moves over) another fill, the "invisible" graphic suddenly pops into view again (**Figure 16.33**).

If the graphic elements of your Flash file contain colors that are not part of the current color palette, you must tell Flash how to deal with those colors when creating GIFs for the published movie.

To control colors that are not in the current color palette:

1. From the Dither pop-up menu of the GIF tab of the Publish Settings dialog box (**Figure 16.34**), *choose one of the following options:*

   - To replace the missing color with the closest match from the current palette, choose None.

   - To simulate the missing color by applying a regular pattern of colors from the current palette, choose Ordered.

   - To simulate the missing color by applying a random pattern of colors from the Web 216 palette, choose Diffusion. (You must also choose Web 216 as your Palette Type in Step 2 for Diffusion to work.)

2. From the Palette Type pop-up menu, choose a color table for use with this GIF (**Figure 16.35**).

continues on next page

USING HTML FOR ALTERNATIVE IMAGES

Your choices are Web 216 (the standard 216 Web-safe colors), Adaptive (only colors used in your movie; 256 colors maximum), Web Snap Adaptive (a modified Adaptive palette, substituting Web-safe colors for any near matches to colors in the animation that are not Web safe), and Custom (the color table specified in Step 4).

3. If you chose Adaptive or Web Snap Adaptive as the Palette Type, in the Max Colors field, type the number of colors that you want to use.

This option allows you to further limit the size of the color table available for the GIF and, thus, reduce file size.

4. If you chose Custom as the Palette Type, load the custom palette (**Figure 16.36**).

Click the ellipsis (...) button. In the file-import dialog box that appears, navigate to the custom palette, select it, and click Import (Mac) or Open (Windows).

✔ Tip

■ You don't have to turn your entire movie into an animated GIF. You can tell Flash to publish a subset of the movie's frames. Assign the label #First to the first keyframe of the subset; assign the label #Last to the keyframe that ends the subset. Flash creates an animated GIF from that range of frames.

Figure 16.36 When you choose Custom as the Palette Type, you must type the file name in the Palette field. Click the ellipsis to open a dialog box for locating the file.

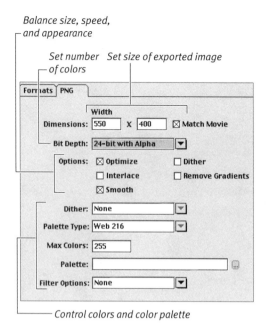

Balance size, speed, and appearance

Set number of colors   Set size of exported image

Control colors and color palette

Figure 16.37 The options for publishing PNGs are similar to those for publishing GIFs (described earlier in this chapter).

Using Other Publish Settings

In the preceding exercises, you learned about the specific publish settings for Flash and GIF files. Flash's Publish Settings dialog box also contains tabs for PNG, JPEG, QuickTime, and RealPlayer formats. You can choose an HTML template that publishes GIF and JPEG images as alternatives to Flash for viewers who lack the Flash Player.

To publish PNG files:

1. Open the Flash file for which you want to create an alternative PNG image.

2. Choose File > Publish Settings.
   The Publish Settings dialog box appears.

3. Choose the Formats tab.

4. Choose Flash, PNG Image, and HTML.

5. In the HTML tab, from the Template pop-up menu, choose User Choice.
   This template creates an HTML document that uses JavaScript to check the viewer's browser for the Flash 5 plug-in. If the plug-in is not available, the HTML calls for the viewer's browser to display the PNG you're about to publish.

6. Choose the PNG tab, and set its options (**Figure 16.37**).

7. Click Publish.

To publish JPEG files:

1. Open the Flash file for which you want to create an alternative JPEG image.

2. Choose File > Publish Settings.
   The Publish Settings dialog box appears.

3. Choose the Formats tab.

4. Choose Flash, JPEG Image, and HTML.

continues on next page

5. In the HTML tab, from the Template pop-up menu, choose User Choice.

This template allows Flash to create an HTML document that uses JavaScript to check the viewer's browser for the Flash 5 plug-in. If the plug-in is not available, the HTML calls for the browser to display the JPEG that you're about to publish.

6. Choose the JPEG tab, and set its options (**Figure 16.38**).

7. Click Publish.

To publish QuickTime 4 files:

1. Open the Flash file for which you want to create a QuickTime movie.

2. Choose File > Publish Settings.
The Publish Settings dialog box appears.

3. Choose the Formats tab.

4. Choose Flash, QuickTime, and HTML.

5. In the HTML tab, from the Template pop-up menu, choose QuickTime.

This template allows Flash to create an HTML document that lets the browser display the QuickTime movie you're about to publish.

6. Choose the QuickTime tab, and set its options (**Figure 16.39**).

7. Click Publish.

To publish RealPlayer files:

1. Open the Flash file for which you want to create a RealPlayer file.

2. Choose File > Publish Settings.
The Publish Settings dialog box appears.

3. Choose the Formats tab.

4. Choose Flash and RealPlayer.

Set the size of the JPEG image

Set the amount of compression — *Allows image to appear gradually as it downloads*

Figure 16.38 The options for publishing JPEGs help you balance file size (download time) against quality.

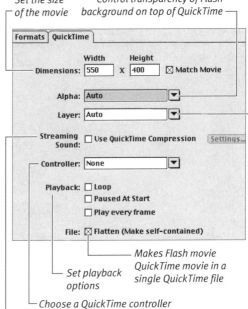

Conrtol where Flash plays in stacking order of QuickTime tracks

Set the size of the movie — *Control transparency of Flash background on top of QuickTime*

Makes Flash movie QuickTime movie in a single QuickTime file

Set playback options

Choose a QuickTime controller

Export streaming sound to QuickTime sound track

Figure 16.39 Set the options for publishing QuickTime movies in the QuickTime tab.

USING OTHER PUBLISH SETTINGS

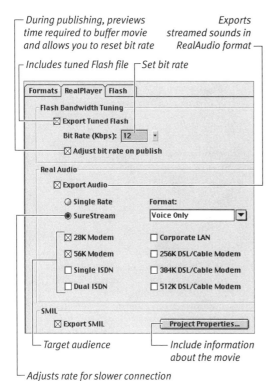

During publishing, previews
time required to buffer movie
and allows you to reset bit rate

Exports
streamed sounds in
RealAudio format

Includes tuned Flash file · Set bit rate

Target audience

Include information
about the movie

Adjusts rate for slower connection
and network slowdowns

Figure 16.40 To create a file for viewing your movie
with RealPlayer, set the options in the RealPlayer tab
of the Publish Settings dialog box.

5. In the Flash tab, from the Version pop-up menu, choose the appropriate Flash version for the version of RealServer that will host your files and the version of RealPlayer viewers use.

RealServer 8, for example, handles Flash versions 1 through 4. RealServer 6 and 7 can deal only with Flash 2. RealPlayer 8 supports Flash 4 content; RealPlayer G2 and 7 do not. (RealPlayer G2 and 7 will, however, alert viewers to update to RealPlayer 8 when they access a RealPlayer file with Flash 3 or 4 content.)

6. In the Flash tab, in the Audio Stream section, click the Set button.

7. In the Sound Settings dialog box that appears, from the Compression menu, choose Raw.

8. Click OK to dismiss the dialog box.

9. In the Publish settings dialog box, choose the RealPlayer tab, and set its options (**Figure 16.40**).

10. Click Publish.

✔ Tip

■ Neither the *Using Flash* manual nor Flash's online help system describes the RealPlayer publishing options. Macromedia has posted an article outlining the process at *http://www.macromedia.com/support/ flash/publishexport/realplayer/realplayer. html*. You can also find information about producing for RealPlayer at *http://service.real.com/help/library/ guides/production8/realpgd.htm*.

Creating Projectors

Projectors are self-sufficient run-time applications. To play a projector file, you simply double-click the projector icon. Projectors are an excellent way to distribute movies directly to people, such as to e-mail a Flash-animated greeting card to a friend. Projectors are platform-specific, but you can make projectors for both platforms from either platform.

To create a projector:

1. Open the Flash movie from which you want to publish a projector.

2. Choose File > Publish Settings.
   The Publish Settings dialog box appears.

3. In the Formats tab (**Figure 16.41**), *choose one of the following options:*
   - To create a projector that runs on a Mac, choose Macintosh Projector.
   - To create a projector that runs in Windows, choose Windows Projector.

4. Click the Publish button.
   As it creates the projector files, Flash displays the Publishing dialog box, which has a progress bar and a button for canceling the operation. Flash places the projector files in the same location as the original Flash movie. A projector has a distinctive buttonlike icon (**Figure 16.42**).

✔ Tip

- If your projector movie includes any Load Movie or Get URL actions, you must keep the additional files at the same hierarchical level as the projector. Place the projector and its ancillary files together in one folder; otherwise, the projector can't find the files to load.

Figure 16.41 To create a run-time version of your movie, choose Windows Projector or Macintosh Projector in the Formats tab of the Publish Settings dialog box. There are no other options for formatting projectors.

Figure 16.42 The projector is a stand-alone run-time file. Double-click the icon to launch the projector.

Setting MIME Types on Your Server

For browsers to recognize and display Flash files, the server that delivers the SWF (Flash Player) files must identify for the browser what type of files it's serving. This information is called the MIME type. The intricacies of server administration are beyond the scope of this book, but this section provides a basic description of the MIME types and the Flash suffixes to add to your server's configuration files. (Check out Macromedia's Flash Support and Developers Center at *http://www.macromedia.com/support/flash* for technical notes about setting MIME types on specific servers.)

To identify a MIME type:

Do one of the following:

◆ For files published as Flash versions 2 through 5 or exported as Flash Player, add the MIME type application/x-shockwave-flash and the associated suffix .swf.

◆ For files published as Flash Version 1 or exported as FutureSplash Player, add the MIME type application/futuresplash and the associated suffix .spl.

Playing Macintosh Projectors Created in Windows

When you publish a Macintosh projector on a computer running the Windows operating system, Flash gives the projector the extension .hqx. That extension indicates a file encoded in binhex format. Macintosh users need to translate the file by using a program such as BinHex or StuffIt Deluxe to play the projector on the Mac OS.

To set additional parameters for Macintosh servers:

1. For servers hosting movies published as Flash versions 2 through 5, *do the following:*

   ◆ Set the Action parameter to Binary.

   ◆ Set the Type parameter to SWFL.

   ◆ Set the Creator parameter to SWF2.

2. For servers hosting movies published as Flash Version 1 or FutureSplash Player, *do the following*:

   ◆ Set the Action parameter to Binary.

   ◆ Set the Type parameter to TEXT.

   ◆ Set the Creator parameter to Fspl.

✔ Tip

■ You can use Netscape Navigator to check whether the MIME type has been set properly on the server where you're posting your Flash movies. In Navigator, surf to a movie on the server that you want to check. From Navigator's View menu, choose Page Info (or Document Info). In the window that appears, click the Embed link for the .swf file. Navigator lists the MIME type for the Embed URL in the bottom frame of the browser window (**Figure 16.43**). See whether the type displayed there matches the MIME type that you need.

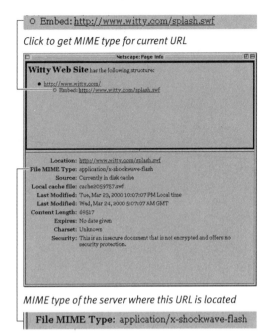

Click to get MIME type for current URL

MIME type of the server where this URL is located

Figure 16.43 The View > Document Info (or View > Page Info) command in Netscape Navigator lets you see whether the MIME type has been set correctly on the server where your Web site is located.

Figure 16.44 To export a single frame of your movie, choose File > Export Image.

Figure 16.45 The export dialog box allows you to select an export format, name your file, and navigate to the location where you want to save the file.

Exporting Flash to Other Formats

When you export Flash movies, you can export the entire movie or just one frame. Flash exports to a variety of formats that are not included in the Publish Settings dialog box: for both Mac and Windows, Adobe Illustrator and EPS; for Mac only, PICT and QuickTime Video; and for Windows only, Bitmap (BMP), Enhanced Metafile, Windows Metafile, Windows AVI, and WAV. Although the options for the export formats differ, the basic process is always the same. The example used in the following sections exports to Illustrator format, which preserves the vector information from your Flash graphics.

To export a single frame to Illustrator format:

1. Open the Flash file that contains the frame that you want to export to another format.

2. In the Timeline, move the playhead to the frame that you want to export.

3. From the File menu, choose Export Image (**Figure 16.44**).

   The Export Image dialog box appears (**Figure 16.45**).

4. Navigate to the location where you want to save the file.

5. Type a name in the Save As (Mac) or Filename (Windows) field.

6. From the Format (Mac) or Save As Type (Windows) pop-up menu, choose Adobe Illustrator format.

   Flash adds the proper extension, .ai, to your file name.

continues on next page

7. Click Save.

The Export Adobe Illustrator dialog box appears (**Figure 16.46**).

Whenever your chosen export format requires you to set further parameters, Flash displays those parameters in a dialog box after you click Save. For Illustrator format, the additional parameter is a version number.

8. Choose the version to which you want to export.

9. Click OK.

Flash displays the Exporting dialog box, which contains a progress bar and a button for canceling the export process.

To export the entire movie to Illustrator format:

◆ Follow the instructions in the preceding exercise, but in Step 3, from the File menu, choose Export Movie, or press ⌘-Option-Shift-S (Mac) or Ctrl-Alt-Shift-S (Windows) (**Figure 16.47**).

When you chose Export Movie, Flash creates a separate Illustrator file for each frame of the movie and numbers the files sequentially.

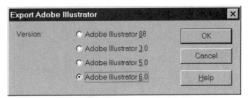

Figure 16.46 Whenever an export format requires additional settings, a dialog box with format-specific options appears when you click Save in the Export dialog box. You can export to four versions of Illustrator, for example.

Figure 16.47 To export all the frames of your movie, choose File > Export Movie.

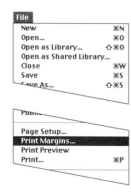

Figure 16.48 To define print settings for frames of your movie, choose File > Print Margins.

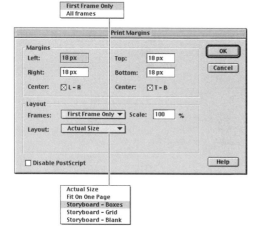

Figure 16.49 The options in the Print Margins (Mac, top) and Page Setup (Windows, bottom) dialog boxes enable you to print the frames of your movie as single pages or as storyboard layouts.

Printing from Flash

In Flash, you can print frames of a movie as individual pages or print several frames per page in a storyboard layout. You choose how many frames each row in the storyboard contains. Flash sizes the frames accordingly. Use Flash's Print Margins command to choose layout options.

To print a single frame:

1. Open the Flash movie that you want to print.

2. From the File menu, choose Print Margins (Mac) or Page Setup (Windows) (**Figure 16.48**).

   The Print Margins or Page Setup dialog box appears (**Figure 16.49**).

3. From the Frames pop-up menu, choose All Frames.

4. From the Layout pop-up menu, choose Fit on One Page.

5. Click OK.

6. From the File menu, choose Print.

   The Print dialog box appears.

7. Type the desired frame number in the From and To fields.

8. Click Print.

✔ Tip

■ If your Macintosh printer isn't capable of printing PostScript, be sure to check the Disable PostScript checkbox.

To print storyboard thumbnails:

1. Follow steps 1 through 3 of the preceding exercise.

continues on next page

2. From the Layout pop-up menu, *choose one of the following options:*

- ◆ To outline each movie-frame rectangle, choose Storyboard-Boxes.
- ◆ To print the frames in a grid, choose Storyboard-Grid.
- ◆ To print just the graphic elements of each movie frame, choose Storyboard-Blank.

The layout parameters appear.

3. In the Frame (Mac) or Frames Across (Windows) field, type the number of frames that you want to print across the page.

Flash prints as many as 128 frames in a single storyboard row.

4. In the Story Margin (Mac) or Frame Margin (Windows) field, type the amount of space that you want to use between frames in your layout.

5. Click OK.

6. From the File menu, choose Print.

The Print dialog box appears.

7. If you want to print only some pages of your thumbnails, type those page numbers in the From and To fields.

8. Click OK.

Flash creates the thumbnails, using the options you specified (**Figure 16.50**).

✔ Tips

- ■ To view your layout before printing, choose File > Print Preview. Flash displays a preview of your movie in the page layout that you've chosen.

- ■ To print the scene and frame number below each frame in the layout, choose Label in the Print Margins (Mac) or Label Frames in the Page Setup (Windows) dialog box.

Storyboard boxes

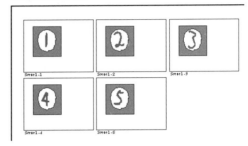

Storyboard grid

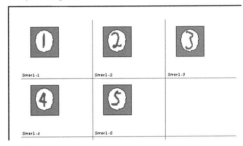

Storyboard blank

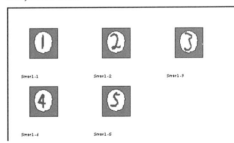

Figure 16.50 The Layout menu of the Print Margins (Mac) or Page Setup (Windows) dialog box offers three storyboard options: movie frames alone, frames set inside a grid, or each frame outlined in a box.

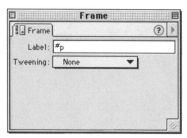

Figure 16.51 To define keyframes that print when viewers choose Print from Flash Player's contextual menu, select the keyframe and enter #p in the Label field of the Frames panel.

Figure 16.52 In your browser, Control-click (Mac) or right-click (Windows) to access the Flash Player's contextual menu. Choosing Print outputs all the pages defined as printable.

Printing from Flash Player

Flash 5 gives you the option of letting your viewers print some or all of a movie directly from Flash Player. You can allow viewers to access a print command from Flash Player's contextual menu. By default, the contextual menu's Print command prints every frame in the movie. You restrict printing to certain frames by labeling them as printable in the original Flash document. You can also create buttons for printing frames of your Flash movie.

To set frames to print from the contextual menu:

1. Create a Flash document with keyframes in frames 1 through 3.

   Place different content in each frame to make it easy to tell which frames you've actually printed.

2. In the Timeline, select Keyframe 1.

3. Access the Frames panel.

   If the Frames panel is not currently open, choose Modify > Frame or Window > Panels > Frame.

4. To define the selected frame as printable, in the Label field, enter #p (**Figure 16.51**).

5. In the Timeline, select Keyframe 3.

6. Repeat Step 4.

7. Publish your Flash movie, and view the resulting Flash Player file in your browser.

8. To access the contextual menu, Control-click (Mac) or right-click (Windows) anywhere in the movie window.

   The contextual menu appears (**Figure 16.52**).

continues on next page

PRINTING FROM FLASH PLAYER

9. Choose Print.

Flash prints frames 1 and 3, skipping Frame 2.

✔ Tips

- If you don't define particular frames as printable by labeling them #p, the contextual menu's Print command prints each frame in the movie.

- If you define more than one frame as printable by labeling it #p, when you publish the movie, Flash will display a warning message in the Output window, letting you know that there are multiple frames with the same label name. In this case, you can just ignore the warning.

To set frames to print from a button:

1. Open the file you created in the preceding exercise.

   Frames 1 and 3 of this file already contain the frame label #p. Even when you set a print action, you must define the printable frames with this frame label.

2. Place an instance of a button in Keyframe 1.

3. Select the button.

4. Access the Object Actions panel.

   If the panel isn't currently active, click the Show Actions button in the launcher bar.

5. From the Add Statement menu, choose Actions > print.

   Flash updates the Actions list to look like **Figure 16.53**.

6. In the Actions list, select the second line of code.

   The parameters for the print action appear in the Parameters pane (**Figure 16.54**).

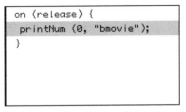

Figure 16.53 Attaching a print action to an instance of a button is another way to give viewers the ability to print frames of your movie.

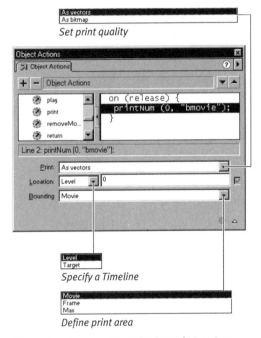

Figure 16.54 The parameters for the print action allow you to control print quality and print area, in addition to targeting a particular Timeline for printing.

7. To set print quality, from the Print pop-up menu, *choose one of the following:*

- ◆ To print at high quality, without transparency, choose Vector.
- ◆ To preserve transparency effects, choose Bitmap.

8. To designate which Timeline to print when you have loaded more than one movie, from the Location menu, *choose one of the following:*

- ◆ Choose Level, and enter the level number.
- ◆ Choose Target, and enter the target path.

9. To define the print area, from the Bounding pop-up menu, *choose one of the following options:*

- ◆ To use an object in a particular frame as a template for setting the print area, choose Movie.

  For the Movie option to work, you must also define the template frame. Select the frame containing the template object, access the Frame panel, and enter #b as the frame label.

- ◆ To vary the print area to enclose just the objects in each frame and scale those objects to fit the page, choose Frame.

- ◆ To make the print area large enough to print all the objects in all the movie's frames, choose Max.

PRINTING FROM FLASH PLAYER

To disable printing from Flash Player:

1. Open the Flash file for which you want to disable printing.

2. In the Timeline, select any frame.

3. Access the Frame panel.

4. In the Label field, enter !#p.

   When you publish the file, the Print option is unavailable from Flash Player's contextual menu (**Figure 16.55**).

✔ Tip

■ You can remove the contextual menu from your published Flash Player file by unchecking the Display Menu checkbox in the HTML tab of the Publish Settings dialog box.

Figure 16.55 Attaching the label !#p to any frame in a movie (top) grays out the Print option in the contextual menu in Flash Player (bottom).

KEYBOARD SHORTCUTS

Shortcuts for Commands

COMMAND	WINDOWS	MACINTOSH	MENU
100% (View)	Ctrl-1	⌘-1	View > Magnification
Actions Panel (Show/Hide)	Ctrl-Alt-A	⌘-Option-A	Window
Add Shape Hint	Ctrl-Shift-H	⌘-Shift-H	Modify > Transform
Align (Text) Center	Ctrl-Shift-C	⌘-Shift-C	Text > Align
Align (Text) Left	Ctrl-Shift-L	⌘-Shift-L	Text > Align
Align (Text) Right	Ctrl-Shift-R	⌘-Shift-R	Text > Align
Align Panel (Show/Hide)	Ctrl-K	⌘-K	Window > Panels
Antialias Text	Ctrl-Alt-Shift-T	⌘-Shift-Option-T	View
Antialias	Ctrl-Alt-Shift-A	⌘-Shift-Option-A	View
Bandwidth Profiler (Show/Hide)	Ctrl-B	⌘-B	View (in Test Movie mode)
Blank Keyframe	F7	F7	Insert
Bold (Text)	Ctrl-Shift-B	⌘-Shift-B	Text > Style
Break Apart	Ctrl-B	⌘-B	Modify
Bring (Selected Item) to Front	Ctrl-Shift-Up	⌘-Shift-Up	Modify > Arrange
Bring (Selected Item) Forward	Ctrl-Up	⌘-Up	Modify > Arrange
Character Panel (Show/Hide)	Ctrl-T	⌘-T	Text, Window > Panels
Clear (Stage)	Backspace	Delete	Edit
Clear Keyframe	Shift-F6	Shift-F6	Insert
Close (File)	Ctrl-W	⌘-W	File
Convert to Symbol	F8	F8	Insert
Copy (Selection)	Ctrl-C	⌘-C	Edit
Copy Frames	Ctrl-Alt-C	⌘-Option-C	Edit
Cut (Selection)	Ctrl-X	⌘-X	Edit
Cut Frames	Ctrl-Alt-X	⌘-Option-X	Edit
Debug Movie	Ctrl-Shift-Enter	⌘-Shift-Enter	Control
Decrease (Tracking)	Ctrl-Alt-Left	⌘-Option-Left	Text > Tracking
Default (Publishing)	F12	F12	File > Publish Preview
Deselect All	Ctrl-Shift-A	⌘-Shift-A	Edit
Duplicate (Selection)	Ctrl-D	⌘-D	Edit
Edit Grid	Ctrl-Alt-G	⌘-Option-G	View > Grid
Edit Guides	Ctrl-Alt-Shift-G	⌘-Shift-Option-G	View > Guide

Shortcuts for Commands *(continued)*

COMMAND	WINDOWS	MACINTOSH	MENU
Edit Symbols	Ctrl-E	⌘-E	Edit
Enable Simple Buttons	Ctrl-Alt-B	⌘-Option-B	Control
Export Movie	Ctrl-Alt-Shift-S	⌘-Shift-Option-S	File
Fast (View)	Ctrl-Alt-Shift-F	⌘-Shift-Option-F	View
First (Scene)	Home	Home	View > Goto
Frame (Add)	F5	F5	Insert
Frame Panel (Show/Hide)	Ctrl-F	⌘-F	Modify, Window > Panels
Frame-by-Frame Graph (Show)	Ctrl-F	⌘-F	View, in test movie-mode
Grid (Show/Hide)	Ctrl-'	⌘-'	View > Grid
Group (Selected Items)	Ctrl-G	⌘-G	Modify
Guides (Show/Hide)	Ctrl-;	⌘-;	View > Guide
Hide Edges (Show/Hide Selection Highlight)	Ctrl-H	⌘-H	View
Import	Ctrl-R	⌘-R	File
Increase (Tracking)	Ctrl-Alt-Right	⌘-Option-Right	Text > Tracking
Info	Ctrl-Alt-I	⌘-Option-I	Window > Panels
Instance Panel (Show/Hide)	Ctrl-I	⌘-I	Modify, Window > Panels
Italic (Text)	Ctrl-Shift-I	⌘-Shift-I	Text > Style
Justify (Text)	Ctrl-Shift-J	⌘-Shift-J	Text > Align
Keyframe (Add)	F6	F6	Insert
Last (Scene)	End	End	View > Goto
Library (Show/Hide)	Ctrl-L	⌘-L	Window
Lock (Group)	Ctrl-Alt-L	⌘-Option-L	Modify > Arrange
Lock Guides	Ctrl-Alt-;	⌘-Option-;	View > Guide
Movie (Properties)	Ctrl-M	⌘-M	Modify
Movie Explorer Panel (Show/Hide)	Ctrl-Alt-M	⌘-Option-M	Window
New (File)	Ctrl-N	⌘-N	File
New Symbol	Ctrl-F8	⌘-F8	Insert
New Window	Ctrl-Alt-N	⌘-Option-N	Window
Next (Scene)	Page Down	Page Down	View > Goto
Open (File)	Ctrl-O	⌘-O	File
Open as Library	Ctrl-Shift-O	⌘-Shift-O	File
Optimize (Curves)	Ctrl-Alt-Shift-C	⌘-Shift-Option-C	Modify
Outlines (View As)	Ctrl-Alt-Shift-O	⌘-Shift-Option-O	View
Panels (Show/Hide, including Toolbox)	Tab	Tab	View
Paragraph Panel (Show/Hide)	Ctrl-Shift-T	⌘-Shift-T	Text, Window > Panels
Paste (Clipboard Contents)	Ctrl-V	⌘-V	Edit
Paste Frames	Ctrl-Alt-V	⌘-Option-V	Edit
Paste In Place	Ctrl-Shift-V	⌘-Shift-V	Edit
Plain (Text)	Ctrl-Shift-P	⌘-Shift-P	Text > Style
Play (Movie)	Enter	Return	Control
Previous (Scene)	Page Up	Page Up	View > Goto
Print	Ctrl-P	⌘-P	File
Publish Settings	Ctrl-Shift-F12	⌘-Shift-F12	File

Shortcut for Commands *(continued)*

COMMAND	WINDOWS	MACINTOSH	MENU
Publish	Shift-F12	Shift-F12	File
Quit	Ctrl-Q	⌘-Q	File
Redo	Ctrl-Y	⌘-Y	Edit
Remove Frames	Shift-F5	Shift-F5	Insert
Remove Transform	Ctrl-Shift-Z	⌘-Shift-Z	Modify > Transform
Reset (Tracking)	Ctrl-Alt-Up	⌘-Option-Up	Text > Tracking
Rewind	Ctrl-Alt-R	⌘-Option-R	Control
Rulers (Show/Hide)	Ctrl-Alt-Shift-R	⌘-Shift-Option-R	View
Save As	Ctrl-Shift-S	⌘-Shift-S	File
Save	Ctrl-S	⌘-S	File
Scale and Rotate	Ctrl-Alt-S	⌘-Option-S	Modify > Transform
Select All	Ctrl-A	⌘-A	Edit
Send (Selected Item) to Back	Ctrl-Shift-Down	⌘-Shift-Down	Modify > Arrange
Send (Selected Item) Backward	Ctrl-Down	⌘-Down	Modify > Arrange
Shape Hints (Show/Hide)	Ctrl-Alt-H	⌘-Option-H	View
Show All	Ctrl-3	⌘-3	View > Magnification
Show Frame	Ctrl-2	⌘-2	View > Magnification
Snap to Grid	Ctrl-Shift-'	⌘-Shift-'	View > Grid
Snap to Guides	Ctrl-Shift-;	⌘-Shift-;	View > Guide
Snap to Objects	Ctrl-Shift-/	⌘-Shift-/	View
Step Backward	,	,	Control
Step Forward	.	.	Control
Streaming (Show/Hide)	Ctrl-Enter	⌘-Enter	View (in Test Movie Mode, with Bandwidth Profiler active)
Streaming Graph (Show/Hide)	Ctrl-G	⌘-G	View (in Test Movie Mode)
Test Movie	Ctrl-Enter	⌘-Enter	Control
Test Scene	Ctrl-Alt-Enter	⌘-Option-Enter	Control
Timeline (Show/Hide)	Ctrl-Alt-T	⌘-Option-T	View
Undo	Ctrl-Z	⌘-Z	Edit
Ungroup	Ctrl-Shift-G	⌘-Shift-G	Modify
Unlock All	Ctrl-Alt-Shift-L	⌘-Shift-Option-L	Modify > Arrange
Work Area (View)	Ctrl-Shift-W	⌘-Shift-W	View
Zoom In	Ctrl-= (equals sign)	⌘-= (equals sign)	View
Zoom Out	Ctrl-— (minus sign)	Command-— (minus)	View

Shortcut for Accessing Tools and Manipulating Elements

OPERATION/TOOL	WINDOWS	MACINTOSH
Arrow tool (select in Toolbox)	V	V
Arrow tool (temporary access)	Ctrl	⌘
Brush tool (select in Toolbox)	B	B
Constrain (ovals to circles, rectangles to squares, lines and rotation to 45-degree angles)	Shift-drag	Shift-drag
Convert corner point to curve point (subselection tool)	Alt-drag	Option-drag
Create new corner point (arrow tool)	Alt-drag a line	Option-drag a line

Shortcut for Accessing Tools and Manipulating Elements *(continued)*

OPERATION/TOOL	WINDOWS	MACINTOSH
Drag a copy of selected element on Stage	Ctrl-drag	Option-drag
Drag a copy of selected keyframe unit in Timeline	Ctrl-drag	Option-drag
Dropper tool (select in Toolbox)	I	I
End open path (pen tool)	Ctrl-click	Control-click
Eraser tool (select in Toolbox)	E	E
Hand tool (temporary access)	Spacebar	Spacebar
Show/Hide all but one layer	Alt-click active layer's eye column	Option-click active layer's eye column
Ink bottle tool (select in Toolbox)	S	S
Lasso tool (select in Toolbox)	L	L
Line tool (select in Toolbox)	N	N
Link/unlink layer to mask or motion guide layer	Alt-click a layer icon	Option-click a layer icon
Lock/unlock all but one layer	Alt-click active layer's padlock column	Option-click active layer's padlock column
Magnifier tool (select in Toolbox)	M, Z	M, Z
Magnifier zoom-in tool (temporary access)	Ctrl-Spacebar	⌘-Spacebar
Magnifier zoom-out tool (temporary access)	Ctrl-Shift-Spacebar	⌘-Shift-Spacebar
Move keyframe unit in Timeline	Click-and-drag	Click-and-drag
Nudge selected element down 8 pixels	Shift-Down arrow	Shift-Down arrow
Nudge selected element to the left 1 pixel	Left arrow	Left arrow
Nudge selected element to the left 8 pixels	Shift-Left arrow	Shift-Left arrow
Nudge selected element to the right 1 pixel	Right arrow	Right arrow
Nudge selected element to the right 8 pixels	Shift-Right arrow	Shift-Right arrow
Nudge selected element up 1 pixel	Up arrow	Up arrow
Nudge selected element up 8 pixels	Shift-Up arrow	Shift-Up arrow
Nudge selected element down 1 pixel	Down arrow	Down arrow
Oval tool (select in Toolbox)	O	O
Paint bucket tool (select in Toolbox)	K	K
Pen tool (select in Toolbox)	P	P
Pencil tool (select in Toolbox)	Y	Y
Rectangle tool (select in Toolbox)	R	R
Select multiple layers	Shift-click	Shift-click
Select noncontiguous layers	Ctrl-click	Control-click
Set fill and stroke color simultaneously	Shift-click with the dropper tool	Shift-click with the dropper tool
Show outlines for all but one layer	Alt-click that layer's outline column	Option-click that layer's outline column
Subselection tool (select in Toolbox)	A	A
Switch magnifier tool temporarily from zoom-in to zoom-out and vice versa	Alt	Option
Text tool (select in Toolbox)	T	T

INDEX

INDEX

INDEX

INDEX

O

object actions, 352, 371–404
Object Actions panel
  accessing, 383, 388, 437
  Add Statement menu, 445, 450, 459, 460
  Insert Target Path button, 450
  Message field, 460
  Parameters pane, 384, 389, 444, 452, 459
OBJECT tag, 477, 478
object-oriented scripting language, 385
objects, 357, 385
On Mouse Event action, 386, 388–390
  event parameters, 389
  triggering events
    key press, 394–395
    mouse events, 388–390
  varying response of buttons, 391–393
on (press) action, 392, 394
on (release) action, 386, 387, 388
onClipEvent action, 401
  event parameters, 403
onion-skinning feature, 270–271
  fine-tuning tweens, 330, 332
  positioning keyframe shapes, 309
  previewing tweened shapes, 281
  repositioning shape hints, 316
  viewing animated buttons, 381–382
open paths, 48
opening
  Libraries, 196–197
  Library folders, 201
  panels, 20
  separate browser windows, 443–445
operators, 357
optimizing movies, 466–468
organizing
  actions, 355
  Libraries, 200–202
  sounds, 409–410
orienting graphic elements
  to a motion path, 298–299
  See also reorienting elements
outlines
  converting to fills, 139
  drawing an oval outline, 39
  editing on inactive layers, 183
  filling with solid colors, 52
  onion skin, 270
  selecting part of, 77
  shape tweening fills with, 312
  viewing layer contents as, 179, 181
oval tool, 39–40
ovals
  drawing an oval outline, 39–40
  pencil tool for drawing, 44
  transforming into rectangles, 308–309
Over state, 374, 378–379
overlapping sounds, 419–420

P

padlock icon, 181
Page Setup dialog box, 497
paint bucket tool, 52–53
  bitmapped fills applied with, 235
  changing fill colors with, 117
  editing fills across layers with, 184
  filling outline shapes with solid colors, 52
  gradient fills applied with, 132
  setting gap closure, 53
  Transform Fill mode, 236–238
Paint modes (brush tool)
  Paint Behind, 163
  Paint Fills, 162
  Paint Inside, 165
  Paint Normal, 54–56
  Paint Selection, 164
painting
  gradients used for, 133
  leaving fills intact, 163–164
  leaving lines intact, 162–163
  restricting to one area, 165
  selected fills for, 164
palettes, color, 487–488
panels, 20–25
  closing, 21
  custom panel sets, 24–25
  default panel sets, 22, 25
  entering values in panel fields, 26
  grouping, 23
  opening, 20
  repositioning, 21
  resizing, 21
  separating from groups, 22
  windows vs., 23
  See also names of specific panels
paragraph attributes, 65–67
  alignment, 65
  indentation, 67
  line spacing, 67
  margins, 66–67
Paragraph panel, 65–67
Parameters pane
  Frame Actions panel, 440, 441, 453
  Object Actions panel, 384, 389, 444, 452, 459
parentheses, in ActionScripts, 436
Paste command, 192–193
Paste in Place command, 193–194
Paste Special command (Windows), 86–87
pasting
  frames, 256–257, 324–325
  graphics imported through the Clipboard, 230–231
  selections, 85, 86–87
    across layers, 192–194
    onto active layers, 185
  special pasting options, 86–87

New from Peachpit Press